The
BRITISH COLUMBIA
WINE
COMPANION

JOHN SCHREINER

Now you know how I know all that stuff about B.C. wine.

Enjoy,
1997.

ORCA BOOK PUBLISHERS

Canadian Cataloguing in Publication Data

Schreiner, John, 1936 –

The British Columbia wine companion

ISBN 1-55143-061-4

1. Viticulturists — British Columbia — Biography. 2. Viticulture — British Columbia — History. 3. Wine and wine making — British Columbia. 4. Wineries — British Columbia — History. I. Title.

TP559.C2S36 1996   663'.2'09711   C96-910302-6

The publisher would like to acknowledge the ongoing financial support of The Canada Council, the Department of Canadian Heritage, and the British Columbia Ministry of Small Business, Tourism and Culture.

Cover design by Christine Toller

Cover photograph by Jeff Barber/INFocus Photography

Printed and bound in Canada

Orca Book Publishers
PO Box 5626, Station B
Victoria, BC Canada
V8R 6S4

Orca Book Publishers
PO Box 468
Custer, WA USA
98240-0468

10 9 8 7 6 5 4 3 2 1

This book is dedicated to Maureen, Alison and John,
whose friends always hand them the wine list
on the assumption that something rubbed off from Dad

INTRODUCTION

This book was prompted by the frustration at not having a handy source for looking up details about British Columbia wines and the industry when I was researching and writing *The Wineries of British Columbia*, which was published in 1994. Once I had begun to create my own reference aid, the project took on a life of its own. I soon turned up nuggets of information, some surprising and some highly amusing, that had to be passed on.

To begin with, I perceived a need to record the salient points about British Columbia wine history. As short as that history is, it is important to know where we have come from to appreciate how much has been achieved in a very few years. It also is important to verify or correct some assertions (such as the romantic but untrue notion that Father Charles Pandosy started the wine industry in the Okanagan). The history has been broken into vignettes organized generally around the lives of the people who made the history.

Beyond history, many of the grapegrowers have been interviewed and profiled here. Every winemaker will say that wine is made primarily in the vineyards. Oddly enough, very few wineries have yet given the growers recognition on their labels, even when single-vineyard wines are produced. Even those who do identify vineyards lack the space on already crowded labels to tell consumers anything about the growers. I had long wondered who was the person behind *Hainle Estate's* Elisabeth's Vineyard wines and I expect many Hainle fans also asked that question. That individual is Elisabeth Harbeck, one of the growers whom I have profiled here, and hers is a story of courage and determination. The portrait of the industry that emerges from reading the anecdotal sketches of the growers should enrich our appreciation of the wines.

This is a very dynamic industry, having grown from thirteen wineries in the early 1980s to about fifty. I profiled a number of wineries in the 1994 book that planned to open over the subsequent three years. Even so, additional wineries have emerged — wineries such as *Carriage House, Gersighel, Larch Hills, Stag's Hollow* and *Slamka Cellars.* The entries on those wineries, along with updates on ownership changes of others, make this volume a supplement to, but not a replacement for, *The Wineries of British Columbia.*

This book is as complete as time and limitations of imagination permit. This book could not have been done without the willingness of the people interviewed and profiled to talk about their lives and their aspirations.

AAA

ACACIA: A warmly aromatic wood occasionally used for wine barrels in addition to or as a supplement to oak. *Domaine de Chaberton Estate Winery* in Langley was the first British Columbia winery to release commercially an acacia-aged wine, a chardonnay from the 1994 vintage. Five other wineries also conducted acacia trials. Its major advocate in the Okanagan has been Hungarian-trained winemaker *Elias Phiniotis*, who, aware of the long-time use of acacia in Hungary, became the British Columbia agent for the Hungarian cooperage in the Tokay region that makes these barrels. He believes the wood imparts a delicate honey/blossom aroma and underlines a white wine's bright gold colour without imparting the tannin and the vanilla flavours of oak. Domaine de Chaberton experienced what co-owner Ingeborg Violet described as "a very overwhelming response" to its chardonnay. The winery had a dozen acacia barrels for the 1995 vintage, with plans to add more. Each barrel contains at least three hundred bottles of wine.

ADAMS, PETER (1911 –): An erudite British wine consultant based in London, Adams almost single-handedly upgraded the wine selection of six Canadian liquor boards, including British Columbia. After graduation from Oxford with a master of arts degree, he began his wine career in 1933 with his family's firm of wholesale wine merchants, Adams & Sons. He retired in 1967, after Adams & Sons had merged with another firm, only to launch a second career as a consultant. The Liquor Control Board of Ontario, which had dealt with Adams & Sons, asked him to find an English wine merchant prepared to emigrate to Canada and join the LCBO to improve the board's scant knowledge of European wines. Adams found a candidate but when the arrangement fell through, Adams offered his services. He advised Ontario on wines from 1967 to 1985. Nova Scotia, New Brunswick, Prince Edward Island and Manitoba subsequently retained him as well.[1]

British Columbia retained Adams in 1975. "My first visit to British Columbia showed a list with almost no foreign wines," recalled Adams, who helped the newly formed Liquor Distribution Branch develop an intelligent and contemporary wine offering. "His advice is absolutely invaluable in terms of building a complete and balanced wine list for the Province," Tex Enemark, deputy minister of Consumer Affairs, told the newly appointed general manager of the LDB, Bob Wallace, in August 1978. Adams advised British Columbia until 1988 and continued his consulting career in Britain until retiring in 1995.

ADELHEID'S VINEYARD: Vineyard designation for wine made by Hainle Estates from grapes grown by Heidi (Adelheid) and Roland Heller in a vineyard near Okanagan Falls. See *Heller.*

ADVERTISING: The government of British Columbia took control of the sale of alcoholic beverages in 1921 as an alternative to direct prohibition that the temperance forces would find acceptable. It follows, then, that government would see the advertising of such beverages as inappropriate. Initially, all advertising was banned; and when print advertising was permitted in the 1930s, the advertisements included the disclaimer that they were not being published by the Liquor Control Board. The government allowed neither broadcast advertising of liquor nor billboards and took such a dim view of promotional material that information brochures were not allowed into liquor stores until 1981. The ban on broadcast advertising became untenable once American television stations began accepting advertisements from Canadian brewers and distillers and beaming the material back across the border. In 1971, a government inquiry recommended that British Columbia permit radio and television advertising. Instead, British Columbia in September 1971 banned *all* liquor advertising, with the only strong protest in the legislature coming from Social Credit backbencher Herb Capozzi, whose family owned **Calona Wines**. The liquor companies simply moved advertising to publications that originated outside British Columbia, while continuing to use American television and radio. Vic Woodland, the general manager of the Liquor Control and Licensing Branch, then pressured the Canadian brewers not to advertise on a specific Bellingham, Wa., channel because 80 percent of its audience was in British Columbia. This policy fell apart after Molson Breweries began exporting its beer to the Pacific Northwest — and advertising on Seattle television stations.

Television advertising on American channels available in British Columbia by cable so irritated the British Columbia government in the late 1970s that it re-fused listings to producers who advertised. In a briefing memorandum to his successor as deputy minister at Consumer Affairs, Tex Enemark wrote: "There has been a policy in place for about a year of not listing any American wines that are *heavily* advertised on American television, and thus Gallo have no listings."[2] This led to persistent pressure from the United States, which wanted more of its wines listed in British Columbia. (Only six American wines were listed in 1974, rising to a modest twenty-eight by the beginning of 1979.) The government had rescinded the futile print advertising ban in the fall of 1972 but beer and wine advertising was not permitted in electronic media or at sports arenas until 1982.

AGENT STOCKING PROGRAM: Inaugurated in 1979 by the British Columbia Liquor Distribution Branch, this program shifted the responsibility for warehousing products to be sold through the LDB to agents and producers. A 45 percent growth in new product listings since 1975 totally overtaxed the LDB's warehousing capacity in Vancouver. The LDB either had to build a massive new warehouse of its own or ask its suppliers to lease their own space in existing commercial warehouses. It was not difficult to see which solution would benefit the LDB; when the suppliers objected, the government hired consultants Urwick Currie, whose report in September 1978 showed that the suppliers as well as the LDB would benefit. Indeed, the consultants concluded that even consumers would benefit since they would not have to absorb higher prices to pay for a new LDB warehouse, which was estimated to cost $25 million.[3]

Overcrowding was not the only problem the LDB was solving. Its own warehouse operations had been marked by a chaotic lack of security — there was not even a fence around the warehouse. In November 1977 Charles Ruddick, then a newly appointed director of warehousing for the LDB, warned general manager Keith Warnes in a memorandum that "a theft of scandalous size could take place at any time and would remain unidentified for a considerable period of time ... Compared to operations which handle groceries and hardware, we are wide open to theft and abuse. There are many indications from those people associated with the warehouse, that widespread theft and abuse is taking place ..."[4] Security was tightened as the warehouse, with the advent of the agent stocking program, became the LDB's distribution centre. Private warehouses took over storing liquor inventories in the province.

Perhaps because of strenuous resistance at the time from Canadian distillers, no other provincial liquor board copied the agent stocking program.

ALCOHOL FOUNDATION OF BRITISH COLUMBIA:

This organization was created in 1951 as a privately run, but government-funded, body dedicated to dealing with alcoholism. In 1957 it arranged to have two beds available at Vancouver General Hospital for male alcoholics, with financial support from the British Columbia Hospital Insurance Service. However, the beds were often given over to what the hospital called more orthodox cases due to general overcrowding. In 1960, the Foundation opened a two-bed treatment facility in a private nursing home.[5]

ALCOHOL RESEARCH AND EDUCATION COUNCIL:

A pro-temperance lobby formed in 1952 by the Vancouver Council of Churches and the British Columbia Temperance League. In the 1960s, it changed its name to the Alcohol-Drug Education Service. See *Prohibition*.

Don Allen (photo courtesy of John Schreiner)

ALLEN, DON (1925–):

A retired naval captain turned winemaker and grapegrower, Allen was born in Revelstoke, B.C., the son of a railroad engineer but, perhaps more important, the descendant of a long line of brewers. His Irish ancestors had a brewery in Ireland; his great-grandfather ran a brewery in Toronto in the last century and his grandfather, who once won a gold medal at a Vienna fair for entering the best lager, established a brewery in Revelstoke because of the quality of the springwater. (He would rather have made whisky but the government denied him a license.) Don Allen joined the naval reserves when he was sixteen; too young either to drink or to fight, he was sent to study electronics at the University of New Brunswick before going on convoy duty in 1944 as an electronics technician.

His wine education began near the end of the war when Allen, now a petty officer, serviced the electronics on a French warship in Halifax and lunched in the officers' mess. "They had four thousand bottles of good French wine right down in the bilges," he discovered. "I got in the habit of going down and servicing this French ship." He began making wine at home in 1948 when he was stationed in Victoria, using locally sourced grapes. His hobby blossomed into a second career after he left the navy in 1972 and purchased a six-acre vineyard near Westbank. Within three years he replanted hybrid varieties with pinot noir, merlot and chardonnay (obtained from Washington state) and with the same Alsace clone of auxerrois that *George Heiss* had imported. At the same time, Allen took a correspondence winemaking course from the University of California at Davis. "On an amateur basis, I won dozens of top prizes in the wine shows," he says. In 1980, when *Uniacke Estate Winery* was established, Allen was the winemaker for the first two vintages, making a challenging range of both whites and reds. "We made pinot noir and we made merlot," Allen says. "They were both barrel-aged — this was pioneering." He left the Uniacke job to pay more attention to his own vineyard's burgeoning production. Allen's professional viticulture included grafting vines that were imported for the Becker project when it began in 1977; and being one of the authors of a booklet that assessed the results of the project some years later. In 1996 he was still cultivating more than 2,000 vinifera vines — including chardonnay and merlot — in his Westbank vineyard, now completely surrounded by a housing subdivision.

ANDERSON, LAWRENCE L. JR.: He was the cost-cutter that Imperial Tobacco named president of *Growers' Wines* in 1969 when Imperial, the controlling shareholder, unhappy with the wine division's anemic profits, decided to shift long-time president *Brian Roberts* upwards into the chairman's post. By the following year, what he called the company's non-performing assets were for sale. These included the *Beau Séjour* vineyard (which the company had purchased in 1966), a loganberry farm in Central Saanich and extra warehouses in Vancouver and Victoria. "Our aim is to maximize profits, and to that end a tight new cost control system has been adopted that gives a check on each department on a monthly basis," he told the 1970 annual meeting. Anderson moved on in the summer of 1970 to run an Imperial-owned food company in San Francisco. See *Lloyd Schmidt.*

ANDERSON, STANLEY F. (1921 –): The Johnny Appleseed of winemaking, Anderson taught thousands — indeed, hundreds of thousands — of people across North America to make wine, both through three books on home winemaking and through Wine-Art Sales Ltd., the retail chain for home vintners that Anderson launched in Vancouver in 1959. It was a ground-breaking venture: the city police in Vancouver tried to close his first store, arguing that it was as illegal for a private store to sell Burgundy yeast as it would have been to sell wine. That threat passed when the Crown prosecutor, reluctant to lay frivolous charges, convinced Anderson to cover the store's window displays, obscuring them from the street.

Anderson was born in Vancouver, the son of a butcher. "My mother made fruit wine," Anderson said, recalling that the wine was sweet and that his father refused to drink it. Yet when Anderson himself first made wine in the late 1940s, he began, unsuccessfully, with his mother's recipe for potato champagne. "It foamed all over the floor," he recounted. A high school graduate, Anderson went to work with the Borden dairy company, intending to become a product researcher until the company put him on the road as a salesman. He began asking food technologists inside and outside the company for information on winemaking and, finding no expertise in Vancouver, sought knowledge farther afield. He wanted to know why homemade wine was so bad when homemade baking generally tasted better than store-bought baking. He found a rich source of information in Suzanne Tritton, a well-regarded British consulting enologist whose clients included Harvey's of Bristol. (A winemaker at *Growers' Wines* in Victoria, when approached by Anderson, scoffed at the notion that *anyone* could make wine at home.) She was employed by Grey Owl Laboratories which sold to home wine- and beer-makers in Britain. Anderson learned that he could improve his amateur wines with good equipment and proper wine yeasts and he became one of Grey Owl's regular customers. A dapper man with a silver tongue, Anderson also discovered that wine was a far better milk salesman's door opener than gossiping about sports. When winemakers among his business associates discovered that he had a source of reliable supplies, they began ordering

through Anderson, who obliged as a personal favour until the volume of orders became substantial. "God," he said to himself, "it seems to me I could make a living doing this."

With $500 of savings, Anderson set up Wine-Art as a mail-order business, but also with a retail store on a high traffic block in an affluent neighbourhood of Vancouver's West Broadway Street. He reasoned, correctly, that his clientele would not be the ethnic winemakers who bought zinfandel and muscat grapes by the ton on Commercial Street every fall. "What we wanted were people who were serious hobbyists," he said. Such as the professor from the University of British Columbia who dropped into the store one day, desperate for an inventive hobby. "The most creative thing I do as a professor of English is polish my shoes in the morning," he told Anderson. "Can you teach me to make wine?" Many of his customers were from the same social milieu. "We have a mailing list of 8,000 names and about every tenth has the prefix *doctor*," Anderson said in a 1967 interview.[6] "I remember being in bed with the flu," he recalled later. "It was the winemaking season and there were six doctors around my bed — not one of them interested in my health, just the health of their wine and how could I resolve their problems."[7]

The original store showed a modest loss of $113.54 on sales of $5,186 in its first twelve months of business, which ended May 30, 1960. Undaunted, Anderson incorporated the company that fall. Wine-Art sales reached $25,000 in the year ended May 30, 1961, and the business showed a profit of $839. In the next year, sales almost doubled to $47,000 and the profit almost quadrupled to $2,900 as Wine-Art opened its first branch in Victoria.[8] This was a somewhat risky expansion, considering that the Liquor Control Board and its redoubtable chairman, **Lt.-Col. Donald McGugan,** were based in Victoria. But Anderson had survived a run-in with the colonel earlier, having told McGugan that Wine-Art would not mind being prosecuted because the publicity would be good for the business. "They left me alone," Anderson said. McGugan told *Vancouver Sun* writer Frank Walden in 1964 that it was legal for amateurs to make wine from Okanagan grapes but when California grapes were used, the LCB expected the home vintners to remit a tax equal to what they would have paid for wine bought in a liquor store. This unenforceable rule was ignored by the authorities.[9] When Anderson gave winemaking courses at night school in Vancouver, the local temperance forces protested, inadvertently generating publicity for Anderson: *Vancouver Sun*'s famed cartoonist Len Norris lampooned the protesters in a typically gently barbed cartoon.

The business grew primarily by word of mouth, as Anderson discovered one year when a $30,000 television advertising campaign by Wine-Art generated so little response that only one new customer was logged by the stores during the month in which it ran. By 1964 Wine-Art's mail-order business from Ontario suggested that the company needed to open a store there. Anderson figured he needed $10,000 but when his banker offered to lend only $3,000, he decided to sell a franchise instead. The partner he signed up, a close friend from his Borden days, was E.A. (Buzz) Arthurs who mortgaged his house to open a

Wine-Art store. No doubt Arthurs had second thoughts after the grand opening sale, on a Thursday in 1965, yielded a mere $4.37 in sales. "Thursdays are always a quiet day," Anderson mumbled lamely to his partner. Happily for Arthurs, business improved substantially and, when Anderson retired in 1986, Arthurs and his family acquired Anderson's interest in the total Canadian Wine-Art business. Anderson credited the early survival of Wine-Art in part to the fact that no competitors emerged until the company was ten years old and solidly established in Canada.

In 1969 Wine-Art — by this time with franchises across Canada — made its ill-fated move into the United States with the establishment of Wine-Art of America, a master franchiser based in San Francisco. The catalyst was **Wallace Pohle,** who, when he was the winemaker at the Andrés winery in Port Moody, obtained some sherry yeast from Wine-Art and who, with several partners, obtained the master franchise for the United States. Wine-Art of America "was a flamboyant enterprise that expanded very swiftly to sales of $6 million in four years," Anderson wrote later in a personal memoir. The operation garnered publicity with such stunts as pressing grapes on Hollywood Boulevard, and steamed ahead to have about fifty franchised stores. "But it was poorly managed and under financed; cost accounting was poor; quality control was inadequate." After Wine-Art of America went bankrupt in 1973, most of the American stores closed.

Years of giving winemaking recipes to his customers led Anderson to write (with the editorial assistance of Raymond Hull, a professional writer) *The Art of*

Making Wine. Published in paperback in 1968, it immediately became a nonfiction best seller and has remained in print for several decades, selling more than 350,000 copies, very likely the most popular book for home winemakers in North America. The book had its shortcomings, predating as it did a number of technical breakthroughs which have made home winemaking much more successful, among them winemaking yeasts that were easy to use. When Wine-Art started, wine yeast cultures were provided in agar in test tubes. Anderson vividly recalled one customer returning the yeast sample with a note that she was "appalled" at the tricky task she was being called upon to do. The first dry yeasts that Anderson found were prone to generating hydrogen sulphide during fermentation, a defect that even if corrected, generally left the wines with a rubbery aftertaste. Eventually, he sourced dry wine yeasts from American and British suppliers that could be simply sprinkled on the *must* to begin working and that fermented cleanly. The winemaking book was followed by *The Art of Making Beer* (since Wine-Art also sold beer-making supplies) and, with Dorothy Anderson, *The Advanced Winemaker's Guide,* published in 1989. For a number of years, beginning in 1970, Wine-Art customers also received, without charge, a quarterly magazine published by Anderson. Called *The Amateur Enologist,* it contained an eclectic range of articles, from profiles of California winemakers to useful technical articles by Anderson and contributing writers.

Because fruit wines were popular in the 1950s, Wine-Art secured early concentrates from Summerland Sweets Ltd., the company formed in 1966 by F.A. (Ted) Atkinson to commercialize products developed at the **Summerland Research Station** when he was its director. Anderson found that these were "marvelous for winemaking ... The apricot concentrate was so cheap and so good that the [commercial] wineries finally got on to making apricot wine." Amateurs were making ten gallons of wine with three dollars worth of concentrate. Some of the initial grape concentrates came from Spain and were not very good. "The technology there was terrible," Anderson said. "They were producing concentrate to sweeten sherries. It was never intended to be made back into wine. And they packaged it in unlined metal tins, which meant you had a very metallic-tasting wine. The breakthrough for concentrates came when I discovered Australia. First of all, they had an enormous amount of quality grapes and they had the highest technology in the world for making concentrate."

While Anderson later took enology courses in California, he acquired a good deal of his knowledge by experimenting with the products he sold. "We made five gallon test batches of wine probably three times a week in our laboratory," he recalled. "As soon as we knew it was wine, we'd throw it away. We made thousands of batches a wine. A winemaker makes wine once a year; we made wine fifty-two weeks a year." In the late 1970s Anderson also hired **Elias Phiniotis**, who had a doctorate in viticulture and three years' experience in a Cypriot winery before emigrating to Canada in 1976. When Phiniotis, who had been unable to find work, first applied for a job as a laboratory technician, Anderson demurred that he could not afford to hire him. "Surely you could pay me as much as I'm getting for driving a truck," Phiniotis replied. Anderson agreed and Phiniotis spent two years as the Wine-Art technical director before becoming a winemaker in the Okanagan. Years later, Anderson still remembered his contribution with immense gratitude. "It was bloody marvellous," Anderson said.

After Anderson retired, he moved to Vancouver Island, to a comfortable house with a fine view of the morning sun rising over Cowichan Bay. He continued making wine here for his own consumption; as well, Anderson provided neighbourly consulting advice to **Hans Kiltz** when the latter established **Blue Grouse** winery not far away in the Cowichan Valley. And he continued to collect royalties on his winemaking books, comfortable in the belief that he likely converted more British Columbians to drinking wine than any other single person.

ANDRÉS WINES LTD.: Canada's second-largest winery and now headquartered in Winona, Ont., Andrés was founded in 1961 at Port Moody, a suburb of Vancouver, by the entrepreneurial ex-brewer **Andrew Peller**. He would have started the winery in Ontario but he had worn out his welcome with Ontario's liquor regulators when, as a brewery owner, he found a way around the rules against advertising: he formed an ice company with a similar name to the brewery and advertised the ice. When Peller applied for a winery licence, the regulators responded with impossible conditions. He got a better reception in British Columbia which then had only two wineries and saw the advantage of encouraging a new one. The impact of Andrés on British

Columbia has been profound, extending from the creation of **Baby Duck** to the support of **Inkameep Vineyards** and the early encouragement of the planting of vinifera grapes. See **Andrew Peller** and **Baby Duck**.

ANSCOMB, HERBERT (1892–1972): By the time he entered the legislature in 1933 as one of four members from Victoria, Anscomb had been successful both as a brewery owner and as general manager of Growers' Wines Ltd., beginning in 1927. An Independent in his first term, Anscomb ran successfully in 1937 as a Conservative and ultimately became finance minister and later (in 1950) his party's leader. He was brazen in the use of his power to secure the interests of Growers'. In 1940 he had a hand in blocking T.G. Bright & Co. from opening a plant in British Columbia to bottle its Ontario-made wine.[10] Very few Ontario wines or even European ones were listed by the Liquor Distribution Branch; the first California wines were listed only in 1962. See **Growers' Wines**.

APPLEBY, TED: Wine educator Appleby represented the Wine Council of British Columbia in the late 1970s as a wine ambassador. Born in London, he interrupted a career in insurance to become an officer in the Royal Navy in the Second World War. After emigrating to Canada in the 1950s, he became a bartender, a club manager (he spent ten years as lounge manager and wine advisor to the Vancouver Board of Trade), a wine writer and a lecturer in wine at Douglas College and the Vancouver School Board. Appleby was as remarkable for his dapper appearance and gentle personality as he was for the wine knowledge he had acquired.

ARNOLD, EDWARD (1937–): Born in Steveston, B.C., the son of a fisherman, Arnold became a food chemist and was apprenticing with a Toronto brewery when in 1965, wanting to return to British Columbia, he talked *Andrew Peller* into hiring him for the *Andrés* winery at Port Moody. "One of my better moves," Peller wrote in his autobiography. "Arnold turned out to be an invaluable asset." By 1970 he was the chief winemaker at the big Andrés winery in Winona, Ont. Brights lured him away in 1976 and promoted him to president in 1978. He retired in 1994 and turned to consulting.

ASIAN MARKETING: Even though the wineries of British Columbia are naturally positioned to export to the Pacific Rim, they have found it challenging to develop sustained sales in those markets. It has not been for lack of trying. One of the first significant marketing thrusts was undertaken in 1987 when *Harry McWatters* of *Sumac Ridge* probed the market in Taiwan with a shipment of one thousand cases. In November of that year, a group of Okanagan wineries, including Sumac Ridge and *Gehringer Brothers*, displayed their products in a wine show in Japan.

ASSOCIATION OF BRITISH COLUMBIA GRAPE GROWERS: See *Grape Growers Association*.

AUXERROIS: Sometimes called pinot auxerrois, this white wine grape was first imported to the Okanagan from Alsace in 1975 by *George Heiss, Sr.*, one of the owners of *Gray Monk*. Invariably, the grape produces an attractively fruity table wine.

AVERY'S TROPHY: This trophy, named after the late Ronald Avery, a renowned British wine merchant, was won at the 1994 International Wine and Spirits Competition in London by *Mission Hill* for its 1992 Grand Reserve Barrel Select Chardonnay (of which 3,000 cases were made). Given for the best chardonnay in the competition, it was one of the most important international awards won to that date by a wine from British Columbia. The trophy succeeded for the first time in capturing the serious attention of the influential British wine writers, including Hugh Johnson who had earlier trivialized British Columbia wines in brief and erroneous entries in his books that signaled his lack of respect for the wines. The award, which Mission Hill publicized effectively, also lifted business confidence generally among British Columbia wineries and that in turn led to expanded vinifera plantings and to the recruitment of other foreign-trained winemakers.

---

[1] Adams's correspondence with author, January 1996.

[2] Tex Enemark papers; memo December 19, 1978, to Peter Bazowski

[3] Currie, Coopers & Lybrand Ltd.: B.C. Liquor Distribution Branch, *Costs and Benefits of Import Agent Stocking Program*, September 22, 1978.

[4] Tex Enemark papers; memo by C.E. Ruddick to Keith Warnes, November 21, 1977.

[5] Sherene Brookwell, Anna Green and Judith Lougheed, *Ladies Don't Drink*, book was sponsored by Health and Welfare Canada; copy in City of Vancouver Archive.

[6] *The Province*, June 1, 1967.

[7] Interview with author, 1995.

[8] Stanley F. Anderson scrapbook.

[9] *Vancouver Sun*, September 26, 1964.

[10] Robert A. Campbell, *Demon Rum or Easy Money*, p.99. (See SOURCES for complete reference.)

BBB

BABY DUCK: Created by *Andrés Wines* in 1971, this was the best-selling domestic wine in Canada during that decade. The Port Moody winery previously had created a 7 percent alcohol sparkling wine called Chanté, which, because lower alcohol attracted less tax, was cheaper than conventional sparkling wines. Several American wineries in the 1960s had become quite successful with sparkling pink wines called Cold Duck. (The name comes from an old European tradition of combining the remains from all the wines at a party in a single bowl and calling the result the cold end; the German word for end sounds much like the German word for duck — hence, Cold Duck for a pink wine blended from reds and whites.) When Andrés introduced a version to Canada in the mid-1960s, it was a huge success even though *Joseph Peller,* then the winery's president, "could not believe it was a serious beverage."[1] Cold Duck, with 12 percent alcohol, was quickly followed by Chanté. From there, it was a short step to blending red and white Chanté wines and calling the result Baby Duck, because of the lower alcohol. A carbonated wine, Baby Duck was made from labrusca grape varieties such as concord and bath, with a soft-drink sweetness that appealed to a great many consumers. The success was not left to chance: Andrés advertised it heavily on television, even hiring an animal psychologist to advise how the ducklings should behave in the commercials. The Canadian success led Andrés to export it to Britain in 1979. Despite a $2.5 million advertising campaign there, Baby Duck flopped in Britain. In its review, the *London Sunday Times* wrote: "The drink, purple, sparkling stuff, tastes like black currant wine gum dissolved in a glass of Andrews Liver Salt. Served extremely cold—preferably on a stick—you might be amused by its presumption."[2]

The initial success of Baby Duck triggered a series of copycat "mod" wines, as the industry liked to call them, with brand names such as Canada Duck from Calona, Love-A-Duck from Ste-Michelle, Kool Duck from Jordan, Sparkling Daddy Duck from Casabello and Fuddle Duck from the Ben Ginter winery (known at various times as Uncle Ben's and as Golden Valley). The name, Fuddle Duck, was inspired from an exchange in the House of Commons during which Prime Minister Pierre Trudeau was accused of mouthing an obscene epithet at one of his political tormentors and he lamely explained that he had only said "fuddle duck." Ginter quickly recognized a winning brand name.

The menagerie of sparkling wine brands copying the Baby Duck style by the late 1970s also included Cold Turkey and Baby Deer from Jordan; Baby Bear from Ste-Michelle and Sparkling Arctic Bear (oddly enough, a red wine) from Casabello; Yellowbird from Uncle Ben and Snobird from Jordan. All were confections concocted from water, sugar and grape juice otherwise unwanted for respectable table wine. All are now extinct species with the exception of Baby Duck. See also *Sparkling Wine.*

BACO NOIR: The French hybridizer

François Baco created this variety in 1902 by crossing a vinifera variety, folle blanche, with a native American riparia variety. The resulting dark-skinned grape makes medium-bodied reds with good acidity. These workmanlike reds can be elevated in quality with aging in wood, as **Calona Wines** discovered when a slack market demand for reds forced the winery to store a substantial inventory of both 1987 and 1988 baco noir in large casks. The wines developed a roundness and complexity; in the early 1990s, Calona began marketing the wines under premium labels and encouraging some growers to replant since most baco noir had been uprooted in the 1988 vine pull (the government-backed program paying growers to pull out almost 2,000 acres of grapes deemed undesirable for premium wines). According to records of the British Columbia Grape Marketing Board, twenty-two acres of baco noir had been in production in 1987.

BALDWIN, GUY: Winemaker at *Andrés Wines* in Port Moody in the mid-1960s, who was one of the creators in 1966 of Chanté, a low alcohol (7 percent) sparkling wine which preceded and inspired *Baby Duck*. When *Joseph Peller* took over management of Andrés from his father, he determined to upgrade the winemaking at Port Moody since there had been quality-control problems (refermenting bottles) under *Wallace Pohle*, the original winemaker. Peller went to California and interviewed about a dozen candidates before agreeing on a three-year contract with Baldwin, who was then a cellarmaster and quality-control chemist at Christian Brothers. When Baldwin left Andrés, he resumed his winemaking career in California.

Sam Baptiste (photo courtesy of John Schreiner)

BAPTISTE, JAMES (SAM) (1952–): The laconic general manager of *Inkameep Vineyards*, Baptiste was born and raised in Oliver, B.C. His eclectic education included two years of survey engineering at the University of Victoria, two years in applied sciences at a college in San Diego and, finally, two years at Wenatchee Valley College, where in 1988 he got an associate degree in horticulture, specializing in tree fruits and grapes. Baptiste credits having worked as a student in the sun-baked Inkameep vineyard with forming his determination to get an education. "I didn't want to be out there, digging holes and picking rocks for a living," he says. Ambitious and brash, he served eight years as chief of the Osoyoos Indian Band when, at age twenty-four in 1976, he was one of the youngest elected chiefs in British Columbia. He resigned in 1984 to go to college in the United States. When he returned, armed with his agricultural education, he took over as the vineyard manager in 1990. His slight build belies Baptiste's willingness to be hard-nosed when necessary. "I've fired the three toughest guys on this reserve," he says.

BARNAY, JOHN (1940–): Big-framed and booming-voiced, Barnay likely is the most experienced grapegrower no longer in the industry, courtesy of the free trade agreement. "It need not have happened," says the former general manager of Monashee Vineyards, who admits to crying when the more than two hundred acres of Monashee vines were ripped out in 1989. Barnay believes that if the wine industry had been given a transition period to adjust — as were other deeply impacted industries — many Okanagan vineyards would have made a much smoother conversion to vinifera grapes than was the case. All Barnay has to show for his quarter century in vineyard management are rich memories and a quarter acre of grapes (mostly schönburger) at his home in Penticton. "I couldn't see myself without a grape around," says Barnay, now office manager for *Munckhof Mfg.*, an Oliver producer of vineyard and orchard equipment.

Born in Penticton, Barnay was the son of an orchardist. Afflicted with hay fever, he avoided agriculture when graduating from high school, spending about five years in a series of manufacturing jobs. In 1965 he was hired by Pacific Vineyards, then planting its property south of Oliver. Three years later, he moved to a more senior job (and a minor partnership) at Monashee, a few hundred yards down the road. One of the largest vineyards in the Okanagan, Monashee was one of the first (in 1973) to start using a mechanical harvester. That enabled Barnay, who had had 120 pickers on the payroll the year before, to harvest the 1973 vintage with half a dozen people; he sat at the controls of the harvester from dawn to dusk and beyond if necessary. Barnay believes that the reduction in payroll costs enabled Monashee vineyards to overcome its other challenges.

The largest was the continual replanting that was required because the wineries kept changing their minds on what grapes they required. Barnay says that Monashee always had perhaps forty acres (sometimes more) of the vineyard not producing because it was being replanted. "Some blocks were replanted three or four times." The original plantings included about seventy acres of bath grapes, a red concord variety that owed its popularity to being the base grape for Baby Duck and that wine's imitators. Once the Duck fad cooled, bath gave way to such varieties as foch, rougeon, Okanagan riesling and verdelet. The surplus of red varieties and the popularity of white wines in the 1980s led to more replanting. By mid-decade the premiums for white varieties gave Monashee its three best years from 1986 through 1988. However, the vineyard had been slow to convert to premium vinifera since the wineries buying Monashee grapes seldom insisted on those varieties. Monashee's owners willingly accepted payments under the grape adjustment program to uproot all the vines after the 1988 harvest. Ironically, new owners have redeveloped the vineyard largely with premium vinifera varieties.

BARREL FERMENTATION: This historic winemaking technique achieved new popularity in the 1990s throughout the world for making premium wines. Winemakers have found that wines pick up oak flavours less quickly during fermentation and integrate those flavours better with the wine's fruit than when a finished wine is aged in oak. Why this is so is a matter of conjecture. The accepted explanation is that portions of the barrel's interior are coated with lees (dead yeast cells primarily), limiting the oak flavour transfers. In British Columbia **CedarCreek** in 1990 was one of the first wineries to begin barrel fermenting certain premium white wines regularly. For example, the winery's 1994 semillon was barrel-fermented in 450-litre oak puncheons.

BARRELS: See *Cooperage*.

BARRIQUE: French for barrel, this word generally describes 225-litre oak barrels. An oak container twice the size is called a puncheon.

BATES, HAROLD (1942–): A distinguished, silvery-haired, self-described "man of few words," winemaker Bates left *Sumac Ridge* in 1996 to become an Anglican priest. Born in Niagara Falls, he received a microbiology degree from the University of Guelph and joined *T.G. Brights & Co.* in 1967, where he had a hand in making the well-known Brights President Canadian Champagne. "While we were living in Ontario" — the "we" referring to his wife, Darlene, a nurse — "we had an obsession to go winemaking in the United States or Australia." In 1971 he joined United Vintners at its big Fresno winery in California, spending the next six years there and learning to work under pressure. "We did 150,000 tons of grapes every crush and bottled 100,000 cases a day," he recalls. One of his Guelph classmates, *Bob Claremont*, was then the winemaker at

Calona Wines and in 1977 recruited Bates, who was ready to return north of the border. "I missed Canada." Bates spent the next five years at Calona and had become that big winery's operations manager by 1982 when he took a sabbatical from winemaking, first to teach at a boy's school in Edmonton and then to run a group home in Kelowna for four years. He returned to winemaking at Sumac Ridge in 1987, helping the winery launch Stellars' Jay and its other sparkling wines.

BATH: A red American hybrid grape comparable in labrusca character to concord, the variety was released commercially in New York in 1962 — just in time to be planted widely in the Okanagan later that decade. It provided the grapey flavours in *Baby Duck* and its imitators and was the most important red variety until 1971, when de chaunac outstripped it in production quantity: 1,547 metric tonnes compared to bath's 1,455 tonnes. De Chaunac was a better grape for the dry red table wines then coming into demand. The bath variety clung to a healthy second place through the 1975 harvest. Production declined rapidly after that year because wineries began refusing it, finding bath useless for making the dry European-style table wines then coming into vogue.

B.C. WINE NOTES: See *Nicholas Grimshawe*.

B.C. WINE NEWS: Free distribution newsletter published since 1991 by the communications division of the British Columbia Liquor Distribution Branch.

B.C. WINE TRAILS: Quarterly industry newspaper published in Summerland since 1991 by *Dave Gamble.* It is essential reading for those who need to stay in touch with wineries in British Columbia.

BEAU SÉJOUR: When Growers' Wines bought Okanagan Mission Vineyards Ltd. in 1965 from *Frank Schmidt*, the property was renamed Beau Séjour, a name that also became a brand for wines that Growers' produced. The vineyard has had several owners since and now is divided between *Leo Gebert*, owner of *St. Hubertus* winery, and his brother, Andy.

BEAUPRÉ WINES (CANADA) LTD.: See *Potter Distilleries.*

BECKER, DR. HELMUT (1927– 1989): The influential head of Germany's Geisenheim grape breeding institute from 1964 until his death, Becker first toured the Okanagan Valley in 1976 at the invitation of his first Canadian-born student, *Walter Gehringer*, then an assistant winemaker at Andrés. Becker already was familiar with the Pacific Northwest, having provided the famed Geisenheim clone of riesling in 1972 to a winery in Idaho, where the grape proved suitably hardy. Impressed with the potential of the Okanagan, Becker supplied, free of charge, a selection of twenty-seven vinifera varieties for trial in three-acre test plots, one at a vineyard at Okanagan Mission run by Glen Wood, and the other at Monashee Vineyards near Oliver. These trials ran from 1977 to 1985 and proved the viability of several varieties — notably pinot blanc, ehrenfelser, müller-thurgau and riesling — that have become a foundation for the industry in the 1990s. "Your soil is young, fresh, virgin," Becker said in a 1985 interview. "They grow like hell."[3] Among the handful of reds supplied by

Becker was St. Laurent, an old French variety noted for hardiness; it was one of the few that was not widely accepted by growers.

BECKER PROJECT: This was the vinifera trial in the Okanagan from 1977 to 1985 under the supervision of German grape scientist *Dr. Helmut Becker.*

BELLA TERRA VINEYARDS: See *Stan Dunis.*

BELLA VISTA VINEYARDS: The most northerly winery in British Columbia, Bella Vista was established in Vernon in 1994 by fifteen fun-loving investors and partners, led by *Larry Passmore*, the operator of a successful store for amateur wine and beer production. Self-described bohemians, the partners involve themselves and visitors to the attractive mountainside winery in hard work in the vineyards and raucous tastings in the winery.

BENNETT, W.A.C. (1900–1979): The nondrinking premier of British Columbia from 1952 to 1972, Bennett paradoxically was an investor in and president of *Calona Wines Ltd.* in its initial years. Bennett, who bought a hardware store in Kelowna in 1930, had become a close friend of *Cap Capozzi*, whose Bernard Avenue grocery story was just three doors away from the Bennett store. Bennett and Capozzi travelled the province in the early 1930s, selling shares in the winery. The nondrinking Bennett was being strictly entrepreneurial: he saw the winery creating jobs as well as markets for local fruit. He resigned in December 1941, writing Cap Capozzi: "Now that I am elected a representative in the Provincial Legislature, and as

Calona Wines does a considerable proportion of its business with the provincial government, I do not think it would be proper for me to retain a financial or directing interest in the company. As you know, I have sold all my shares...." Bennett had accumulated 5,237 shares; they were sold to a businessman named Gordon Finch.[4]

His sons R.J. and William (who also became premier) toyed briefly with growing grapes on their ranch north of Kelowna after *Growers' Wines Ltd*. offered them a contract in the 1960s, primarily to keep them from growing for anyone else.

BIOLLO, ANTHONY S. (TONY) (1917–1971):

Penticton-born son of an Italian immigrant, Biollo was a construction contractor by trade but a grapegrower by choice. He began trial plantings in the 1950s at his home in Penticton's West Bench area, made his own wine and once even sought (unsuccessfully) a winemaker's job with a Quebec winery. Biollo claimed to have been the first person hired by *Andrew Peller* when the latter was starting Andrés in 1961.[5] In 1964, having left Andrés, he persuaded *Evans Lougheed* to organize *Casabello Wines*. Biollo became its production manager until a brain tumour claimed his life.

BIRD CONTROL: Certain birds have voracious appetites for ripe grapes and, if protective measures are not taken, flocks will strip entire vineyards prior to harvest. *Cherry Point* winery on Vancouver Island was forced to delay its opening one year when birds got most of the 1992 vintage before the pickers, despite electronic alarms meant to frighten

birds away. In the following year, Cherry Point deployed nets over the entire vineyard. An increasing number of growers have now resorted to nets as the routine defence.

The most basic measure for discouraging birds is to frighten them with noisemakers that mimic the sound of discharging firearms, coupled with actually shooting birds from time to time when they begin to ignore the noisemakers. The effectiveness of these measures is far from complete. In a 1985 article, the Farm Credit Corporation's magazine *Encounter* reported that when Gray Monk's *George Heiss, Sr*. was asked about vineyard problems, he drew a pistol from his pocket. "The starlings are bad but the robins are even worse. You can shoot one off a wire and the guy sitting next to him will watch the body fall and say 'Oh look, Fred just fell off the wire,' then he'll hop down and eat your grapes. They are fearless and stupid and very difficult to control."[6] In general, noise-making devices need to be deployed early in the season and must be moved about the vineyard to keep the invading flocks of birds off balance. But if the birds become accustomed to these devices, they soon ignore them. Recordings of starling distress calls have proved effective in frightening off flocks. Other occasionally effective devices include kites bearing hawklike images or helium-filled balloons that dangle hawk replicas. *Jenny White*, one of the proprietors of *Mistral Vineyard* south of Oliver, claims success at deterring birds after populating the vineyard with a horde, literally, of scarecrows, clad in cast-off clothes and topped with fierce visages painted onto empty plastic milk containers. One large Okanagan vineyard has experimented with photo-degradable netting that can be draped over rows of vines prior to harvest, giving three to four weeks of protection before breaking down sufficiently in sunlight that the netting does not impede harvesting equipment. There also is an effective chemical, Measurol, which, when sprayed on vines, makes the grapes unpalatable to birds. However, it is not approved for use in Canada. The most unconventional (but barely effective) weapon against starlings was the ultra-light aircraft flown by Monashee Vineyards manager *John Barnay*, a keen amateur pilot who once herded a huge flock away from his vineyard during a two-hour aerial dogfight one calm afternoon. He zoomed back to the vineyard for a four o'clock meeting. The starlings were back thirty minutes later.

Give the birds credit for discerning taste. The growers had far fewer problems with birds when the vineyards were full of labrusca varieties. "Concord is not a very big priority food for starlings," Washington State authority **Dr. Walter Clore** wryly said at a 1974 growers' meeting in the Okanagan. "We didn't have any problems with birds until we started planting some of the wine grapes." In the Okanagan, growers had begun to plant more palatable wine grapes in the 1960s and the word of good eats quickly spread through the bird kingdom. At the request of grapegrowers, the British Columbia agriculture ministry inaugurated a starling control program in 1972, setting out fifteen starling traps between Vernon and Osoyoos that year and a further six the following year. The traps caught 38,000 birds during those two years. As large as that figure seems, even the ministry acknowledged it was insignificant compared with the size of the flocks. "Trapping is not reducing the population quickly enough to benefit the growers to any extent," a provincial pest control officer told a growers' meeting in January 1974.[7] The ministry continued trapping birds for some time while searching for bird repellents.

Dr. Clore told that 1974 meeting that robins were more difficult to deal with than starlings. "We can scare the starlings out of the vineyards and they stay out most of the day, but robins, they just fly up and come back," Clore said. "They even sit on the end of the cannons." But **Dick Cleave**, a veteran Okanagan vineyard manager, argues that the starling is the single most troublesome bird. Native to Britain, the starling was brought to North America in the nineteenth century as a house bird. Those that escaped or were released soon bred large flocks which thrive because there are few natural predators. To grape and fruit growers in western North America, the migratory starling is a major economic problem. "I've seen starling damage where they've taken five or six tons in fifteen minutes and what they have not eaten has fallen to the ground," Cleave says. "You have to be very vigilant with them, dawn until dusk, seven days a week."[8]

BLACK SAGE VINEYARD: This 115-acre vineyard north of Osoyoos was established in 1993 when *Sumac Ridge* purchased part of what had been the Monashee vineyard. The sandy property, affording dramatic views of the valley below from its slightly rolling southward-facing slope, had been idle since the vines were pulled out after the 1988 vintage. Its proven ability to grow grapes had caught the ambitious eye of Sumac founder **Harry McWatters**. **Dick Cleave**, who was named Black Sage's vineyard manager, says: "Harry and I had been talking for years and years and years about acquiring some of this land and planting good grapes — vinifera grapes, reds in particular." Some 96,000 grape vines, including cabernet sauvignon, cabernet franc and merlot, were imported from France and planted that year. Canadian plant quarantine authorities, worried that vine viruses might also be imported, required that all imported vines that year get a hot water bath before leaving the nursery. When the Black Sage plants began to grow, a quarter of them either were found to be dead or weakened seriously by the treatment, a serious setback. However, the vines that survived are thriving and ultimately the grapes will be processed in a winery that is planned for a knoll at the northeast corner of the vineyard, a location with the site's best views.

BLACK WIDOW VINEYARDS & ACCESSORIES LTD.: This name encompasses a small vineyard near Okanagan Falls and a business of extroverted owners Matt and Alice Leak, whose T-shirts in wine bottles are among the more original of wine accessories. The name, of course, is a reminder of the Okanagan's large population of black widow spiders, creatures feared for the toxic sting of the females. Leak believes the fear is overdone. "They are very pretty and very shy," he has found. "They mind their own business and you rarely see them in the house." Leak has registered the name because he believes it would be suitable for a winery; Leak's son, Kevin, a commercial tree planter, has shown interest in operating the vineyard one day.

A large friendly man with a booming voice, Leak was born in Edmonton in 1932, the son of a farmer, and lived much of his life in Drayton Valley, an Alberta oil industry community. At various times, he owned a large insurance brokerage, built and operated a golfing resort and was a co-owner and pilot of an air charter company. He retired in 1988 when severe arthritis forced him to relinquish his pilot's licence. The search for a dry climate brought Leak and his wife to the Okanagan in 1990 and to the rugged property now called Black Widow. He refused to let his arthritis and several artificial joints deter him from planting grapes. "What else could you put in that was viable for this area?" he said. He has two thousand vines, equally divided between pinot noir and pinot blanc, and sells most of the fruit to **Wild Goose Vineyards**, which is just across the road from his property. Leak, who knew nothing about winemaking before moving to the Okanagan, has taken to producing about four hundred gallons a year. "Just in case of sickness," he winks.

The novelty T-shirts packaged in wine bottles were launched in 1995 after the Leaks mastered the trick of bottling the cartoon-embellished garments. Using a special lapidary saw, Matt Leak cuts each wine bottle in half, enabling one carefully folded shirt to be placed inside. The two halves are rejoined with tape and a wrap-around label totally covers the cut. The bottles are then sealed with shrink-wrap capsules. The T-shirts are adorned with colourful images of two winemaking friars christened Brothers Herman and Jake by Matt Leak, their creator, whose own zest for life is mirrored in the bucolic grape-stomping clerics.

BLUE GROUSE VINEYARDS: Established in 1993 by **Dr. Hans Kiltz**, a former veterinarian, Blue Grouse is a farmgate winery in the Cowichan Valley based on a vineyard originally developed by **John Harper**, a veteran grape nursery operator. The winery's production includes pinot noir, pinot gris, müller-thurgau, and bacchus.

BLUE MOUNTAIN VINEYARD AND CELLARS: Established in 1992 near Okanagan Falls by veteran grower **Ian Mavety** and his wife, Jane, this estate winery has produced some of the Okanagan's most sophisticated table wines and sparkling wines. The winery has focussed closely on four primary grape varieties, pinot blanc, pinot gris, chardonnay and pinot noir. Mavety grows other varieties, including riesling, in his extensive vineyard but believes that the microclimate at his location approximates the growing conditions of Burgundy. The successive vintages of full-bodied pinot noir and barrel-fermented chardonnay made at Blue Mountain aim for the style of Burgundy. In its initial years the winery sold all of its wines directly to private customers or to prestige restaurants, offering only its sparkling wine through the British Columbia liquor stores. This shrewd strategy enabled Blue Mountain to retain the maximum revenue from its wine sales.

BOWEN, DR. JOHN (1914–): One of the developers of the cider-making process for Growers' apple cider, Bowen was born in Vancouver and, after getting a master's in microbiology from the University of British Columbia in 1937, spent three years as a bacteriologist for the Fraser Valley Milk Producers' Co-operative. After three years in the air force, he joined **Growers' Wines Ltd.** in Victoria as an understudy to winemaker **Dr. Eugene Rittich** who was thinking of retiring. But because Rittich, a year later, was no closer to retiring, Bowen moved to Ottawa and the federal department of agriculture for two years until, in 1948, he won a transfer to the research station at Summerland. It was here in the 1950s that he and Summerland's director, F.A. Atkinson, developed at fruit-grower request the method for making cider from the Okanagan's abundant sweet eating apples. Traditional cider in Europe is made from tart apples not especially appealing on their own. Bowen's method involved pressing the juice from Red Delicious and the more acidic Jonathan apples in a 75 percent/25 percent blend. This juice was sweetened and then fermented with wine yeast, with fermentation stopped before the cider was fully dry. It was then carbonated — Bowen called it "a half-baked champagne process" — and bottled. The first commercial quantities were bottled at a brewery in Princeton; the inventory and the process was acquired by Growers', which scored a long-lasting success with the cider. Subsequently, Bowen took his doctorate at Bristol University in Britain in 1962, doing his thesis on the ecology of yeasts in English cider. After returning to Summerland, he was in charge of winemaking trials until he retired in 1975. He also authored a pamphlet on winemaking and, in the fall of 1971, taught a four-session winemaking course at Okanagan College, one of the first such courses in the Okanagan.[9]

BRAUN, JACK (1927–): Born in Herbert, Sask., Braun grew up in communities in the Fraser Valley, left home to go to work when he was fourteen, becoming literally a jack of all trades. He spent thirty years in Alberta in construction and subsequently owned and operated Bronco Industries, a manufacturer of recreational vehicles in High River. Braun sold the business in 1983 and, looking for what he termed "something different," bought a rugged ten acres of sage brush and pine on Oliver Ranch Road, south of Okanagan Falls. Encouraged by a neighbour's new vineyard, Braun began planting in 1988. On four rocky slopes, three of which pitch steeply into a sun-drenched bowl, Braun grows almost a dozen different varieties, all vinifera, including cabernet sauvignon, merlot and chardonnay. An independent-minded man who has never joined the growers' association, Braun markets significant quantities to home winemakers.

BREMMER, JOHN (1942–):
Born in Vernon, the son of a fruit farmer, Bremmer was three years into a veterinarian's course at the University of British Columbia when one of his professors steered him into food technology. On graduating in 1965 Bremmer became a production trainee with a commercial dairy in Burnaby. He quickly discovered this to be a "staid and boring" industry and joined Andrés in March 1966 as a laboratory technician. There was plenty of excitement at Andrés where sales took off after brewery workers in British Columbia went on strike. "We made sure that the brewery workers [on the picket lines] were kept supplied with wine during the strike," Bremmer recalls. With wine sales then booming at 15 percent a year, new products like *Baby Duck* were

constantly emerging (Bremmer blended the original Baby Duck formulations for winemaker *Guy Baldwin*). By the time he left Andrés in 1978, Bremmer had risen to general manager and production manager of the Port Moody winery. In 1978 he took on a nine-month assignment to plan a viticulture program for *Jordan & Ste-Michelle*; then he and *Robert Holt* bought eighty-six acres on the Similkameen River near Cawston as the basis for a future winery. The hard winter of 1978–79 wiped out that dream and Bremmer went to work for *Brights* in December 1980, supervising construction of the new winery and subsequently becoming the general manager. He left in 1990 to work as a consultant to the industry and to devote more time to his five-and-a-half-acre orchard south of Oliver. Here in 1995 Bremmer and his wife, Lynn, began converting the property to a vineyard.

BREMMER, LYNN (1951–):
The first female professional winemaker in British Columbia, she was better known as Lynn Stark, having worked under her maiden name to avert confusion when both she and John Bremmer worked in commercial wineries. She was born in Kinnaird, B.C. (a community since absorbed by Castlegar), the daughter of a Cominco smelter worker. After completing a two-year food-processing program at the British Columbia Institute of Technology, Bremmer joined *Andrés* in 1973 as a laboratory technician and was assistant winemaker when she left in 1980 to join John Bremmer on the Similkameen vineyard that he and *Robert Holt* had purchased in 1978 as the basis for an estate winery. After the vineyard had been almost wiped out during the win-

ter of 1978–79, the Bremmers accepted employment at the new *Brights* winery in Oliver, selling their interest in the vineyard to Holt. Starting with the 1981 vintage, Lynn Bremmer was the senior winemaker at the Oliver winery through to the end of the 1992 harvest. She produced a wide range of varietals, including small batches of highly individual wines from Russian grape varieties that had been planted initially at the *Inkameep* vineyard and later by grower *Lanny Martiniuk*. Notable among these were sereksia chornaya (which made a good rosé), matsvani and rkatsiteli, both white varieties. Brights subsequently discontinued these because, with their difficult names, they were hard to sell. In 1992, Lynn and John Bremmer established their own consulting company, Tyme Technologies Inc., serving Okanagan wineries. "We do a lot of analysis in the fall when we look at the vineyards and advise when they should be picked," Bremmer says. "I have set up a small laboratory." Tyme (so-named because the Bremmers grow thyme and other herbs) also has consulted on winery projects in the Caribbean, Romania and Slovakia. The Bremmers have a long history as consulting winemakers, beginning with *Gray Monk* for whom they made wines in 1979, 1980 and 1981.

BRENTWOOD PRODUCTS LTD.: See *Victoria Wineries (B.C.) Ltd.*

BRIGHTS, T.G. & CO.: Now known as *Vincor International Ltd.*, Canada's largest winery, Brights was established in Ontario in 1874. The winery sought to market its wines in British Columbia after the Second World War, with little success since it lacked a winery in the province. In the 1970s Brights considering buying *Calona* and very nearly did buy *Mission Hill* before finally opening its own winery until 1981 at Oliver near the *Inkameep Vineyards*. Five years later Brights took over *Jordan & Ste-Michelle Cellars*, closing the large and almost new Ste-Michelle winery in Surrey to consolidate operations in Oliver. There was further consolidation into the Oliver winery in 1995 after Brights merged with *Cartier & Inniskillin Vintners* in 1994. The Cartier winery in Penticton, formerly the Casabello winery, was closed, with equipment and personnel moving to Oliver. Under the Vincor banner, the historic Brights name largely has disappeared from wines, replaced primarily by two national brands, *Jackson-Triggs* and *Sawmill Creek*. The strategy has been to produce higher quality varietal wines than were associated with the Brights history and to sell them at higher price points.

BRITISH COLUMBIA SCHOOL OF ALCOHOL STUDIES: This summer school, which had its first week-long session in the summer of 1957, was run through the University of British Columbia Extension Department with backing from the Alcohol Research and Education Council and the Alcoholism Foundation of British Columbia. The work of the school involved "personal and social implications of alcohol problems." The philosophic thrust was inferred by the identity of some lecturers: Mrs. E. Willoughby Crawford, British Columbia education director for the Women's Christian Temperance Union, and John Richey, director of education for the Washington Temperance Association, plus a chaplain from the Oakalla Prison and a Salvation Army officer.

BRITISH COLUMBIA WINE AND GRAPE GROWERS COUNCIL:
An organization of this name was proposed to the industry in January 1967 by R.A. McFadyen, who signed himself as acting secretary. This is one of the first recorded attempts to form such an umbrella promotion body for the industry. McFadyen laid out four aims: helping wineries and growers evaluate grape varieties; creating a meeting ground for the exchange of ideas and information; education in wine appreciation; and "to taste wines produced in British Columbia and compare them with those produced elsewhere." The reaction of the wineries was summed up by Growers' Wines president **Brian Roberts** in a memorandum in February to his vineyard manager **Lloyd Schmidt.** "Is this the nut from Keremeos who thinks his grapes are worth $165 a ton? From what I know, he is trying to make a name for himself and is a born troublemaker.... You already have a grape growers association and the various seminars such as the last one in Kelowna bringing the growers and government and wineries together. Do we need another organization? If you wish you might have a quiet word with **Tommy Capozzi** [of Calona] about it. I personally am a little scared of this thing. P. S. I was talking to Tommy Capozzi by telephone today and he agrees that this guy is a nut." Ironically, after Roberts retired from Growers', he went on to run the British Columbia Wine Council, a promotional body formed by the major wineries.[10]

BRITISH COLUMBIA WINE INSTITUTE:
Launched in August 1990, this is the industry body that is responsible for ensuring minimum standards of wine quality in British Columbia, with powers granted under the British Columbia Wine Act of 1990. The Institute supervises the Vintners Quality Alliance program and the regular tastings that award the VQA seal to wines that meet or exceed the quality standards. (Since it is not mandatory for a winery to apply for VQA seals, some producers of top quality wines, for reasons of their own, have not placed their wines before the VQA tasting panels.) The Institute promotes wines to consumers and restauranteurs in Canada and in export markets. It also provides a communication link on wine and taxation policy between wineries and grape growers on the one hand and the provincial government on the other. The Institute's financing includes levies on both grape and wine sales. See **Christine Coletta.**

BRODERSEN, NICK (1930–):
A specialist in growing gewurztraminer and celebrated as such on **Gray Monk**'s Brodersen Vineyard wine, Kaleden grower Brodersen arrived in the Okanagan in 1980, planning semi-retirement as a vineyard owner. He had been raised on a farm in northern Germany where he was born, a descendant from a family with Viking forebears. Lack of opportunity there led him to come to Canada in 1951 where he became an electrician, operating a successful commercial and industrial electrical contracting firm in Vancouver with a partner. He sold his interest in 1972, buying a motel and restaurant in Cranbrook which he operated before moving to Kaleden.

Brodersen, who had studied agriculture in Germany, had first canvassed viticulture in the Okanagan in the mid-1960s. He was not encouraged by a conversation he had with **Dr. Donald Fisher**, then director of the research station at Summerland, who reminded Brodersen that the Okanagan was first and foremost an apple-growing valley. "By heart we are apple growers here," Brodersen recalled being told. But the desire to grow grapes remained, the ambition being realized when, tired of the motel, he bought highway frontage near Kaleden with sandy soil and a southeastern exposure suited to grapes. He began in the spring of 1981 by transplanting young gewurztraminer vines he dug out laboriously from a vineyard in Penticton scheduled to become a housing development. The remaining three acres in his vineyard were planted with vines obtained from a Washington state nursery. Because his mentor was Sumac Ridge co-founder **Lloyd Schmidt**, Broder-sen's first grapes were sold to that winery. Subsequently, he transferred his contract to Gray Monk.

When planning the vineyard initially, Brodersen was advised to plant Okanagan riesling but after attending a seminar on vinifera varieties, he said to Schmidt : "I would like to grow a more exotic variety." Schmidt suggested gewurztraminer and Brodersen has been grateful ever since for the advice. In many ways, Brodersen felt like a pioneer. For example, vineyard supplies were not easily available. "The wire for the trellis system came, I think, from a [dismantled] telephone line in the Peace River country," he recalled. One of the early growers to install finicky drip irrigation, Brodersen had difficulty getting a proper water filter, and resorted to swimming pool filters which proved too fragile; af-

ter weeks of frustration, he finally located a reliable filter. "Today, you don't even plant by yourself anymore," he said. "You just phone up the contractor."

Ted Brouwer (photo courtesy of John Schreiner)

BROUWER, TED (1925–):

A rotund and cheery optimist with infinite patience with bureaucracy, Brouwer steered ***Inkameep Vineyards Ltd.*** through its tumultuous early years, learning grapegrowing as he went until he was completely seduced by viticulture. After he left the vineyard in 1986, he bought a small apple orchard nearby on a property with no vines. "I still would like some grapes," he said wistfully in a 1995 interview.

Brouwer was born in Heemstede, a small town about twenty-five kilometres west of Amsterdam in Holland, the son of a food wholesaler. In 1946 Brouwer enlisted in the Royal Netherlands Army's medical corps and was posted to Indonesia, then still a Dutch colony. In his free time there, he enrolled in courses in tropical agriculture. On returning to

Holland in 1950, he went to work for his father's firm but continued his agricultural studies until, with a group of other ex-army friends, he came to Canada in 1955. After a summer on a grain farm near Medicine Hat, Brouwer moved to Vancouver and spent two years working as a poultry technician at the University of British Columbia. That led to his working on several large turkey ranches until the fall of 1967 when he enrolled in a two-year agriculture course at Northern Lights College in Dawson Creek.

In the summer of 1967 he responded to an advertisement for a vineyard manager at Monashee Vineyards. The job did not materialize because owner **Ed Wahl** decided to run the vineyard himself; but the offer piqued Brouwer's interest in grapegrowing. When he heard that a job was opening at Inkameep, he was able to spend the summer of 1968 there before returning to the college, completing his studies with a term paper on grapegrowing. In the spring of 1969 he took over as the vineyard manager, staying there until February 1986 when he clashed with a newly elected chief of the Inkameep band and was fired. The resulting suit for wrongful dismissal was settled out of court with Brouwer getting a cash settlement to compensate for the abrogation of his contract.

BUCHLER, HANS (1947–):
One of the leading organic grapegrowers in the Okanagan, the lean, lanky Buchler farms a seventeen-acre vineyard tucked into a bucolic, pine-covered valley high above Oliver. In Berne, Switzerland, where he was born, his father was a doctor and his mother a teacher. When he finished college, Buchler spent some time travelling before returning to Switzerland and marrying Christine, a nurse. They lived and worked on his father-in-law's organic vegetable farm in the Swiss winegrowing region known by the appellation *La Cot*, where his interest in grapes and wine began. Land prices being prohibitive in Switzerland, Buchler and his wife emigrated, choosing Canada over New Zealand because Buchler had travelled across Canada in 1976. "I was just overwhelmed by the beauty of British Columbia," he recalls. The raw land they purchased near Oliver was planted to grapes in 1983 after Buchler negotiated a contract to sell the fruit to *Mission Hill*. They originally planted foch, Okanagan riesling and verdelet, along with only two vinifera (gewurztraminer and white riesling). The Okanagan riesling was the first to be replaced — with chardonnay, pinot noir and semillon; half of the foch was uprooted later and the verdelet was pulled out after the 1995 harvest, to be replaced by pinot noir and gamay. The remaining foch plants may have gained a lease on life by the return of this variety to favour. As well, Mission Hill has had commercial success marketing an organic foch wine, made from Buchler's grapes.

The vineyard has been organic since 1988, although Buchler had used herbicides and synthetic fertilizers in the first two years on the property. "But that does not agree with my outlook on farming," he says. Now he gets nutrients into his soils by growing legume cover crops such as peas, vetch and clover, so successfully that some parts of the vineyard are at risk of having excessive nitrogen (which causes the vines to grow too vigorously). Weeds are kept under control with cultivation and by incinerating the young weeds with blasts from a portable propane-fueled flame thrower. The most devastating insect pest in vineyards is the leaf hopper. Buchler has found the populations of these can be reduced with insecticidal soaps and by introducing parasites, some of which are commercially available while others — notably a microscopic wasp called *Anagrus epos* — occur naturally. None of the controls is complete but Buchler is satisfied with establishing a balance between nature and an acceptable amount of damage. "I always have to find the solution which is the least labour intensive," he says.

Dedicated to organic principles, Buchler is a member of the Similkameen-Okanagan Organic Growers Association and has been president of the Association of Certified Organic Growers of British Columbia. With three wineries fully organic in 1995 and with many requests for information from growers, Buchler knows he is no longer pioneering the concept.

BULLDOZER DISEASE: Many Okanagan vineyards have been shaped by earth-moving equipment as growers seek ideal slopes for exposure to the sun. When a vineyard has been contoured so ineptly by the dozer that the soil strata have been mixed and much of the topsoil buried or degraded, the vines just grow poorly. Growers call this bulldozer disease.

BURROWING OWL VINEYARDS LTD.: This 220-acre vineyard north of Osoyoos encompasses much of what was once called *Pacific Vineyards*. It was acquired in 1992 by Okanagan Falls vintner **Albert LeComte**, who renamed the property Desert Rose Vineyard and began replanting acreage idle since the 1988

vine pull. In 1993 Vancouver business-man *James Wyse* purchased the land and, reflecting his interest in conservation, renamed it again for the burrowing owl. In addition to mainstream reds such as cabernet sauvignon and merlot, this vineyard also has trial plantings of three Italian reds — barbera, nebbiollo and sangiovese. "I think sangiovese will be too late but there is no harm in trying," vineyard manager **Dick Cleave** says. "We're looking for the next generation of varieties. An awful lot of merlot and pinot noir have been planted in the valley. You have to expand your horizons." In 1995 the vineyard contracted a portion of its production for eight years to *Calona Wines*, but also began planning an estate winery, with the first crush scheduled for 1997.

BUSNARDO, JOE (1934–): The iconoclastic founder in 1983 of *Divino Estate Winery*, the fiercely independent Busnardo planted his choice vineyard site entirely to vinifera at a time when many growers were only just switching with reluctance from labrusca. Busnardo planted a vast menu of varieties which later enabled him to produce an equally vast table of wines. "I make twenty-five wines," he said. "I have wine for everybody. If a person says he does not like *any* of my wines, he had better stop drinking." He sold the Divino vineyard in 1996 and moved his winery to a new vineyard site in the Cowichan Valley on Vancouver Island.

When he was growing up on a farm at Treviso, north of Venice, and when he studied at a nearby agriculture school, he "never liked any plant but grapes." He came to Canada in 1954, a twenty-year-old bachelor, and by 1967 scraped together enough to buy sixty-eight acres on an eastward-facing sloping bench just south of Oliver. He imported twenty-six varieties of vinifera grapes from Italy and a further fifty-six varieties from the University of California at Davis. Busnardo's planting of pinot bianco (Italian for pinot blanc) was one of the earliest and largest plantings of what now is recognized as a vinifera superbly suited to the Okanagan. He ignored the established wineries and professionals in the Okanagan who urged more hardy hybrid varieties as well as bath, a labrusca grape totally unsuited for table wines. With the wineries not prepared to pay a premium for his low-yielding vinifera, the struggling Busnardo took a job as a heavy-duty mechanic for the city of Penticton and simply neglected his vineyard. "I closed the farm down," he recalled. "I didn't even prune the grapes." His father visited him, shook his head and advised Joe to rip out the vineyard.

The bitter winter of 1978–79 killed the next season's growth on many vines in the Okanagan and destroyed some vines entirely. But Busnardo found that his casually tended vineyard had come through the winter, proving that his faith in vinifera was not ill-founded. By coincidence, the first estate winery regulations had been issued by the provincial government in 1978. Busnardo now decided to get a winery licence. Untrained as a winemaker, Busnardo launched Divino on a wing and a prayer, making wines in the traditional method that he remembered from his father's farm. "I just throw in the grapes and hope for the best," he said at the time. The occasional winemaking mistake slipped by: once, 5,000 bottles of pinot blanc had to be taken off the market after the harmless but unsightly residue of the fining agent began settling out in the bottles. Busnardo survived and learned from such experiences; subsequently, a brother, Guido, began coming from Italy to help with the winemaking which became more sure-handed with each passing vintage.

The vineyard once had as many as 128 different grape varieties, a testimony to Busnardo's undisciplined curiosity about the vine. It also has made for a wide range of releases from the winery, among them several that no one else had. Divino was the only winery to release varietals made from garganega, trebbiano and malvasia, all important to vintners in Italy. Garganega, for example, is the principal grape for the production of Soave, a well-known delicate white made in the northern Italian winegrowing district of Veneto. But Divino has been at a disadvantage with these varietals because, in the British Columbia market it targets, these whites are scarcely known and, as much as Busnardo argues — and rightly so — that consumers should explore wines beyond the mainstream varietals, not many leave the beaten track.

1   Interview with author, 1982.

2   Quoted in a 1980 Canadian Press series of articles written by Leslie Shepherd.

3   Interview with author.

4   Correspondence in Calona Wines Ltd. files.

5   *Penticton Herald*, August 17, 1967.

6   Farm Credit Corporation, *Encounter*, March 1985, in Gray Monk scrapbooks.

7   Proceedings of the third annual Okanagan-Similkameen Grape Grower's Forum, January 15–16, 1974. In Lloyd Schmidt files.

8   Interview with author, June 1995.

9   *Oliver Chronicle*, September 30, 1971.

10   McFadyen letter January 18, 1967, and Roberts's memo dated February 3, 1967, in Lloyd Schmidt files.

CCC

CABERNET FRANC: This vinifera variety produces fine wines in the Loire but is used elsewhere in France primarily as a blending grape. It ripens slightly earlier than cabernet sauvignon, which is one reason why the variety has been planted in the Okanagan, where the growing season can be relatively short. One early advocate of the grape was *Elias Phiniotis* when he was the winemaker at *Calona Wines Ltd.* In 1988 the winery procured grape plants from a Washington state nursery and parcelled them out for trials by three growers, two of which found that the vines thrived. One was *Marcello Ercego* at Kaleden and the other was Joe Fatur at Oliver. Fatur sold his vineyard to *Domaine Combret* in 1992. That winery's first red wine was a richly flavoured cabernet franc from the 1994 vintage. Most cabernet franc in the Okanagan, as in France, is blended with merlot and cabernet sauvignon.

CABERNET SAUVIGNON: This is arguably the best red wine grape in the world; it is certainly the most ubiquitous. Given good growing conditions, the vine adapts easily and almost everywhere in the world, and produces lively berry-flavoured wines capable of elegance and longevity. Almost all the plantings in the Okanagan have been in the Oliver-Osoyoos area because cabernet sauvignon benefits from heat and needs a long autumn to mature properly.

CALONA WINES LTD.: The largest and oldest continuing winery in British Columbia, it was conceived by *Guiseppe Ghezzi,* who put together a syndicate in 1931 to raise $10,000 for the purchase of winemaking equipment. He relied on *Peter Casorso* to tap fellow farmers in the Kelowna area but when the fund-raising fell short, the syndicate in 1932 turned to outsiders, including two of Kelowna's rising businessmen, *Pasquale (Cap) Capozzi* and *W.A.C. Bennett,* who subsequently raised additional funds, largely from the Italian community in Trail. (Thanks to the smelter there, citizens of Trail in the Depression still had cash to invest, unlike the Okanagan's farmers.) Bennett became the president, Capozzi vice-president and Ghezzi's son, Carlo, became general manager; the other directors were drawn entirely from Kelowna's non-Italian business community with the exception of one original member of the Ghezzi syndicate, John Maggiora, who ran the Westholme Hotel in Victoria. While Ghezzi and Casorso sought backing from the Okanagan farmers, Maggiora negotiated with a consulting chemist in Turin, Italy, Dr. Eudo Monti, who wanted to sell certain patent rights to the new venture for $3,000. The chemist arranged the shipment to Kelowna of grape concentrate and equipment for winemaking and fruit concentrating. While the files of correspondence on these transactions are incomplete, the relationship with Monti lasted several years. The winery sent him samples of its first wines to evaluate and invited him to visit Kelowna.[1]

Launched in 1932, the winery was called *Domestic Wines and By-Products Co.* because the investors intended to make not only apple wines but also "ap-

Carlo Ghezzi (left) and Cap Capozzi of Calona Wines (photo courtesy Lina Ben-Hamida)

ple cider ... brandy, alcohol, spirits of all kinds, fruit juices, soft drinks, fruit concentrates, jelly, jams, pickles, vinegar, tomato paste, tomato catsup, tomato juice and by-products of every kind."[2] One early letter to Dr. Monti reports that "we have a large demand for concentrated apple juice from England." The winery had a shaky start. In a booklet written for its fiftieth anniversary, Calona admitted: "The company's original apple wines — Okay Red, Okay Clear, Okay Port and Okay Champagne — were a bitter disappointment. Many bottles refermented on liquor store shelves and had to be thrown out." With experience and with the use of grapes in 1935, the wines improved. The company now called itself *Calona*, a name plucked from a competition among consumers

and not, as some have maintained, because it was the phonetic way in which the Italians spelled Kelowna.

Sales were slow at first, confined mainly to the Okanagan. In the last two weeks of November 1932, the Liquor Control Board sold 262 bottles through its nineteen stores, including 70 bottles at the Kelowna store and 43 in Penticton and Vernon. When Bennett complained, an LCB official wrote: "I think possibly you are unreasonable in expecting any large turn-over on this brand of wine, as it will naturally take you some little time to get it properly introduced." In its first financial statement, for the period from February 28, 1932, to September 30, 1933, the winery had sales of $13,204.19 and a profit of $554.49. In that report Bennett wrote: "The Company has gone through an experimental period, perfecting the manufacture of the different kinds of wines now being sold, and with all the opposition and obstacles it had to contend with, it is gratifying to report that there is a balance on the right side after writing off heavy depreciation."

Barely surviving its first decade, Calona began growing when wartime and a military base at Vernon brought cash and customers into the Okanagan. For example, sales reached $95,236.59 in the year ended January 31, 1942, with a profit of $4,007. In 1951 the winery moved from the warehouse it had rented into a purpose-built winery at what became its permanent Kelowna location. In 1960 the cautious Carlo Ghezzi retired, handing over management to the aggressive Capozzi family: Cap and his three sons. The youngest of the three, Herb, after a successful career as a football tackle with the Montreal Allouettes and the Calgary Stampeders, entered politics in 1966 and was a Social Credit member for Vancouver Centre for two terms. But with Joe Capozzi as production manager and Tom Capozzi as executive vice-president and sales manager, Calona went from being the smallest winery in British Columbia to the largest, overtaking *Growers' Wines* of Victoria. While Growers' products remained in dull packaging, Calona updated both its packages and labels, scoring a particular success with a bottle that resembled a decanter. Calona's sales people also were more aggressive in pursuing listings in the liquor stores. Herb Capozzi's renown as a football player and banquet speaker — where he plugged Calona and usually insisted Calona wines be served — gave the entire Capozzi family and their winery useful recogni-

tion among liquor store clerks awed by celebrity. By 1967 Calona was the sales leader and spent close to $1 million that year on what Cap Capozzi called "the most modern and up-to-date winery in all of Canada."[3] The British Columbia wine industry grew more competitive in 1967 when both Casabello and Mission Hill opened. But at December 1967, Calona had 38.6 percent of the wine sales in British Columbia (and was selling as far afield as New Brunswick), compared with 33 percent for Growers', 15 percent for Andrés, 10 percent for Villa Wines (soon to be acquired by Growers') and 1.5 percent each for Mission Hill and Casabello.[4] According to the *Beverage Alcohol Reporter*, in a November 1968 article, Calona's sales had risen from $478,000 in 1960 to an estimated $3.7 million in 1968.

While wine consumption was already rising quickly, the Capozzi brothers hurried their business along even faster by copying whatever worked for the successful Gallo Brothers in California. When Gallo released fruit wines, Calona followed in February 1968 with Double Jack, Berry Jack and Cherry Jack, fortified with spirits made in Calona's own distillery. At $1.40 for a forty-ounce bottle and $2.70 for an eighty-ouncer, these wines were a hit across western Canada.[5] By the end of the decade, the Capozzi brothers even invited Gallo to buy 49 percent of Calona but balked when Gallo wanted 51 percent. Tom Capozzi later admitted that one strategy adopted from Gallo did not serve Calona well. Like Gallo in the United States, Calona tried to supply the entire Canadian market from one large, efficient winery at a time when Calona's competitors in Canada built smaller wineries in almost every province in exchange for preferred listings in each of those provinces. Calona only opened a second winery in 1973, in St.-Hyacinthe, in an effort to break into the exceptionally protectionist Quebec market. The winery lost money and was sold in 1974 to Andrés.

During the early 1960s archrival Growers' bought 16,882 shares in Calona. There was no possibility of Growers' gaining control since Capozzi Enterprises Ltd., the family company, had accumulated 61,120 shares by 1968 and Tom Capozzi owned another 1,089. Ever the deal maker, Tom Capozzi flew to Montreal and proposed to Imperial Tobacco, Growers' parent, that Growers' buy Calona. Imperial turned him down and Capozzi had to get used to the fact that his biggest competitor, as a substantial shareholder, was receiving Calona's annual report, even if disclosure was minimal (the 1968 report even omitted the annual sales). Growers' president **Brian Roberts** attended the Calona shareholders' meeting on June 28, 1968, grilling the Capozzis on everything from the non-disclosure of sales to the nature of a $21,200 investment by the winery in something called McCan Holdings Ltd. Later, Roberts reported in a memorandum to Imperial Tobacco that this was a 16 percent investment in "a new chain of drive-in restaurants known as MacDonalds [sic]."[6] Roberts added that he conducted himself at his rival's meeting with the "essence of courtesy . . . [But] notice has definitely been served on the Capozzis that they are now being watched like hawks." Evidently, Imperial Tobacco was not interested in keeping that close an eye on the Capozzis. In October 1968 Growers' offered its shares to Capozzi Enterprises for $25

each, an aggressive request, since the Capozzis had a standing offer of only $15 a share. "Because we felt that it was not good business to have a competitor as a shareholder, we purchased these shares," Tom Capozzi wrote to the remaining minority shareholders, offering them same. Most accepted; Capozzi Enterprises had almost 90 percent of the shares when the offer expired. By 1971, Calona was selling wines across Canada (1970 sales were $5.6 million) and the company had decided to open the winery in Quebec. The Capozzi family put the winery back on the market, getting $9.6 million from Standard Brands Ltd. of New York.[7] The new owner was not interested in keeping Calona's stake in the hamburger chain and Calona sold the shares back to McDonald's for $1 million.[8]

Calona's portfolio at this time still was dominated by fortified or sweet wines, often packaged in eccentric bottles (another idea copied from Gallo). Only a quarter of its sales in 1972 were dry table wines. Standard's managers realized that the future would be in table wines and hired a new winemaker, **Bob Claremont**, to produce them. Claremont was given stainless steel tanks and a properly equipped laboratory; and he bought more premium grapes and fewer of the labrusca varieties that had been serviceable for old style products such as Royal Red and the fortified wines. In short order Claremont overhauled the entire table wine portfolio, crafting such wines as Sommet Rouge in 1974 and Sommet Blanc in 1975, both of which were dry and were packaged in standard Bordeaux-style bottles closed with corks. In 1977 Claremont created *Schloss Laderheim*, a white wine cleverly packaged in a brown hock bottle with a Germanic label. In 1981 Schloss outsold **Baby Duck** — 589,000 cases to 571,000 cases — to become the top-selling domestic wine.

While proprietary wines like Schloss have been Calona's bread and butter ever since, the winery also began releasing varietal table wines in the late 1970s, starting with maréchal foch and rougeon and, with the 1981 vintage, expanding to include riesling, gewurztraminer, chenin blanc and chancellor. In the 1990s, under winemaker **Howard Soon,** small oak barrels were installed in the cavernous winery and Calona started making barrel-fermented chardonnays and merlots.

The winery changed owners again in May 1989 when **International Potter Distilling Corp**. of Vancouver bought Calona for $16.9 million from Heublein Inc., an American conglomerate into which Standard had been absorbed earlier. In 1995 Potter changed its name to **Cascadia Brands Inc.,** a name thought better suited for export sales of wine, cider and beer, the latter from a sister company, Granville Island Brewery.

CAPISTRO: This was a brand name under which **Casabello** launched so-called light wines in 1982 — called light because the alcohol was reduced to 7 percent and the wines therefore had fewer calories. The idea seems to have come from the California wine industry where Sebastiani Vineyards of Sonoma in 1981 claimed to be the first to release a light wine. Several other British Columbia wineries soon followed Casabello's lead: **Calona**'s light wine was called Tiffany and was aimed, to quote Calona literature of the day, "primarily to women concerned with their health and lifestyle, as well as to those who follow trends." These wines only were

popular for a few years, until the calorie count-ers moved on to mineral waters and the real wine lovers rediscovered real wine. Sebastiani dropped its light wine in November 1993. "Light wines are not perceived as quality," explained Sam Sebastiani, then the winery's president.

CAPOZZI, HERB (1925–): His successful stint as a tackle with the Montreal Allouettes and later Calgary Stampeders football clubs launched Capozzi as a popular sports banquet speaker where his plugs for Calona Wines were shameless. The Calona sales team also liked to have him along when visiting sportsminded liquor store managers. After completing two terms as a Social Credit backbencher in the British Columbia legislature, Capozzi became a financial promoter on Vancouver's Howe Street. Capozzi again became associated with Calona Wines in 1989 when his partner at the time, Harry Moll, put together the deal in which **International Potter Distilling Co.** acquired Calona.

CAPOZZI, JOE (1922–): Eldest son of Cap Capozzi, he became the production manager of Calona Wines in the 1960s. He was so renowned for his tight-fistedness that one of the long-time winery employees explained away a foolish grin at the funeral of a former Calona manager by saying he imagined Joe Capozzi objecting to the six pallbearers when four would do. Frugality had its limits, however. At a time when private business aircraft still were unusual, Capozzi Enterprises Ltd., the family company, owned a twin-engined Beech Bonanza aircraft as the family's executive plane for business trips around North America. Joe learned to fly it.

CAPOZZI, PASQUALE (1889–1976): Colourful Cap Capozzi — his friends called him Cap while his family called him Pats, a corruption of Pasquale — was the Italian grocer behind *Calona Wines Ltd.* Born at Santo Stephano del Sole, near Naples, Capozzi emigrated to Canada in 1906, worked as a railroad labourer in western Canada until he concluded that he could do better selling groceries. He managed the company store at the smelter in Trail (another source has him running a grocery at Revelstoke) and in 1917 opened a store in Phoenix, briefly a thriving copper mining town with seventeen bars in southern British Columbia, near modern-day Greenwood.[9] Phoenix died with the collapse of copper prices after the First World War and Capozzi headed for the Okanagan. Family legend has it that he settled in Kelowna in 1919 when he spotted a large field of ripe tomatoes there and remarked that an Italian can never starve where tomatoes are grown. The winery in 1932 was the brainchild of *Guiseppe Ghezzi* who believed there would be good business in converting the Okanagan's surplus apples into wines but needed Capozzi's help to raise the money. Capozzi and another Kelowna merchant, *W.A.C. Bennett*, raised much of it from the Italian community in Trail, one of the few islands of prosperity in British Columbia during the Depression. Sales of shares to investors sometimes were closed with what Cap's son, *Tom Capozzi*, called the telegram trick: midway through a meeting with these investors, a prearranged telegram would arrive from the winery trumpeting yet another large order for its wines.

Cap Capozzi stayed in the background at the winery for years. Bennett, even though he did not drink, was its president until he was elected to the British Columbia legislature in 1941. He was succeeded by Kelowna car dealer *Jack Ladd*, who was president until his death in 1957. Cap and his family began buying back the shares that he had sold in the 1930s. By 1960, he was president and he installed sons Tom and Joe in management at the winery, Cap and his family having acquired almost total control of Calona. He remained chairman until retiring in 1971.

Neither a winemaker nor a connoisseur, Cap certainly was a determined partisan of his wines. The most oft-repeated Cap Capozzi story, verified by son Tom, relates that Cap once was panhandled on a Vancouver street by a man who wanted a quarter for a drink. "How do I know," Cap asked, "that you won't spend it on coffee?"

CAPOZZI, TOM (1928–): After being made a director of Calona Wines in 1958 and then becoming vice-president and general manager, Tom brought modern marketing to the winery by the simple strategy of going to California at least once a year in search of ideas. He admired especially the Gallo Brothers and appropriated their packaging and product ideas for the better part of the decade until he was inspired to propose a partnership to them in 1969. When they met at the Gallo offices in California, Ernest Gallo thought the idea had merit — with conditions. Gallo offered to buy a 51 percent interest in Calona with no payment other than lending the Gallo name to the venture. Tom Capozzi angrily retorted: "Mr. Gallo, if I had wanted a job as a salesman for Gallo Wines, I'd have filled out an application."[10]

CARAFE: In July 1974 *Casabello* introduced table wines bottled in distinctive one-litre and half-litre glass carafes, closed with vacuum-sealed metal lids. Both the carafes and the metric measure were firsts in Canadian wine. The design was copied from Paul Masson in California; Casabello spent $20,000 to have the carafe moulds made. The carafes, filled with what *Harry McWatters*, then sales manager, described as "very palatable wines," attracted both consumers and restaurants to the wines. No other British Columbia winery copied Casabello, perhaps because the carafe was costly and required extensive modifications to winery bottling lines.[11] "It put Casabello on the map as far as table wines were concerned," long-time Casabello employee *Maurice Gregoire* said. "It was a real big piece of business that came walking through the door when that happened." However, the carafes were phased out in 1994 after Casabello (by then known as *Cartier*) was absorbed by *Vincor*. The reason was entirely practical: the winery had discovered that, unlike wine bottles, carafes were not thrown out after the wine had been consumed. Consequently, when consumers had all the carafes they could use or store, they began buying other products. Ultimately, the carafe brands ceased to be economic.

CARAVEL RUBY RED: The best-selling brand from *Uncle Ben's Gourmet Wines*, it was sweet and packed a punch with 16 percent alcohol. It was modelled after the market leader, Calona's Royal Red. Both wines are still marketed but Caravel Ruby has 14 percent alcohol today while Royal Red is 12.5 percent.

CARRIAGE HOUSE WINES: Farmgate winery established in 1995 by *David Wagner,* based on an eight-acre vineyard on Black Sage Road (also signed as 71st Street) south of Oliver. Varieties include kerner, pinot blanc, chardonnay, pinot noir, merlot and cabernet sauvignon. The winery name was chosen because Wagner and his Quebec-born wife, Karen, admire the architecture of carriage houses they have seen in eastern Canada, touches of which have been adopted at their Okanagan winery, along with horse-drawn carriages from a local carriage rebuilder.

CARTIER: This was the name that replaced Casabello when a management group acquired that winery and Chateau-Gai in Ontario from John Labatt Ltd. in 1988. The name had a modest history in Canadian wine, starting as the *Chateau Cartier* label that Labatt introduced in 1970 through Parkdale, a Toronto winery it owned. Parkdale was renamed Chateau Cartier Wines Ltd. in 1971, only to disappear when the Toronto winery closed five years later. The revived Cartier corporate name was modified when Inniskillin Wines Inc. was taken over in 1993 and submerged again in 1994 when Cartier and *T.G. Brights* company merged under a new corporate name, *Vincor*. Cartier currently survives only as Vincor brand.

CARTIER & INNISKILLIN VINTNERS INC.: This name was adopted by Cartier after it acquired Inniskillin Wines Inc. in 1993.

CASABELLO: The proponent of this winery, which was established in Penticton in 1966, was a vineyard manager named *Tony Biollo*, a former field man for Andrés when that winery tried to develop a vineyard in the Similkameen Valley in the early 1960s. After a falling out with Andrés, he sold the idea of a winery to Penticton businessman **Evans Lougheed**. Beginning in 1964, Lougheed assembled about forty investors, many his personal friends, and tapped a $100,000 area development grant from the federal government to finance the Casabello winery, an investment that contemporary media reports put at $350,000. That was about half of what had been spent on the competing *Mission Hill* winery, which helps to explain why Mission Hill was effectively bankrupt in two years while Casabello had expanded, investing another $300,000 by 1970.

The name, Casabello, is a corruption of an Italian phrase meaning fine house. A serviceable name, it was an improvement on two dozen or so concocted names that Lougheed scribbled on a piece of paper. Among them: SOVALE, for South Okanagan Valley; LOBIDA, from the names of the three founders, Lougheed, Biollo and Dawson (for local businessman Jim Dawson); and PENVINO, for Penticton winery. The list even included SOAVE, usually the name of a Italian white wine.

Getting the winery built for the first crush in the fall of 1966 was a race against time. Because no local companies could supply stainless steel tanks, Casabello ordered them from London, Ont. — only to have the railroad lose the shipment for ten days. The winery also was equipped with three large California redwood storage vats and a number of used Portuguese brandy barrels. (Within five years the winery had more than seven hundred oak barrels.) For the first vintage, the winery made 60,000 gallons of wine from 250 tons of grapes; 60 percent of the grapes were obtained in the Okanagan, the remainder from California. **Wallace Pohle,** the Californian who had been the first winemaker at Andrés, was the consulting winemaker for the first two vintages, with German-born **Thomas Hoenisch** being hired in 1967 as resident winemaker. The two had worked together at Andrés.

The winery opened under blistering 98°F heat on August 18, 1967, with nine wines for its guests and for the market; and the selection grew over the next year. The range of brands extended from a Canadian Riesling to a herb-flavoured May wine, a Canadian Pink Sauterne, sherries and a port, as well as a Canadian Burgundy, described on the label as a "very dry red table wine" that should be served "slightly chilled." Casabello wines reached the market a month earlier than Mission Hill. By the end of 1967, Casabello had sold 12,000 gallons of wine compared with Mission Hill's 9,730 gallons. But together, they accounted for less than 3 percent of a market dominated by Calona. New entrants at that time suffered because there were few self-serve liquor stores and no other opportunity to promote the products aggressively. Casabello's first labels were two-colour oval labels printed on in-expensive brown paper (Lougheed thought this a distinctive design). More contemporary labels were introduced when the winery's cork-finished "Estate Selection" varietals were released in 1973. Casabello's strategy at the time was the production of varietal table wines, using Washington state-grown vinifera while growers in the south Okanagan (including Lougheed's son-in-law *Walter Davidson*) planted vinifera. The strategy was seriously set back when the severe winter of 1969 destroyed many vinifera plantings.

Although winery tours were prohibited at the time, Lougheed had the foresight to build the winery on Penticton's Main Street, rather than on a cheaper site in the nearby industrial park. Casabello quietly began providing tours until the summer of 1972 when the Liquor Control Board found out and stopped them. When tours were allowed in 1974, it was unclear whether tastings were to be permitted. *Calona Wines* took a chance and opened its tasting room, but Casabello played safe a few more months, providing visitors with maps showing the nearest liquor store. When winery stores were permitted, Casabello was the first in August 1977 to open one.

Casabello's sales grew rapidly, doubling almost every year until the mid-1970s, and the capital needed to support this growth was beyond the resources of the original investors. In 1972 Lougheed agreed to give the Labatt brewing company a five-year option to acquire Casabello for a minimum of $1.5 million, with a formula that allowed Casabello to earn a bonus for hitting aggressive sales targets at the end of the five years. The brewer poured money into Casabello, putting more emphasis on generic wines, including British Columbia's first bag-in-the-box wines. Labatt took over management in September 1977 and spent another $3.5 million to increase Casabello's capacity by half, until it reached 2.5 million gallons of wine storage. Some of the brands (Capistro, for example) were integrated with those of Chateau-Gai, the Niagara Falls winery also acquired at this time by Labatt. When the brewer decided to leave the wine business in 1988, the managers of the wineries acquired the operations and renamed the company *Cartier.* In turn, this company merged in 1993 with *T.G. Brights & Co.* in a new company known as *Vincor International Ltd*. Production at the Penticton winery stopped in March 1994, equipment was moved to the Vincor winery at Oliver and the wine shop closed finally on October 31, 1994. The property was demolished by year end, the well-chosen site having been snapped up by developers for a new shopping centre bearing the name of Evans Lougheed. See also *Carafe; Evans, Lougheed*.

CASCADIA BRANDS INC.: The new name chosen in 1995 by the company that owns *Calona Wines Ltd*. See *Potter*.

CASHMAN, SANDRA: See *Sandra Oldfield*.

CASORSO: This pioneer Okanagan agricultural family[12] — the name in Italy was spelled Casorzo — was established in the valley by Giovanni (John) Casorso (1848–1932), who was born near Turin, Italy, and who arrived in the Okanagan (after a short stop in San Francisco) in 1883 to work as an agriculturist for the missionaries. He homesteaded land south of Mission Creek in 1884 to which he brought his young family from Italy. By the 1930s the Casorso family was raising livestock and selling it through a chain of retail stores in the British Columbia Interior. John Casorso also was one of the large tobacco growers when that crop flourished in the Okanagan in the 1920s; and was so successful with onions that he was crowned Onion King one year. Son Charles is credited in the family history with planting a vineyard on a thirty-five-acre property at Rutland in 1925. Two other sons, Napoleon Peter and Louis, planted grapes on the family's home property, Pioneer Ranch, subsequently managed by son-in-law Bert Sperling. Grandson August continues to grow grapes near Kelowna. Great-granddaughter *Anne Sperling* — her mother Velma was Peter's daughter — became a winemaker.

In November 1931 when *Guiseppe Ghezzi* conceived what was to become *Calona Wines*, he formed a syndicate to raise $10,000 for what was called the Interior Co-operative Association. The investors included Napoleon Peter Casorso and his sister, Mary, and possibly (the documentation is ambiguous) John Casorso, who was a member of the syndicate but who died in April 1932.[13]

CEDARCREEK ESTATE WINERY: In November 1986 Vancouver businessman *Ross Fitzpatrick* took over the struggling *Uniacke Wines*, renaming it for the creek that flows along the northern boundary of the property down to Okanagan Lake. Production has expanded steadily from 610,000 litres in 1987 to 2,100,000 litres in 1996. With the exception of chancellor, a reliable workhorse red hy-

brid variety, this winery has specialized in wines from the premier vinifera varieties. Most of the grapes are grown either in the CedarCreek vineyard south of Kelowna on the east side of the lake, or at the newly planted *Greata Ranch* across the lake. In addition, CedarCreek has long-term contracts with several top growers, including the King Vineyard at Naramata. The winery has targetted a production of 3,800,000 litres by the year 2000.[14]

CENTRE FOR PLANT HEALTH: Known colloquially as the Plant Quarantine Centre, this federal government institution is the technical arm of the Plant Protection Division of Agriculture Canada. The Centre opened in 1912 as a Dominion Experimental Farm and, since 1965, has been the only federal establishment in Canada that screens the import and movement of grape vines within the country. (It also screens tree fruits and ornamental plants.) The Centre occupies forty-eight hectares of gently rolling farmland south of Sidney on Vancouver Island, a location suited for plant testing and quarantine because it is isolated from

the major commercial growing areas in Canada. The mild climate permits the growing of all plants suitable for cultivation in Canada.

Since 1987 the Centre has focussed on keeping plants infected with virus diseases out of Canada. Although grape vines had been imported for as much as one hundred years, Canadian authorities believed Canada had been remarkably fortunate not to have inadvertently imported some of the commercially crippling viruses found in the vineyards of Europe. When the growers and the wineries began sourcing new and better varieties from Europe in the 1980s, the Centre took a more active role in making sure the incoming plants were clean. The first round of significant varietal imports from France early in the 1980s came to an end when the Centre detected viruses on the rootstock. Dr. William Lanterman, the Centre's director, went to France in 1986 and again in 1991 to inspect how the grape nurseries there certified the disease-free status of the vines that were being ordered by Canadian growers. "We were trying to kick-start the industry here because we had been working with a lot of old varieties," Lanterman says. Previously, newly imported vines first went into quarantine for three years at the Centre where the vines were tested thoroughly, only to be released if virus-free. Because there was pressure from growers to convert vineyards more quickly to better varieties, the Plant Protection Division amended its regulations to allow the import of vines from nurseries certified to be virus-free. One German and nine French sources were identified and certified.

As a result, thousands of vinifera vines began entering British Columbia in 1989, enabling growers to replant with preferred varieties such as merlot, pinot noir and chardonnay. But there was another outcome as well. Viruses were detected in 1991 on a small number of German vines, and in 1993 and again in 1995 on some French vines; imports were suspended again from both countries until more stringent screening could be imposed. Canada now requires thorough testing of the nursery mother blocks from which vines are imported, with samples also being tested by the Centre near Sidney. The Centre, in its audit program, takes samples from all commercial shipments from certified nurseries, a safeguard to make sure that nurseries continue to send clean plants. Virus-free mother plants of more than 300 varieties are maintained almost in perpetuity at the Centre. By 1995 six nurseries in France had been certified to export vines and the process for certifying German sources was well underway.

The repeated interruptions of vine imports has been controversial among growers impatient to plant new vineyards. However, Lanterman argues that the Centre and the Plant Protection Division in Ottawa have a difficult but important job to do. "Viruses are different from insects or bacterial diseases that are on the surface of plants," he says. "Viruses are sub-microscopic. They are not readily detectable at ports of entry and are very easy to smuggle." Any easily hidden pocket-sized cutting from a vine might include a virus not yet established in a Canadian vineyard. "Our principal role is the exclusion of those viruses that we don't have." Techniques for eliminating viruses in plants, effective in a nursery, are not practical on a commercial scale. "We have no chemicals available. If an orchard or vineyard is infected with viruses, there is absolutely no way to cure those plants in the field," Lanterman says.

About sixty viruses can be found in grape vines. One common method for detecting them involves grafting buds from a vine to an indicator plant known to be sensitive to certain viruses and waiting, sometimes as long as five years, to see if virus symptoms show up. (Generally used indicator vines include pinot noir.) "We can detect all the known diseases through these indicator plants," Lanterman says. "The disadvantage is the time. We can't wait that long for results any more." The small number of sap-transmitted viruses can be detected, if present, within two weeks by smearing ground-up vine leaves onto certain annual plants, a commonly used one being a weed called *Chenopodium quinoa* or lamb's quarters, and waiting for symptoms to show. As well, Lanterman's staff also can use a variety of laboratory tests to detect specific viruses in one or two days. The laboratory tests have been developed to detect what are believed to be the most serious viruses. Leaf-roll virus is one of the most common in the world and one of the most damaging because it reduces yield as much as 50 percent and also delays grape ripening.

The paradox that viruses showed up in 1993 on plants from previously certified French nurseries is simply explained: when importing growers began asking for clones or varieties that the nurseries did not have in their own plots, the nurseries obtained the desired vines from other sources, some of which turned out to be tainted. In other instances, virus problems had developed in plots subsequent to those plots having been tested and found clean. Controlling the transmission of viruses is never easy; and since viruses are widespread in Europe, less effort is directed at those that are the least economically harmful. "France refers to itself as the cradle of grape vines," Lanterman said early in 1995. "They feel that if you grow vines, you are going to have these diseases and you just have to deal with them. But we are in a very different situation in Canada. We have an industry with a tremendous freedom from viruses. British Columbia is one of the least virus-infected grapegrowing areas in the world because of these controls."

However, Canadian vineyards are not quite so free of major viruses as had been thought. In 1995 a survey managed by the Centre sampled vines from 11,000 acres of grape vines across Canada to determine whether four major viruses may have slipped through the net in earlier vine imports. It turned out they had. The survey found samples of Arabic Mosaic virus, fanleaf virus and two leaf-roll viruses. While the survey suggested that disease problems are not extensive, it confirmed the viruses exist in Canada and, under trade agreements, Canada will no longer be able to ban vine imports to exclude viruses now proved to be here already.

Once a virus becomes established in a vineyard, it is very difficult to eradicate, even when the plants are removed and the soil is fumigated. The nematode worms that spread the viruses from plant to plant as they feed on roots usually survive on old roots too deep to be pulled out or reached by fumigation and will contaminate newly planted vines when their roots contact the remaining old roots. Those growers in British Columbia unfortunate enough to have planted virus-infected plants were not permitted to propagate those plants and were required to burn all the cuttings when the vines were pruned. However, the vines can remain in production although a severe virus infection will reduce productivity and fruit quality. Leaf-roll viruses, for example, reduce plant growth anywhere from 10 to 70 percent, slow the ripening of the fruit, reduce its sugar content and its colour. Since the impact varies with the variety of vine, growers in Canada, like those elsewhere, have little choice but to manage vineyards to minimize the virus problems.

CHANCELLOR: One of the best of the hybrid red grapes — it was the most widely planted red hybrid in France in the 1940s — chancellor was first planted in the Okanagan in the early 1960s. It became the signature red varietal for *Sumac Ridge*, whose founders, *Harry McWatters* and *Lloyd Schmidt*, had been familiar with the variety while they were still at *Casabello*, for chancellor was used in some of that winery's best blends. The wines typically possess bright berry aromas and flavours, with notes of cherry, and none of the bitter finish so common to other hybrids. Until New York grapegrowers named it in 1970, the hardy, disease-resistant variety simply was called Seibel 7053, one of many varieties created by a nineteenth century French plant breeder named Seibel.

CHARDONNAY: One of the great white grapes and certainly a popular one, chardonnay put British Columbia on the world wine map in 1994 when *Mission Hill*'s 1992 Chardonnay Grand Reserve

won the prestigious *Avery's Trophy* at a major London wine competition. The following year *Domaine Combret*'s 1993 vintage won a bronze medal at the Chardonnay du Monde competition in Burgundy, while in 1996 four British Columbia producers, including *Mission Hill*, *Calona*, *Combret* and *Domaine de Chaberton* won medals there (see *Competitions*). Okanagan chardonnays are crisp and fresh, usually with delicate citrus-like fruit, although barrel-fermented examples show more body and complexity. As the awards show, Okanagan producers have achieved qualities competitive with their peers elsewhere.

CHASSELAS: A vinifera vine usually identified with Switzerland, chasselas was first planted in the Okanagan by error. When *Richard Stewart* began planting the vineyard in 1963 which today supports the *Quails' Gate* winery, a nursery in Washington state from which he had ordered diamond, a labrusca variety, sent him chasselas mislabeled as diamond. Stewart discovered his good fortune several years later when a professional enologist identified the vines correctly. Writer Jancis Robinson, in her excellent book *Vines, Grapes and Wines*, suggests that chasselas "may be the oldest known vine variety cultivated by man." Unhappily, the vine is susceptible to frost and yields rather neutral wines. Only a few wineries (including Quails' Gate, of course) have released a varietal chasselas. Perhaps the most eloquent comment on the grape's future for British Columbia is that Swiss-born *Leo Gebert* has dropped it from the line at his *St. Hubertus* winery.

CHATEAU JONN DE TREPANIER: British Columbia's first estate winery, it opened in 1978 at Peachland. In 1979 the owner, *Marion Jonn,* sold it to *Bob Claremont,* the former winemaker at *Calona Wines*, who renamed the property Claremont Estate Winery and Vineyards.

CHATEAU STE. CLAIRE ESTATE WINES:

This winery was originally known as Chateau Jonn de Trepanier and then Claremont; the name was changed in 1986 when it was purchased by *Goldie Smitlener,* a devout Roman Catholic, whose choice of name was inspired by her admiration for the Poor Clares, an order of nuns.

CHATEAU WOLFF:

Scheduled to be opened in 1997 in a vineyard at the edge of Nanaimo, this is the most northerly winery on Vancouver Island. See also *von Wolff.*

CHEERS: In March 1984 the British Columbia Liquor Distribution Branch replaced its quarterly product catalogue with *Cheers,* a quarterly magazine that included informative articles as well as the LDB's product listings. The franchise to publish the magazine was awarded to Western Canada TV Week Ltd., which planned to recover its costs by selling advertising. The government, meanwhile, expected to save the $32,000 it was spending each year on the product guide. *Cheers* lasted only six issues, doomed by its own stiff advertising rates and by the government's rules. For example: the magazine was not permitted to carry advertising on the outside back cover, traditionally one of the most valuable pages to advertisers in any publication. When the LDB resumed publishing the product catalogue itself, it kept the popular magazine format.

CHELOIS: A red hybrid grape developed in France, it achieved modest popularity in the Okanagan because the variety ripens early and yields soft, fruity and inoffensive wines.

CHENIN BLANC: An ancient French vinifera not widely grown in the Okanagan because it needs a long growing season, chenin blanc in British Columbia typically yields refreshing, appley whites, sometimes with bright acidity.

CIPES, STEPHEN (1944–):

Born in Manhattan, the son of a professor of dentistry, Cipes was an ambitious New York real estate developer when, in search of a change of lifestyle, he moved to the Okanagan in 1986. The sixty-acre farm on Chute Lake Road, south of Kelowna, that he bought, included a thirty-eight-acre vineyard. Cipes converted the property to a fully organic farm, with the grapes supporting his *Summerhill Estate Winery* which opened in 1992. An advocate of New Age philosophy, Cipes has built a pyramid on the property because he believes Summerhill's already fine sparkling wines are even better when aged in the pyramid.

CLAREMONT, BOB (1943–1994):

An influential Okanagan winemaker during his tenure at *Calona Wines*, Claremont's British Columbia career also had an unfortunate financial conclusion when his Claremont Estate Winery and Vineyards went into receivership in 1986. He had rebuilt a career as a winemaker at Culotta Wines Ltd., Oakville, Ont., when he died of a heart attack in the midst of the 1994 vintage.

Born in Toronto, Claremont intended to become a brewer after graduating in microbiology from the University of Guelph but, unable to find a brewery job, he became a laboratory technician at the Jordan winery near St. Catharines. After a year, he went to work in 1968 as a winemaker at a winery called St. Julian in Paw Paw, Michigan. There are a number of wineries on the eastern shore of Lake Michigan in communities with such mellifluous names as Kalamazoo and Keeler and Paw Paw. The St. Julian winery was founded in 1921 in Windsor by an Italian immigrant and was relocated to Michigan after the Americans ended Prohibition in 1933. Claremont had a challenging four years there, learning how to make seventeen different wines from just two grape varieties then vinted at St. Julian, niagara and concord. "It was excellent experience," Claremont recalled some years later, a typical note of Claremont swagger in his account. "I got my hands dirty and I really enjoyed it."[15] Calona Wines recruited him in February 1972, to help chief enologist **William Finley**. Finley left in 1973 and Claremont took over as chief winemaker under the new management that had succeeded the **Capozzi** brothers when they sold Calona. One of his first tasks was overhauling Calona's stable of jug wines that came in baroque bottles. "We had without a doubt the ugliest goddamn packaging," Claremont said. An impressive range of soundly made brands soon began to emerge: Sommet Rouge in 1974 and Sommet Blanc in 1975 were dry British Columbia table wines made to compete with generic reds and whites from Bordeaux. Popularly priced Italian reds were challenged by Palazzo Reale. Claremont's biggest hit at Calona and probably in his career was **Schloss Laderheim**, a German-style white ini-

tially made primarily from Okanagan riesling grapes. It was released in 1977 and became Canada's largest selling domestic wine by the early 1980s, only to be knocked from its throne when the Liquor Control Board of Ontario began pricing it higher than other domestic wines. (With good reason: Schloss had become so successful that Calona had to supplement its limited quantities of Okanagan grapes with bulk wines imported from California.) Not everything that Claremont created at Calona was successful: Maisonneuve Mousseux Rouge, his answer to sparkling red Burgundy, despite its handsome packaging, flopped when it reached the market in the late 1970s.

Claremont left Calona after British Columbia decided to permit estate wineries in 1978. While he was looking for a property, *Chateau Jonn de Trepanier* at Peachland — the first estate winery to open in 1978 — came on the market. With several silent partners putting up the money, Claremont bought the winery for $1 million. Two days before the start of the crush in 1979, Claremont took over and was lucky that the newly installed winemaking equipment functioned smoothly for him. "My only regret is that it is much too big," Claremont said later.[16] "I'd much have preferred to start from scratch. There's too much business involved in all of this." That was an exasperated reference to his distaste for dealing with governments and bankers. The marketing was handled by his wife, Lee (they were subsequently divorced), whose refined aesthetic taste led to Claremont being the first estate winery with a label by a British Columbia artist — New Denver watercolourist Les Weisbrich. The first wines under the

Claremont label included a verdelet and an Okanagan riesling. For the most part, the winery stayed with the hybrid varieties such as foch and rougeon because that was what was already in the thirty-five-acre vineyard. There were several vinifera varieties, among them merlot, pinot noir, semillon, gewurztraminer and pinot blanc. Claremont's intention was to expand gradually the quantity of vinifera but he never had the time. The high interest rates at the time undermined the winery's economics while the winery's reputation suffered when some indifferently made wines slipped through to the market. By early in 1985 a Vancouver Stock Exchange-listed company, Simpatico Wines Ltd. of Richmond, announced it would acquire the Claremont winery in an exchange of shares. That deal fell through that spring and the winery went into receivership in December 1985, to re-emerge next year under new ownership as **Chateau Ste. Claire.** Claremont moved to Ontario and re-established his career there.

CLARK, NICK (1945–):
The entrepreneurial first president of the **British Columbia Wine Institute** when it was formed in 1990, Victoria-born Clark has had significant impact on the British Columbia wine industry since entering it in 1975. A 1968 graduate in industrial engineering from the Hamilton Institute of Technology, Clark was recruited from a management job at the Canadian post office to become the first director of purchasing for the Liquor Distribution Branch in Vancouver where he was one of the proponents of the so-called **Agent Stocking Program.** This was a crafty program under which the wine and spirits agents selling to the LDB were effectively

required to take over from the LDB the responsibility for warehousing products. The LDB thus reduced its inventory costs by millions and generated more profit for the government. In 1981, Clark partnered with wine merchant **Anthony von Mandl** to buy **Mission Hill** winery at Westbank. Clark, who initially owned a quarter of the shares, served as president until selling his interest in 1989 to take a year's sabbatical with his wife Norah and their two daughters. A consulting assignment he did in 1990 on exporting British Columbia wines led to the newly formed Wine Institute giving Clark an eighteen-month contract to be its first chief executive. By the time he stepped down, the Institute was firmly established, with the highly effective VQA program in operation. See **Vintners Quality Alliance.**

CLEAVE, RICHARD (DICK) (1946–):
After more than twenty years as a vineyard manager in the south Okanagan, the lean, windburnt Dick Cleave, as he is generally called, has lived the roller coaster of seeing major vineyards build to full production with the wrong varieties, only to have to start over again. With a hint of frustration in his voice, he calculates that he has planted and replanted about eight hundred acres. However, the most recent plantings of the vineyards in his charge have been exclusively vinifera, including the premier red varieties — cabernet sauvignon, merlot and pinot noir — upon which serious wine industries can be anchored. "My philosophy is that you don't have a wine industry until you have good reds," Cleave contends. "They are the best."

Cleave, who speaks with a twangy Suffolk accent, was born in Ipswich on the English Channel coast, into a career military family. "I'm the first one that went into agriculture," he says. After studying at an agricultural college in Suffolk and working with a farming company, Cleave settled into what looked like a technical and sales career with an agricultural chemicals firm. But in 1972, fed up with Britain's inflationary economy, he and his wife, Adrienne — who had previously lived in Canada — emigrated to British Columbia. "I've never regretted it," Cleave says. He managed a vegetable farm at Grand Forks, B.C., until 1975 when vineyard owner Harry Shannon recruited Cleave to run Shannon Vineyards north of Osoyoos. The following year the partners in Shannon Vineyards acquired the adjoining *Pacific Vineyards* and the youthful Cleave found himself in charge of nearly five hundred acres of vines. He went to *Covert Farms* in 1979, returning to Shannon and Pacific in 1984. Cleave stayed on after the 1988 pull out of vines to manage the residual eighteen acres of pinot blanc that had not been uprooted. In 1991 he established his own vineyard on Black Sage Road (as the residents call 71st Street), planting fourteen acres of premium varieties and giving himself the option of establishing a small winery. However, his first love is growing grapes, leaving others to make the wines. In 1993, when new owners acquired the land that once was Shannon and Pacific, Cleave, who had now formed a management and contract planting company with Osoyoos orchardist Robert Goltz, once again became manager of the adjoining vineyards, now called *Black Sage*, *Sunset* and *Burrowing Owl*. When fully planted, they will total four hundred acres, heavily committed to red varieties

suited to this sun-drenched bench on the east side of the Okanagan Valley. "If we are going to grow reds anywhere in British Columbia, this is the place to start — because of the soil type and the climatic conditions," Cleave believes.

Cleave's grapegrowing experience ranges from the labrusca and hybrid varieties common in the mid-1970s to the vinifera that have now mostly replaced them. "Viniferas are far easier [to grow]," Cleave maintains. "Their water requirements are probably 50 percent or less what a hybrid needs." The explanation lies in the production demanded of the vines. Where growers once accepted twenty-five pounds of grapes per vine from hybrid varieties as normal, the vinifera are cropped at eight to ten pounds from each vine. The resulting grapes deliver more intense and concentrated flavours to the wines, notable particularly in exceptional vintages like 1994 when low yields due to natural causes produced rich wines seldom seen before in the Okanagan. "Growing vinifera is pretty much a new game to all of us," Cleave admits. "If we keep the number of plants up per acre and the pounds per vine down, we're going to get that intensity nine out of ten years."

CLORE, DR. WALTER J. (1911 –): A
native of Oklahoma, Clore obtained a doctorate in pomology from Washington State University in 1947 but switched his professional interest shortly thereafter to grapes and asparagus at the university's experimental station at Prosser, Wash. His research helped the state's fledgling wine industry nurture premium vinifera grapes in Washington, a state then (and still today) where the major grape variety was concord,

grown primarily for juice. The versatile Clore also helped concord growers improve their crops. The Washington State Asparagus Association named him "Mr. Asparagus" in 1969 and the Washington State Grape Society named him Man of the Year in 1977. He retired from the university in 1976 but has been active since as a consultant to winegrowers in the United States and in British Columbia. Clore began visiting the Okanagan in the 1960s and has records of five official trips between 1973 and 1980 to lecture and consult with grapegrowers in British Columbia. "I couldn't understand," he said later, "if we were growing the hardier viniferas successfully in Washington, why the more favourable areas of the Okanagan wouldn't be able to do likewise."[17]

COBBLE HILL: See *John Harper.*

COLD DUCK: Led by Chateau-Gai in Ontario in April 1970,[18] Canadian wineries scored a big marketing success with carbonated pink wines called Cold Duck. *Andrés* and *Growers'* introduced their versions that spring in British Columbia while *T.G. Brights & Co.* released one in Ontario. The idea of what the public called pink champagne came from the United States where Cold Duck wines had been marketed for a decade but suddenly became popular at the end of the 1960s. The name was a pun on a German phrase, *kalte ende,* referring to the tradition of mixing the "cold ends" or party leftovers in wine bottles in a punch bowl. Duck in German is *ente,* an easy slip of the lip at the conclusion of a good party. The Cold Duck wines had the usual 11 to 12 percent alcohol of most table wines but, being sparkling,

attracted the higher tax traditionally imposed on luxury wines like champagne. In short order, Andrés realized that 7 percent sparkling wines were taxed at a lower rate; the winery jumped through that loophole to create *Baby Duck* and that less expensive wine quickly eclipsed the success of Cold Duck.

COLETTA, CHRISTINE (1955–): Perhaps it is the rebellious streak in her nature that has made Coletta effective as the executive director of the *British Columbia Wine Institute*, a post she assumed in 1992. Born in Vancouver into a family of educators, she did not wait until her teen years to chafe against schooling. "I actually hated kindergarten," she admitted later. "When you are surrounded by educators, the last thing you want to do is be educated yourself. My only diversion through high school was sports. Solitary sports — nothing that involved team sports."

When she was fifteen years old, she talked Denny's, a family restaurant chain, into hiring her. "That's where I got my restaurant bug. Before that, I was painfully shy and quite a loner. It forced me to develop human relations." Three years later she joined Denny's alumnus Bino Felix when he began his Bino's restaurant chain. That led to a series of hotel and restaurant jobs and a three-year stint with the Hotel Industry Education Advisory Committee, creating and giving training programs. As averse as she was to formal education, she revelled in eighteen-hour days learning and passing on experience gained on the job. Managing restaurants created opportunity to acquire wine knowledge on the job.

Volunteering for the *Vancouver Playhouse International Wine Festival* in 1982 pulled Coletta further into wine-related work. When the Society of Wine Educators (SWE), a United States-based group, held its annual convention in Vancouver in 1986, Coletta was hired to coordinate the events in Vancouver. Sumac Ridge's *Harry McWatters*, an ardent SWE member, had beenU bringing that year's conference to British Columbia. McWatters was the first chairman of the British Columbia Wine Institute when it was formed in 1990. When *Nick Clark*, the Institute's first executive director, resigned, McWatters asked Coletta, who was then doing conference organization for the Canadian government, to compete for the job. She was chosen from among eight candidates.

"The job really intrigued me," said Coletta, who opened the office in her home because that suited her work habits, which include beginning at four or five in the morning. She expanded the job well beyond chatting up liquor store managers and other buyers of British Columbia wines. "My attitude is blaze ahead, boldly go forward and do, do, do. Eighty-five percent of what you do will be spot on and the other 15 percent you'll be forgiven for." Since 1992 the Institute has increased significantly the awareness of British Columbia wines in restaurants; it has moved ahead with a strategic plan for the industry and it has begun to develop export markets for British Columbia wine. While most wineries had no difficulty selling their VQA wines in British Columbia throughout the mid-1990s, Coletta looked down the road to a time when more wineries with more wines might saturate the home market. "You don't go looking for a new market when you have oversupply," Coletta has argued. "You do it five years ahead." Funded primarily by levies on the wine industry, the Institute's increasing menu of duties includes supervising the all-important VQA tasting panel. While established wineries need not submit wines, it generally is advantageous to do so since wines that merit the VQA seal sell more readily and at better prices than most non-VQA wines. All new wineries during their first three years are required to have their wines passed by the VQA panel as technically sound (even if not meriting VQA) before the wines are allowed to go to market. "The government feels it would be very detrimental to our image if we had ten new wineries out there, cranking out wine that was technically unsound," Coletta says. "The process is to provide feedback to these people. Some of them are opening with very little winemaking expertise. We don't get involved in the approval process for new wineries. What we do is assist new wineries when they identify themselves to us. Each winery has different challenges to face. We don't view it as being our business to hold their hands and get their business into operation but we can provide them with some information to make it easier for them."

COLLINGS, BILL (1934–):

A former teacher, Collings traces his passion about wine to having won third prize in 1969 for the first wine he ever made, a blackberry wine with fruit from a backyard patch. His wife, Joan, also credits the Portuguese rosé wines that once enlivened Friday evening dinner. After moving to a country home near Okanagan Falls in 1989, and never intending to grow grapes, the Collings planted a vineyard all the same and became industry activists, with Bill president of the 140-member Association of Grape Growers of British Columbia and Joan a director of the **British Columbia Wine Institute**.

Born in Kamloops, the son of a pulp mill consultant, Collings himself spent three years working in an Alberta pulp mill until enrolling at the University of British Columbia in 1959 and emerging with a master's degree in education. He spent twenty-five years as a Vancouver high school teacher, specializing in English, history, art history and geography. His winemaking mentor was Charles Plante, a fellow teacher and a legendary home winemaker. Collings himself became a prize-winning amateur vintner, joining with three other partners to buy a Similkameen Valley vineyard in the mid-1970s. The vineyard interest was sold in 1979 when the Collings, now wanting their own country property, bought raw land near Okanagan Falls with a site for a house. Seven acres of vineyard was developed for the practical reason that the revenue would pay the taxes. Dissuaded initially from planting either sauvignon blanc or semillon, the Collings devoted three acres to Okanagan riesling and one to pinot noir. They retained the Okanagan riesling after the 1988 pullout but as the hoped-for market among home vintners eroded, they replaced the variety with pinot noir, pinot meunier and johannisberg riesling. The single largest planting at their vineyard consists of 4,000 pinot noir vines. In spite of Bill's winemaking skills, the Collings are firm that they will not open a farmgate winery. "Never, never, never," Bill Collings said. "I know everyone in the business — and I know all the trials and tribulations."

COMBRET, OLIVIER (1971 –): Born in France and educated at the renowned *Montpellier* wine school there, he is the winemaker at **Domaine Combret**.

COMBRET, ROBERT (1931 –): The French-born proprietor of **Domaine Combret** which was opened in 1994 by Robert Combret, his wife, Maite, and his son, Olivier. They formerly owned Chateau Petit Sonnailler, a winery in Provence where the Combret family has made wine for many generations. After selling that winery in 1991, they emigrated to the Okanagan where, they knew, the dry climate made it relatively simple to grow healthy and high-quality grapes. Robert Combret was familiar with the Okanagan, having completed his master's degree in agriculture in 1958 at the University of British Columbia. His thesis, completed during several months at the Summerland Research Station, was on apple storage, since grapegrowing then was a minor industry with varieties totally uninteresting to a French vintner.

COMPANIONS OF OKANAGAN GRAPES & WINE: Formed in 1991 under the sponsorship of **B.C. Wine Trails,** this award honours pioneering contributors to the British Columbia wine industry. The initial Companions were the families of pioneer growers *J.W. Hughes, Frank Schmidt, Martin Dulik* and the *Casorsos*. The 1995 inductees were founders of three original estate wineries: Joe and Barbara **Busnardo**, George and Trudy **Heiss**, and Harry and Cathy **McWatters**.

COMPETITIONS

Every winery aspires to display medals, trophies and ribbons won in competition for these not only recognize achievement by winemakers but also send signals of excellence to consumers. Some competitions are more rigorous than others but there is no guide to which awards have more weight. Indeed, some European competitions in the 1960s and 1970s tended to award medals to virtually all wines for which entry fees were paid. "My personal view ... is that such competitions have practically no validity," wrote Conal R. Gregory, the editor of the *International Wine & Food Society Journal* in a 1982 letter to a Canadian wine writer.[19] The standard of today's competitions is higher and more reliability can be read into the awards. However, it is worth remembering that the wines with an established international reputation for superior quality (such as Bordeaux's classified growths) are unlikely to compete. Not only is it unnecessary for a prestige winery to compete but there always is the risk of being humiliated by a little-known new winery.

It also is worth remembering that wine evaluation is highly subjective. "Wine competitions are for the most part like playing roulette," suggests winemaker **Eric von Krosigk.** "In a given competition there are so many variables, real and subjective, that the given results are for the most part not reproducible." The results depend "on the experience level of the tasters — what type of wines they might have tasted, their individual threshold sensitivities, their personal or regional preferences in wines, their ability to remember smells and taste, what they ate the night before, their emotional well-being that day, group dynamics, temperature of the wines, type of tasting glass used, number of wines being tasted at one sitting, order in which the wines are lined up — to name a few. The judging is only as good as the judges." The existence of variables does not invalidate wine awards since a mediocre wine is unlikely to win in any well-run competition. What it means is that bronze medal wines may please some consumers more than gold or silver medal wines. In general, good wines will win medals in more than one competition and capable wineries will win awards consistently.

Within British Columbia, the premier competition, with the judging panel consisting of wine writers, Liquor Distribution Branch staff and restaurateurs, is the **Okanagan Wine Festival**, first established in 1982 as **Septober.** At the first competition in Kelowna, 47 wines were entered and five gold medals were awarded. The 1995 competition also handed out five gold medals, but after judging 112 wines, a ratio of winners to entrants that suggests more aggressive standards of adjudication.

The international competitions in which British Columbia wines are entering have much more credibility than those of which Conal Gregory wrote. The International Wine & Spirits Competition held annually in London is the one where **Mission Hill** in 1994 won the **Avery's Trophy** for Best Chardonnay for its 1992 Grand Reserve Barrel Select Chardonnay. The Mission Hill wine was matched against 220 other chardonnays from around the world, more than enough to assure that the competition was rigorous and the award was merited.

The Paris-based Office International de la Vigne et du Vin (OIV) sponsors or provides the regulatory framework for competitions in several of its forty-four member countries. The competitions draw their credibility from the fact that the OIV, founded in 1924, is an organization dedicated to serious research of matters related to wine, including health. British Columbia wineries that have won awards at OIV competitions include **Domaine de Chaberton** (silver medals in Mendoza, Arg., in 1995 for its 1993 chardonnay and its 1993 botrytis-affected ortega) and **Domaine Combret** (bronze for its 1993 chardonnay at the 1995 Chardonnay du Monde competition in Burgundy, in which 348 chardonnays from twenty-one countries were entered). At the Chardonnay du Monde competition in 1996, at which 494 wines were entered, silver medals were won by **Calona** and Domaine de Chaberton and bronze medals were won by **Mission Hill** and Domaine Combret. A pattern of consistency can be seen to emerge.

A French competition of rising importance is the Blaye-Bourg International Wine Challenge, which began in 1976 as a local competition for Gironde wines. Wines from other nations were entered first in 1981. By 1995 the competition attracted 4,150 entries, a third of them non-French. British Columbia's Domaine Combret won its first medal in 1994 at Blaye-Bourg for a riesling from the winery's debut 1993 vintage.

The InterVin International Wine Competition, which was launched by Toronto wine writer Andrew Sharp in 1986 and grew to an important international competition in eastern North America, tackled the credibility issue of competition medals by raising the standards significantly in 1996. Over its years InterVin has grown to accept many entries from around the world and has awarded medals generously. In 1995 the competition awarded about eight hundred medals, more than one hundred of them gold. The one British Columbia wine to score a gold that year at InterVin was the **Gehringer Brothers** 1994 riesling icewine. In subsequent competitions, gold-medal wines need to score ninety points (raised from eighty-five) on the one-hundred-point judging scale and all gold medal wines are retasted blind by a second panel; if that panel does not confirm the gold, a third panel, unaware its decision is final, will taste the wine in question a third time and award a medal based on this judging. Sharp estimated that no more than five or six gold medals would be awarded for each thousand wines judged. Unquestionably, the competing wineries see these standards as too stringent despite assurances that InterVin's silver and bronze medals now command more esteem. On the liquor store shelf, a silver or bronze medallion is never as good as a gold one.

In the United States, more than fifty wine competitions are held each year, most of them small regional affairs. However, about a dozen attract one thousand wines or more which assures tough competition. One of the largest is the Los Angeles County Fair, which draws about 2,000 entries a year and which awarded fourteen medals to British Columbia wines in 1995. These included four golds: Gehringer Brothers won gold and best white of the show for its 1994 pinot gris and a gold for its 1994 riesling icewine; **CedarCreek** won gold for its 1994 ehrenfelser; and **Sumac Ridge** won gold and best of class for its 1993 pinot blanc.

Winning wineries often take advantage of modern labelling technology to festoon each bottle of a winner with gold, silver or bronze medallions. Clearly, this promotes sales since, as winemaker von Krosigk says, "an award should indicate that a chosen wine has reached at least an above average quality level. However, having said that, the individual consumer's palate may not agree with any of the judging results. Which brings us back to the most important rule of enjoying wine: *trust your own palate.*"

COOPERAGE: This term encompasses storage vessels used in a winery for the wines before they are bottled and is derived from the word *cooper* — someone who makes barrels. Except for the experimental lots of wine that are kept in glass carboys usually twenty to twenty-five litres in capacity, wines are stored in one of three types of cooperage. Food-grade polyethylene tanks are popular with small wineries because these are the least expensive storage vessels. Stainless steel tanks are widely used as fermentation tanks and for blending and storing wines. While more expensive than plastic, stainless steel tanks are easier to clean, are impervious to air and are entirely neutral storage containers. Stainless steel tanks came into use in the 1930s in the wine industry and plastic tanks have become widespread only in the 1980s. Wood cooperage, on the other hand, has a long history in wine and today is regarded as mandatory to the production of many premium table wines. The oak imparts additional flavours: French oak adds vanilla aromas and subtle spiciness while American oak adds bold, sweet notes, all of it adding complexity to wines. At the same time, the texture of wines softens attractively during maturation in barrels.

In British Columbia, the first large oak vats were acquired by *Growers' Wines* around 1930 when Growers', just launching its first grape wines, bought vats from the Christian Brothers winery in California — the vats having become surplus there as a result of the American Prohibition. In 1977 when the Growers' Victoria winery closed and the new *Jordan & Ste-Michelle* winery opened in Surrey, the vats were rebuilt and placed in a cellar below the Surrey tasting room. Built with thick staves of French oak, the 100 ovals ranged in capacity from 750 to 1,400 gallons. *Robert Holt*, then general manager of the winery, spent $200,000 on the project, hiring a cooper in California to do the job. "We had the cooper take them completely apart, shave about an eighth of an inch from inside of all the wood, put them back together and sandblast and refinish the outside." Holt neglected to get the expenditure authorized, having concluded that the vats were worth saving for their aesthetic value in the tasting room as well as for their practical use. Ste-Michelle used the vats to store red and fortified wines; the cellar was a high point during the wine tours. When the winery was demolished in 1990 after being sold to *Brights*, some of the vats were sold to wineries in the United States. "But most went to firewood," Holt lamented later.[20]

The other winery to use large vats was *Calona Wines*, which stored its reds in large tanks made either of oak or redwood. In the early 1980s, at the urging of *Elias Phiniotis*, then the winemaker, the oak vats were also rebuilt and the interiors were shaved to rid them of crusts of tartaric acid accumulated in decades of wine storage. As a result, the vats regained an ability to impart an oak complexity to the red wines that were maturing therein. Calona's award-winning rougeons of the 1987 and 1988 vintages developed some of their round richness in these vats.

Casabello was the first of the commercial wineries to make a significant commitment to small (typically 225 litres) oak barrels. Shortly after the winery was established in 1966, it began acquiring used barrels, primarily barrels that previously had been used to transport Portuguese bulk brandies and sherries to North American liquor boards which then sold the empty barrels. These were well-made quality oak barrels, so good that the British Columbia board at one time, to the intense irritation of barrel merchants **Sweeney Cooperage Ltd.,** began selling them separately from its run-of-the-mill used whisky barrels. Casabello aged some of its best red wines in these barrels, including several acclaimed vintages of pinot noir. The barrel cellar was disbanded in the 1970s when Casabello de-emphasized oak-aged varietals. Only in the 1990s have oak barrels again become widely used by British Columbia wineries.

Used barrels still have a role, both for practical and esthetic reasons. In 1995 **CedarCreek**, which had used only French oak to that time, increased its barrel population dramatically by buying two hundred three-year-old American oak barrels from the Napa Valley cabernet sauvignon specialist, Silver Oak Cellars (eighty of which were resold to other wineries). "We decided that was a good way to get a large number of barrels for red wine," winemaker **Ross**

Mirko says. "The price was great." Good used barrels are a fraction of the $250 – $300 for each barrel of new American oak and the $700 – $800 for each new French oak barrel. Worldwide demand has made French oak barrels more expensive than the grapes for the wine going into them. In any event, many winemakers prefer a mixed barrel population: new barrels, which can impart pronounced oak flavours to wines, alongside barrels that have been already used for one to three vintages of wine and no longer will overpower wines with wood flavours. And used barrels are just as effective as new barrels for softening and rounding the texture of wines during barrel-aging. There is always the risk of importing bacterial problems into the cellar with the used barrels if the previous owner had less than impeccable sanitation in the winery. Several Okanagan wineries, notably **Mission Hill,** have purchased new American oak barrels produced in a French style in cooperages in California. "The way we can expand our barrel program is to look at American oak," Mirko suggests. "French oak is just so prohibitive now." The choice of French or American oak also depends on the style of wine desired by each winemaker and on the wine.

While important to quality winemaking, barrels are inherently risky. "Barrels need real vigilance," Mirko says. Because wood is slightly porous, wines stored in wood undergo constant evaporation through the wood. Thus, barrels are topped up regularly — at least once a month — to minimize the head space that will develop and which, if not attended to, can expose wines to excessive oxygen. There is also a risk that barrels, especially used ones, will begin to harbour micro-organisms that can spoil wines. Happily, the alcohol in wine is an adequate defence against such spoilage, as long as the barrel remains filled and clean. Used barrels, when empty, are fumigated with sulphur, the all-purpose winery sterilant, and ideally are refilled as soon as possible. While barrels involve far more work and risk than stainless steel tanks, they are essential for most premium wines. "There's no substitute for barrels," Mirko says. "I love working with barrels. I like the way the wine reacts in barrels — the way the flavours develop with oxidative aging."

CORNISH, EARL (1932–): When Earl Cornish was preparing to retire from his career as a heavy duty crane operator, he and his wife, Joanne, bought a home in 1981 at Kaleden with a postage-stamp gewurztraminer vineyard. "The basic reason was to have my life savings on something I would walk around on rather than on a piece of paper with numbers on it," Earl said. "The vineyard didn't mean much to me." A perfectionist, he began tending the vines himself after an unsatisfactory experience with leasing it to another grower. His proudest moment came in 1994 when *Jackson-Triggs* produced an exquisite and rare late harvest wine from his gewurztraminer — rare because a fully mature gewurztraminer seldom retains the acidity needed for late harvest wine. "When I read the back label, I feel pretty humble," Cornish said, referring to the gold type that proclaimed: "This vineyard has been individually selected for its ability to produce Gewurztraminer of the highest quality." The vineyard was planted in 1978, four years before Cornish took over, with plants supplied by *Casabello,* on southeastern sloping land backing against a high bluff. The soil changes from rocky near the bluff to loam and heavy clay and finally to what Cornish describes as beach sand.

Born in Penticton, Cornish is a ninth generation Canadian on his father's side. His mother was born in Italy and came to Canada in 1924. Her father, Dominic Blasutig, had come to Nanaimo in 1914 as a coal miner, immigrating from Udine in northeastern Italy. In the garden behind his modest home on Nanaimo's Terminal Avenue, he maintained a small vineyard and was still making his own wine when he was in his eighties. "He wouldn't let anyone else touch his vines," Cornish said. This agricultural heritage rubbed off on the entire Cornish family, the members of which return (with their spouses) each year to harvest the grapes. As many as thirty people congregate for what has become a three-day Cornish harvest festival each vintage.

COVERT FARMS: In the lee of McIntyre Bluff, the landmark geological feature of the Okanagan Valley just north of Oliver, there is an expansive plateau that Californian-born George Covert (1910–) purchased in 1959, converting the ranch land into the valley's largest mixed fruit and vegetable farm. For many years until all of the wine grapes were pulled out after the 1988 harvest, Covert Farms also was one of the single largest grape producers.

Known as a shrewd investor and a driving entrepreneur, George Covert was a successful wholesaler and shipper of fruit and vegetables in California. He was unaware of the Okanagan until one of his customers in Calgary chanced to mention the valley as a source of apricots. Covert soon travelled north to see

Covert Farms (photo courtesy of Crofton Studios Ltd.)

for himself and promptly bought six hundred acres of sandy, pine-covered ranch land just below McIntyre Bluff. The land had no water but Covert had an irrigation line built from the valley 450 feet below (and later drilled an artesian well to fill a storage reservoir) and began growing tomatoes and onions. He began adding grapes in 1962, beginning with Okanagan riesling, white diamond and bath, the usual varieties planted in the late 1960s. Subsequently, some of the labrusca varieties were replaced with French hybrids, notably maréchal foch. In 1978 when the vineyard reached its full extent of 180 acres, Covert Farms leased one of the first mechanical harvesters in the Okanagan in order to cope with a chronic labour shortage. George Covert stopped using the machine after one vintage because it left too many grapes unharvested while damaging the vineyard trellis.

In the 1980s when wineries were scrambling for white grapes, Covert Farms was asked to replace its foch with a white variety. The hard-headed Covert family — George's son, Mike (1944–), a University of British Columbia agriculture graduate, had become general manager — instead had the grapes crushed, selling the juice in 1985 and 1986 to home winemakers and to juice drinkers. "People who liked the grape juice *really* liked it," said Diane Covert, Mike's wife, also a UBC agriculture graduate and a marketing manager at Covert Farms. "And people who didn't like it said it tasted like prune juice." This digression into the juice business enabled Covert Farms to maintain its foch acreage until the wineries once again were asking for red grapes. However, that happy situation lasted only a few years until the provincial and federal governments paid growers in 1988 to rip out wine grapes, like foch, that were judged too mediocre for making premium wines. The Coverts pulled out all their grapes except ten acres of table varieties and bitterly declined immediately to re-plant with vinifera, instead planting eighty acres of exotic apples. "We just decided that governments make up their minds and three years later are likely to change their minds," Diane Covert said. "Farming is long-term and government is not." Various other crops, including corn, asparagus, potatoes and melons, took over at Covert Farms. It was 1996 before Mike Covert felt comfortable enough with the wine industry's progress to agree to plant twenty acres of vinifera, mostly chardonnay and merlot, for the nearby *Vincor* winery.

CROWSNEST VINEYARDS: Farmgate winery opened in 1995 near Cawston by *Hugh* and *Andrea McDonald*. Based on a twelve-acre vineyard, the winery produces auxerrois, riesling, chardonnay, kerner, merlot and pinot noir.

[4] Memorandum in Lloyd Schmidt files.

[5] Ibid.

[6] Memorandum by Brian Roberts, July 4, 1968, in Lloyd Schmidt files.

[7] *The Province*, May 3, 1971.

[8] Tom Capozzi, in interview with author, 1995.

[9] Rosemary Neering, *A Traveller's Guide to Historic British Columbia*, (Vancouver, Whitecap Books, 1993) p. 126.

[10] Anecdote recalled by Tom Capozzi in interviews with author in 1983, 1994.

[11] Interview with author, May 15, 1982.

[12] Victor Casorso, *The Casorso Story*. (See SOURCES for complete reference.)

[13] Ibid.

[14] CedarCreek Estate Winery "Business Plan and Financing Proposal, April 1996."

[15] Interview with author, 1983.

[16] Ibid.

[17] Correspondence in author's files.

[18] *The Financial Post*, October 31, 1970.

[19] Letter to author.

[20] Interview with author, 1995.

---

[1] Copies of letters in personal files of Linda Ben-Hamida.

[2] *Calona Wines: Golden Anniversary,* booklet published by the winery in 1982.

[3] The President's Report for the year ended December 31, 1967, for Calona Wines Ltd.

DDD

DAL'ZOVO, LAURENT (1966–): Born into a family of restaurateurs in Paris, Dal'Zovo is a graduate of the winemaking school at *Montpellier*. Although he worked at several wineries in France and spent two years as a technical advisor to the French Union of Enologists, a vintage spent at Grand Cru Vineyard in California's Sonoma Valley left him determined to work in North America where he discerned that winemaking is not as circumscribed by tradition as in France. In 1991 he accepted an offer to work at Hillebrand Estates, a large premium Ontario winery which was acquired in 1994 by *Andrés Wines*. The new owners transferred Dal'Zovo in August 1994 to their winery at Port Moody, B.C., where he teamed with winemaker *Tony Vlcek* to launch the premium Peller Estates wines. He returned to France in June 1996, becoming a winemaker with a Banyuls co-operative in southwestern France.

DAVIDSON, WALTER (1944–): Raised on a Penticton-area farm, Davidson was pursuing a career as a teacher in Quesnel when his father-in-law, *Evans Lougheed,* convinced him in 1974 to buy a hundred-acre-plus vineyard on a plateau overlooking Osoyoos. It had been developed by Lougheed with his brother Alan and with several founding shareholders of *Casabello Wines* to produce fruit for the winery; the shareholders now wanted to sell it. One-quarter of the vineyard was planted to an admirable range of vinifera grapes, including pinot noir, merlot, carignan among the reds; and chenin blanc, chardonnay, grey riesling, sauvignon blanc, semillon and johannisberg riesling among the whites. Davidson added another ten acres of vinifera, leaving the remainder of the vineyard in hybrid varieties. This noble vinifera thrust ended late in October 1978 on a day when the temperature plunged abruptly from shirt-sleeves at lunch to freezing water lines in the early evening — and stayed cold. Because the vines had not yet become dormant, almost all were frozen to the roots except for the semillon. This was a major financial blow to Davidson who had insurance only on the surviving hybrids, coverage then not being available for vinifera. Davidson prudently replanted with hybrids: foch, verdelet and seyval blanc. These comprised the bulk of the thirty-seven acres of grapes Davidson retained after the 1988 pullout when he removed about eighty acres of vines to plant exotic apple varieties. Subsequently, the verdelet and the seyval blanc also have been removed, victims to lagging winery demand. "I'd sooner grow apples," Davidson says, adding with a chuckle: "In this family, that's heresy."

DE CHAUNAC: Red hybrid grape variety also known as Seibel 9549 because it was one of many hybrids that emerged from the nursery of Albert Siebel (1844–1936), one of France's most prolific grape breeders in the late nineteenth and early twentieth century. It was among the many varieties imported from France in 1947 by *T.G. Brights & Co.* for propagation in Ontario vineyards. The variety, which generally produces a light red with no particular complexity, propelled the transition in Ontario winemaking from labrusca to hybrid varieties. In 1970 the Finger Lakes Wine Growers Association of New York, with an eye to commercially acceptable varietal names on labels, began assigning names to the more important hybrids. This variety was first called *cameo*. After the Canadian Wine Institute objected that this was a proprietary name belonging to one of its members, the grape was renamed *de chaunac* in 1972 to honour Adhemar de Chaunac, who was the winemaker at Brights from 1933 until he retired in 1961 at age sixty-five. De chaunac grapes were planted in British Columbia during the 1960s and by 1974 the variety, with six hundred acres planted, was the province's most important. It proved a useful blending grape but, because of its simple flavour profile, de chaunac never generated a following as a variety table wine. Most of the vines were pulled out in 1988.[1]

DEGUSSEM, DIRK (1946–): The proprietor, with his family, of *Gersighel Wineberg* south of Oliver, DeGussem was born on a farm near Ghent, in Belgium's Flanders Fields. "We were potato farmers," he says. His enthralment with grapes began in 1966 when he went to Pomerol in France as a picker. He returned to the family farm but in 1970, after marrying, he and his wife Gerda moved around Europe and even, in 1981, spent six months in South Africa, in search of a place where he could grow grapes and make wine. Along the way he developed a taste for poetry. DeGussem not only writes poetry in English and in Flemish; with his long, undisciplined hair and flashing eyes, he looks the part and is prone to uttering mysterious aphorisms and references to Homer in conversation with visitors to his winery.

DeGussem brought his family to Canada in 1986, buying an orchard and vineyard on the west side of Highway 97, between Osoyoos and Oliver. In 1989, the fruit trees were replaced with more vines, among them premium varieties such as pinot noir, pinot blanc and chardonnay. The Gersighel farmgate winery opened in the summer of 1995 with two vintages of pinot blanc for sale and chardonnay still to be bottled. Unhappily, none of the 1994 vintage of pinot noir survived the assault of the birds; in 1995, DeGussem began protecting his vines with nets. He is enthusiastic about the potential for his site, a sliver of soil wedged between the highway and the low mountains to the west, that shield the vineyard from the late afternoon sun. "This is Burgundy country here," he insists. "When it is too hot, you have problems with pinot noir." He has an acre of this variety and is enthusiastic about it, even while admitting it is a difficult grape to grow and vinify. "You have to look after it like a chicken on a bed," he says, lapsing into one of his aphorisms. Equally mysterious is the winery's label. The fetching damsel stomping grapes in a basket, DeGussem says with an enigmatic smile, is a memory from Europe.

DENBY, LYALL (1923–): Director of pomology and grape research at the *Summerland Research Station* from 1971 until he retired in 1983, the Regina-born Denby joined the scientific staff at Summerland in 1950 after completing a master's degree in agriculture at the University of British Columbia. He was already an authority on ornamental plants, having gained experience working at a Vancouver nursery. At Summerland he gravitated towards vegetables and later toward tree fruits and grapes. He took over the grape program, with emphasis on developing winter-hardy varieties that had been launched by Dr. D.V. Fisher, who had moved on to become Summerland's director. Like many of his professional peers, Denby had reservations about the viability of vinifera grapes. Consequently, Summerland sought to breed varieties with vinifera flavour characters but with the vigour and hardiness of hybrids. The only wine grape from this work that became a commercial variety was the muscat-flavoured **sovereign opal**, produced only by *Calona* as a varietal. Denby said later that other promising varieties were under development when he was diverted from that research to work on the so-called Becker Project, which focused on German vinifera. "I was forced into it," Denby said. "I would have preferred to put much of my own time into the next two generations of crosses. We had some good stuff coming on; opal was only one example."

With a small Canadian delegation, Denby toured the Soviet Union in 1973 and arranged to bring back from a research station in Yalta a number of Russian varieties. These included matsvani and rkatsetelli which were grown at *Inkameep* and which *Brights* turned into interesting varietals in small lots before the winery's accountants decided sales were too small to continue. The Russian varieties now are largely uprooted from Okanagan vineyards.

DIAMOND: This obscure white grape, a hybrid from the eastern United States with some labrusca character, was the most widely planted wine grape in British Columbia during the 1960s. The acreage rose from 166 acres in 1960 to peak at 376 acres in 1966. In 1970, at 330 acres, it still was the most widely grown variety, but was about to be overtaken by de chaunac.[2]

DIVINO ESTATE WINERY: Established in 1983, this Oliver winery was based on one of the oldest all-vinifera vineyards in the Okanagan, including grape varieties originally imported from Italy. Both the cabernet and the merlot from this winery are notable for their distinctive peppery character. The winery owner, voluble Italian-born *Joe Busnardo*, is one of the industry's most lively renegades. With no family member prepared to take over Divino, the seventy-one acre property was sold in 1996 to become *Hester Creek Estate Winery*. Busnardo moved Divino, along with enough finished wines to support five years of sales, to a new thirty-nine acre property in the Cowichan Valley on Vancouver Island. He took with him 50,000 grape plants grown from cuttings made at the Oliver vineyard for planting at the new vineyard. "We don't know yet what will grow on the Island," Busnardo said. "I figure I will do exactly the same mistake I made twenty-nine years ago."

DOCKSTEADER, BILL (1928–): In 1984 this successful Vancouver car dealer, with brother Don, acquired *Okanagan Vineyards*, formerly *Vinitera,* an estate winery that had opened in 1979 south of Oliver but subsequently went into receivership. Unable to turn the business around, the Docksteader brothers withdrew in 1987.

DOMAINE DE CHABERTON: Opened

July 1991, as a farmgate winery, it soon upgraded to the status of an estate winery. Production is supported by a large vineyard on carefully contoured south-facing slopes in the Fraser Valley, literally within sight of the United States border south of Langley. Owners are Paris-born **Claude Violet** and his German wife, Ingeborg, who emigrated to British Columbia in 1980. Violet traces his roots in the wine industry back to the seventeenth century. In this century, his family owned the company that produced Byrrh, a popular French aperitif. When that business was sold, Violet, who also is trained as a banker, pursued a career as a wine merchant in Europe before coming to Canada. The winery, named for Violet's family farm in the south of France, is the only estate winery with its own vineyard in the Fraser Valley. Because the growing conditions here are cooler than in the Okanagan, Domaine de Chaberton has specialized in aromatic white wines — bacchus, madeleine angevine, madeleine sylvaner — best suited to the cool conditions.

DOMAINE COMBRET: Established in 1994, this winery is a technical showpiece perched on a hillside overlooking the Okanagan Valley south of Oliver, with a tasting room taking full advantage of the view. The winery, owned by **Robert Combret** and his family, specializes in chardonnay, riesling, cabernet franc and gamay, all made to exceptional standards. The winery's debut vintage 1993 riesling won a silver medal at the International Wine Challenge at Blaye-Bourg near Bordeaux and the debut 1993 chardonnay, competing with 348 chardonnays from around the world, scored a bronze at the 1995 Chardonnay du Monde competition in Burgundy. Winemaker **Olivier Combret** and his father Robert credit their vineyard's soil, or *terroir*, for the quality of the wines but credit also must go to tradition: generations of the Combret family had been growing wine in Provence in the south of France since 1638 before moving to the Okanagan in 1992.

DOMESTIC WINE AND BY-PRODUCTS CO.: This was the pedestrian original name for **Calona Wines Ltd.** The new name was chosen in 1936 after a province-wide competition which was won by an entrant from the Fraser Valley. The prize: $20 and a case of wine.

DOSMAN, ROGER (1948–): With his wife, Nancy, Dosman is the owner of **Dosman Vineyards** near Duncan on Vancouver Island. Born in Vancouver, Dosman got a bachelor's degree in urban geography from the University of British Columbia but took over his father's automobile body shop in 1976 and ran it successfully until selling it twelve years later. He spent the next four years searching for vineyard property before buying a ten-acre farm in the Cowichan Valley. The varieties planted primarily are grapes for cool-climate white wines: bacchus, sieggerebe, kerner, schönburger and auxerrois. Also being cultivated are two red varieties from Europe, agria and dunkelfelder, which have never before been produced as varietals in British Columbia.

DOSMAN VINEYARDS: Since 1993, this ten-acre property near Duncan gradually has been converted to a vineyard to support a farmgate winery scheduled to open in 1997 or 1998.

DOTTI, HELMUT (1939–): Austrian-born winemaker trained at Weinsberg whose career in Canada began at Growers' Wines Ltd. in 1964, including an assignment at the company's winery in Moose Jaw, Sask. Dotti subsequently worked for several other wineries, including Mission Hill in 1981, Okanagan Cellars in 1986, and CedarCreek.

DRINKWATER, BILL (1928–): Until the unusually cold November of 1985, Bill Drinkwater's Basque Vineyards was one of British Columbia's most northerly vineyards — and the only one in the Thompson River valley. The grapes were high quality but the site was not.

Drinkwater was born in Vernon to a pioneer family that had come to British Columbia as loggers in the late 1800s. Trained as a mathematics and history teacher, he bought six acres in east Kelowna in the mid-1960s which included three acres of grapes, primarily diamond, a labrusca variety. As his interest in grapes grew, he bought a twenty-seven-acre property with an orchard and a vineyard in the Belgo district, northeast of Kelowna. Here he grew maréchal foch and himrod, among other hybrid varieties. He also involved himself in grower politics and was president of the B.C. Grape Growers Marketing Board in 1978. By that time Drinkwater concluded that the Kelowna vineyard did not get enough heat units to mature his grapes to optimum levels. He sold that property and, after an extensive search, bought one hundred acres of sagebrush-covered land in the Basque district on the east flank of the Thompson, about ten miles south of Ashcroft, a small ranching and mining community. (The area gets its name because a pioneer set-tler came from the Basque region of Spain.) Temperature readings indicated that this site in summer had heat units comparable to those at the very south end of the Okanagan. In 1980, after installing an irrigation system on the arid site, he planted premium varieties including johannisberg riesling, chardonnay, gewurztraminer and chancellor. Both Sumac Ridge and Calona bought Drinkwater grapes, with Sumac Ridge producing a vineyard-designated chardonnay.

But on the night of November 17, 1985, the temperature plunged to -28°C and stayed bitterly cold for a week. Most of the vines were frozen through to the roots since there was no protective snow cover on them (very little snow ever falls in the Basque region). The Drinkwaters had buried the vines with earth in previous years but found this was too costly and damaged the fruiting buds on the vines. Few vines, with the exception of chancellor, were alive in the spring of 1986 and the Drinkwaters sadly switched to growing tomatoes, peppers and other vegetables. The vineyard posts remained in place for several more years as Drinkwater vacillated about restoring the vineyard. When the posts were removed, he regretted not replanting with cuttings from those few hardy vines that had survived the killer freeze. He continued to collect temperature data until he sold the property and retired in 1993, noting bitterly that there had never been another freeze as severe as the 1985 one. However, had Drinkwater persisted, the immense flocks of starlings that descended on the Basque Vineyards each fall likely would have defeated him. He admitted later, after a trial with netting, that he was too upset at the number of owls and kestrels trapped to consider the permanent use of nets over the vineyard.

DUDA, MEL (1951 –): Since planting his vineyard in 1984, this Okanagan Falls grower has specialized in vidal, a white hybrid variety that grows vigorously and produces full-blown fruity wines, particularly when used for icewine. Unhappily for Duda, the variety has fallen from favour. With the market price for the variety no longer attractive, Duda in 1996 was considering switching to another variety.

The son of a farmer, Duda was born in Dauphin, Man., and raised in Penticton where he worked twenty years, until 1992, for a manufacturer of recreational vehicles. In 1981 he purchased ten acres of rugged undeveloped property south of Okanagan Falls, an area he knew well from hunting there as a youth, and where he and wife Lynn built a home. Told only two acres were plantable, Duda bulldozed and contoured the property until eight and a half acres were suitable for agriculture. He concluded that grapes were the only viable crop and on four and a half acres planted 4,500 vines, all vidal obtained from neighbouring grower *Ian Mavety*. Problems with frost in one area caused him to shrink the vineyard to three acres. At the same time Duda also established a nursery for ornamental evergreens, a business that has assumed the priority in Duda's farming, if not in his heart. "There's something to grapes," he says wistfully.

DULIK, DANIEL (DEN) (1939–): Born in Kelowna, Dulik learned the art of grapegrowing from his father, Martin, gradually taking over the operation of the Pioneer Vineyard at the very end of Hughes Road, east of Kelowna. The amiable, barrel-shaped Dulik is one of the few growers who made the jump from labrusca grapes to vinifera without a significant stop with the hybrids. The first of the vineyards planted by *J.W. Hughes,* Pioneer was given over entirely to labrusca table grapes, many of which were sold to wineries for the fortified pop wines popular in the 1960s. With the exception of a small planting of maréchal foch, Den Dulik declined to plant hybrids because he did not think those varieties were sufficiently better than his labrusca. (After all, his vivacious wife Patricia, an accomplished home food processor, was able to win awards with her home-made whites made from diamond grapes.) However, in 1978 Dulik — and his even more sceptical father — were persuaded by *Jordan & Ste-Michelle* winemaker *Josef Zimmerman* to plant white riesling. Zimmerman argued that, if the variety was hardy enough for German vineyards, it would also thrive in Kelowna. The clay-loam vineyard, because of its southwesterly slope, is one of the warmer sites among the vineyards east of Kelowna. The Duliks planted five acres and, over the next decades, learned that Zimmerman was right. At the first industry-wide competition in 1982 (at *September*), the winery won a gold medal for a 1981 riesling special reserve made from Dulik grapes. Pioneer Vineyard, now with twenty-nine acres under vine, also includes bacchus and optima (also Zimmerman recommendations), pinot noir, pinot blanc, chardonnay and pinot meunier. "I'm happy with them all," Dulik says.

DULIK, MARTIN (1907–1987): Born in Czechoslovakia, Dulik came to Canada when he was fifteen and, after a decade in Saskatchewan, he and his new bride came to the Okanagan, looking for work. In 1934 Dulik was hired by *J.W. Hughes* to work on the Pioneer Vineyard just southeast of Kelowna and ultimately became a foreman. In 1944, when Hughes began selling the vineyard to his foreman, Dulik agreed to buy the Pioneer Vineyard. The terms (which were extended to other foremen as well) were unusual but then neither Dulik nor the others had ready cash. Dulik acquired the vineyard over seven years by paying the income tax on the crop and giving Hughes the proceeds from half the crop.[3] Grapes were sold both to the fresh market and to *Growers' Wines* in Victoria, with the wine grape market becoming the major market with the expansion of wineries in the 1960s. Dulik also was one of the leaders in the 1961 formation of the *Grape Growers Association*.

DULIK, SUSAN (1962–):

Born in Kelowna into one of the pioneer grape-growing families, Susan Dulik was drawn irresistibly to the wine industry by the infectious enthusiasm of the winemakers who continually visited the family's Pioneer Vineyard. When she asked for work at *Jordan & Ste-Michelle*, the winery to which her family then sold grapes, she was offered a tour guide's post in 1980 at the Ste-Michelle winery in Surrey. "I just had a ball," she recalls. After three years she was promoted to sales and administration work and stayed with the winery until it closed in 1990, took a year's sabbatical and then came back to the industry, first working with *Cedar-Creek* and then with *Summerhill*.

"I decided I wanted to open my own winery," she said. Winemaker *Eric*

von Krosigk, her mentor at Summerhill, instilled the belief that good wine begins with good grapes. Susan Dulik had not been a great student of viticulture before but she joined her family at Pioneer Vineyards in 1992 and was surprised that she enjoyed vineyard work. She soon began making trial batches of wine in preparation for the farmgate winery planned to open in 1997 under the name, *Pinot Reach.* Susan Dulik's wines are clean and fresh, the result of a minimalist style of winemaking that dictates interfering with the wines as little as possible. "I just leave them alone — keeping them incredibly clean but letting the wines be," she says.

DUNFIELD, ROBB (1959–):

This Vancouver-born artist's courageous career received significant impetus after *Calona Wines* began featuring his oil paintings on its premium wines in 1991. Dunfield paints all of his canvasses by manipulating the brush with his mouth because he is paralyzed below the neck, the result of a broken vertebrae suffered at age nineteen in a thirty-foot fall to the pavement from the balcony of an uncompleted building. An active athlete prior to the accident, Dunfield began painting during his rehabilitation to fill the time. "The days were long and boring," recalls Dunfield, who now also has become a motivational speaker. "The art work allowed me to get lost in my own little world and to express myself, the way I used to in sports. Then I had someone offer me money for one of my paintings. That's when I really started to enjoy it." He was already producing art for calendars and cards when Calona commissioned label art. "I was definitely struggling," he admits. "They opened a lot of doors for me. I was selling my paintings for substantially less than I am now."

The first wine distinguished with a Dunfield label was the winery's 1987 Rougeon Reserve, with an initial production run of three hundred cases priced at $10 a bottle. "I remember saying that Calona has never sold a bottle of wine over $10 in its entire history," recalled *Ian Tostenson*, who was just then taking over as president of Calona's parent company. The eye-catching labels depicting a British Columbia scene propelled the wine's success; Calona soon dared to price its top wines aggressively. The Dunfield labels, allied with label commentary by winemaker *Howard Soon*, were appearing by 1996 on all of Calona's flagship wines — and they began to attract collectors. Dunfield's arduous technique limits his annual output of canvasses so that each print is likely to have a three-year life on a specific label before being replaced. The original canvasses, some of which have been acquired by Calona, are limited by Dunfield's reach to a maximum size of twenty inches by thirty inches. He paints in oils because water colours dry too quickly. For scenic inspiration, he augments limited trips to the outdoors with his vivid imagination and memories of his youth. Dunfield and Soon seek to match the label scenery with the character of the wines which Dunfield — whose father was a keen home winemaker — gets to taste. "I am more of a red wine drinker than a white wine drinker," the artist says.

DUNIS, STAN (1953–): "Working with plants is almost like a religion," maintains Dunis, a former and future grape-

grower on a historic vineyard south of Oliver. He treated the 1989 grape pullout program as a sabbatical from viticulture, going back to university and becoming a registered nurse. But when he began planting pinot blanc in 1996, Dunis once again was pursuing a long-term dream of establishing his own winery.

He was born in what was then Yugoslavia, near the Italian border in what has since become Croatia, the son of an engineer who refused to join the Communist Party and thus put himself and his family at risk. So in 1960 the Dunis family slipped out of Yugoslavia with only the clothes they were wearing, ultimately making their way to Canada. Stan Dunis and a high school friend, Regina-born Jim Shkrabuik, teamed up in 1981 to buy a vineyard south of Oliver which they called Bella Terra. About seventy acres under contract to Andrés, the vineyard was part of a much larger parcel on the east side of the valley below Black Sage Road that had been planted in the mid-1950s. It was then called the Blue Sage Vineyard, and once had been the largest melon farm in Canada! The major portion of the property was purchased by the Ritchie brothers who are believed to have planted the first de chaunac grapes in the Okanagan in 1962, under an agreement to supply *Andrés*. Much of the early de chaunac acreage in the valley owed its existence to cuttings from there. *Eden Raikes*, one of the founders of the Grape Marketing Board, bought the vineyard in the early 1970s; when he left in the latter part of that decade to become a developer in Hawaii, the vineyard was owned briefly by Vancouver developers. Dunis and Shkrabuik bought it when the developers got into financial trouble. They continued to supply Andrés with French hybrid grape varieties, frequently winning praise from the winery for the quality of their reds.

With the free trade agreement in 1988, the partners were faced with the choice of replanting or accepting the compensation for pulling out the vines. They had just recently converted a quarter of the property to vinifera varieties but realized that they could not keep up their mortgage payments without continuing to sell the now-unwanted red hybrids. They agreed to have all the grapes pulled out in exchange for the compensation. "It wasn't overly generous but it was fair," said Dunis. Subsequently, he acquired his partner's interest, sold a portion of the vineyard to neighbour **Lanny Martiniuk,** and let the remainder lie fallow while pursuing a nursing career. The 1996 planting of pinot blanc, which Dunis considers one of the best varieties for the Okanagan, takes him full circle. When he and his partner began planting vinifera in the mid-1980s — "and a lot of people laughed at us" — pinot blanc was one of the varieties. Dunis now owns a total of twenty-three acres (mortgage-free), with about eighteen acres of plantable land.

---

[1] Hudson Cattell and H. Lee Stauffer, *Wines of the East: The Hybrids.* (Lancaser, PA: Eastern Wine Publications,1978.)

[2] British Columbia Ministry of Agriculture, vineyard surveys.

[3] Ruth Saari, Forty-One Years on the Pioneer Vineyard — *Forty-fifth Report of the Okanagan Historical Society,* pp. 112–116.

EEE

EHRENFELSER: This grape produces aromatic dry white wines and intensely flavoured dessert wines from British Columbia vineyards. Developed in 1929 at **Geisenheim,** this is a cross of riesling and silvaner. Its name was inspired by a nearby ruined castle, Schloss Ehrenfels.

EISWEIN: This is the German word translated in Canada as icewine but occasionally still used by some producers. See **Icewine.**

ELISABETH'S VINEYARD: A vineyard designation on pinot blanc and pinot noir wines made by **Hainle Estates** from grapes grown by **Elisabeth Harbeck.**

ELMES, GARRON (1972–): The first South African-born winemaker to work in the Okanagan, Elmes handled the 1995 debut vintage for **Lake Breeze Vineyards** at Naramata and made appealingly clean and fresh wines despite working in a winery then not yet adequately equipped. Born in Capetown, Elmes was drawn to wine despite being raised in a business family (plastics and injection moulding). "I shot off in a completely different direction," he said. "It was just something I always wanted to do." He earned a diploma in 1993 at the Elsenburg Agricultural College in Stellenbosch, choosing that school over the University of Stellenbosch because the three-year program is solidly practical. Each of the ten students in the final year is assigned a portion of a vineyard, the challenge being to bring those grapes to maturity and make two wines, one white and one red. Elmes won his diploma with

the production of about 4,000 bottles of a blush wine from ruby cabernet and 2,500 bottles of an off-dry white from an obscure local grape variety. After graduation, Elmes moved swiftly through a variety of jobs to polish his skills. Never reluctant to take on a challenge, he once spent two and a half months taking 100,000 bottles of methode champenoise wines through the final finishing steps before releasing them to market for his employer, a merchant who had bought the unfinished wine for quick resale. After this assignment Elmes became the farm manager and assistant winemaker at Stellenzicht Vineyards, a mid-sized premium winery.

Having spent three weeks after wine school touring wineries in France, Elmes had an expressed interest in working outside South Africa, not for political reasons, he adds, but simply because he "wanted to go somewhere and do something different." In mid-1995 his family learned that Lake Breeze owner Paul Moser — who had also been in the plastics business in South Africa — was looking for a winemaker in Canada. "One day my mother said, 'How would you like to go to Canada?'" Elmes remembers. Two weeks later he was on his way, arriving in the Okanagan before the grapes had even begun turning colour. It gave him a chance to learn something about the varieties he would have to work with. He had a key role in helping secure the necessary winery equipment before vintage. Moser had only purchased the vineyard in late 1994 and was moving so fast towards establishing the winery that the only equipment in place when Elmes arrived were two stainless steel tanks — one of which did not fit into the new winery's buildings. Elmes and Moser continued to move at top speed, locating winemaking equipment as far afield as Switzerland and assembling an assortment of tanks, several of which were too large for the individual lots of wine that Elmes made. The winemaker confessed to "a lot of sleepless nights" because he was forced to commit the cardinal sin in a winery: not all of his tanks could be filled to the very top. Elmes protected those wines from oxidation by filling the head space in each tank with nitrogen, an inert gas. To be positively assured, he refreshed the nitrogen cap almost daily. "It was a bit of a nightmare but it worked out fairly well," he said modestly. In fact it was better than that, for none of his first wines made in Canada showed any trace of oxidation. By the 1996 vintage Elmes was given a fully-equipped winery, including new oak barrels with which he planned barrel-fermented chardonnays and full-bodied reds. Delighted to find morio muscat grapes in the Lake Breeze vineyard, Elmes also began to explore making a fortified dessert muscat in the classic South African style. "There are a lot of different things I would like to start playing around with," said Elmes, clearly having made a personal commitment to the Okanagan.

ENEMARK, TEX C. (1940–):

Appointed deputy minister of Consumer and Corporate Affairs on January 1, 1977, Enemark was the gunslinger for *Rafe Mair*, his minister, in accelerating the overhaul of liquor regulation in British Columbia that had begun three years earlier under the previous administra-

tion. A native of Prince George and a law school graduate, Enemark's enthusiasm for Liberal politics took him to Ottawa as an executive assistant to Ron Basford, then the senior British Columbia cabinet minister there. Enemark subsequently had become a partner in a government relations firm in Ottawa when Mair lured him back to the west coast in November 1976. The ministry, created by the previous New Democratic government, had been enlarged to include, among other duties, responsibility for the retailing and regulation of beverage alcohol which previously (and subsequently) resided with the Attorney General. Putting liquor under Consumer Affairs heralded a more open and commercial attitude for what was a highly controlled product.

An activist who seldom runs out of ideas, Enemark once sent 2,500 "Smile" buttons to the general manager of the Liquor Distribution Branch, asking: "Will you please see to it that employees in the LDB who are in contact with the public are supplied with a button?" Most of his initiatives had more substance. Immediately after becoming deputy minister, he proposed a $2 million "major program to try to change drinking habits." The other senior bureaucrats showed little enthusiasm. In a series of angry memos to them in March 1978, Enemark groused bitterly that "the inter-departmental campaign on liquor moderation appears to be now definitely down the drain."[1] The Liquor Moderation Campaign, as it was called, finally began in late 1978, with an initial $1 million budget derived from a five-cent-a-bottle surcharge on LDB sales. The program lasted only five months, lapsing after Mair and Enemark moved to other assignments in government. The surcharge, however, lasted for several years before it was killed. Other Enemark ideas fared better. The LDB's antiquated administration was updated by the installation of $2 million worth of computer equipment — although it took Enemark a year to sell this idea through the bureaucracy.

One contentious Enemark initiative was his proposal that the private sector, not the LDB, provide the major warehousing in Vancouver for imported wines and spirits. Because the LDB had so increased its product offerings, it urgently needed a new warehouse. "We are ... in this situation," Enemark wrote to Mair in March 1978, "because of many years of neglect." Consultants Urwick Currie had told the government that the LDB warehouse was inadequate to accommodate inventories then averaging 275,000 cases a month. In the succeeding four years the LDB inventories had doubled. The alternative to leasing or building new space was to have wine and spirit companies find their own warehousing for any additional products they intended to stock. Some of the agents for imported products complained until Enemark told them that agents not participating in what was called the Agent Stocking Program would receive no new listings from the LDB. Although Enemark was transferred to become deputy minister of deregulation, the Agent Stocking Program was implemented by the end of 1979.

It was also in Enemark's time in the ministry that the government finally countered the succession of brewery strikes that had occurred in the 1970s. When another one was called in the summer of 1978, the LDB branch invited American brewers to ship beer to British Columbia. In June and July that year the LDB received almost 2 million cases of American beer or ten times what it had imported the year before. This summer enabled the American brewers to gain a foothold in British Columbia. That strike also increased wine consumption sharply and *Calona Wines* — which already was coping with the runaway success of *Schloss Laderheim* — sought permission to import 25,000 gallons of wine in bulk, rather than grapes or concentrates, from the United States. Enemark not only agreed, he extended the privilege to the other commercial wineries, provided that the imported wine comprised 20 percent of volume of wine made from British Columbia grapes, the formula already in place for grape imports. As it happened, Calona imported 118,022 gallons of wine from California in the twelve months to September 1978.[2]

ENOLOGIST: The professional designation for winemaker; some European books still prefer the more archaic spelling, oenologist.

ERCEGO, MARCELLO (1935–): In the province of Vicenzo in northern Italy where Marcello Ercego grew up, it seemed to him that everybody grew grapes and made wine, including his farmer father who also required his help after school. "When you are a little kid, what do you do?" he shrugs. "When the old man is out there, pruning grapes, you got to go and clean the canes and prepare. That's the way people learn." Years later, he put those vineyard skills to work at his well-tended eight-acre Kaleden property where, with the help of a tractor affectionately called Toby, he grows chardonnay, gewurztraminer, chancellor, cabernet franc and merlot. He also makes his own, quite drinkable, wine. "I drink store-bought wine and I get sick," maintains Ercego, who also argues that the best way of crushing red grapes is still the original way his father taught him: with clean, bare feet.

Ercego — the pronunciation is err-chay-go — left Italy in 1957 after having learned to be a bricklayer. In Vancouver he earned his living in construction until an injury and subsequent arthritis led him, on a doctor's recommendation, to move to the Okanagan in search of a drier climate. He and his wife, Anna Maria, initially lived on a property in Kaleden with only a few acres of vines. Ultimately, Ercego, who was now helping build houses in the Okanagan, agreed to partner his neighbour and childhood acquaintance Silvio Bicego in buying and splitting an advantageously priced but abandoned thirteen-acre orchard and gravel pit. Ercego thought he would have a house and a few cattle. The local authorities told him that he could only keep horses, not cows. "I don't like horses," Ercego says. Bicego took five acres for his own vineyard while Ercego had his rough, overgrown site expensively contoured and terraced to create the ideal site for growing grapes. "The hill had been so bad that you couldn't walk on it," Ercego recalls. The slopes are still steep but not too steep for Toby, the small four-wheel-drive Japanese tractor that Ercego calls "my right-hand man" and that provided the agility threatened by Ercego's returning arthritis. "He'll do anything I want."

At first, Ercego planted the vineyard entirely to Okanagan riesling, virtually all of which came out after the 1988 vintage, to be replaced primarily by vinifera. Ercego still offers a vigorous defence of the Okanagan riesling as a winemaking grape, insisting that the fermentation needed to take place on the skins. Indeed, he was unhappy even to take out the grapes. "I cried that time, I tell you," he recalled. He protested to the newspapers and wrote to government before finally giving in. "We can't have everything, can we? Sometimes we have to take the good with the bad." His southern-sloping vineyard, with deep gravel under the topsoil, has enabled Ercego, a grower for **Calona**, to mature his vinifera and earn bonus payments most years. "The sun hits me in the morning," he notes. "I believe the morning sun makes the good fruit."

ESTATE WINERIES: Originally called "cottage" wineries, these are the mid-sized wineries producing wine primarily from grapes grown in their own vineyards. (Sumac Ridge's savvy **Harry McWatters** claims to have been the winery owner who pressed the government successfully to ditch the term "cottage" for the upscale "estate" designation.[3]) Consumer Affairs Minister **Rafe Mair,** whose ministry authored the regulations, believed that small wineries based on their own vineyards would produce premium wine from better grape varieties than were then being processed by the major wineries. **Tex Enemark,** Mair's deputy minister, laid out the rationale in a memorandum to Tourism Minister Grace McCarthy, who was preparing for a speech in Kelowna in the autumn of 1978. "In Europe and in California, one of the most pleasant things a tourist can do is to tour the small vineyards and taste the product of the small specialized winery, and as the small winery goes, so the large winery will follow." [4]

The guidelines were published early in 1979 by the British Columbia Liquor Control and Licensing Branch, an arm of Mair's ministry. Estate wineries were limited to a maximum annual production of 30,000 gallons (about 180,000 bottles) and they were expected to own twenty acres of vineyards. Subsequently, the ceiling was raised to 40,000 gallons, not including production sold outside British Columbia. The rationale for the limit? Government concluded that this was a viable size for a family-operated winery. Estate wineries were limited to extracting a maximum of 150 gallons of juice from each ton of grapes, a rule intended to prevent estate wineries from adding water and sugar to wines, an unfortunate but legal practice of the commercial wineries at the time. (Quality wines cannot be made by adding water; in most of the wine world, the practice is illegal.) Four of the first seven estate wineries encountered serious financial problems, largely because the wines were of indifferent quality. Of the original seven, three have thrived under the founding owners: **Gehringer Brothers, Gray Monk** and **Sumac Ridge**.

EWERT, BRUCE (1963–): Born in Prince George, the son of a pipeline tech-

nical executive, Ewert grew up in California and Vancouver where he took an engineering degree with a food technology bent at the University of British Columbia. Soon after he graduated in 1986, he joined *Andrés* as a quality control supervisor at Port Moody. Two years late he was transferred to Andrés' Winona winery in Ontario as an assistant winemaker. Within eighteen months Ewert had become the winemaker at the company's Truro winery, where he spent two years until transferring back to Port Moody. This trip around Andrés gave him experience with large vintages — the Winona plant was processing 5,000 tonnes of grapes a year — and with making wine in Truro with raw materials mostly from California, Spain and Argentina. He left Andrés in 1994 for a winemaking sabbatical to Australia, returning to British Columbia in mid-1995. He subsequently became a consulting winemaker for sister wineries **Sumac Ridge** and **LeComte**.

[1] Tex Enemark papers; memorandum March 22, 1978, to Richard Vogel, deputy attorney general.

[2] Tex Enemark papers, letter to D.W. Shaw of Davis & Co., December 20, 1978.

[3] Interview with author, May 1982.

[4] Tex Enemark papers; memorandum to Grace McCarthy, September 7, 1978.

FFF

FABER: This white grape variety is a German cross developed in 1929 and popular there because the quality of the white wine it makes approaches the classic riesling. It has been grown only by *Blue Grouse Vineyards* on Vancouver Island but proprietor *Hans Kiltz*, not having enough to support a varietal wine, removed the variety from his vineyard, leaving only a few vines so that, he said, it would not be "extinct" in British Columbia.

FARMGATE WINERY: The British Columbia government in 1989 announced regulations to permit grapegrowers with vineyards not large enough (less than twenty acres) to support *estate wineries* to open small wineries, called farmgate wineries (because the wines must be sold entirely from the farm "gate"). Maximum production allowed was 45,000 litres a year, a quarter of that allowed for estate wineries. See also *Lang Vineyards.*

FATHOM: When *Hainle Vineyards* released a portlike dessert wine in 1995, wine lovers in British Columbia were asked to propose an original name since international regulations prevent Canadian wineries from using *Port* as a wine name. The competition drew 617 entries from 120 entrants (1 person alone submitted 76). The successful entry was Fathom, submitted, Gloria Barkley, a writer in Coquitlam. The first release under this label was a 1993 vintage made from baco noir grapes. See also *Pipe.*

FERGUSON, ROBERT (1950–): The partner and winemaker at *Kettle Valley Winery* in Naramata, Ferguson was born in Hamilton and became a chartered accountant in Vancouver after graduating from the University of Western Ontario. His interest in wine developed from making wine at home with *Tim Watts*, his brother-in-law and now his partner. Ferguson moved to the Okanagan in 1992 after he and Watts acquired and planted the vineyard for their winery.

FERMENTATION: This is the process in which grape juice is converted to wine through the action of yeast turning the grape sugar into alcohol. Yeast spores are found naturally in vineyards and wineries and a basket of grapes left in a warm place will ferment on its own. Because uncontrolled ferments can yield vinegar as easily as wine, most winemakers crush grapes or place juice into clean, temperature-controlled tanks and add yeast strains specifically cultured for wine. For example, yeasts capable of thriving at cool temperatures are used in white wine production while yeasts tailored to warmer temperatures are used for red wines. The fermentation period, which typically lasts five to fifteen days, is perhaps the most critical few days in the life of a wine, which is vulnerable to microbiological spoilage until a protective level of alcohol has been created. Along with acidity, alcohol gives wine its stability. In the making of icewines and other dessert wines, the unusually high sugar content of the juice may slow the fermentation process which then will last weeks, months or — very rarely — years. With these wines, the winemaker relies on the higher than normal acidity of the juice to keep the fermenting juice healthy until alcohol levels approach 9 to 12 percent. Yeast strains lose their vigour as alcohol rises above 12 percent. The fermentation process is a vigorous one, visually resembling boiling because the natural sugar is converted not only to alcohol but also to carbon dioxide. During active fermentation, enough carbon dioxide is released from bubbling vats of wine that fatal concentrations can collect in a poorly vented building.

FINLEY, WILLIAM E: Consulting winemaker whose credits include chief enologist at Calona during the 1960s and winemaker at Okanagan Vineyards in the early 1980s.

FITZPATRICK, GORDON (1960–): A Vancouver-born 1983 economics graduate of the University of British Columbia, Fitzpatrick has absorbed both the wine and political interests of his father Ross Fitzpatrick, the owner of *CedarCreek Estate Winery*. After leaving college, the young Fitzpatrick went to Ottawa as a special assistant to Jean Chrétien, then the Minister of Energy, Mines & Resources. After the Liberals lost the 1984 general election, Fitzpatrick spent a year travelling in Europe before returning to Vancouver for a strategic planning post with Westcoast Transmission Co. In 1986, he joined Viceroy Resource Corp., a Vancouver mining company headed by his father, where he became vice-president, corporate relations, and secretary. He also took time off to be director of operations in Western Canada for Chrétien when the then future prime minister still was Leader of the Opposition.

After the elder Fitzpatrick in 1986 took over the *Uniacke* winery, Gordon was involved in developing the labels and marketing plans to relaunch the winery as CedarCreek. Over the next decade the appeal of wine grew until he decided in the summer of 1996 to take charge of the business side of the winery. "The wine business is a very personal business," he believes. "People do it because they love the business."

FITZPATRICK, ROSS (1933–): The proprietor of *CedarCreek Estate Winery*, Fitzpatrick is the Renaissance Man of British Columbia wine, given his many other interests. He was born in Kelowna, the son of a fruit-packing-house executive and the grandson of farmers who had settled in the Okanagan in 1913. Fresh from the University of British Columbia with a commerce degree, Fitzpatrick worked for a royal commission on the fruit industry, then enrolled at Columbia University in New York for a master of business administration degree and in 1963, before having time to write a thesis, he went to Ottawa as an executive assistant to Liberal cabinet minister John Nicholson. Fitzpatrick's three years in Ottawa left him with a lifelong interest in politics and a close friendship with Jean Chrétien, then an ambitious young politician from Quebec who became the prime minister of Canada, with Fitzpatrick managing Liberal Party affairs in British Columbia for Chrétien. The business career that Fitzpatrick took up after returning to the West from Ottawa in 1966 included a successful aircraft parts brokerage firm in Seattle, a successful Calgary oil company and a successful Vancouver company, Viceroy Resource Corp., with a gold mine in California.

Fitzpatrick's entry into the wine business was a matter of chance. He sought an Okanagan orchard as a weekend hobby farm and found an attractive lakeside property on the Okanagan Lake south of Kelowna, just across the road from struggling **Uniacke Wines**. When the owners of this winery decided to sell in 1986, Fitzpatrick bought it, renamed it after Cedar Creek which flows through the property, and soon found winemaking more compelling than apple growing. A demanding taskmaster and a perfectionist, Fitzpatrick changed the winemaker at CedarCreek three times in the first decade under his ownership, in a quest to produce both red and white table wines of award-winning finesse.

FLETCHER, JOHN (1949–): A veteran of the Canadian wine industry, Fletcher jokes that his expertise is in closing wineries. But as a partner in the team that took over **Hillside Cellars** in mid-1996, he does not intend to be closing any more wineries in his career.

Fletcher was born in Brantford, Ont., the son of a welder who had recently emigrated from Britain. After studying chemical engineering at Mohawk College in Hamilton, Fletcher went to work in 1971 as a quality control technician in the Jordan winery in St. Catharines. In short order, he was being shuffled around the company's far-flung operations: from winemaker at the Calgary winery in 1973 to the operations manager at Selkirk, Man., where Jordan opened a small winery and bottling plant in 1975. Three years later he was back in Calgary as manager and winemaker. The experience closing wineries began in 1980 when **Jordan & Ste-Michelle**, as it had become known, had Fletcher close wineries in Selkirk and Moose Jaw, Sask. In 1985 he was on hand to close the Calgary winery and then

moved to Jordan's new winery in Surrey, B.C., where he was operations manager. Five years later that winery closed. The production and many of the staff moved to what is now the **Vincor** winery on Oliver. Of course, Fletcher was on hand to help close the Cartier winery in Penticton in 1994 after the merger of Cartier and Brights to form Vincor.

In 1996, coming up on his twenty-fifth year in the wine business, Fletcher began looking for a career change. "I have always had a passion about winemaking," he said. "It was time for me to think about doing it myself." He had come close to striking out on his own when he moved to Oliver in 1990, buying a small orchard and giving thought to an estate cidery. He changed his mind after looking into the difficult regulatory climate and the limited market. The chance to realize his ambition arose when a Calgary businessman, **John Hromyk**, asked Fletcher to be his consultant in Hromyk's search for a winery acquisition in the Okanagan. The partnership turned out to be controversial within Vincor, which itself had entertained buying the Divino vineyard earlier in 1996, resulting in Fletcher and the big winery parting company. Hromyk and Fletcher went on to acquire **Hillside Cellars** in mid-1996. Fletcher, the former closer of wineries, immediately set about doubling the capacity of Hillside.

FLOHR, ULRIKE (1955–) AND AUGUST (1943–): Late in 1995 the Flohrs, newly arrived in Canada from Germany, purchased the **Joe Petronio** vineyard, one of those choice vineyards on the **Golden Mile** south of Oliver and applied such a teutonic discipline to an already intelligently planted vineyard that neighbours were already commenting on the orderliness of the farm by the following spring. The discipline should not be surprising. Ulrike Flohr, who was born in Bavaria as was her husband, had worked for the West German border police while August pursued a successful twenty-year career as a salesman of stationery products. Both chose to emigrate to Canada after extensive travel. Ulrike, who learned English at school in Ireland, lived for a time in Adelaide and developed a familiarity with the Barossa Valley and its wines. August spent two extensive vacations in British Columbia. "We like Canada," Ulrike Flohr says. "This is a free country." They arrived as business immigrants and, also having a modest agricultural background, were steered into grapegrowing at the recommendation of a government official. Their ten-and-a-half-acre vineyard is planted almost exclusively to vinifera grapes, including chardonnay, chenin blanc, riesling, gewurztraminer and merlot. Additional acreage was planted to pinot noir in 1996. The Flohrs immediately made up for their lack of specific viticultural knowledge by taking all the available courses with the result that they were reported to want to start a winery. In fact, the vineyard in 1996 had three years remaining under its contract with a major winery and the Flohrs have every intention of honouring that. "We are German," Ulrike Flohr says simply. "We must be correct."

FRASER, MAJOR HUGH NEIL (1885–1970):

Born in Montreal of a military family that had been in Canada since 1810, Major Fraser is remembered now in British Columbia wine circles as the owner of what later became the **LeComte Estate** vineyard near Okanagan Falls. After service in the First World War (two years on the front, two years as a prisoner of war), Fraser decided to settle in the Okanagan after visiting a friend there in 1919. He bought a large farm on Hawthorne Mountain which, legend has it, was then so remote that his bride departed after a few months, leaving a note signed "S.Y.L." for "See you later." The story may be apocryphal. The major, who planted the first grapes on the property, retired to Penticton after selling it. A dignified, erect figure who owned numerous elegant collies (and buried a dozen of them under headstones behind what is now the winery), Fraser's community activism ranged from presidency of the local Society for the Prevention of Cruelty to Animals to a director of the Red Cross. His gun collection was donated to the Penticton Museum.

FREE TRADE: The Canada-United States Free Trade Agreement of 1988 triggered the most dramatic improvement in quality, but also the greatest upheaval, in the history of the British Columbia wine industry. The industry had developed over half a century, protected in some small degree by tariffs but primarily by government policies that gave domestic wines both price and listing advantages over imported wines. For example, the Liquor Distribution Branch since 1977 had guaranteed each commercial winery sixty-six liquor store listings; and it marked up imported wines by 115 percent but only marked up domestic wines by 66 percent. These policies had been challenged by other wine producing nations and Canada, in world trade negotiations in the late

1980s, agreed to eliminate the protections. The FTA with the United States accelerated that commitment.

Free trade was feared by the Canadian wine industry because the majority of its products then were made chiefly with inferior wine grapes and the wines were not competitive with imported wines. In British Columbia, the federal and provincial governments established a $28 million adjustment fund, the major portion of which paid growers to uproot inferior vines and, if they wished, to replant with premium European varieties. After the 1988 harvest in British Columbia, 110 of the 200 growers pulled out about 1,335 hectares of vines and took compensation payments. The grape harvest plunged from 18,000 tonnes worth $13 million in 1988 to 3,000 tonnes worth $3 million in 1989. According to Calona Wines' *Ian Tostenson*, even more vines might have been pulled out but Premier Bill Vander Zalm insisted that some viticulture base had to be preserved. The commercial wineries, to protect their preferred listings with the *Liquor Distribution Branch,* agreed to give six-year contracts to remaining independent growers, whose four hundred hectares generally were planted in premium varieties. Before the vine pull, the most widely planted varieties included Okanagan riesling (white) and maréchal foch (red). After the pull, the remaining ten most widely planted varieties were johannisberg riesling (fifty-eight hectares), verdelet (forty-nine), pinot blanc (thirty-two), gewurztraminer (twenty-seven), chardonnay (twenty-one), ehrenfelser (twenty-one), vidal (twelve), bacchus (eleven), seyval blanc (eleven) and maréchal foch (ten).[1] Subsequently, most of

the verdelet also was replaced. By 1995 almost three hundred hectares of new plantings had been added, almost exclusively focused on vinifera.

While apprehension about free trade was widespread, the *Mission Hill* winery took the contrary view from the outset, aggressively signing up growers until it controlled 20 percent of the vineyards remaining after the pullout. "The formula is working for us," *Nick Clark*, then president of Mission Hill, said in one newspaper interview in April 1989. "I think free trade is going to force everyone in the industry to become more conscious of competition and not take anything for granted. The wine industry is 80 percent bulk wines and 20 percent premium quality wines. The bulk wines are going to suffer because of free trade but the premium quality wines will survive because the demand for excellent taste will always be there." Clark was encouraged by the model of successful wineries in Washington state where "people will sacrifice drinking wine altogether if it's not grown there." Mission Hill accelerated its production of varietals from premium grapes.

The British Columbia government, besides compensating those who decided to quit growing grapes, unveiled a premium wine policy in the fall of 1989. The policy permitted smaller vineyard owners — the optimists who believed in winegrowing in the Okanagan — to establish *farmgate wineries*; it increased the production ceiling of *estate wineries* to 40,000 gallons a year from 30,000. The commercial wineries, to replace the volume of grapes lost to them in the pullout, were allowed to import bulk wines, bottle them in British Columbia and sell them at domestic wine prices. To get that privilege, the commercial wineries agreed to contract most of the remaining grapes for six years through to the end of the 1994 vintage. With the exception of Mission Hill, none of the commercial wineries initially were enthusiastic. Six of the eight commercial wineries hired a lawyer to lobby against the premium wine policy. "My clients weren't aware of more competition at the time of the negotiations," lawyer Stan Wong complained to the *Oliver Courier* in September 1989. They were particularly irritated the farmgate wineries would be allowed to sell wines directly from the vineyard without paying the liquor board markup.

The government was not swayed and the policy worked. By 1995 the premium wine policy had been so successful in establishing a quality wine industry that wineries, including the commercial ones, were scrambling to contract growers and to buy vineyard property. Wine quality had improved so dramatically that consumers were demanding British Columbia wines. Perhaps the key to the success of the premium wine policy was the creation of the *Vintners Quality Alliance* (VQA), a program to identify and market the top quality British Columbia wines. Nick Clark, after he left Mission Hill, became the first chief executive of the *British Columbia Wine Institute* in 1990; in the eighteen months he remained there, the Institute succeeded in marketing the concept that VQA wines were the quality wines from British Columbia.

FROST PROTECTION: See *Winter damage.*

---

1   Official 1990 Yearbook, Okanagan Wine Festival, p. 26.

GGG

GAMAY: This red-skinned, white-fleshed grape makes the agreeably fruity reds of Beaujolais. In the Okanagan the leading producers are **Blue Mountain** and **Domaine Combret**. Other growers have modest plantings of gamay noir, believed to be a lesser clone of pinot noir. These wines also are pleasantly light and fruity and often are more enjoyable when served slightly cool (but not chilled).

GAMBLE, DAVE (1940-): The chronicler of wine industry news in his quarterly newspaper, *B.C. Wine Trails*, Gamble was born in Armstrong, B.C., and worked as a broadcaster in the Okanagan until he became editor of the *Summerland Review* in 1971. He purchased the newspaper a decade later, publishing it until he sold it in 1990. He and his wife, Lynn, briefly considered establishing a farmgate winery before launching *B.C. Wine Trails* in August 1991. A companion annual, *Wine Trails of the Wine Regions of Ontario,* has been published by Gamble since the spring of 1992. Gamble writes most of the detail-packed articles in *B.C. Wine Trails* with a friendly and supportive tone, reflecting his view that "the whole industry has a warm familial aspect to it." That includes Gamble's newspaper: his oldest daughter, Dawn Weins, does typesetting and his son Scott, a Penticton graphic artist, assists in design. The publication, which is available without charge in most wineries or by a modest subscription covering postage, has a quarterly circulation between 15,000 and 20,000.

GEBERT, ANDY (1965-): Swiss-born Gebert apprenticed as a plumber but gravitated towards horticulture before emigrating to Canada late in 1989 and then acquiring part of the vineyard his brother, Leo, had owned since 1984. In 1994 Andy Gebert became a partner in *St. Hubertus Vineyards*, almost immediately making his mark by convincing his winemaker brother that the winery should also begin using barrels rather than finishing all of its wines in stainless steel cooperage.

GEBERT, LEO (1958-) AND BARBARA: Swiss-born proprietors of *St. Hubertus Vineyards,* the Geberts purchased a fifty-five-acre vineyard in 1984 at Okanagan Mission. Having worked part time in Swiss vineyards, they desired a rural lifestyle in a mountain setting but could not afford farmland in Switzerland. Leo was a banker and a plastics fabricator but pined to be a farmer until he could pursue that goal in the Okanagan. A third of their vineyard was sold in 1990 to Leo's brother Andy.

GEHRINGER BROTHERS ESTATE WINERY: Since opening in 1986, this winery consistently produced wines in a meticulously clean style that brothers Walter and Gordon Gehringer learned during their enological studies in Germany. Hallmark of the style are white wines finished with the addition of sweet reserve (unfermented fresh grape juice), which reinforces the wine's natural fruitiness and softens the acidity. The Gehringers released their first totally dry table wine (a johannisberg riesling) in 1987, subsequently keeping it in their lineup and in 1996 adding several other superb dry wines in a new reserve range. The winery also earned renown for its icewines which it began producing in 1991. One of British Columbia's more remarkable icewines was the Gehringer 1991 chancellor, a rare red *icewine* with which the winery won a number of awards. This is a thoroughly family-operated winery, with the brothers drawing on help and support from their father Helmut and their uncle Karl Gehringer.

GEHRINGER, GORDON (1959–): A co-proprietor of Gehringer Brothers Estate Winery, Gordon Gehringer was born in Oliver and trained as a winemaker at Weinsberg in Germany. A shy, self-described "man of few words," he occupies himself in the winery and in the adjoining vineyard and leaves public relations to his older brother, Walter.

Walter Gehringer (photo courtesy of Andrés Wines)

GEHRINGER, WALTER (1955–): Born in Oliver, Walter Gehringer in 1978 became the first Canadian to graduate from the *Geisenheim Institute* in Germany. Returning to Canada, Walter Gehringer worked for *Andrés* in Ontario and British Columbia while the vineyard south of Oliver, purchased in 1981 by the Gehringer family, was planted in the varieties desired for the estate winery that opened in 1986. It is operated by Walter and his younger brother Gordon, with their father Helmut and uncle Karl as silent partners.

GEISENHEIM INSTITUTE: This famed Rheingau viticultural research station founded in 1872 has had a profound impact on winemaking in British Columbia. The late *Dr. Helmut Becker*, Geisenheim's long-time director of grapevine breeding, guided the trials in the Okanagan from 1978 to 1985 that led to varieties such as ehrenfelser and pinot blanc becoming established in the valley. Numerous graduates of Geisenheim's rigorous winemaking course have worked in British Columbia. Among those currently active: *Walter Gehringer* and *Eric von Krosigk*.

GERELUS, LARRY (1952–): A Winnipeg-born actuary, Gerelus and his accountant wife, Linda Pruegger, are the owners of *Stag's Hollow Winery & Vineyard,* which opened near Okanagan Falls in 1996. The son of a railroader, Gerelus began making his own wine and touring wineries in the late 1970s. "I don't know whether it was making wine so much as the lifestyle I saw out here that really attracted me," he says, trying to explain why a professional would become a winegrower. "I enjoy wine very much but I also like to grow plants." After visiting the Okanagan in 1974 for the first time, he was determined to live in the valley, but initially as a fruit grower. He recalls being impressed by several table wines from the newly opened *Sumac Ridge Estate Winery* in 1981. "Since then, it had been in the back of my mind to get into the business. When I discovered the wines, I didn't want to buy an orchard any more — it was going to be a vineyard."

Tall, boyishly slim and soft-spoken, Gerelus became an insurance actuary after graduating with a commerce degree from the University of Manitoba, working in Toronto and Winnipeg before moving to Calgary in 1979 as a consultant. Along with his wife, he worked for major oil companies and then became an independent financial planner. After buying his Okanagan Falls vineyard in June 1992, Gerelus and his wife became regular commuters from Calgary until moving to the Okanagan in 1996 when construction of the winery began. The vineyard previously had been owned by a grower named Joseph Grgich who had planted it, on the direction of a winery, to three acres of vidal and four of chasselas. "I almost dislike chasselas," Gerelus says. "I found it a very watery, nondescript wine. It was grown by Joe because *Mission Hill* asked him to grow it." After his contract ended with the winery, Gerelus had all of the chasselas vines grafted over in 1995 to pinot noir and merlot. He also had a third of the vidal acreage grafted over to chardonnay. However, he retained two acres of vidal, a variety notable for intense flavours, for the production of late harvest wines. "It was a very fast way of changing the vineyard over," he says of grafting new varieties onto mature trunks. The technique was pioneered in the Okanagan by *Paradise Ranch*; Gerelus employed the same expert crew to switch over his vineyard. Approximately 90 percent of the grafts succeeded and by 1996 the Stag's Hollow vineyard was back to 80 percent of normal production.

"I truly believe that wines are made in the vineyard," Gerelus insisted after four years experience at Stag's Hollow. The vineyard is a sun-drenched bowl, with the vines planted in well-drained gravel or sand, a terroir typical of this part of the Okanagan. Gerelus quickly changed the trellising in the vineyard, adopting a system that spreads the canopy so that the leaves have the maximum exposure to the sun. He concluded he was on the right track viticulturally one year when his chasselas, which seldom reached optimal ripeness without losing its natural acidity, achieved 110 percent of the target maturity while still retaining acidity. He earned a bonus from the winery. During his years as a commuting vineyard operator, Gerelus struggled for methods of minimizing bird damage, installing noise cannons and getting his father, now living in Kelowna, to patrol the vineyard when he was not there. Gerelus decided against nets which trap birds indiscriminately and opted for an idea suggested by his neighbour, *Adolf Kruger*, one of the owners of *Wild Goose Vineyards* — electric deterrents. Gerelus fashioned electrified perches throughout the vineyard after a test of giving birds the hot foot proved effective. "I've spread it out over the whole vineyard and I have lost minimal amounts of grapes," Gerelus says. "I'm willing to live with the very slight damage."

Since both Gerelus and his wife know all about business plans and financial projections, it was clear from the start of their vineyard ownership that they needed to create a winery. Their modest acreage would not support them from grapes alone, while additional vineyard land had become too expensive. "I did not want to complicate my life by working at a second job," Gerelus said.

"Besides, the wine route was more exciting. It also allowed me to control the process from the beginning to the end. I don't think it is going to make us rich but it will give us a nice living." The first vintage of Stag's Hollow wines were custom-produced in 1995 at the Sumac Ridge winery since Gerelus had no wine production facilities on his property — and, indeed, was still living in a trailer when not in Calgary. The well-planned and tastefully designed winery, a striking green-roofed building nested into the side of a slope, was completed before the 1996 crush. Not evident is an intriguing design feature — the building is geothermally heated and cooled by fluids that are pumped through a closed system of pipes drilled to a depth of 1,000 feet. Gerelus calculates his heating and cooling costs, both for a residence and for the winery, will only be several hundred dollars a year.

Stag's Hollow debuted with two table wines from vidal, one dry and one in an off-dry style that accentuates the variety's already intense flavours of peaches. Also released from the 1995 vintage is a chardonnay-pinot blanc blend and a barrel-aged pinot noir. While Gerelus already has the ability to make wine as an amateur in small lots, he is employing professional consultants initially. "I'd be foolish to try to do it on my own without the technical assistance of a good winemaker," he recognizes. "There is too much to know to do it right." At full production, Gerelus expects to be producing and selling perhaps 8,000 gallons of premium wines each year. Using a consulting winemaker flows from the same strategy that had Gerelus build a distinctive winery rather than start out, as many farm wineries have, in humble quarters. "I wanted to create a boutique image," he says. "To me, if I want to create a quality product, I need a quality image. The two go hand-in-hand. The image can tarnish very quickly if we do not do it right from the start."

GERSIGHEL WINEBERG: Farmgate winery on Highway 97 between Osoyoos and Oliver that opened in 1995. Flemish-born owner **Dirk DeGussem** drew the inspiration for the name from the names of his three grown children, Gerd, Sigrid and Helgi. Sons Gerd and Helgi help their father run the vineyard and the winery. The six-acre farm, purchased by the DeGussem family in 1987, is planted primarily to pinot blanc, pinot noir and chardonnay.

GEWURZTRAMINER: This is quite possibly the most frequently misspelled grape variety on restaurant wine lists and in wine literature. Even **Gray Monk Cellars,** which produces some of British Columbia's best white wines from the variety, was embarrassed by its printers in a 1990 winery brochure. Twice, and in bold-face type, the spelling was *Gerwurztraminer.* The wines from this variety are notable for lively, spicy fruit flavours and aromas. The wines are best served as aperitif wines or with substantially flavoured foods such as roast turkey, Chinese food and even mild curries.

GHEZZI, CARLO (1899–1963): Born in San Bonifacio near Verona in Italy, he interrupted his technical school education to enlist in the Italian air force when he was seventeen. While he learned to fly, the war ended before he could be thrust into combat. In 1921 he emi-

Carlo Ghezzi in the Calona Winery, 1943 (photo courtesy of Linda Ben-Hamida)

grated to Canada, apparently to join his father. Like his father, he changed his surname to Ghezzi from Brena (signing himself as Carlo Brena Ghezzi). Having some chemical and technical training, Carlo succeeded his father as the winemaker at **Calona Wines**, subsequently also becoming general manager until he retired in 1960. A quiet, formal man, Carlo Ghezzi was troubled through-

out his life by an energy-sapping heart condition. He managed the winery as carefully and cautiously as he managed his own finances. While he doted on his only daughter, Linda, she also recalls an occasion when he flatly refused her money for the movies. In a fit of pique, she tore down all of the no-smoking signs in the winery.

Giuseppi Ghezzi
(photo courtesy of Linda Ben-Hamida)

GHEZZI, GUISEPPE (1867–1943):

The real founder of *Calona Wines Ltd.*, Guiseppe Ghezzi lived a life dramatic enough for the opera. To begin with, Ghezzi was not his real name. He was born Cleto Candido Desiderato Patrizio Brena at San Bonifacio, a community southeast of Verona in northern Italy. Brena, as he was known until he came to Canada, was the son of an orphan, Camillo Brena, whose surname came from his mother because the father was unknown. The entrepreneurial Cleto Brena, after completing technical school studies and getting married in 1892, established his own business in San Bonifacio making cravats and other silk products. Throughout his life, he dressed as elegantly as only a silk manufacturer would. An adventurer, he also was driving in automobile races in Rome as early as 1905. Brena's business appears to have suffered a serious reversal, causing him to set out for North America without his family in 1912 to rebuild his fortunes, choosing a new name in the new world. Settling in Winnipeg, Ghezzi worked first in the Winnipeg office of a firm of Italian wine merchants, Luigi Calissano & Figlio of Alba. Subsequently, he had a leading role in the mid-1920s in organizing a colony for Italian farmers near the Winnipeg suburb of St. Boniface, the name of which had a comfortable resonance.

Ghezzi family records offer no clues as to why he moved on to Kelowna in 1931, organizing a syndicate of investors to fund a winery, with his son Carlo, as the winemaker. Ghezzi's wife had died in Italy in 1922 and some of their five children (all with given names starting with C) began to follow the father to North America. One son became a wine merchant in New York; one daughter married an Italian businessman in Modesto, Ca.; and another settled in Yakima in Washington. Family recollections have Ghezzi visiting his far-flung family and remarrying (a soprano who had performed at Milan's famed La Scala opera house). Ghezzi, who was Calona's winemaker throughout 1933, eventually moved on, returning to Italy permanently in 1938. He died at San Bonifacio five years later.

Ghezzi's credit as instigator of the winery rests on a one-page handwritten document by him, dated November 25, 1931. It describes an agreement drawn up earlier that month, providing for a group of investors to lend $10,000 to the Interior Co-operative Association to purchase equipment for a winery. Ghezzi himself contributed $1,500 to the investment pool, followed by Peter *Casorso* ($1,000); Mary Casorso ($250); and a Victoria hotel operator, John Maggiora ($1,250). When Ghezzi's original pool of investors came up short, Kelowna businessmen *Pasquale (Cap) Capozzi* and *W.A.C. Bennett* joined the syndicate in 1932, with Bennett providing the leadership until he entered politics in 1941.[1]

GIDDA BROTHERS: These three Punjabi-born brothers have emerged as Okanagan growers with commercially significant vineyard acreages. Their father, Mehtab Gidda, emigrated to Canada in 1962; having been a wheat and vegetable farmer in India, he soon was operating an orchard near Westbank and planted grapes as early as 1972. The farm operations subsequently were taken over and expanded by his three sons. Sarwan, the eldest, trained as an accountant; Norm got a bachelor of science degree from the University of Alberta; Cal, the youngest (born 1958) studied business administration and then learned to be a heavy duty mechanic.

The brothers, who also grow apples, have thirty acres of grapes in several vineyards near Westbank and a forty-one-acre property called Sunrise Vineyards south of Okanagan Falls. The Westbank vineyards now are planted almost entirely to white vinifera, including chardonnay, with gamay being the only red. Sunrise Vineyards, owned by Gidda Brothers since 1991, has some of the same whites but also has merlot and cabernet franc. Both vineyards were contracted to wineries in 1995 but Cal Gidda says that the entrepreneurial brothers have considered establishing a winery.

GINTER, BEN (1923–1982): Born in Poland but raised in Swan River, Man., Ginter was a bombastic entrepreneur who earned a fortune building highways in northern British Columbia and lost most of it in the beer and wine business. He became a brewer after buying the idle plant of the Cariboo Brewing Company in Prince George in 1962, at first planning to turn the site into storage for construction equipment. Local business people persuaded him to reopen the five-year-old brewery, which Ginter then called Tartan Industries Ltd. because he liked Scottish tartans. Ginter was in trouble continually with the bureaucrats who regulated the liquor business because he always made his own rules. When British Columbia banned liquor advertising in 1971, two of Ginter's senior employees, encouraged no doubt by their boss, launched a company that sold soft drinks in beer bottles, including a ginger ale called Uncle Ben Pale Dry Ginter Ale.

In 1970, Tartan took over the nearly bankrupt *Mission Hill* winery. Always the egotist, Ginter changed the winery name to Uncle Ben's Gourmet Wines Ltd. The product line was expanded to include such outrageous brands as Fuddle Duck, a pop wine modelled on Andrés' highly successful *Baby Duck*. The name was inspired after Prime Minister Pierre Trudeau was accused of mouthing an obscenity in the House of Commons and protested he had merely said "fuddle duck." Despite such inventive wine marketing, Uncle Ben's was in receivership by 1978, having been caught up in an earlier labour dispute that originated in a Ginter brewery and resulted in union members in British Columbia boycotting all Ginter products.

Earlier, Ginter had turned to the government in late 1976 for help in breaking the stranglehold the three national brewers had over sales through hotels and taverns. *Tex Enemark*, the deputy minister of Consumer and Corporate Affairs and a Prince George native, suggested to the government that hotels be required to buy at least 10 percent of their draught beer from a British Columbia brewery. "It is the only way of arresting the trend towards the independents going bankrupt, and providing an opportunity for other breweries to be founded in the future," Enemark argued in a memorandum to **Rafe Mair**, his minister, on February 2, 1977.[2] Enemark added that "the Ben Ginter empire is likely to collapse and largely be dismembered, unless Ginter can get back into the beer business." Neither **Keith Warnes**, general manager of the Liquor Distribution Branch nor **Vic Woodland**, general manager of the Liquor Control and Licensing Branch were, Enemark confessed in a subsequent memo, "favourably disposed to giving any privelege [sic] to Mr. Ginter ... " Subsequently, the idea "was most emphatically rejected" by the cabinet, as Enemark wrote a year later when a pair of Prince George businessmen sought to buy Ginter's Prince George brewery from the receiver. Meanwhile, **Brights** sought to buy the winery but Ginter, with fresh financing, topped the $800,000 Brights' bid by $10,000 and took back his winery, running it until it was sold in 1981 to **Anthony von Mandl**. Ginter died of a heart attack in 1982.

GIVTON, ALBERT (1945–): A Vancouver businessman and wine collector, Givton published *The Wine Consumer*, a well-produced but acerbic newsletter which appeared quarterly from the spring of 1985 to the winter of 1990. "The ability to call 'a spade a spade' has always been our forte and although some disliked this aspect of *The Wine Consumer*, most respected us for that," Givton wrote in his editorial in the final issue.

Born in Cairo, Givton took pride that his birth year was 1945, one of Europe's greatest wine vintages in the century. "Overall, there hasn't been a better vintage," he said in a 1985 interview. The son of a banker and a nurse, he grew up in Israel where he served in the Israeli army (as a corporal in intelligence) in 1967 during the Six Day War. The following year he considered settling in the United States, where he would have been accepted immediately only if he volunteered to go to Vietnam. Thus, he chose Canada in 1968, clerking in a Montreal hardware store while attending George Williams University. He returned to Israel for an economics degree at the Hebrew University of Jerusalem and then, in 1973, settled in Vancouver where in 1974 he founded a real estate development company. He also began to study and taste wines seriously at this time and in 1977 launched a private and elite tasting club called Le Tastevin. So formidable is Givton's wine knowledge and personality that, when he announced in 1995 he would cease running the club, the rest of his executive chose to wind it up rather than carry on without him. A passionate lover of fine Bordeaux wines, Givton also was a founder and later chapter head of the Commanderie de Bordeaux, one of Vancouver's most exclusive wine-tasting groups.

The newsletter grew from Givton's frustration with the mediocre wines that agents and the **Liquor Distribution Branch** were offering consumers in British Columbia. "There is such a jungle of junk out there," he complained. He maintained his objectivity by refusing samples: all the wines his panels tasted were purchased. Over the newsletter's six years, one of Givton's regular targets was the LDB; he raged against everything from "the exorbitant price of Champagnes" to salespersons who were not knowledgeable. The LDB had the last word, refusing to distribute his newsletter because, Givton believed, it was too frankly critical about poor products in the liquor stores. He also criticized restaurant wine lists, most of which he believed were unimaginative yet overpriced. He believed that government should permit consumers, if they wished, to bring their own wines to restaurants, a standard practice in Australia. "I for one would eat out much more often if I could bring a special bottle of wine to a favourite restaurant," he wrote.

The Wine Consumer's treatment of British Columbia wines pulled no punches when the wines were pedestrian, or worse. Example: **Andrés** in 1987 bottled a limited edition of its Domaine d'Or Superieure White for the seventy-fifth anniversary of Port Coquitlam, the winery's home. "Pale colour," the newsletter complained. "Sugary-candied manufactured nose. Thick, sweetened oily liquid. No fruit or grape varietal there. A composite chemical product made by a chemist. Artificial junk." In the summer of 1987, the newsletter had its panel taste more than a dozen British Columbia commercial whites, such as **Schloss Laderheim,** which was one of only two described as "pleasant, everyday whites." The others? "A painful experience." It must be said that varietals from estate wineries received kinder treatment, perhaps because the estate wineries had begun to make wines with more character and interest. Not that estate wineries always got off lightly. In the spring of 1986, Givton's panel tasted eleven red wines, including Bacaro, a proprietary red from **Divino Estate Winery**. "This is the worst wine I have ever tasted and having tasted more

than 7,000 wines over the past 15 years, this wine will always be remembered," Givton wrote. "Absolutely foul, wicked wine. Divino's fermenting bath water."

The newsletter spawned a book by Givton in 1988, called *Wine Wise*, published by Brighouse Press of Vancouver. It rated seven hundred wines then available in British Columbia, drawing on the tastings done for the newsletter. Givton's newsletter ceased publication with the winter 1990 edition because, even with 800 subscribers subscribers, "we can no longer ignore the economics of this venture." He wrote tartly that *The Wine Consumer* had more readers than subscribers, thanks to "the photocopying problem which is surely the curse of any publisher."

GOLDEN MILE: This is what growers call the superb bench of vineyard land on the west side of the Okanagan Valley south of Oliver. In reality, it extends for several miles, consisting of rocky but moisture-retaining soil. Because it is high above the valley floor, tucked against the mountains to the west, it escapes the worst of the desiccating winds which, in March and April, can kill more vines in the south Okanagan than does the winter cold. The wineries on this favoured bench include **Domaine Combret, Tinhorn Creek, Gehringer Brothers** and **Divino**. Walter Gehringer argues that the eastern exposure of these vineyards is an advantage compared to the more conventional western exposure. The reason: the morning sun warms the vines gently while the afternoon sun in summer is blistering, stunning vines into temporary inactivity each afternoon. The vines on the eastern side of the valley south of Oliver continue to be baked by the extreme sunlight long after the Golden Mile gets relief from shade as the sun sinks in the west.

GOLDEN VALLEY WINES LTD.: The

Mission Hill winery operated under this name during its second round with **Ben Ginter** as owner. The first Ginter incarnation of the winery was called Uncle Ben's Gourmet Wines; it went into receivership in 1978 but Ginter bought the assets and ran it again until 1981 when it was sold to a group headed by **Anthony von Mandl.**

GRAPE AND WINE INSTITUTE OF BRITISH COLUMBIA: This industry as-

sociation was formed in 1981 with J.P. (Jack) Meadows as its general manager. The initial membership included the commercial wineries, the new estate wineries, the **Grape Growers Association** and the Grape Growers Marketing Board. Meadows ran it from his home in a Vancouver suburb but he stepped down in 1983 after the wineries decided to relocate the institute office to Kelowna. Then the estate wineries formed their own association and the grapegrowers also dropped from the membership. Finally in mid-1984, the Institute folded, leaving behind a host of unresolved problems, among them the **red wine surplus**, the rising tide of imported wines and the government's refusal to permit grocery store sales.

GRAPE GROWERS ASSOCIATION: The

Association of British Columbia Grape Growers was set up under provincial legislation in 1961. In 1970 the Grape Growers Marketing Board was formed, empowered under an order-in-council to negotiate grape purchase contracts with the wineries.

GRAY MONK ESTATE WINERY: This

postcard-perfect winery opened July 27, 1982, based on a vineyard at Okanagan Centre cultivated since 1972 by **George** and **Trudy Heiss**, two European-trained hairdressers who had met in Edmonton and then moved to the Okanagan in search of a rural lifestyle. The winery's name was inspired by George Heiss's affection for the grape variety, pinot gris, whose Austrian synonym, *grauer moench,* translates as gray monk. The grape produces the dry, fruity white wine that has been the flagship varietal for the Heiss winery since it launched itself with 350 cases of 1980 vintage pinot gris.

This is one of the most northerly vineyards in the Okanagan, a fact celebrated in Latitude Fifty, Gray Monk's successful generic white wine. Latitude 50 north, generally regarded as the practical limit for viticulture in the northern hemisphere, runs through Kelowna airport — and Gray Monk is still farther north. However, the vineyard's ideal southwestern exposure benefits from light and heat reflected from Okanagan Lake and is protected from frost because the lake, believed to be 1,500 feet deep at this point, moderates winter temperatures. The property was a tree fruit orchard but the Heisses switched to the high quality vinifera grapes that George had been reading about in German viticulture literature borrowed from his grapegrowing father-in-law, Hugo Peter, who lived nearby. Heiss sought to import vines from Europe, with kerner being the first of these varieties to arrive. From a research station at Colmar in Alsace (one of France's more northerly wine regions) Heiss imported 3,000 auxerrois vines, 50 pinot gris and 10 gewurztraminer vines. While these became the foundation for the vineyard, other vinifera (including riesling, bacchus and ehrenfelser) were planted later.

On occasion, Heiss has paid the price of being so far north. Most of the vineyard's ehrenfelser vines failed to survive the rugged 1981 winter. The winery also suffered a major setback after the sharp November 1985 cold snap reduced the entire Okanagan grape crop by a quarter. Gray Monk's own vineyard production dropped by two-thirds and the winery had only enough fruit from its own vines and contracted growers to make 41,000 litres of wine, although its sales had reached 100,000 litres a year. In a move that put Gray Monk at odds with other estate wineries, it sought to import grapes from the United States to maintain its production. Both **Sumac Ridge** and **Uniacke** opposed this and British Columbia Agriculture Minister James Hewitt refused, pointing out that the estate winery rules specifically required the use of only British Columbia grapes. The crisis for Gray Monk (and other estate wineries) was averted when the commercial wineries, which are allowed to import grapes and bulk wines, diverted some of their British Columbia grapes to the estate producers. "They still aren't the varieties we needed," Trudy Heiss said in November 1986. "We'll have enough gallonage but it will mean some interesting marketing strategies."[3] They managed to produce three-quarters of their 1985 output.

The Heisses wanted a winery licence as early as 1975, but the government did not create an estate winery licence category until 1978. Beginning with the 1980 vintage, they began building an inventory of wine and planning their winery. The first two vintages were made and cellared at the **Brights** winery in Oliver after Gray Monk's rezoning application was stalled by the Central Okanagan Regional District, delaying the construction of the winery until the spring of 1982. **John Bremmer** and **Lynn Stark**, then at Brights, handled the winemaking during Gray Monk's initial three vintages; **George Heiss, Jr.**, who took over as winemaker, was then completing his training in Germany.

Gray Monk made an impressive debut that fall. In the first Okanagan wine competition (in which forty-seven British Columbia wines competed), the winery's 1981 pinot auxerrois was awarded a gold medal by a panel of winemakers and a silver by a separate panel of five judges. The winery's 1981 gewurztraminer also earned a gold from the public at the competition's consumer tasting (where the public selected their favourites by ballot) while the pinot auxerrois got a silver from the public. For several years, the winery's brochures printed the growing list of awards garnered by Gray Monk — until the list simply got too long. In the early years, the wines often aped the style of German wines, right down to the baroque typography and terminology on the labels. One example: kabinett, a term drawn from German wine law where it defines quality attributes of wines. Gray Monk sprinkled its labels with such terms, even though they are generally incomprehensible to consumers who have not grown up in the German tradition. Vancouver agent Pierre Doise, Gray Monk's representative from 1984 to 1990, convinced the winery to simplify the labels; he also suggested the release of the dry Alsace-style gewurztraminer reserve. Vintage Consultants Ltd. of Vancouver, who took over in 1991 from Doise as the Gray Monk agent, had the winery redesign its labels completely. Gray Monk moved into the 1990s without the baggage of a German heritage which, however deeply felt, was neither understood nor relevant in the British Columbia market. The smart, cleanly designed new labels translated immediately into substantial increases in sales.

GREATA RANCH: Once one of the largest orchards in the Okanagan, the Greata Ranch, since being acquired in 1994 by *CedarCreek Estate Winery*, has been redeveloped with thirty-five acres of premium grapes and an elegant residential community on the western shore of Okanagan Lake south of Peachland. The property is named for G.H. Greata, who came from Manitoba in 1895 to homestead here. After securing water rights and building an irrigation line from a nearby creek, Greata planted the first apple trees in 1901. Greata sold the ranch in 1910 and it was run for the next fifty-five years by John T. Long and his brothers. The Long family vastly expanded fruit production, established a packing plant and a warehouse, served both by rail and by lake steamers. A 1949 article in the *Family Herald and Weekly Star* reported that the orchard's average annual crop totalled 485 tons of cherries, pears, apricots, plums and peaches; and the packing house also handled a prodigious quantity of apples from the area. The ranch declined dramatically after a killing 1965 frost, changing owners and direction many times in subsequent years, including an unsuccessful and incomplete 1984 attempt to turn the property into a condominium development. It had become a derelict eyesore, littered with old buildings and discarded appliances, until CedarCreek took it over and began planting vines in 1995.

GREGOIRE, MAURICE (1947–): Born in Kelvington, Sask., and raised in the Okanagan, Gregoire was a summertime construction worker with the firm building the *Casabello* winery in 1966. When the grapes arrived that fall, Gregoire joined the winery and was there until it closed in 1994, after being acquired by *Vincor*. Gregoire then became Vincor's production manager in western Canada.

GRIFFITH, ROY (1935–): It is probable that no one has sold more bottles to the British Columbia wineries than Roy Griffith, in a career that started with Dominion Glass in 1954. Born in Vancouver in 1935, he considered briefly becoming a chiropractor until he went to work for the glass company, then one of two Canadian manufacturers of bottles and jars. Dominion Glass had one plant in Redcliff, Alta., which produced bottles from 1915 until it closed in 1989. With the expansion of the wine industry and of food processing, it also operated a second western plant in Burnaby from 1965 to 1985. Its rival was The Consumers' Glass Company of Toronto, which opened a plant in 1969 in Lavington, near Vernon in the Okanagan. Consumers' took over Dominion Glass in 1989.

Griffith began calling on the wine industry in 1960 about the time that *Andrés* was opening in Port Moody. The wineries in western Canada initially were unable to order bottles similar to those used in Ontario because the Ontario industry retained the designs for its own use. The wineries in the West simply bought generic whisky bottles, accounting for the widespread use of gallon jugs, half-gallon jugs and forty-ounce bottles — all with screw caps.

One of his first accounts was **Calona Wines.** Griffith began calling on the Kelowna winery just as the Capozzi brothers were taking charge. "Joe Capozzi, with his travelling to California, came back with some wine bottles from a company called Gallo and he said 'I want them.'" Griffith had Dominion's design department modify the designs — the more popular looked like bowling pins — for the imperial measurements used in Canada. The distinction that these designs gave to Calona products coincided with the opening of the first self-serve liquor stores. Griffith believes that the new bottles helped Calona's dramatic sales growth during the 1960s. "The other wineries had all this mundane packaging," Griffith says. Not for long. By the mid-1960s competitors also began to adopt both more shapely bottles and conventional wine bottles.

The 1971 launching of Andrés' **Baby Duck** (and the copycat sparkling pop wines) generated a demand for bottles that could contain pressure. "I can remember having to do a fast study on my own about pounds per square inch and pressures. I got a hold of a manual from Liquid Carbonic, and then had to send copies down to our design department in Hamilton, because they didn't know how to approach this. It was a west coast phenomenon." While conventional champagne bottles were available — **Brights** had been producing its President Champagne since the 1950s — the bottles weighed thirty-five ounces each because of their heavy walls and the punt (the conical indentation in the bottom

of a bottle), all designed to contain more than six atmospheres of pressure. The pop wines did not need such heavy bottles because they were only pressurized three to five times atmospheric pressure. The Duck bottles weighed about twenty-one ounces and were less costly because they contained less glass and therefore were made more quickly.

As the only bottle manufacturer in the West for many years, Dominion Glass had a lock on the market. It also was vulnerable; when rival Consumers' did market research in the mid-1960s, asking whether customers wanted choice, the answers were overwhelmingly yes. Consumers' then scouted various locations in the Okanagan before picking Lavington. According to Griffith, Calona's **Capozzi** brothers believed they had talked the company into locating in Kelowna and angrily refused to deal with Consumers' when Lavington got the plant. Ultimately, Consumers' prevailed but it took fifteen years.

When the companies amalgamated, Griffith joined Richards Packaging Inc., a major Canadian distributor of glass packaging, and he continued to call on the wineries. The business has changed significantly since 1990. Not only are there more wineries but some of the proprietors are ordering distinctive European- and American-made bottles as well as the standard wine bottles made in Lavington.

GRIMSHAWE, NICHOLAS (1949–): In 1983, Grimshawe launched *B.C. Wine Notes*, the first independent newsletter dedicated exclusively to British Columbia wines. He also formed the first independent wine tasting club for British Columbia wines: fourteen people attended the inaugural meeting in May

1983. Born in Britain, the son of a nurseryman who emigrated to Canada in 1957, Grimshawe's wine interest was piqued while he trained as a chef in Ontario. When he tired of cooking for large groups, he moved to Vancouver in 1972 to become a freelance food and wine writer and subsequently discovered British Columbia wines. However, both the newsletter, which achieved a circulation of more than three hundred, and the wine society were premature and both closed at the end of 1984. Grimshawe went on to manage a shop dedicated to British Columbia wines in The Hudson's Bay Co.'s main store in Vancouver until 1987 when the shop was franchised to a group of estate wineries. Grimshawe then joined The Bay's staff as a departmental manager.

GROWERS' WINES LTD.: In 1923 farmers on the Saanich Peninsula on Vancouver Island who were growing loganberries established this winery on Quadra Street in downtown Victoria to produce sweet, portlike loganberry wines. (The berry was developed by an Oregon horticulturist named Logan who crossed raspberry and wild blackberry.) The five founders of the winery were William Bickford, Philip Holloway, Neil Lamont, Clarence Oldfield and Harry Tanner and their first two brands were Logana, made entirely with loganberries, and Vin Supreme, a blend of loganberries and blueberries.

The winery owed its initial success to *Herbert Anscomb*, an accountant who ran the Victoria Phoenix Brewing Company before investing in Growers', which he managed from 1927 to 1955. By 1936 he had consolidated all the loganberry wine brands under Growers',

having purchased first *Richmond Winery* and then *Victoria Wineries (British Columbia) Ltd.* The latter — called Brentwood Products Ltd. when it opened in 1927, changing its name two years later — had ex-jockey Stephen Slinger as its winemaker and sold its wines primarily under the Slinger brand. These brands remained in the portfolio of Growers' and its successor wineries for more than fifty years. The British-born Anscomb juggled business with a long political career: he was reeve of Oak Bay, then mayor of Victoria, and sat from 1936 to 1952 as a Conservative in the British Columbia legislature. As the province's minister of finance from 1945 until 1952, he introduced the province's first sales tax, 3 percent, in 1948. As a cabinet minister, Anscomb ensured that his winery's products enjoyed secure listings in government liquor stores. Anscomb's political links with the government in Ottawa also enabled Growers' to get a distillery licence in 1936, then the only Canadian winery with that privilege. The alcohol was used to fortify wines and to make some of the first wine-based cocktails. One example: 45 Per, made with rum and loganberry brandy.[4]

After pioneer grapegrower *J.W. Hughes* accepted a ten-year contract from Anscomb, Growers' began buying wine grapes in the Okanagan valley in 1932, shipping them by rail and boat to Victoria for processing, where the wines were matured in the eighty large oak casks that Anscomb bought from the Christian Brothers winery in California during the American Prohibition. By 1959, when Growers' was buying about 1,000 tons of grapes annually, the winery began crushing the grapes in the Okanagan (on the vineyard operated by

Frank Schmidt) and shipping the must to Victoria in 500-gallon glass-lined vats. A contemporary newspaper account noted: "A crusher has been installed in the heart of the Okanagan vineyard at Lakeside, and the pulp is each day pumped into tanks mounted on trucks for fast shipment to Victoria. Each truck carries 3,000 gallons and the journey is made overnight so that the temperature of the juice will remain low." Crushing near the vineyards obviously improved the wines. It rained during the bounteous 1969 harvest and the wet grapes certainly would have begun to spoil had they been shipped to Victoria for crushing, as had been done for so many years.

Anscomb sold Growers' in 1955; it was first purchased by a syndicate of Vancouver businessmen that included Coleman Hall (better known later for his investments in the Vancouver Canucks professional hockey team) and a retired banker, Francis Lumb. Late in 1959 Vancouver stationer Ernest C. Warner took over, to the evident delight of general manager **Brian Roberts,** who wrote to grower Frank Schmidt: "We have a new controlling interest in the Company in the person of Mr. Ernest C. Warner, who is an exceptionally capable, vigorous and successful businessman. Mr. Lumb remains President, and the Company carries on in the same way, except that we have a very much more aggressive outlook and will make every possible effort to expand and develop."[5] A Growers' advertisement in the *Kelowna Courier* in May 1962 signalled the new outlook: "If you are interested in growing grapes for wine production Growers' Wine Company of Victoria will give long term contracts and if necessary financial assistance." Between 1962 and 1965 Growers'

gave long-term (seven-to-ten-year contracts) to thirteen growers, including R.J. and Bill Bennett, sons of **W.A.C. Bennett** and owners of a ranch north of Kelowna. The Bennetts never became significant growers.

Warner wanted wineries in every province and by 1964 Growers' was completing an Edmonton winery and announced plans for one in Moose Jaw, Sask. "The opening of all-weather roads over the Rockies and the improvement of trucking facilities makes it possible for us to deliver grapes to Edmonton at comparative costs to Victoria and Vancouver," Roberts said in 1964.[6] Roberts, the glue that held Growers' together through the tumultuous decades after Anscomb, was general manager and later president from 1956 to 1976. Imperial Tobacco bought Growers' in 1965, changing the name to Ste-Michelle after a popular wine brand controlled by Castle Wines Ltd., a Growers' subsidiary in Saskatchewan. When the cigarette company's brief diversification into wines ended, Jordan Wines Ltd. of Ontario bought Growers' in 1973, merging it with Villa Wines, Jordan's subsidiary in New Westminister (originally called West Coast Wines Ltd. when incorporated in 1960). In 1976 **Jordan & Ste-Michelle Cellars Ltd.** was adopted as the winery's national name. The Victoria winery was closed in 1977, replaced by a new $7 million winery in Surrey, with a storage capacity for 4 million gallons and room to be tripled. However, after the market for domestic wineries stalled in the 1980s, Jordan & Ste-Michelle was acquired by **T.G. Brights & Co.** who closed and dismantled the Surrey winery in 1990. The Growers' name survives as a popular brand of cider. In 1962 Growers' took over the production and marketing of apple cider that had been developed by scientist **Dr. John Bowen** for Sun-Rype in Kelowna.

GUIDI, ENRICO (1917–1993): Born in Kelowna of Italian immigrant parents, Guidi joined **Calona Wines** when he was seventeen. In his forty-three-year career there, he rose to become the cellarmaster, a post in which he was responsible for blending hundreds of wines.

GUTTLER, DIETER (1945–): Winemaker for **Jordan & Ste-Michelle** in British Columbia from 1972 until 1976 when he was transferred to a sister winery in Ontario as the company's national vice-president for production. Subsequently, Guttler was a founding partner of Vineland Estates winery in Ontario and then became an independent grape-grower near Vineland, Ontario. Born in Germany, he grew up in South Africa where he apprenticed as a winemaker before completing his enology studies at the **Geisenheim Institute** in Germany. After running a premium winery in South Africa owned by the Rothmans Group, Guttler was transferred to Canada after Rothmans acquired control of Jordan & Ste-Michelle and found he had to make wine from inferior grapes in the decrepit Victoria winery formerly known as the **Growers'** winery. "It was a plain shit-house, that's all it was," Guttler remembers. "It was absolutely unbearable there." He believed money spent to renovate the old building, whose unsani-

tary wooden floors were soaked with fifty years of spillage, would be wasted and he joined general manager **Robert Holt** in pressing for the new winery that subsequently was opened in Surrey in 1979.[7]

Guttler also gets some of the credit for initiating a program by Jordan & Ste-Michelle to provide its growers with johannisberg riesling vines from nurseries in Germany. For any cooperating grower, the winery financed the importation of the vines; the growers made no repayment until the vines were in production three to four years later. Before Jordan & Ste-Michelle was taken over in 1989, it had the largest acreage of johannisberg riesling under contract in British Columbia and Ontario of any commercial winery. The variety took over from the inferior Okanagan riesling as the most widely planted white grape in the Okanagan, and Ste-Michelle Riesling was a top-selling table wine in British Columbia.

---

[1] Personal files of Linda Ben-Hamida.

[2] Tex Enemark papers.

[3] Article by Mike King in *Kelowna Super Shopper*, November 5, 1986, p. 7: clipping in Gray Monk scrapbooks.

[4] Brian Roberts to author, 1982.

[5] Lloyd Schmidt files: letter from Brian Roberts to Frank Schmidt, January 11, 1960.

[6] *The Financial Post*, September 26, 1964.

[7] Interview with author, 1996.

HHH

HAINLE, SANDRA: Born in Saskatchewan, Sandra Hainle graduated in 1980 from the law school at the University of Saskatchewan. Moving to Kelowna in 1983 to practise with a small law firm, she met and subsequently married Tilman Hainle. She resigned her law partnership in 1989 to help her husband run Hainle Vineyards, both because she was "burned out" with law and because more help was needed at the growing winery. With a sense of humour as dry as Tilman Hainle's table wines, she deals with tasks from wine marketing to writing a consistently good newsletter for the winery. Among the newsletter's features are recipes researched by Sandra Hainle and her mother-in-law, Regina, to complement the wines produced there.

HAINLE, TILMAN (1958–): Born in Stuttgart, Hainle grew up in the Okanagan after his parents, Walter and Regina, emigrated to Canada in 1970 and, after a few years in Vancouver, purchased a property near Peachland. Walter Hainle's passion for winemaking and the vineyard he planted seized his son's imagination. "I can place the 'blame' squarely on my dad's shoulders," Tilman Hainle says. His father was determined to establish an estate winery soon after neighbour **Marion Jonn** secured the first such licence in 1979. Tilman, on graduating from high school, completed a program in viticulture and enology in 1982 in Weinsberg, a practical winemaking school in Germany. He practised his craft during the next four vintages at **Uniacke** estate winery near Kelowna prior to the opening of Hainle Vineyards in 1988.

HAINLE VINEYARDS ESTATE WINERY: Established in 1988 near Peachland, this family-owned and -operated winery is best known for producing dry table wines in a highly individual style. Everything about this winery reflects the rigorous and uncompromising discipline of the proprietors, Tilman and Sandra Hainle and Tilman's mother, Regina Hainle. This was the first winery (in 1995) to be certified as a fully organic grower and producer of British Columbia wines, meaning that the winery avoids herbicides and pesticides in its vineyards. It was the first winery (again in 1995) to get a so-called "J" licence, a new designation in British Columbia that allows wineries to sell food and to sell wine by the glass. Hainle also became the first British Columbia winery (in 1995) to establish its own home page on the World Wide Web (the address is http://www.millennia.net/hainle/). Included on that web site is the winery's highly literate newsletter.

HAINLE, WALTER (1915–1995): Born in Germany, Hainle was an overachieving textile salesman until a serious ulcer attack in 1970 led to a lifestyle change, on doctor's orders. Hainle emigrated with his wife, Regina, and son Tilman to Vancouver and, after running an apartment block for a few years, moved to the Okanagan. Already interested in winemaking, Hainle had begun buying Okanagan riesling grapes and making wine in his West Vancouver home in 1971. The Hainle family settled on a steeply pitched property above Peachland where Walter planted vines and regained robust health as a farmer. When Tilman graduated in 1982 from Weinsberg, a German winemaking school, the vineyard became the base for the family-operated *Hainle Vineyards Estate Winery*. Walter Hainle is believed to have been the first vintner in Canada to make *icewine*, a tradition in Germany but practically unknown in British Columbia before the Hainle family arrived. Active in the winery until the last, Walter Hainle died in the vineyard on January 1, 1995. The winery's newsletter recounted: "Walter had celebrated New Year's Eve with family and friends in his usual fine form. At about 2 PM the next day, he went for a hike with our dogs. A fall down a steep embankment on our property ended his journey."[1] See *Icewine*.

HAMILTON, JAMES (1943–):

The grandson of an English wine merchant who perished in the sinking of the *Lusitania* during the First World War, James Hamilton is among those who pioneered grapegrowing on Saltspring Island. Born in Vancouver, he became enthralled by the Gulf Islands during summer sailing vacations with his parents. As a young man, Hamilton studied at universities in British Columbia, dabbling in engineering and arts before drifting into meteorology. After several years as a meteorologist, Hamilton launched a business manufacturing computer peripherals, including printer ribbon; selling the business in 1988, he then became a real estate developer until 1992 when he bought six acres on Saltspring Island and called it *Madrona Valley Farms*, after the madrona trees, better known as arbutus trees. "I grew up always wanting to be a farmer," he confides. "There's nothing to beat walk-ing through a vineyard on a summer evening. It's magic, somehow. You don't want to leave."

The farm's rich, southward-facing slopes have been planted with both fruit trees and filbert trees. But Hamilton also began planting müller-thurgau vines in his first year and other varieties since, cautiously limiting himself to about one hundred vines each year. "It's marginal," he believes. "I wouldn't put the whole farm into grapes." After four years he had less than an acre under vine but has several more acres available if the vineyard proves viable. Beside müller-thurgau, the vines include pinot noir, pinot blanc, pinot gris and ortega. "Pinot noir seems to be the hardiest," he found. He has tried chardonnay but does not believe it ripens consistently on the island where the climate is dry but not nearly as hot as the Okanagan. Whether or not Hamilton proceeds to develop a farm winery will depend on how the vineyard performs over several years. "You go through a lot of learning years before you can go into production," he believes. He has quickly discovered Saltspring Island's unique challenge to grape cultivation. The island's abundant wild blackberries support large resident swarms of wasps, which find ripe grapes as nourishing as ripe berries. "The wasps have become entrenched here and it is a massive problem," he says.

HARBECK, ELISABETH (1944–):

Her skill and determination as a grower for the *Hainle* winery earned Elisabeth Harbeck recognition with a vineyard-designated wine, the Elisabeth's Vineyard pinot blanc and pinot noir, beginning with the 1989 vintage, the first year in which her grapes were purchased by

Hainle. She was born in Basel, Switz., the daughter of a professor of medicine. "My parents liked to drink a good glass of wine and we had good quality wine in our cellar," she recalled. Trained as an intensive care nurse, she emigrated to Canada in 1983 with her husband, Philipp, a German-born anesthetist who, looking for a house with a vineyard, found a home near Okanagan Falls with land sloping towards Vaseaux Lake in the distance. "He just knew this hillside was the place where he wanted to have his vineyard," Elisabeth Harbeck said. They decided on pinot blanc and pinot noir, with Philipp planning a high quality sparkling wine from pinot blanc. Planting started in 1985 but, unhappily, Philipp died the following spring from complications following routine eye surgery. Left to raise three children alone, Elisabeth Harbeck abandoned plans for a winery even though a cool aging cellar had already been prepared.

Harbeck also was unlucky with the initial plantings: three-quarters of the vines failed to grow, likely because they had been improperly stored over the previous winter in the nursery from which the vines had been purchased. She replanted, ultimately developing a four-acre vineyard dedicated to the two pinot varieties. Additional acreage is available but Harbeck, with an affinity for nature, has preserved much of it for a menagerie of animals that includes ducks, horses, half a dozen assorted dogs and about thirty cats. She sold her first grape crop in 1988 to **Sumac Ridge** but balked at taking viticultural orders from the winery. "I thought I should have a word too as a grapegrower because I am together with my plants more than the winery is." When **Walter Hainle** called

one day, looking for grapes, Elisabeth Harbeck agreed to switch. "The way Tilman [Hainle] wanted the grapes was more the way I liked to grow. And I also like the way that he keeps the grapes of each grower separate. I try to get a good quality grape and I don't like my grapes to [be mixed] with someone else's." Since 1993 she has adopted organic practices in the vineyard. The outcome of not using artificial fertilizers has been reduced yields. "I think in the long run it is not bad," she said. The lower yields have translated into earlier maturing fruit with more intense flavours. "With organic growing, you don't force the plant so much to produce."

HARPER, JOHN (1915–):
One of British Columbia's most determined independent grape nurserymen, Harper has devoted a life to horticulture. Born in Calgary, he was growing and exhibiting vegetables by his eighth birthday. After graduating from high school, he moved into the hospitality industry, working as a cook for Canadian Pacific, both on the company's trains and in its hotels in the West, where he began to learn about wines. His wine education blossomed in Europe during the Second World War, when he served as a catering manager for a Canadian forces hospital in Britain. He opened his first plant nursery in Steveston after returning from Europe but he established his reputation with a nursery he operated in Cloverdale for twenty years. He also worked as a fieldman both for **Andrés** and for **Jordan & Ste-Michelle.** At Cloverdale, Harper had so many experimental grape varieties there that, when he moved to a farm on Vancouver Island south of Duncan, in 1983, he took 160 varieties

for the modest vineyard he planted there. Harper moved to Vancouver Island in search of a quieter life and lower property taxes. Unhappily for him, a group of promoters fastened onto the vineyard as the basis for a company whose research in tissue culture would qualify the company for money under the ill-fated Scientific Research Tax Credit program. While some serious tissue research was done, some of the moneys vanished on nonscientific projects before the federal government cancelled the entire program. Harper had had little to do with the SRTC program; he was entirely focussed on the development of what could have been Vancouver Island's first cottage winery. His promoter partners had a company on the Vancouver Stock Exchange called Bitec Development Corp. which announced early in 1984 that $1.5 million was to be raised for Cobble Hill Estate Winery and Vineyards Ltd. The plan called for a fifty-acre vineyard which, optimistically, would produce and sell 180,000 bottles of wine annually by the fourth year of operation. Harper developed about half the vineyard acreage but the winery was never financed. In 1990 the vineyard was acquired by *Hans Kiltz* who used some of the Harper plantings to produce wines for his own *Blue Grouse Vineyards* farmgate winery which opened in 1993. Meanwhile, Harper and his wife, Verna, moved to a nearby twelve-acre property he called Ayle Moselle where a new vineyard and nursery was established.

HARRIES, HU (1921–1986): An Edmonton consulting economist, Harries and his family in 1975 purchased *Paradise Ranch* near Naramata, subsequently developing a sixty-acre vineyard.

HARRIES, JEFFREY K. (1956–): While Edmonton-born Harries and his wife, Leona, are both doctors in the Okanagan, they actively manage *Paradise Ranch*. Aptly named for its beauty, the ranch includes vineyards on benches high above and overlooking Okanagan Lake north of Naramata. The property was purchased by the Harries family in 1975 and the vineyards have been developed with a number of investors (about 140) buying partnerships. Initially planted to hybrid grape varieties in the early 1980s, the vineyards struggled to become economically viable. Harries declined to pull out grape vines in 1988 when growers were paid to get rid of less desirable varieties. "I thought it was obscene that the government should be paying you to destroy something," Harries said. On a more practical level, the vineyard only qualified for minimum compensation, based on the limited production of its young vines. Subsequently, most of the vines were grafted over to premium varieties and in 1995 *Mission Hill Vineyards* signed a five-year contract for the grapes.

HAWTHORNE MOUNTAIN VINEYARDS: After *LeComte* vineyards changed owners in 1995, *Harry McWatters,* the new proprietor, unveiled Hawthorne Mountain Vineyards as the name on the label for premium wines released from the winery from 1996 onward. The height of land on which the winery is located is known as Hawthorne Mountain, after the two Hawthorne brothers who were the original homesteaders.[2]

HEALTH: Research in the 1990s has suggested that wine consumed regularly but also moderately (moderate generally means no more than half a bottle a day, taken with food) is beneficial. In particular, red wines contain elements that are antioxidants and that also reduce the build-up of cholesterol deposits in blood vessels, thus reducing coronary disease. Obviously, wine needs to be integrated with a healthy lifestyle of exercise and good nutrition. However, wine is not without problems for some. Red wine also may trigger headaches for migraine sufferers while asthma sufferers may have reactions to wines containing comparatively high amounts of sulphur. Many wineries have learned to reduce sulphur levels to a minimum, and occasionally eliminating sulphur entirely, with sterile handling and bottling of wines.

HEISS, GEORGE SR. (1939–): Co-founder of *Gray Monk Estate Winery*, Heiss was born in Vienna. Both parents were hairdressers; his father (also George) was a three-time world champion hair stylist. After apprenticing with his parents, George worked his way around Europe and then abroad, ending up in Edmonton in 1960 where he met another young hairdresser, Trudy Peter. They married in 1962 and successfully operated two hair salons in Edmonton until, in a career change in 1972, they bought an orchard overlooking the lake at Okanagan Centre and set about developing a vineyard and winery there. Although self-taught as a viticulturist, George Heiss has led in the successful introduction of high quality European wine grapes to the Okanagan. A man of many interests, he took up scuba diving as a hobby in 1988. He need not go far to pursue that interest: the expanse of Okanagan Lake that can be viewed from the Gray Monk winery is believed to be as deep as 1,500 feet, far beyond any scuba diver's dive limit.

HEISS, GEORGE JR. (1962–): Born in Edmonton, he was sent to Germany when he was eighteen to become a winemaker. He apprenticed at the prestigious Louis Guntrum Weinkellerei at Neirstein and then took his professional courses at Weinsberg, graduating in 1984. A winemaker with monastic dedication to his cellar, Heiss is respected for crafting consistently flavoursome white wines.

HEISS, STEVEN (1967–): Also born in Edmonton, he is a computer systems analyst who joined his brother and his parents at Gray Monk in 1994, increasingly taking over marketing and public relations jobs suited to his easy, personable style. In 1995 he began a five-acre vineyard not far from the Gray Monk winery, with siegerrebe planted and viognier planned.

HEISS, TRUDY (1941–): Co-founder of *Gray Monk,* she was born Waltraud Peter in Rostock, a German community on the Baltic where her father, Hugo Peter, was a machinist and millwright. Her parents fled what was then East Germany, coming to Canada in 1952 and settling in Edmonton. Her parents bought a pear orchard near Okanagan Centre in 1968. Hugo Peter converted it to a vineyard, teaching himself viticulture from professional publications obtained from Germany. His enthusiastic letters about the Okanagan persuaded Trudy and George Heiss to move there as well. Trudy, a hairdresser, soon was as capable on a tractor as in a hair salon.

HELLER, ROLAND (1944–) AND ADELHEID, (HEIDI) (1943–): The Hellers are the owners of the twenty-two-acre Adelheid's Vineyard just south of Okanagan Falls, a site they chose in 1991 with the help of the late *Walter Hainle*, who also suggested the name. "Adelheid is an old Germanic name that Walter and husband Roland like very much; I don't," says Mrs. Heller, who prefers to be called Heidi. The Hellers call Walter Hainle the "father of the vineyard; his spirit is there." Almost all of their grapes are sold to *Hainle Vineyards Estate Winery.*

Roland Heller, a telecommunications technologist, was born in Stuttgart, the capital of the Baden-Württemberg region of southwest Germany, so renowned for its wines that the city — which has vineyards well within city limits — is known as the metropolis between forests and vines. Heidi Heller, a software coordinator, was born at Neuhausen, thirty kilometres south of Stuttgart, a town better known for its cabbage than its wines. "In this region," she recalls of Baden-Württemberg, "wine is part of the daily life. The seasons smell — of wine, cider, onion quiche, rye bread and sauerkraut." The Hellers vacationed in the Okanagan in 1978, visiting with Hainle, a family acquaintance, and in 1982, following a lifelong ambition of Roland's, emigrated to Canada and settled in Edmonton, where they worked with Hewlett Packard.

The vineyard was acquired because they admired Hainle's lifestyle and decided, ultimately, to retire to the vineyard. "As Walter always said," Heidi Heller recalls, "once you walk the rows up and down every day, you will discover the meaning of life all over." Beginning in 1992, the Hellers planted pinot noir and merlot. In subsequent years, they have added chardonnay, lemberger, pinot gris and kerner, tailored for the requirements of the Hainle winery. There also is a small quantity of maréchal foch, sold to the nearby *Wild Goose* farmgate winery.

HELMER, FRANZ: A Geisenheim-trained winemaker, Helmer joined *Growers' Wines* in 1955, spending much of his Canadian career there. In 1983 he became the winemaker at Beaupré Wines (Canada) Ltd., a short-lived winery opened in Langley that year by *Potter Distilleries* and closed when *Calona Wines* and Potter merged in 1989.

HESTER CREEK ESTATE WINERY: Established in 1996, this is the successor to *Divino Estate Winery* whose property south of Oliver changed owners that year. The Divino name followed its founder, *Joe Busnardo*, to a vineyard on Vancouver Island while the new owners of the Oliver-area vineyard named their winery after a creek that flows by the property.

The seventy-two-acre vineyard, despite the ramshackle winery, fetched more than $3 million when the mercurial Busnardo decided to relocate his operation to thirty-nine unplanted acres in the Cowichan Valley. "I figure I will do exactly the same mistake I made twenty-nine years ago," Busnardo said of the new vineyard. The so-called mistake was the planting of vinifera grapes against all advice. Because the vineyard, in fact, was successful, Busnardo was able to command a generous price from the new owners who appreciated getting fully mature vines. "It's an advantage," says Hester Creek president *Hans Lochbichler*. "That's why we didn't mind to pay the price."

Lochbichler, a former restaurateur, took over the vineyard and the winery in partnership with Vancouver pub owner Henry Rathje and winemaker **Frank Supernak**, formerly the winemaker at the nearby **Vincor** winery. They launched the winery with 200,000 litres of carefully selected wine from Busnardo's inventory (Busnardo shipped the rest of his stock, enough for five years of sales, to his Vancouver Island facility). Supernak immediately prepared to have the wines qualified for the **VQA** seal, a sharp contrast to Busnardo who declined to have anything to do with the **British Columbia Wine Institute** or its VQA program. Like Lochbichler, Supernak expects good quality grapes from the estate. "The vineyard is immaculate."

HILLSIDE CELLARS: This tiny farmgate winery, located right on Naramata Road, was established in 1990 by Czech-born **Vera and Bohumir Klokocka**, based on a sun-drenched vineyard that was an orchard when they bought the property in 1979. The varieties grown and vinified there — and often available in small quantities primarily from the wine shop at Hillside — include cabernet sauvignon, gamay, pinot auxerrois, riesling and dry muscat, the latter a winery specialty. The winery was acquired in mid-1996 by a group headed by **John Hromyk** and **John Fletcher**, who undertook a significant expansion both of the winery and of production.

HIMROD GRAPE: This white seedless grape, one of whose parents was the thompson seedless variety, was developed in New York state as a table grape and released commercially in 1952. When cuttings arrived in British Columbia,

750 ml   11% alc./vol.

Canadian
Rhine Castle

White Wine / Vin Blanc
PRODUCT OF CANADA   PRODUIT DU CANADA
JORDAN & STE-MICHELLE CELLARS LTD., SURREY, CANADA

enough were provided to **Frank Schmidt** that he could propagate the variety. A fruity early ripener with high sugar, its potential as a wine grape, compared to the white labrusca grapes then being used, galvanized **Growers' Wines Ltd.** president **Brian Roberts** to send this urgent note to Schmidt in July 1960: "Don't sell a single plant" because the wine from the variety was "*very* promising.... If we can get a listing & get the jump on all the others — Himrod table wine may yet make you famous.... Don't sell a stick to anyone else. Keep the variety for yourself & we can give you a good deal. Try to keep the other growers disinterested. Don't mention a word to anyone...." A provincial survey of vineyards that year found that Schmidt had 2,200 himrod vines on four acres, with, according to a footnote to the survey, plans for a "future fifteen acres of himrod on new land as plants become available."

Schmidt kept the variety largely to himself (**H.D.Powell** had a hundred plants in 1960). Roberts, in a letter dated January 30, 1962, wrote: "At the present stage this is top secret. We hope to be bringing out a delightful off-dry white table wine about the middle of the year made partially from Himrods. You did not give us enough last vintage to make the wine entirely from Himrods. The big secret is that we want to call the wine

'Okanagan Mission' and the reason for the great secrecy is that the name is probably not registerable — because it is the name of a geographical place." However, the winery chose to call the wine Canadian Liebfraumilch and kept the brand on the market at least through 1967 when a group of German wineries took legal action, prompting Growers' to change the name to Rhine Castle.

Schmidt was released from the order not to sell himrod vines and other Okanagan growers soon planted some. So did many home gardeners when, in the fall of 1963, Schmidt's vineyard in newspaper advertisements urged: "Grow grapes right in your own back yard." Vines were sold in bundles of six for $5, with responses from as far afield as Seattle. Surviving himrod vines today are limited chiefly to backyard grape arbours. One massively sprawling original vine from Frank Schmidt's day still was producing abundantly in 1995 in the front yard at **St. Hubertus**, the farmgate winery now occupying part of what was Schmidt's vineyard.

HOENISCH, TOM: Winemaker at *Casabello Wines* from 1967 to 1980. The son of a winemaker in Alsace, Hoenisch emigrated to Canada in 1960, worked as a chemist for *Andrés* for four years, spent three years making wine in the United States and was lured back in 1967 by job offers from British Columbia's newest wineries at the time, Casabello and *Mission Hill*. Hoenisch also became a personal friend of *Dr. Walter Clore*, an influential viticulturist in Washington state, and was strongly influenced by Clore's views that vinifera grapes could and should be grown in the Okanagan. Casabello itself planted varieties such as semillon, pinot noir, chenin blanc, chardonnay and riesling on a vineyard at Osoyoos. Abrasive and determined, Hoenisch believed it essential to have vinifera grapes and suggested that the hybrid varieties were only suitable as "fill in or blending material."

HOLT, ROBERT (1945–): A native of Niagara Falls, Holt was enrolled in engineering at Queens University in Kingston when his father alerted him to a well-paying summer job in 1967 as an assistant production manager at the *T.G. Brights & Co.* winery. "I wasn't really interested in the wine business," Holt admitted later. Yet he agreed to join the winery in the fall of 1968 as assistant production manager, after graduating and hitchhiking in Europe. His brashly aggressive style — "they were too slow for me" — got Holt fired three years later. Unfazed, Holt enrolled at McMaster and in 1973, when he got his master's degree in business administration, he was snapped up by Jordan Wines as assistant to the president. In 1975 Holt was sent to Victoria to manage the former *Growers' Wines*, now known as *Jordan & Ste-Michelle*.

Holt undertook one more study on relocating the aging Victoria winery, whose wine-soaked wooden floors after fifty years of production made sanitation next to impossible. "There had been already eight to ten studies done over time," Holt discovered. "Every time it got down to the crunch, it was going to cost several million dollars." Holt and his winemaker, *Dieter Guttler,* calculated that it would take $5 million to gut and rebuild the Victoria winery. They advised against sinking capital into an unsuitable old facility far from the Okanagan vine

Robert Holt (photo courtesy of John Schreiner)

yards when, for perhaps an additional million or so dollars, an efficient new winery could be built on the mainland. Holt found property in Surrey, chosen because the freight costs of delivering finished product to market from Surrey were much lower than from Penticton, where there was also property available. He also reasoned that the winery likely would attract more tours if readily accessible to Vancouver. When Jordan & Ste-Michelle in 1977 built what Holt considered "the best winery in Canada and as good as most in North America," the facility incorporated an attractive tasting room. With a storage capacity for 4 million gallons and a flexible design to triple the size, the winery was one of the largest in British Columbia. Armed with modern winemaking equipment, Holt now moved Jordan & Ste-Michelle dramatically towards varietal table wines, based initially on imported vinifera grape varieties from California such as ruby cabernet and grey riesling. These were to be an interim measure until the winery's contract growers in the Okanagan could begin delivering vinifera such as the johannisburg riesling that the winery had urged on growers.

However, the winery's head office in Toronto directed that Holt concentrate on producing branded jug wines, notably Toscano and Ruby Rouge. Holt disagreed with the strategy. "I had argued long and hard that that was terminal, that we could not compete with the *vin ordinaire* coming in from other countries; that we would be dead if we did not concentrate on the high end," Holt recalled. This difference of opinion led him to resign in 1979 to run a vineyard in the Similkameen Valley that he and **John Bremmer** had purchased the year before. This was Holt's second foray towards a winery of his own: in 1976 he had negotiated the purchase of a Washington state vineyard and had already resigned from Jordan ("They even had a nice going-away party for me") when the seller had a change of mind and Holt returned to Jordan. His 1979 resignation was permanent; but he and Bremmer were thwarted when the severe damage of the 1978–79 winter killed most of the vines and reduced the forty-six-acre vineyard's production to barely 30 tons in 1979 from 400 tons the year before. The vineyard could no longer support two partners. Bremmer joined **T.G. Brights & Co.** while Holt began re-propagating the vineyard. In 1986 an executive recruiter convinced Holt to become general manager (later president) of Sun-Rype Products Ltd., the big Kelowna food processor, and his brother Bill moved from Ontario to manage the vineyard. In the 1988 grape pull, Holt uprooted about thirty acres, reducing the vineyard to a vinifera core, subsequently adding more vinifera until 1994 when he offered fifty-five of the property's eighty-six acres for sale. What remains also keeps alive the dream of a winery. "I just may decide to put some nice reds in there on the south end of the vineyard," Holt believes. "Pinot noir does really well down there."

HOOD, JOHN (1941–) AND JANE (1947–): If John Hood is correct in his view that the best grapes grow on rocky soil, his vineyard on the southern slope of the *Golden Mile* is a choice location. Boulders removed from his rugged twelve acres now are an abundant part of the landscaping around the family home, and there are more than enough stones remaining between the vines to improve the vineyard's favourable microclimate. "The rocks, although I curse them daily, hold the heat at night," Hood maintains. The sardonic label for the wines he makes from his own grapes is Stone Acres.

A compact man with reddish blonde hair, John Hood was born in Mission City, B.C.; his wife, Jane, was born in Vancouver. Education graduates of the University of British Columbia, they came to Oliver in 1964. A practical man, John Hood accepted a teaching job there because the salary offered was several rungs up from the usual starting salary for new teachers. He retired in 1996, having risen to become principal of the Oliver Elementary School. When the Hoods decided to move into the country in 1975, the property they bought happened to have vines on it and the owner needed some time to build a new house next door. That suited John Hood for it meant he could learn grapegrowing under the tutelage of the seller. "I did my apprenticeship before I moved in," he says. "People told us we were crazy, that it would never work." That advice merely reinforced their determination to do it right. The vineyard had an eclectic selection of varieties, including delaware, white diamond, Okanagan riesling, de chaunac and "a few other oddballs." The best wine variety being grown was chancellor, sold to *Sumac Ridge*, the winery that popularized table wines from this, the most harmoniously flavoured of the red hybrid grapes. Hood replaced the labrusca varieties in his vineyard with vidal and seyval blanc while most of the Okanagan riesling and de chaunac were replaced with pinot blanc. Hood retained a row each of the latter two varieties because he discovered a demand for these from the amateur winemakers that buy some of Hood's grapes. Further fine-tuning of the vineyard has seen the seyval blanc, no longer in demand from wineries, replaced with pinot blanc, while merlot, some grafted onto vidal trunks, has come to occupy a third of the Hood vineyard. In 1996 when he could obtain no merlot plants from France, he planted an acre of gamay noir, a variety that was available. Hood has thought out carefully the selection of varieties. "If I ever do sell this place, and somebody were interested in starting a farm winery, the balance of grapes would be fairly attractive." The vidal also is out of favour with wineries but Hood has kept a small number of vines for himself. A skilled home vintner, he made an *icewine* from those grapes in 1995.

HOUSE OF ROSE: This farmgate winery just north of Kelowna was opened in 1993 by Vern Rose, who has been growing grapes on a seven-acre farm he

purchased in 1982 when he retired from teaching school in Alberta. Located on the Rutland Bench, the site is among the cooler vineyards in the Okanagan, which is why Rose attended a New Zealand seminar in cool-climate viticulture in 1988. That fired his enthusiasm to open a winery. He is among the few who have maintained faith in hybrid varieties such as foch, Okanagan riesling and verdelet, which grow well in his vineyard. He also has merlot, chardonnay and auxerrois.

HROMYK, JOHN (1960−):
The tall and boyishly youthful president of Vintage Holdings, Inc., Hromyk, a former magazine publisher, emerged in the British Columbia wine scene as the leader of the team in mid-1996 that acquired *Hillside Cellars* farmgate winery at the outskirts of Penticton. The purchase was concluded after an intense and disciplined six-month search for an entry into the industry by Hromyk and his partners.

Born in Vancouver, Hromyk — the H is silent — is the son of an education professor whose forbears emigrated to Alberta from the Ukraine after the First World War. After getting a degree in communications from Simon Fraser University in Vancouver, John Hromyk carved out a publishing career. Basing himself in Calgary, he launched in 1988 a magazine called Homes and Ideas, aimed at readers interested in home renovation and redecoration. He credits a food and wine section in the magazine for developing his interest in wine. Hromyk, who sold the magazine in 1993 but remained active in other publishing ventures, got serious about the wine business at the beginning of 1996. He took time off from other busi-

ness and vowed to himself he would find a property in British Columbia within four months. Three wineries were on the market at the time — Hillside (one of whose owners died in 1995), *Chateau Ste. Clair* and *Divino* — and Hromyk took a long look at all three. He was within days of acquiring Divino on May 31, by far the largest of the three with a 72-acre vineyard, when one of the investors in his group backed out. With Chateau Ste. Clair essentially out of production, Hromyk and his backers then settled on Hillside, a well-regarded winery with a five-acre vineyard and, with a 1996 output of 2,500 cases, definitely a going concern. "It gave us a chance to get a foot in the door," Hromyk said. "And it gave us legitimacy."

Hromyk's key partner is *John Fletcher*, veteran former production manager at *Vincor*'s Oliver winery and since mid-1996, the vineyard and winery manager at Hillside. An ambitious team, they planned immediately to double the winery and to acquire additional vineyard property. The product offering from Hillside has been based on the successful wines, 90 percent of which have been sold from the winery, that former owner *Vera Klokocka* had been making.

HUGHES, JESSE WILLARD (J.W.):
A talented Iowa-born horticulturist, Hughes in 1927[3] planted raw land east of Kelowna for the development of what was known as Pioneer Vineyards. The original vine cuttings were purchased both from the *Wilcox* vineyard at Salmon Arm and from Ontario. The initial commercial production was sold as fresh fruit across western Canada but in 1930 the first grape contracts — the agreed price was $100 a ton — were signed by

J.W. Hughes (on ground) helps with baskets of table grapes, circa 1929 (photo courtesy of Lloyd Schmidt)

Hughes with *Victoria Wineries (B.C.) Ltd.* The credit for contracting the first grapes usually goes to *Growers' Wines Ltd.* because it acquired Victoria Wineries at this time.[4] In 1937, having sold his first vineyard, Hughes purchased about 235 acres at Okanagan Mission, where current producers *St. Hubertus* and *CedarCreek* are located. Beginning in 1944, he began to transfer the vineyards to his farm managers who paid him half the gross profits each year for seven years and received title to the vineyards at the end of that period. *H.D. Powell* took over the Mission Vineyard in 1944; *Martin Dulik* the Pioneer Vineyard in 1945; *Frank Schmidt* the upper portion of the Lakeside Vineyard in 1949. The Great West Vineyard was split among four growers in 1946: George Nemeth, Tor Tuovilla, Bill Bata and Roy Francis.[5] Besides growing grapes, Hughes devoted twenty acres to commercial production of peonies, tulips and gladioli. Unusual

for a grapegrower, he welcomed wild birds onto his land. Back in 1940 Mr. Hughes had many strange birds at Cedar Creek. In 1958 amateur historian Primrose Upton, in a centennial book, *The History of Okanagan Mission*, wrote: "There were pigeons, pheasants, ducks, geese, chickens, turkeys, peacocks, bob white quail, and partridge. Now all that remain are the peacocks."[6] Hughes died in Kelowna in 1976.

HYBRIDS: When this term is used in the British Columbia wine industry, it refers to grape varieties created by crossing two different grape species, for example, crossing *Vitis labrusca* or *Vitis riparia,* two native North American species, with Europe's *Vitis vinifera*. The nineteenth- and early twentieth-century French plant breeders, who developed many of the hybrids in a search for disease-resistant vines, are still remembered in the names of some hybrids. Baco noir was named for Maurice Baco; seyval blanc for Bertille Seyve-Villard; vidal for J.L. Vidal. One of the most prolific hybridizers was Albert Seibel, who churned out a long list of vines simply designated with his name and a number, such as Seibel 9549, Seibel 9110 and Seibel 10878. In North America, these hybrids first were widely grown in Ontario and New York and in 1970 the Finger Lakes Wine Growers Association gave more commercially acceptable names to the popular Seibel hybrids. Thus, 9110 became verdelet, 10878 became chelois, 5898 became rougeon and 7053 became chancellor. The name assigned to 9549 was "cameo" but the Canadian Wine Institute objected, in part because that already was a proprietary name used by one Canadian winery. In 1972 it was agreed to call 9549 de chaunac, named after Adhemar de Chaunac, the veteran winemaker at *T.G. Brights & Co.* in Niagara Falls who had convinced his company to import many hybrid varieties from France.[7] The European Union no longer permits the use of hybrid varieties in the production of "quality" wines, which includes all wines made under controlled appellation rules. Hybrid varieties still may be used in wines that qualify for the *Vintners Quality Alliance* in British Columbia, even though

most hybrids were pulled out after the 1988 harvest. The poor wines formerly made from, for example, ineptly grown de chaunac or the characterless verdelet earned such a bad reputation for hybrids among consumers that most wineries cannot sell even well-made examples for reasonable prices. As a result growers and wineries alike have switched to the more remunerative vinifera vines and wines. However, an unexpected surge in red wine demand in the mid-990s revived interest in such full-flavoured hybrids as maréchal foch (originally Kuhlmann 188-2 after hybridizer Eugene Kuhlmann), rougeon and chancellor.

[1] *Hainle Vineyards Newsletter*, February/March 1995.

[2] Correspondence with Eric von Krosigk, February 1996.

[3] Merril Hughes, J.W.'s son, says the first twenty acres were planted in 1927. Other sources put the date at 1926, which may have been when Hughes acquired the property.

[4] John Vielvoye's 1971 article, p. 21.

[5] Ibid. p. 22.

[6] Primrose, Upton: *The History of Okanagan Mission*, p. 78; in British Columbia Archives.

[7] Hudson Cattell and H. Lee Stauffer, *The Wines of the East: The Hybrids* (Lancaster, PA: Eastern Wine Publications, 1978).

III

ICEWINE

A dessert wine remarkable for its room-filling aromas and intense flavours, icewine was first made in the Okanagan in 1973 by **Walter Hainle**. This was a decade before the first commercially available Canadian icewine was made by Hillebrand Estate Winery in Ontario, establishing a category in which Okanagan and Niagara icewines have rivalled Germany, the birthplace of these wines, in both quantity and, many will argue, in quality. Canadian vintners, unlike their German peers, can count on the required freezing temperatures chilling their vineyards almost every year, either in November or in December, turning the grapes into near-marbles which, when pressed, yield very sweet, concentrated grape juice while leaving behind the water content as crystals of ice. The first vintage in the Okanagan in which a number of other wineries joined the Hainle family in making icewine was 1991 when an unexpected cold snap on October 29 caught several vineyards with grapes for late harvest wines still on the vines. The first vintage of extensive icewine production was 1994.

Walter Hainle (photo courtesy of Dave Gamble)

In his native Germany, Hainle knew icewines only as a consumer, having been a textile salesman before coming to Canada. "It wasn't something that figured very prominently in what he knew about wines from that area of Germany where we came from," his son, **Tilman Hainle**, says. The family came from Württemberg and their favourite local producer, Weingut Graf Adelmann, was not an icewine producer or even a significant maker of the sweeter wines fashionable in Germany. "He came at the whole subject of wine from an amateur enthusiast's point of view," Tilman says of Walter. "Growing some grapes on his own property and making some wine from it was a dream from a long time ago."

Karl Kaiser, the Austrian-born winemaker at **Inniskillin** and now one of Canada's most experienced icewine makers, has found historical references that an icewine was made by chance in 1794 by a grower in Franconia when an early frost caught some of his grapes still on the vines. Kaiser thinks it probable that wines of this style were produced earlier, since Europe endured unusually cold winters throughout the eighteenth century. (The English Channel was partially frozen during one brutally cold winter.) But deliberately made German *eiswein* lacked its own category under German wine law prior to the 1970s, being labelled simply as *auslese* or late harvest. The category was established in part because vintners discovered they could sell *eiswein* at a premium over late harvest wines. The comparative rarity and the exotic novelty of icewines support their premium pricing. Frozen grapes yield a concentrated essence whose volume at best is one-fifth of the juice normally available for wine. "To mass-produce icewine is an oxymoron," insists winemaker Tilman Hainle.

In 1971, one year after emigrating to Canada, Walter Hainle began making wine at home, mostly from Okanagan riesling. Two years later an early frost occurred before picking had been completed in the Summerland vineyard of his friend, Ludwig Littau, from whom he was buying grapes, giving Hainle the opportunity to make between 30 and 40 litres of icewine. It was the start of an annual tradition. "The only year that we never made icewine was 1977," Tilman says. "We would have been able to make it but we were still relying on the grapes from Ludwig Littau's place and he got antsy. The birds were after the grapes and he said, 'Walter, get them off — I can't hang onto them anymore.'" Stubbornly, Hainle picked the grapes and placed them in the walk-in freezer at a Summerland butcher shop for several days before pressing, a technique now called cryogenic vinification and occasionally employed in the United States and Australia to simulate icewine. The Hainle experiment was not successful. "The result was very disappointing," Tilman recalls. "The wine had a frosty taste — the wine equivalent of freezer burn. No fruit. It was an interesting experiment and to us it proved you have to do it the natural method."

Beginning in 1978 the Hainles began making icewine from Okanagan riesling grapes grown in their own vineyard at Peachland which had been purchased in 1972. Once other wineries began making icewines in the 1990s, contracting wineries agreed to pay growers by November 1 for grapes reserved for icewine, no matter when they were picked, thus shifting the risk of crop loss to the winery from the grower. In 1991, when **Summerhill** reserved a block of riesling at **Paradise Ranch** near Naramata, a mild winter ensued and the necessary sharp frost did not occur. The grapes were finally picked the following March when the vineyard manager complained that the vines had to be pruned before spring. "We had paid for 5 tonnes of grapes and we maybe got half a tonne of raisins," recalls **Eric von Krosigk,** then the Summerhill winemaker. He produced an elegant dessert wine called *El Nino* (for the warm ocean current in the Pacific) which, in half-litre bottles, retailed for $62; even at that price, the winery failed to cover the cost of the grapes. "That was prestige," von Krosigk said. (The Canadian practice is to vintage date the wine for the year in which the grapes are grown rather than the year in which they are harvested.) The dry Okanagan climate minimizes the risk that grapes reserved for icewine will rot on the vines before harvest. "The grapes are generally very healthy going into their late-ripening phase," Tilman Hainle says. "All you have to worry about then is protecting them from predators." At different times of the season, that can include birds, bears and coyotes; some growers have experienced 80 percent losses.

By late October winemakers with grapes set aside for icewine begin paying especial attention to the forecast, waiting for the first arctic front to move down from the north. Alerted by changing weather patterns, wineries have their pickers (almost always volunteers) standing by on short notice for the call to get into the vineyards by dawn, or sooner, if picking is being done at night by tractor light. The icewine picking threshold temperature is -8°C. At warmer temperatures, the juice pressed from frozen grapes, while still quite sweet, will be too dilute for quality icewine. Yet if the thermometer drops towards -20°C, the honey-like juice — the little that can be pressed from the hard grapes — will be difficult to ferment and the wine will be overly sweet. Ideal picking temperatures are -10 to -14°C. The winemaker's dilemma at -8°C is whether to pick or gamble that it will get a little colder. At the Hainle vineyard in 1978, there were two icewine pickings, one on November 8 at about -8°C, and the second four days later at -12°C. As it happens, the wine was not released for sale until 1991, three years after the Hainle winery opened. "It had in a sense slipped our collective memories that there was this carboy of old icewine that was doing very well," Tilman recalls. "We were taking stock of what was in the cellar and we realized that this would be wonderful to release, and with some fanfare." The 108 bottles of November 14, 1978, icewine, because it was the sweeter and more intensely flavoured of the two batches, was released on May 1, 1991, at $45 a half-bottle, while the 157 bottles of its older but slightly lesser sibling were priced at $35 when released in December 1991. "My dad's belief was that it always has to be a rare item," Tilman says of the small production.

A grape now reviled for table wine, Okanagan riesling perhaps was the best available at the time to Walter Hainle. "Back then, getting any vinifera was extremely hard," Tilman says. "At its best, Okanagan riesling had some very interesting exotic fruit characteristics and a spice and floral impression on the palate. I thought it did better in the dessert wine category where you were used to dealing with strong and unusual flavours rather than in the table wine category where a winemaker would try to tone down those flavours. At its worst, Okanagan riesling can be extremely foxy, with medicinal and chemical tones." The Hainles made their last Okanagan riesling icewine in 1982; it was the first sold to the public in January 1989 after opening the winery store. The Hainles switched to white riesling for icewine in the 1983 vintage. The first wine that brought acclaim to the winery was the 1987 icewine, which picked up a number of awards, including best of show at one of the Pacific National Exhibition competitions.

Many producers have discovered that icewines are surefire award winners — wines whose intense aromas and lush tropical flavours seduce judging panels as readily as they seduce consumers. The white riesling has been the preferred variety for icewine, first because the vines are durable enough to take the stress of nurturing fruit well beyond the usual harvest, and second because the variety matures to great elegance and is suited to prolonged cellar-aging. *CedarCreek's* award-winning icewines are made only from riesling. *Summerhill* and *Gehringer Brothers Estate Winery*, among others, have also used such varieties as ehrenfelser, gewurztraminer, traminer among the whites and pinot noir and chancellor among the reds, the latter being portlike curiosities. *Lynn Bremmer* produced a medal-winning icewine at *Brights* from vidal, a sturdy-skinned variety that can be left on the vines longer than usual and that yields intensely tropical aromas in the wines.

Missouri-born *Dr. Alan Marks*, who took over at Summerhill from von Krosigk, describes his first Canadian icewine, Summerhill's 1994 riesling, as "quite an experience." The grapes were picked during a three-day period in late November, mostly at night with temperatures as low as -21 °C. Under such conditions, grape clusters generally can be snapped off the vines readily; at times, individual grapes can simply be shaken into picking buckets although winemakers generally prefer that stems also go into the press to form juice channels through the frozen cake in the press. Remembering the bitter cold in the vineyard, Marks contends that icewine vintages should be filmed so that consumers appreciate the justification for $40 a half-bottle. Such is the mystique of icewine that it is seldom difficult to get pickers, as uncomfortable as it is to be in a vineyard during frigid nights and early mornings; picking stops if the temperature rises above -8 °C or if the sun starts trying to defrost the grapes. Many wineries have turned icewine picking into an end-of-harvest festival, with food, hot beverages and a party atmosphere. Regina Hainle, Tilman's mother, traditionally greets pickers at the winery with mulled wine, onion quiche and croissants. "Everyone gets sent home with a bottle of icewine and an Icewine Crew T-shirt, which is great for sporting at the beach in the summer," Tilman chuckles. At the **Vincor** winery in Oliver, former winemaker **Frank Supernak** and fellow employees turned out for a round-the-clock party when the frozen grapes were being harvested. "You need a little bit of a festive air to get people to come and pick grapes for you," Marks suggests.

Making icewine is as hard on the equipment as it is on the people. Hainle first crushes his grapes (others bypass this step), a practice that plugs crushers but, once the frozen mass is in the press, increases juice extraction. Pressing requires either hydraulic basket presses or sturdy old bladder presses capable of pressures as high as 90 pounds per square inch. This is a far higher pressure than is needed or desirable for table wines and equipment does break. In fact, the newer models of membrane presses now being introduced to wineries are not capable of the necessary high pressures. "You start the pressing very gently, to make sure that you keep your juice channels open as long as possible," Tilman Hainle says, describing a process that can last most of the day. "You just let the pressure rise. You keep the pressure on until your juice extraction has slowed to a dribble." Typically, all wineries crush and press outside or in wineries with doors left open to admit the winter cold, since the icewine grapes must not be allowed to thaw.

The challenge continues into the winery because the sugar content of icewine juice, by volume, usually is between 35 and 45 percent, depending on how intensely frozen the grapes are when pressed. This saturated juice is a hostile environment to wine yeast, since the sugar weakens yeast cells by dehydrating them. "The crucial thing in icewine making is to make a strong yeast culture," Marks says, echoing other winemakers. At **Quails' Gate**, which began making riesling icewine in 1993, winemaker **Jeff Martin** gets yeasts (he uses three strains) working actively in an aerated starter before inoculating the juice. **CedarCreek** doubles the amount of yeast and the amount of yeast nutrient and warms the juice to kick-start the fermentation — and even then, it will be ten days before the fermentation begins to drop the sugar level noticeably. In general, most wineries let the fermentation proceed about three months, stopping it (by chilling the wine) when the alcohol level is in the 10 to 12 percent range. At this point, half of the natural sugar remains unfermented. Martin believes that icewine then should be

QUAILS' GATE
VINEYARDS ESTATE WINERY

1994
RIESLING
ICE WINE

10.4% alc/vol   375ml
Product of Canada   Produit du Canada

bottled promptly and allowed to develop nuances of bouquet and flavour in the bottle. As always, Tilman Hainle goes his own way: like his father before him, he leaves his icewines alone until fermentation stops naturally, at between 15 and 17 percent alcohol, leaving wines that are less sweet than mainstream icewines and, with age, that can develop nutty, sherrylike flavours. "To market a drier style icewine is going against the flow but we are no strangers to that," he says. He also differs with the majority who release icewines by their first birthday (he has only done that once) when the wines already have very showy aromas but still have a sharp, acidic edge. "You should release it when it is mature," Tilman contends. "The wine has to be in balance. There is no sense in releasing something that will eat away at your teeth." But all winemakers agree that icewines generally are being consumed far too young. "If people would buy them and set them aside for five years, the wines will be better," promises Martin. "There is so much potential there."

There is enough in a half-bottle (350 ml) of icewine for six to eight servings, although a partly consumed bottle will remain sound for a week or so in a refrigerator. *St. Hubertus* has begun selling its icewines in 200 millilitre bottles, if only to make the wines more accessibly priced. Arguably, icewines are best served on their own, lightly chilled, simply because the aromas and tastes are so spectacular. However, many chefs have seen the increasing selection of these wines as an intriguing culinary challenge. To release its 1993 *Jackson-Triggs* riesling icewine, *Vincor* organized a dessert competition among the chefs at Whistler where the judges gave first prize to a dessert with hazelnut and banana flavours. "We try and steer people away from having it with really sweet desserts," *Sandra Hainle* advises. "I usually suggest a very conservative approach with it and will recommend desserts that are based on pastry, fruit, cheese and nuts as the best bet to show the wine really well. If you get into chocolate or added sugar, you will alter the character of the wine or your experience of the wine. One of the classic food matches we have had it with are baked brie coated with almonds in egg white and brushed with a tiny bit of honey." Because icewines are rare and expensive, they are typically reserved for special occasions. "That might be a shame," she says. "Maybe you should open a nice wine just because it is Tuesday night."

The Okanagan Icewines of the 1994 Vintage

WINERY	VARIETY	PICK DATE	PICK TEMPERATURE	QUANTITY
CedarCreek	Riesling	December 6	N.A.	1,000 half-bottles
Gehringer Bros.	Riesling	December 4	−12°C	2,400 half-
Gray Monk	Ehrenfelser	December 8	−8°C	2,100 half-
Hainle	Riesling	December 3	−15°C	170 litres
Inniskillin	Chenin blanc	December 3	−15°C to −18°C	1,600 litres
Jackson-Triggs	Riesling	December 4	−15°C	1,600 litres
Lang	Riesling	November 21	−10°C	380 litres
LeComte	Gewurztraminer	December 4	−13°C	550 litres
Peller Estates	Ehrenfelser	December 8	−12°C	80 cases
Peller Estates	Riesling	December 8	−12°C	50 cases
Peller Estates	Vidal	December 8	−12°C	50 cases
Peller Estates	"Trinity" *	December 8	−12°C	50 cases
St. Hubertus	Northern Red	November 21	−10°C	50 litres
St. Hubertus	Riesling	November 21	−10°C	180 litres
Summerhill	Riesling	November 21–22	−15°C to −18°C	1,600 litres
Tinhorn Creek	Kerner	December 3	−9°C	700 litres
Quail's Gate	Riesling	December 5	−15°C	700 litres

* blend of riesling, vidal and ehrenfelser

INKAMEEP VINEYARDS: At 215 acres in size in 1995 and one of the Okanagan's largest commercial vineyards, Inkameep was judged an "apparent failure" after its first decade. It survived, now selling more than $1 million worth of quality wine grapes each year. Today, *Sam Baptiste*, the vineyard's ambitious general manager, envisions several thousand more acres planted to grapes in the Osoyoos Indian Band's reserve, which stretches from Oliver to Osoyoos along the eastern slopes of the Okanagan Valley here.

In 1966 *Andrés Wines*, then five years old and wanting an assured source of grapes, sought, but was refused, a long-term vineyard lease on Osoyoos Band land. The following year, however, the Band reconsidered the opportunity, in concert with the federal Department of Indian and Northern Affairs and one

Agnes MacDonald, who proposed she would supply vinifera vines from Germany to the project. (MacDonald withdrew from the venture before planting began.) With Ukrainian-born Balthaser Bachmann as vineyard manager (he had been running the Andrés vineyard at Cawston), a development plan was drawn up. The Band invested $60,000 and Indian Affairs $428,000. Andrés was to provide technical advice through Bachmann. A man nearing seventy at the time, he was described in a letter by an Indian Affairs official as "an older man with set ideas and minimum patience [who] has not worked on a Reserve before and has difficulty realizing that the people he is advising have not the background in grapegrowing that he has."[1] Bachmann declined the job as foreman, preferring to be an advisor, and Jim Stelkia, a Band member, was chosen

Ted Brouwer (photo courtesy of John Schreiner)

as foreman, with **Ted Brouwer**, who was still finishing a community college agriculture course, joining Inkameep initially as project manager. Andrés' founder, **Andrew Peller,** acknowledged that

Brouwer "had no experience with vineyards" but was "a smart man [who] learned the best methods from all over the world. He certainly knew how to work."[2] Brouwer believed that all agriculture has common principles. "I find apple growing more difficult than growing grapes," he said. "There is a way of adapting yourself. You have to take an interest in how things progress. You grew up along with the grape." An almost scientific record-keeper, Brouwer filled 104 diaries of data during his eighteen years with Inkameep. Unfortunately, enthusiasm was no substitute for experience, as the events of 1968 showed. Because an irrigation system was not installed until late summer, the newly planted sixty-three acres of vines had to be watered by hand, causing a $20,000 labour cost overrun. "The failure to install a satisfactory irrigation system until mid-August resulted in a 20 percent [vine] loss through drought," according to a project review of the vineyard done in 1977 for Indian and Northern Affairs and signed by Fred Walchli, then its regional director in British Columbia.[3] Frost in December knocked off another 20 percent.

That inauspicious start set the tone. "The new year [1969] began with no money for wages, and consequent labour problems," the Walchli review continued, alluding to the perennial difficulty in getting the bureaucrats to release Inkameep's operating funds as they were needed. Brouwer, who took over as the full-time manager this year, described the vineyard's initial years as "a struggle that was unbelievable." He attributed some of the problems to the way Indian Affairs disbursed funds. "We got actually piecemeal financing and you got piecemeal results," he said later. On occasion he got personal bank loans to meet the payroll, being reimbursed later when the money arrived from Ottawa. In 1969, he could not hire enough planters until the summer school break; this was much too late to plant and many new vines, with no chance to become dormant for winter, were damaged by an early October frost. By February 1970 the vineyard project had burned through $267,000 of its capital yet, with eighty-three and a half acres planted, was well behind schedule. However, Inkameep harvested its first 35 ton crop that fall, marking the event with an official opening where **Joseph Peller** was made an honorary chief, shared a peace pipe and picked up the bill for the event. Plantings remained stalled in 1971 but the existing vines produced 153 tons of grapes which were sold for $26,900, covering about half the vineyard's wage bill. In September 1971, the vineyard incorporated so that it could borrow additional funds from a federal government program. Brouwer recalled: "The bank at that time said, 'Hey Brouwer, an organization of this size should have sufficient funds available to carry out an operation of this size.'"

"The company planted 49,000 vines in 1972," Walchli reported. "However, the pattern of the previous years was repeated; funds were received too late to ensure that adequate labour was on hand." Once again, vines were planted later in the spring than they should have been and many, not fully dormant by the fall, were damaged by cold weather. Then on January 4, 1973, a week of cold weather after a long spell of mild weather caused what Walchli described as "almost wholesale destruction of the new plantings, as well as

severe stunting to many of the older plants, particularly those planted in 1969." No vines were planted in 1973 while the damage was assessed. It was bad: the 1973 harvest was only 60 percent of the 252 tons produced in 1972. Uncertain how severely vine productivity had been hurt, Brouwer ordered a very light pruning to preserve a large number of buds — with the result that 1974's crop was almost double that of 1972. The vineyard then compensated by pruning the over-cropped vines aggressively and the 1975 harvest dropped to 235 tons. This was, however, the first Inkameep vintage taken off with a new mechanical harvester, acquired because of the perennial labour shortage. The best news for 1975 was that Andrés sponsored an experimental planting of vinifera vines — johannisberg riesling, ehrenfelser and scheurebe — purchased from the **Geisenheim Institute** in Germany. This marked a turning point for Inkameep which had been planted initially to Okanagan riesling, foch, de chaunac and other hybrid varieties.

Planting was suspended after the 1973 freeze, in part because the major wineries now decided they did not want the white varieties scheduled for Inkameep. The vineyard, with land ready for cultivation, sought to generate cash with corn in 1974 and with vegetables in 1975. Once again misfortune dogged the project. The vegetable crops soaked up the labour pool, preventing Inkameep from doing any significant planting. In the late summer, much of the bounteous tomato crop rotted in the field due to a shortage of labour. Sixty acres of corn planted in 1976 were ploughed under after a cold spring and unusually wet summer. The grape harvest that year also was poor. Walchli's report, which was done just after that harvest, called the vineyard an "apparent failure." He did not blame Brouwer, having recognized that "the position of the vineyard manager is unenviable" because of the energy Brouwer expended on dealing with the real culprits, the departmental bureaucrats, who had impeded developing Inkameep to the two hundred-acre vineyard planned at the outset. "While staggering investments were made in capital improvements," Walchli wrote, "little concern was given to planting the vines, upon which the ultimate success of the project would depend.... The circumstances reflect the deep-rooted belief that Indian-operated projects will ultimately fail."

Despite that devastating report, the promise of new funds from Ottawa enabled Brouwer to carry on, this time with a significant planting of white vinifera vines imported from Geisenheim, in early 1977. "There were 83,000 plants and Andrés underwrote the whole thing," Brouwer recalled. The backing by a major winery enabled Brouwer to do the usual juggling of his finances (Ottawa's disbursements being late as usual), stalling suppliers such as Air Canada — which flew in the vine cuttings — as much as six months. Inkameep managed to plant another 90 acres that spring, bringing its size to about 250 acres. Production was 465 tons in 1977 and 735 tons in 1978; and Inkameep had operating profits. The vineyard's profile improved further when Andrés in 1977 released Inkameep Red and Inkameep White, two of the Okanagan's earliest vineyard-designated wines. Then the notorious 1978–79 winter killed 15,000 of the Geisenheim vines and damaged

the vineyard's mature vines so badly that grape production plunged to 107 tons in 1979 and did not recover to the 1978 level until 1982.

Amid the rebounding optimism of 1980, Simons Resource Consultants of Vancouver was hired to produce a major feasibility report on what was called Wolf Creek Farms Vineyards. The concept was to develop a new five hundred acre vineyard (80 percent in white varieties) on the Osoyoos Reserve, with Andrés and T.G. Brights each to purchase the production of two hundred acres and the remainder to be marketed to other wineries. Four locations were studied, including two near the current vineyard, with the preferred site being a bench on the east side of Osoyoos Lake. "A new vineyard will certainly lend more feeling of pride to the Osoyoos band and utilize prime land for which there does not appear to be other plans," Simons commented in its 1984 report.[4] Had it gone ahead, about $6 million would have been invested over five years, with all of the planting done in the first two years. This audacious plan was stillborn; by this time, the wineries were struggling with a surplus of red wines and wanted growers to pull out vines.

Brouwer meanwhile had begun encouraging an estate winery based on Inkameep's production. Indian Affairs, perhaps understandably given the financial struggles of the vineyard, wanted nothing to do with the idea — but the T.G. Brights & Co. winery from Niagara Falls did. After failing to acquire the Mission Hill winery in 1978, Brights seized the opportunity to develop a winery north of Oliver, not far from the vineyard, in a $1.9 million building financed by Inkameep Vineyards Ltd. with

ny's leading grape-breeding stations. In any event, vines do not produce enough wood to yield cuttings for new vines until their third year. Forced to rely on its own resources, the vineyard did not fully replace the losses of 1979 until 1986.

In 1983, however, the vineyard began to show its potential by producing 1,000 tons for the first time. Cold weather then reduced the 1984 vintage to 750 tons and selective pruning was a factor in 1985 production dropping to 625 tons. This was a factor in the confrontation between Brouwer and the Osoyoos Band which led to Brouwer's abrupt departure in February 1986 (and a subsequent out-of-court settlement in Brouwer's favour). His successor, **Kenn Visser**, inherited a vineyard on the turn: it produced 1,100 tons that fall and turned a tidy profit.

The Missouri-born Visser, who had lived in the Okanagan since 1980 and who was a manager at **Covert Farms** before being hired for Inkameep, soon found himself considering strategies to help Inkameep survive the free trade agreement Canada and the United States signed in 1988. Along with most other growers, Inkameep got rid of unwanted grape varieties (foch, de chaunac and Okanagan riesling), pulling out 107 of the 255 acres then in production. That still left Inkameep as B.C.'s largest producing vineyard; and while it had contracts for its remaining grapes through the 1994 vintage, Visser and the Osoyoos Band probed the winery option again with the production of **Nordique Blanc,** a white wine aimed initially at export sales. The market trials in New York and Chicago gained significant media attention for Inkameep but ultimately the label was licenced to

a loan on commercial terms from the federal government. The winery, now operating under the **Vincor** name, was opened in 1981. "Without my suggestion and the gut feeling that we could do something with a winery, Vincor would not be there," Brouwer asserted later. Sam Baptiste was chief of the band when the winery agreement was negotiated. "It almost didn't happen," he recalled. Some of his fellow chiefs were opposed, telling him at a meetings of chiefs: "Sam, the biggest problem on every reserve is alcoholism — and you're putting in a winery!" His first reaction was to call off the talks with Brights but he changed his mind after the meeting. "I thought about it and I decided it was none of their business."

Ironically, the Geisenheim vines imported in 1977 set back the planting of the vineyard. The federal plant health authorities discovered viruses among the vines, stopped Inkameep from importing more Geisenheim vines to replace the losses and quarantined the entire vineyard for several years, which prevented Inkameep from sending vine cuttings out to nurseries for propagation. "We had brought those plants in on the assumption that those plants were free of any contaminated viruses," Brouwer recalled. It should have been a safe assumption, Geisenheim being one of Germa-

Summerhill Estate Winery and the vineyard continued to sell its grapes, negotiating new three-year contracts for them in 1995.

Baptiste has presided over replanting Inkameep with vinifera. The new vines have included thirty acres of chardonnay along with plantings of merlot and pinot noir and scheduled plantings of cabernet franc and sauvignon blanc. In 1995 the vineyard still retained twenty-six acres (of 215 planted) in two workhorse red hybrids, chancellor and baco noir, that may ultimately give way to red vinifera. He also has had some struggles with the weather but they have been a far cry from Ted Brouwer's experiences. In part, this reflects the knowledge that has been gained in vinifera growing. Newly planted chardonnay were caught by freezing temperatures in early 1991 but this time most of the vines survived. "I'd never grown chardonnay before and I found out how hardy it is." Baptiste also has adopted conservative techniques. "Every time there is a bad freeze, I take the ones that survive and I take cuttings," he says, arguing that these are stronger plants. "I also hill my young plants [ploughing a protective blanket of earth against the base of the vines each fall] until they are three years old." He has great confidence in Inkameep's ability to grow quality grapes. "There's going to be a surplus of grapes in a few years," Baptiste predicted in a 1995 interview, "but there will never be a surplus of premium grapes."

INNISKILLIN OKANAGAN: In 1975, when Inniskillin Wines Inc. was established near Niagara-on-the-Lake in Ontario, it was Canada's first modern estate winery, producing wines so consistently superior that it set the pace for all estate wineries. Owners *Donald Ziraldo* and *Karl Kaiser* also became major forces behind the development of Canadian wine standards leading to the *Vintners Quality Alliance* programs in Ontario and British Columbia.

In 1992, Inniskillin merged with the *Cartier* wine group which, subsequently, merged with *Brights* to form *Vincor.* That association led in 1994 to Inniskillin establishing what is effectively an estate winery in the Okanagan, with Kaiser making wine in the Vincor plant at Oliver, using grapes grown at the nearby *Inkameep* vineyard. "The gods are with us," Ziraldo said, referring to the remarkably high quality of the 1994 vintage in the Okanagan. In its debut year, Inniskillin Okanagan produced about 3,000 cases of wine: pinot blanc, chardonnay, pinot noir and merlot, along with a modest quantity of icewine. With the wines being well received, production was doubled in 1995. One reason for the instant success of the wines was the eye-catching Inniskillin Okanagan label, based on ancient petroglyphs in the hills above the vineyard.

Estate winery rules in British Columbia, at least in 1995, called for such a winery to have a separate facility. Ziraldo and Kaiser held back at first, cellaring the wines at the large Vincor plant. "My idea is to build the market before we build ourselves a monument," Ziraldo said. The winery that will emerge is likely to stand apart, judging from the concept that was forming in Ziraldo's mind in 1995. He believes a cave winery built into the hillside above the Inkameep vineyard would provide ideal temperature control, save energy — and provide a unique experience for visitors.

INQUIRIES: Since 1950 there have been three public inquiries into liquor regulation in British Columbia. What each one had to say about wine reflected the importance — or lack thereof — of wine in British Columbia at the time.

Harry H. Stevens chaired the first commission,[5] which was appointed in September 1952, held twenty-seven public hearings around the province, considered two hundred briefs and, as requested by the government, reported by the end of that year. The inquiry was concerned mostly with the licensing of establishments that sold liquor to the public, a lively issue when it was discovered that the breweries had more than $1 million outstanding in loans to hotels and beer parlours. The Commission recommended against this practice.

That the Commission did not advocate a return to Prohibition is remarkable, given its breathless discovery that the "extent of alcoholism in Canada ... and the increasing magnitude of the problem created by this disease, which fastens itself on our social fabric like a cancerous growth, has shocked us almost beyond words." One brief suggested that there were 30,000 "uncontrolled drinkers or alcoholics" in British Columbia. The Commission recommended that the government extend a provincial education campaign on drinking to all school grades; and that an alcohol research foundation be established.

Some of the briefs suggested all-night liquor stores, as had been done for a time during the 1930s. "There is no reason in our opinion why a liquor-store should be open all night any more than a dairy or any other establishment," the Commission snapped. On the other hand, it did recommend more efficiency

in the stores. "It has been brought to [our] attention ... that persons entering a Government Liquor Store must pass their order through three different individuals before they receive service of the article they wish to buy."

Stevens and his two fellow commissioners had little to say about wine-making. "... They have not had sufficient time to secure the technical knowledge to offer specific recommendations in regard thereto ... However, evidence has been submitted that the public have been denied the opportunity of purchasing wines of their choice through the tendency of the Liquor Control Board to limit stocks of imported wines. It has been alleged to your Commissioners that some Canadian wines stocked by the Liquor Control Board contain an unusually high alcoholic content, considerably in excess of reputable brands of imported wines."

The second commission,[6] appointed in January 1969 and reporting in March 1970, was chaired by Judge Charles W. Morrow of Vernon, who was assisted by the Roman Catholic Archbishop of Vancouver, Martin M. Johnson, and by Edward M. Lawson, the long-time director of the Teamsters Union in British Columbia. They listened to 4,934 pages of testimony from 153 witnesses and received another 5,000 letters. The terms of reference simply asked them to look into the "distribution, sale and consumption of spirituous, vinous and malt liquors." As the commissioners said in the preface to their report: "A sizable segment of the public had been complaining over an extended period about many facets of the sale, distribution and consumption of alcoholic beverages."

The Morrow Commission, whose

sensible recommendations initially fell on largely deaf ears, was not overwhelmed that some people are alcoholics. The government should be able to "harness [the] temperance unions and the moderate drinkers who constitute 95% of the beverage alcohol consumers to alleviate the tragedy of alcoholism." The commissioners believed that the Stevens recommendations had resulted in "rigid rules, regulations and strictures ... interpreted and implemented by an authoritarian Board.... The Commission's view at this time is that many of the restrictive regulations promulgated over the years have become onerous and repulsive to many people and that if alcoholic beverages are to be allowed, the fewer restrictions surrounding their sale the better."[7] This was hardly the view of Premier W.A.C. Bennett, a teetotaler. The Morrow Commission recommended allowing distilleries, wineries and breweries to advertise in all media (subject to a code laid down by the report). Yet the Bennett government banned all *advertising* in 1971, the year *after* Morrow reported.

The Morrow Commission, besides recommending that all licenced dining rooms have British Columbia table wines available by the carafe, fulminated against excessive restaurant and LCB wine prices. "We believe that the public would hold your Commissioners 'flagrante delicto' if we did not comment upon the gouging of the consumer in the high markup of wines both by the Liquor Control Board and by dining room licensees.... The consumer finds it costly to enjoy a meal complemented by wine." The commissioners found instances where Chateau Pontet [one of the rare Bordeaux chateaux then listed in British

Columbia] was sold by the LCB for $6 but resold in restaurants for as much as $14. "In our opinion this gouging is most reprehensible.... It would seem to your Commissioners that if the word 'control' is to be meaningful it should be in this area." There should be "severe sanctions against those who through high markups deny many people the experience of gracious eating and drinking habits."[8] The government subsequently limited the restaurant markup on wines to 100 percent of their retail price.

Morrow did lay the seeds for the substantial changes inaugurated by Dave Barrett's government after it took office in 1972, including splitting the **Liquor Control Board** and relocating a more focussed retailing arm to Vancouver. The mood for reform was continued in the policy changes in 1977 and 1978 under Consumer Affairs Minister **Rafe Mair** which bolstered the British Columbia wine industry (successful lobbying by the Grape Growers Marketing Board accelerated the changes). For the first time, British Columbia wineries were permitted to create promotional pamphlets and distribute them in liquor stores. The government allowed wineries to open on-site retail stores and to offer tours and tastings. The wineries were given more freedom to advertise than was permitted either breweries or distilleries. The markup on domestic wines was reduced to 46 percent from 66 percent; highly visible end-of-aisle displays of British Columbia wines appeared in liquor stores. And the government agreed that the growing number of domestic wines in bottles sealed with corks rather than screw caps should be integrated in liquor store shelves with imported cork-finished wines, in the apparent hope that the prestige of being among the imports would rub off on British Columbia wines, many of which now appeared under pseudo-labels such as **Schloss Laderheim**. These changes reversed the decline in British Columbia wine sales that had begun earlier in the decade.

The third inquiry,[9] appointed in February 1987, took so much interest in wines that the members and some of the staff even travelled to the United States to visit wineries. The review panel — Chairman John Jansen, Larry Chalmers and James Hewitt, all Social Credit members of the legislature — were asked to look at all liquor policy. This inquiry received 400 briefs, 1,200 letters and even a few petitions. The inquiry revisited all of the concerns of the two previous ones and made some of the same recommendations (such as mandatory substance abuse programs in all grades in school). On wine, it supported the preferential treatment then given the British Columbia wine industry: domestic wines then were marked up only 50 percent (15 percent in the case of estate wines) compared with 110 percent on imported wines. As well, British Columbia wineries were guaranteed a quarter of the shelf space in liquor stores. Ironically, the Canada-U.S. Free Trade Agreement signed in 1988 coupled with a ruling against Canada under world trade rules forced British Columbia to gradually abandon the preferential pricing for domestic wines.

The Jansen Commission, like the Morrow Commission, concluded that the prices of top imported wines were excessive and recommended a clever markup system that, to take an example, would have rolled back the retail price of a $30 bottle of wine to $23.95.

The three members said the government should continue the 110 percent markup on the first $6.40 of a standard bottle but should only mark up the rest by 25 percent. The idea was not implemented.

INTERNATIONAL POTTER DISTILLING CORP.: The successor to **Potter Distilleries Ltd.**, this company acquired **Calona Wines** in 1989. The company changed its name in 1995 to **Cascadia Brands Inc.** See also **Ian Tostenson.**

IRVINE, BARRY (1941–) AND SUE (1946–): Born in Vernon, a member of a pioneering family, Barry Irvine earned a doctorate in biology (specializing in insect physiology) from Case Western Reserve University in Cleveland and was doing post-doctoral studies at the University of California in Los Angeles when he and his wife decided in 1970 to take over her parents' 150 acre orchard near Naramata. Barry Irvine also taught at Okanagan College for twenty years, beginning in 1974. Sue Irvine was born in Penticton and grew up on the family orchard. She took a degree in English and psychology at the University of British Columbia, where she and Barry met.

As tree fruits became less remunerative, the Irvines converted the Naramata site to grapes. It was a gutsy decision, first because they planted vinifera (primarily pinot blanc), and second, because none of the wineries they approached would contract their grapes; and without a contract, they could not get a licence from the Grape Marketing Board. After their member of the legislature took up their case, **Okanagan Vineyards** agreed to buy the first 2,000 tons of pinot blanc they harvested in

1986. As it happened, Okanagan Vineyards immediately resold those grapes to *Gray Monk*. Beginning in 1987 *Sumac Ridge* began buying the Irvine grapes, turning them into one of Sumac Ridge's best-selling dry whites. "The challenges are so stimulating both in the growing of the grapes and the desire to increase our understanding of wine that it appalls us we stayed in the tree-fruit business as long as we did," Sue Irvine said in a 1989 newspaper interview.

The vineyard led Sue Irvine, a life-long community activist, to become an executive member of the *Grape Growers Association* and its representative on the *Okanagan Wine Festival*, where she was co-chair for two years and chair for three more years, from 1988 through 1990. An effective organizer, Irvine had the festival operating on a solid business-like basis when she left. Remarkably involved, Sue Irvine also was a school trustee and chair for nine years, and a member of the board of governors at the University of Victoria. In the 1993 federal election, she was an unsuccessful Progressive Conservative candidate.[10] The Irvines sold half of the vineyard in 1995, Barry having retired the year before from Okanagan College, and bought a forty-foot ocean-cruising sailboat, moored on Vancouver Island. The ten acres of precious pinot blanc that they retained is the right size, they believe, to be managed between ocean cruises. The section they sold now hosts *Lake Breeze Estate Winery.*

1   A.B. Ash, regional agricultural supervisor for Indian Affairs, in a letter April 26, 1968, to Jim Stelkia of the Osoyoos Band; in Ted Brouwer personal files.

2   Quoted in Andrew Peller, *The Winemaker*. (See SOURCES for complete reference.)

3   Inkameep Vineyards Ltd. Project Review, January 1977, prepared by F.J. Walchli, Regional Director General, British Columbia, Department of Indian and Northern Affairs. Copy in Ted Brouwer personal files.

4   *Inkameep Vineyards: Analysis and Forecast*, copy in Ted Brouwer personal files.

5   *Report of the British Columbia Liquor Inquiry Commission*, 1952; in City of Vancouver Public Archives.

6   *Report of the British Columbia Liquor Inquiry Commission*, (Ottawa: Queen's Printer, 1970.)

7   Ibid. p. 13.

8   Ibid. pp. 96–97.

9   *Liquor Policies for British Columbians*, 1987.

10 *Okanagan Business*, September 23, 1989, p. 5.

JJJ

JACK WINES: *Calona Wines* launched this family of fortified pop wines early in 1968 after producing a trial 40,000-gallon lot in 1967. The wines were so well received that 260,000 gallons were made in 1968. The wines were Double Jack, made from apples; Cherry Jack; Berry Jack (loganberries) and Grape Jack. All were fortified to a resounding 20 percent alcohol with spirits that Calona made in its new distillery. (Indeed, in 1968, thirteen of Calona's wines were similarly fortified.) The winery recommended that the Jack wines be served well chilled, "for entertaining or after dinner." They were called Jack wines because the original intention was to call the apple wine Applejack. This was not allowed by the regulators since Applejack is distilled apple brandy by definition.[1]

JACKSON, ALLAN H. (1951 –): A native of Hamilton, Jackson joined the research department of John Labatt Ltd. in 1977 immediately on completing his doctorate in chemistry at McMaster University. His doctoral work on the chemical components of wine included hilariously remembered research on the chemical difference between *Baby Duck* and Chambertin. (Jackson noted wryly that the difference was small but fundamental.) In 1981 Jackson transferred from Labatt's in London to its wine division in Niagara Falls and he ultimately emerged as the wine group's technical director. He gained experience both in Canada and at the Labatt-owned Lamont winery in Bakersfield, Ca., an old facility that was still fermenting in concrete vats when Labatt took it over. It was at Lamont that Jackson became close friends with *Donald Triggs,* then running the California winery. When Labatt decided to sell its wine division in 1988, Jackson galvanized the wine group's management to buy it and convinced Triggs, who had left Labatt some years earlier, to rejoin as the head of the group. Jackson now is the executive vice-president of *Vincor International Inc.* and, as such, is the senior technical officer in Canada's largest winery.

JACKSON-TRIGGS: Launched in September 1992 as a brand of what was then *Cartier Wines,* it has since become the flagship label for *Vincor International Inc.* The label incorporates the surnames of *Donald Triggs* and *Allan Jackson*, the president and executive vice-president, respectively, of Vincor.

The idea was conceived by Triggs, who sought to emulate the successful President's Choice labels of the grocery giant Loblaw Companies Ltd. "There is a proprietary nature to the wine business," he reasoned. But since he was president of a large corporate winery, he thought it inappropriate to have just his name on the label and he asked Jackson to share the billing with him. "We had a real partnership," Triggs said. "If I had his name on the label, I would be certain to have his commitment."

Virtually all of the wines bottled under the label are varietal wines. Triggs and Jackson had discerned that varietal wine sales were growing as consumers moved up from once-popular generics, such as their own Alpenweiss. After merging Cartier with **Inniskillin,** they considered using Inniskillin's prestige label as the varietal flagship. In the end, they settled on Jackson-Triggs, in part because Inniskillin lacked national distribution. Some of the early Jackson-Triggs varietals, in bottles with white labels, were blended from imported wines but by 1995, black-labelled Jackson-Triggs varietals featured Canadian-grown **VQA** wines. In British Columbia, Vincor produced about 5,000 cases of Jackson-Triggs VQA wines in 1995 and, based on vineyards coming into production, projected producing 15,000 cases in the 1997 vintage. "We can sell everything we make," Triggs said.

Vincor's total catalogue includes about 160 products but the Jackson-Triggs wines get extra attention. "Do we taste every bottling of Jackson-Triggs?" Don Triggs asks rhetorically. "You bet!" No detail eludes them, including the writing of the back labels. The partners often spend weekends faxing drafts of back-label copy between each other's homes until they come up with text on which both agree.

JESSACHER, ANTON (1927–): One of the cluster of grapegrowers at Kaleden, Toni Jessacher enjoyed a twenty-eight-year career as an electrician with Canadian Forest Products in Vancouver before buying vineyard land in the Okanagan. Born in the German-speaking South Tyrol (formerly Austrian but Italian since 1918), Jessacher grew up in Innsbruck, Aus., working there for the local power company until he emigrated to Canada in 1954. With little English, he worked for the Powell River Co. in a variety of logging jobs until his language skills enabled him to work as an electri-

cian. After working with construction crews at the Kitimat aluminum smelter, Jessacher had had enough of remote coastal communities and settled in Vancouver, joining Canadian Forest. What drove him to the Okanagan was severe arthritis. "The doctor said I have to move to a drier climate."

One of his acquaintances in the Okanagan was **Nick Brodersen**, another former Canadian Forest Products electrician who had become a grower at Kaleden. One day in August 1983 Jessacher went to visit his friend. "The vineyard looked so lush, so beautiful," Jessacher recalled. "I said to him, is there anything for sale around here?" Brodersen directed him to a five-acre plot nearby with a new house on it but also so broken up by gullies that it seemed an unlikely vineyard site. Jessacher and his Hamilton-born wife, Nancy, a twenty-eight-year career banker, bought it nonetheless, and had the gravelly terrain levelled and contoured into an excellent southeastern slope.

Knowing nothing about grapes, the Jessachers sought advice from **Lloyd Schmidt,** then one of the partners at **Sumac Ridge** and a respected vineyardist. After Schmidt moved to Ontario, Jessacher found other mentors who offered abundant free, if conflicting, advice. "The first couple of years were tough. Finally I read German grape books and decided my own way." On Schmidt's instruction, he planted the vineyard in 1984 entirely to bacchus and grew that variety successfully for a decade before wineries decided the variety was losing fashion. His contract has moved from Sumac Ridge to **Calona** and finally to **Gray Monk**, which has an established market niche for the bacchus as a varietal wine. Yet when all contracts expired after the 1994 vintage, "nobody was really knocking down our door for the bacchus," Nancy Jessacher said. They decided to switch some of the vineyard to the hottest red variety and, in the spring of 1995, hired a professional crew to graft half of the 4,500 bacchus vines over to merlot. Unlike some other growers, Jessacher was not entirely pleased with the result, finding that only 70 percent of the grafted vines grew successfully. It has convinced Jessacher to rely on his own counsel and on the lessons of his hard-earned experience. "I take so much care [in the vineyard that] some people think I am crazy," he said. In his own nursery he has cultivated merlot, cabernet franc and a small number of chardonnay vines for his vineyard. His meticulous touch carries over to home winemaking, also self-taught. His favourite wine? Bacchus with a touch of sweet reserve.

JOHANNISBERG RIESLING: One of the oldest of the great white wine grape varieties, with at least five hundred years of documented history in Germany, the variety increasingly is called either riesling or white riesling or Rhine riesling as it is now being cultivated around the globe, not just in the shadow of Schloss Johannisberg on the Rhine. Much confusion has been caused when the name riesling has been appropriated for varieties whose only similarity is that they also produce white wines, a case in point being the vastly inferior *Okanagan riesling*, now essentially banished from British Columbia vineyards.

The true riesling vines first began to be planted extensively in British Co-

lumbia in the early 1970s when *Jordan & Ste-Michelle*'s German-born winemakers, *Dieter Guttler* and *Josef Zimmerman,* asked growers to plant the variety. The variety since has become a star with a number of wineries. The grape, best suited to the cooler vineyards of the north Okanagan, is exceptionally versatile, capable of being made into crisp and richly flavoured dry wines at one end of the spectrum and seductive icewines at the other end. At *Summerhill*, riesling is used for the winery's best-selling Cipes Brut sparkling wine.

JONES, CHERIE (1969–): The winemaker who joined *St. Hubertus* estate winery for the 1995 vintage, Jones was born in Gisborne, N. Z., an agricultural community that calls itself that country's chardonnay capital. However, Jones became interested in wines while helping pay her way through university by working in wine bars. After getting a bachelor of arts degree, she managed a wine bar for a year in the New Zealand tourist resort of Queenstown. She spent another two and a half years in Europe, including a year completing her wine immersion at a London wine bar. Returning to New Zealand, Jones took the rigorous diploma course in viticulture and enology at Lincoln University where one of her classmates was *Ross Mirko,* who subsequently became the winemaker at *CedarCreek*. After graduating in 1994, Jones joined the Corbans winery in Gisborne to work the 1995 vintage there while Mirko passed her résumé around in British Columbia, resulting in an offer from the rapidly expanding St. Hubertus winery. In Canada, she has been given much more responsibility early in her career than she would have expected to get in the more mature New Zealand and Australian wine industries. "This region is burgeoning as a frontier for winemaking," Jones says of British Columbia. "There are so many opportunities for me here." Jones returned to the southern hemisphere to work the 1996 vintage at a new winery in Marlborough, one of New Zealand's best viticultural regions, but was back in the Okanagan to bottle the 1995 St. Hubertus wines.

JONN, MARION (1929–): The Okanagan's first estate winery, established in 1978, was the grandly named Chateau Jonn de Trepanier. Jonn was the owner's surname, Trepanier comes from the name of the road near Peachland at the end of which the winery is located, and Chateau was swagger. Jonn was born in Bulgaria and raised in Sofia in a family with a winegrowing tradition; his grandfather had a vineyard in the country and made wine eagerly sought after by the local restaurants. A refugee from invading Russian armies, Jonn ended up in Germany in 1944 where he found work after the war with the American army and then studied philosophy at the University of Heidelberg until emigrating to Canada in 1954. Having learned the requisite skills from the American military, he got a data processing job with the Alberta government in Edmonton.

Newly married, Jonn and his wife, Irma, drove to the Seattle World's Fair in 1962 by way of the Okanagan Valley. "I said this is where I want to live," he recalled. Characteristically impulsive, Jonn bought an undeveloped twelve-acre property near Kelowna that year and in 1965 moved to Kelowna when he found a data processing job with a trucking

firm. When he could get no irrigation water, he sold his patch of land and in 1968 bought the property at the top end of Trepanier Bench Road, which already had a house and a small vineyard. Most of the land was so rugged and rocky that Jonn took several years to prepare to plant a large vineyard in 1972. "From the minute I moved there, my idea was to plant and start making my own wine," he said. The varieties planted included Okanagan riesling, foch and rougeon but Jonn now started reading the literature and attending grape forums in Washington and realized that he also could grow vinifera. Beginning in 1974 he began planting johannisberg riesling, pinot blanc, gewurztraminer, merlot and pinot noir.

Jonn's plans for a winery took shape after he met Dennis Culver, a Vancouver accountant and talented amateur winemaker. Culver first bought some of Jonn's grapes and later prepared the winery business plan when Jonn began pestering the government for a licence in 1975. A gambler, Jonn also arranged to have **Mission Hill** crush his grapes and produce wine for him, with the result that the $350,000 winery opened in 1978 with a healthy inventory both of Okanagan riesling and of a red that had matured up to three years in used whisky barrels. He did much of his own winemaking but was careful to get help from experienced professionals, notably **Tom Hoenisch** at Casabello. "I wasn't making my wine blindly," Jonn said. Yet a year after opening the winery, Jonn suddenly sold it when former Calona winemaker **Bob Claremont** offered him just over $1 million. Jonn considered developing a new Okanagan vineyard with his half of the proceeds (his wife, from whom he separated, took the other half). However, he invested in oil and gas stocks, only to see most of his equity wiped out when those stocks collapsed in 1981. Jonn then moved to Ottawa, working again as a computer programmer, until he agreed to take on the development of a vineyard in Venezuela in 1987. Ironically, the investor behind that project was then wiped out in the 1987 stock market crash. Jonn subsequently returned to Canada, living in Toronto as a semi-retired computer consultant, but never abandoning his interest in viticulture. In 1996 he be-

came engaged with several partners in a grand, perhaps even grandiose, scheme to develop vineyards in China and to revive a modern but failed winery there. "I'm back in action again," he exulted after returning from a month-long visit to China.

JORDAN & STE-MICHELLE CELLARS:
See *Growers' Wines Ltd.*

I   *Beverage Alcohol Reporter*, November 1968.

KKK

KAISER, KARL (1941 –): The Austrian-born co-founder and winemaker with **Inniskillin Wines Inc.**, Kaiser got his first taste of viticulture by working in the vineyards at a Cistercian monastery where he was a novice before deciding to become a teacher. Later he helped during the vintage in an Austrian vineyard owned by the grandparents of his future wife, Sylvia. They emigrated to Canada in 1969 so Sylvia could be near her parents in St. Catherines. In Canada Kaiser began making his own wines when he was appalled by the poor domestic wines then available. Kaiser met future partner **Donald Ziraldo** in 1971 while buying vines from the Ziraldo family nursery. Kaiser won an argument that better wine could be made in Ontario by sharing a bottle of his own chelois rosé with Ziraldo. They joined to form Inniskillin in 1974 and remained partners to launch Inniskillin's Okanagan winery twenty years later.

KALAMALKA ESTATE WINERY: Planned for a 1998 opening, this winery is based on the ninety-two acre Sunset Vineyards on Black Sage Road, south of Oliver. Proprietor **Rob Milne** has contracted to sell three-quarters of the vineyard's production to major wineries for several years. But starting in 1996 he began turning some of the rest of the young vineyard's grapes into wine under the supervision of an established winery. When Milne, a Vancouver businessman, began planning the winery, he retained a marketing company to search for a name more regionally resonant than Sunset Vineyards. Kalamalka, which also is

the name of a lake near Vernon, almost one hundred miles north of the winery, appealed to him. It is an aboriginal word meaning "water of many colours."

KEREMEOS VINEYARDS LTD.: This estate winery was established in 1984 just east of Keremeos by three partners: Dick Coleman, Larry Bryan and **Joe Ritlop**. The vineyard and winemaking was handled by Ritlop. It was subsequently reorganized under the name St. Lazlo. Grapegrower Ritlop was now fully in charge.

KERNER: This versatile white grape accounted for only 60 tonnes or less than 2 percent of total production of wine grapes in British Columbia in 1994. However, the wines produced from it that year ranged from bone dry (at **Carriage House Winery**) to icewine (at **Tinhorn Creek**). The variety was developed by plant breeders in Germany and released commercially in 1969, quickly becoming the third most-widely planted vine there because it yields better than riesling and the wine can almost rival riesling's quality. The grape is named after one Justinus Kerner, a nineteenth-century German writer of drinking songs.[1]

KETTLE VALLEY WINERY: Opened in 1996, this Naramata winery is named for the historic Kettle Valley Railroad, some of whose abandoned roadbed and tunnels on the east side of the Okanagan Valley can be seen from the Kettle Valley vineyard. (The railroad operated from 1910 to 1973; a short tourist section reopened near Summerland in 1995.)

The winery debuted with a big barrel-aged 1992 pinot noir and both a 1994 chardonnay and pinot noir. In the 1995 vintage the winery also produced ice-wines from pinot noir and from chardonnay, quite possibly the first time those varieties have been vinted in that manner anywhere. The winery also produces cabernet sauvignon and merlot. Partners **Tim Watts** and **Bob Ferguson** own about nine prime vineyard acres, purchased between 1989 and 1991.

Hans Kiltz (photo courtesy of John Schreiner)

KILTZ, DR. HANS (1938–): The proprietor and winemaker at *Blue Grouse Vineyards* near Duncan on Vancouver Island, Kiltz was born in Berlin and has a doctorate in microbiology. He practised as a veterinarian for twenty years in Africa and Asia. In 1988 he and his wife, Evangeline, moved to Canada to have their two children educated here. They purchased a picturesque farm in the Cowichan Valley previously operated as a vineyard by veteran grapegrower *John Harper*. Kiltz, whose relatives in Germany are winegrowers, continued tending — as a hobby — the vines left behind by

Harper. When the government allowed farmgate wineries, Kiltz secured a licence and opened Blue Grouse in 1993. Specialties based on the seven-acre vineyard include pinot noir, pinot gris, müller-thurgau, bacchus and ortega.

KING BROTHERS: Don King (born in 1951) and Rod King (born in 1953) grew up on an orchard that the King family had operated for half a century northeast of Penticton, overlooking Okanagan Lake. Shortly after the brothers took over the family farm, they decided to convert to grapes. "We didn't see much future in tree fruits," Rod King says, admitting that "prior to 1990, we had never seen a vine planted in our lives." Between 1992 and 1996, they planted forty acres of vines, including chardonnay, merlot, auxerrois, cabernet franc and cabernet sauvignon. The most daring variety on the vineyard's deep, rich loam is syrah. "We've never had a problem growing anything on this site," Rod King says. The vineyard was contracted in 1995 to *CedarCreek Estate Winery*.

KIRSCHMANN, HANNA: Entirely surrounded by residential development, Hanna Kirschmann's beautifully-situated Summerland vineyard produces full-flavoured gewurztraminer grapes, the vines growing in a five-acre bowl that captures the optimum heat units. "To me, it's a special place," said Kirschmann, who changed her mind about selling it in 1996 when her son, Paul, decided to switch from teaching school to helping her grow grapes. German-born Hanna Kirschmann has lived on the property since 1964 when she and her late husband, also called Paul, bought it because they wanted to raise their four children in what was then a rural orchard. Neither had a farming background; he was a miner and Hanna, who became a secretary, was the daughter of a policeman. "I'm not an outdoors person," she says, "but I just love growing things." They converted the orchard to de chaunac and foch grapes in 1968. When her husband died in a 1981 car accident, Hanna took over the vineyard, successfully juggling that and her family with a range of interests extending from ballroom dancing to foreign language study. After the 1988 industry vine removal program, she replanted to gewurztraminer and semillon. After the 1995 harvest, the late-ripening semillon vines came out as Hanna Kirschmann decided to focus entirely on one variety. An orderly harvest with a single variety would give her more time to pursue Spanish studies in Ecuador, one of her favourite South American countries.

KLOKOCKA, BOHUMIR (1935–1995) AND VERA (1942–):

The founders of *Hillside Cellars*, the Klokockas both worked for the Czech state airline (he as a mechanic, she as a ticket clerk) until they defected in 1968, coming to Canada that fall after several months as refugees in Austria. Skiing enthusiasts, they moved to the Okanagan to work at the Big White resort near Kelowna. Bohumir ultimately resumed his trade as a sheet metal worker in the Western Star truck plant in Kelowna. In 1979 they purchased an orchard on Naramata Road, and after converting it to grapes in 1984, Vera Klokocka taught herself to become a winemaker. After she had become a skilled amateur vintner, she emerged as a leader of the band of farm winemakers that successfully pressed the provincial government in 1989 to create the farmgate winery licence for ambitious producers with vineyards too small for the estate winery category. (Others included *Adolf Kruger* and *Guenther Lang*.) After her husband's death, she sold the winery in 1996.

KRUGER, ADOLF (1931 –):

The founder, with his family, of *Wild Goose Vineyards*, Kruger was born in a farming community near Berlin. After arriving in Canada in 1951 and working the harvest on a Manitoba wheat farm, he became an electrical designer and, in his free time, a hobbyist yacht designer. He brought his family to Vancouver in 1964 where he pursued yacht design more aggressively while also working as an electrical draftsman with a firm of consulting engineers. Having become a capable amateur winemaker, he purchased vineyard property near Okanagan Falls in 1983 and began planting the next year. His new career as a grapegrower seemed in jeopardy in 1988 when it appeared probable grape sales to wineries would dry up after the Canada-U.S. free trade agreement took effect. To protect his future Kruger became a leader of the small growers who successfully lobbied the provincial government for farmgate winery licenses.

KRUGER, ROLAND (1964–):

An electronics technician, Roland Kruger dropped that career to work full-time with his father *Adolf Kruger* shortly after family-owned *Wild Goose Vineyards* opened in 1990. The personable Roland handles much of the marketing. His older brother, Hagen, who was born in 1960 and who is a draftsman, also finds time to work in the winery.

---

[1] Jancis Robinson. *Vines, Grapes and Wines*. (See SOURCES for complete reference.)

LLL

LABELS

Thirty seconds: in the judgment of Mission Hill's Vinetta Peek, that is all the time the label on a bottle of wine has to catch the consumer's eye in a liquor store. "They are a huge marketing tool for us," she says of Mission Hill's labels, frequent trend-setters in design and technology. **John Simes,** Mission Hill's award-winning winemaker, says that packaging sells the first bottle of a wine and only then can his wine sell the second. One of British Columbia's more innovative producers of wine labels, Langley's Tapp Technologies Inc., traces its genesis to a 1983 conversation between **Mission Hill** owner **Anthony von Mandl** and Jay Tapp, then a packaging industry executive. Von Mandl expressed frustration that the printing industry seemed unable to produce the intricate labels von Mandl wanted on his wines. A decade later, using million-dollar presses developed in Japan, Tapp won Mission Hill as his company's first label customer. Other large North American wineries have since adopted Tapp labels or sought out other printers with competitive technology, with the result that a profound aesthetic revolution in label design has taken place.

Wineries in British Columbia (and elsewhere) now revise their labels continually in a clamour for the consumer's attention in a very competitive market. One strategy is to create packaging whose very sophistication proclaims that the wine is of high quality. Many icewine producers, who of necessity charge a lot of money for their wines, have adopted seductively sleek Italian bottles whose deep olive gold hues ooze a fashion model's allure. **Quails' Gate Vineyards Estate Winery** signalled that its 1994 Old Vines Foch was a distinguished wine justifying its high price by bottling it in just such a package, finished with a striking three-piece label that included an embossed gold medallion. Only when viewed under a magnifying glass did it become evident that the medallion was merely a design element, not a replica of a prestigious competition's gold medal. In a world of proliferating wineries, clever packaging and striking labels clearly support and advance a winery's struggle to be noticed. It was not always so. Prior to the middle of the nineteenth century, labels were rare, in part because adhesives and printing material were inadequate and in part because fine wines were decanted before being served and identifying silver medallions were placed around the neck of decanters. It also was customary to trademark the corks, if only to discourage fraud. As well, it had been traditional for producers to sell their wines by the barrel to be bottled, if at all, by wine merchants or dining establishments. Paper labels became common about 1860 but even then were fixed on bottles by the sellers rather than by the producers. Estate bottling became routine after the 1920s but label designs, once settled upon, remain static for years.

In any event, the label was more the owner's signature than a point-of-sale marketing device since wine marketing was not as dynamic as it is today. Before self-serve liquor stores — the first one in Canada opened in British Columbia in 1968 — a Canadian consumer wrote his order on a piece of paper, and gave it

to the clerk who retrieved the desired product from behind the counter. The labels had very little to do with the consumer's initial choice. Consequently, labels were simple and inexpensive. When **Casabello** wines launched its first products in 1967, the winery used oval brown paper labels with cookie-cutter fluted edges and with one or at most two colours. Similar kraft paper labels, simple to the point of being dull, were common in the British Columbia industry, a classic example being the label used by now-defunct **Vinitera Estate Winery** for its dry 1979 Okanagan riesling. A large square tawny label framed with a bronze border, it featured a sober sketch of the winery with only the building's red roof tiles giving life to the label. (The medium-dry version of the same wine had a very pale green label but with the same red roof.) It is difficult to understand why the winery abandoned its bucolic 1978 label with a red sun setting on a bright green vineyard and juicy bunch of grapes. The **Chateau Jonn de Trepanier** debut label for its 1977 riesling featured a full-colour scenic vineyard photograph more appropri-

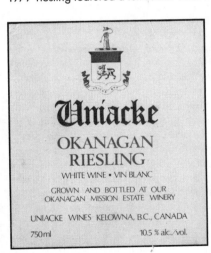

ate to a small-town hardware store calendar. When it came to market, **Uniacke Wines** opted for clean white labels with two colours but with the winery's name, already unfamiliar to consumers, printed in forbidding Olde English script. **Gray Monk** succeeded despite festooning its label with even more difficult German script and terminology, but experienced a major increase in liquor store sales after converting in 1991 to crisp white, black and gold labels that were both elegant and accessible. Label design shortcomings reflected the industry's lack of experience in sophisticated packaging. The 1960s and 1970s were a time, after all, when **Ben Ginter,** a former bulldozer operator, put his own bearded visage on Uncle Ben's wines, very likely the only winery owner in the history of British Columbia to seek immortality on a wine label.

Ginter also was one of the first to take playfulness — as represented by the cuddly duckling on Andrés **Baby Duck** — to the point of outrageous humour, as in Fuddle Duck and Hot Goose. Those were the times. In 1980 a Calgary winery called Stoneycroft Cellars produced a line of carbonated fruit wines under the Fanny Hill brand, named for the heroine of a salacious novel that had been banned briefly in the 1960s. The blackberry wine was called Fanny Hill's Bramble Bush. Because the wines were not as well made as the labels, Stoneycroft soon failed.

By the mid-1970s wineries had begun to grasp the marketing power of labels, however. This was a pivotal decade in British Columbia wine, which had been cloistered from the world by a liquor board uninterested in wines from elsewhere (and probably not interested in wine at all!). Imported wines began to flood into British Columbia after 1975 and the superior packaging signalled that the wines also might be superior (as they

often were). The Okanagan vineyards were slow to plant the grapes needed to compete but the marketers in the wineries moved more quickly. With **Calona** leading the way with **Schloss Laderheim**, the commercial wineries invented European-sounding names by the dozen for what came to be called **pseudo-labels**. The generous interpretation of this strategy was that the vintners were communicating the profound changes being made in their traditional wine styles to emulate the wines of Europe. The cynic would say that the wool was being pulled over the eyes of unsophisticated consumers. In either case, the strategy sold a lot of wine and saved wineries from failing. And the pseudo-label wines, while not what they pretended to be, pleased thousands of consumers; some brands continue to do so today.

The truly profound changes in wine quality in the 1990s and the significant increase in the number of wineries has been a boon to the label industry. The established wineries have revised label design to communicate that there is better wine in their bottles while the new entrants are fighting for recognition. And they are all dealing with consumers who know more and require better information.

When Chateau Jonn de Trepanier released its riesling, the label included the instruction "Serve Chilled" prominently displayed next to the photograph. Next it became popular to advise what foods to match with

the wine: Mission Hill in the 1980s developed a label that included a grid of wine and food recommendations that was forbidding in its complexity. Labels of the 1990s have become minor courses in viticulture and enology, feeding a perceived new level of consumer curiosity. Mission Hill's Vinetta Peek explains: "We aren't putting as much of what I used to call bumpf onto it — the flowery descriptions. We're getting more into technical information, varietal information, and more into educating our consumers in what our wines are all about. They want to know exactly how the grapes were grown, how they were picked, what the weather was like, how many bottles were made. Because they are purchasing this wine and it's now part of their life, they want to know something about it."

Typical of today's hard-sell label is the wine description that **Blue Mountain Vineyard and Cellars** put on its 1992 pinot noir. "Our 1992 Pinot Noir is 100% estate grown, produced and bottled. The vineyards produce a beautiful rich full bodied wine. The complex array of black cherry and berry aromas and flavours make this wine an ideal food companion. Barrel aging has added interesting chocolate and spicy characters." Paradoxically, the winery dropped back-label copy from its labels with its 1995 vintage when the mercurial proprietor, **Ian Mavety**, decided he disliked the practice.

Label design at a small winery generally reflects the owner's values, tastes and budget. At larger wineries like Mission Hill, more money is spent on a design process that is also more scientific, usually starting with a survey of competitive labels from elsewhere in the world. Peek explains: "We bring in all of our competition and we evaluate what works and what doesn't work. We determine where the brand should be positioned and who the target market is. Then we do some rough designs based on that and take them into focus groups." As many as a dozen computer-generated label designs are affixed to wine bottles. "We sit down with our consumers and ask them how these designs appeal to them; and not only our designs but all of our competition. Sometimes it is quite an eye-opener. We get so close to things and we think, this is perfect. And when you put the design into a focus group, they will trash it because it is not what they want." Mission Hill's designers once created an avant garde dark black diamond label that was meant to communicate elevated wine quality in a particular category — only to have the focus group compare it to a shampoo bottle label. "We realized we had gone way too far." Not all wineries can afford the expense of assembling focus groups or test panels to react to new label ideas and will rely on the less-structured approach of taking new design ideas to public tastings and soliciting reactions.

What is required on wine labels by law has expanded substantially since wine production began in British Columbia. The short-lived Richmond Wineries, which was based in Steveston and absorbed by **Growers'**, had a brand called Myrtena. The only copy on the label of Myrtena Grape Wine was the name and location of the winery, the size of the bottle and the words "Fully Matured." The modern label includes not only the bottle size but the name and address of the winery; the type of wine (red or white, for example) in both English and French; alcohol by volume; and an all-important inventory number. By the mid-1990s the inventory number has grown to become an electronically readable bar code, a challenge to the label designer because the code is unattractive. It also is a nightmare to the printer because any minuscule error in reproducing the code can make it erroneous or unreadable, causing the vendors to return the wine. In some export markets, various health warnings also are required.

The breakthrough in creative label design in the 1990s has come with the printing industry's development of pressure-sensitive labels. Traditionally, labels have been glued to bottles. This has forced the design of labels to uniform shapes (square, oblong, round) so that the automatic glue applicators on bottling lines apply just the right amount of adhesive as each bottle passes. Even so, unsightly glue smears on bottles and labels fastened off centre, while rare, are not unusual. Pressure-sensitive labels can be virtually any shape, with two- and three-piece labels possible with modern bottling equipment. Mission Hill's first Vin Nouveau in 1982 carried a square one-piece kraft label which was given over to text telling where the grapes were grown. The 1995 Vin

Nouveau carried a two-piece front label with gold lettering proclaiming the winery's name and its VQA status as well a matching back label briefly telling consumers that a nouveau wine "is the first wine of the new vintage." The package subliminally communicated quality with its sophisticated elegance. The drawback to these intricate labels is cost: it can translate to a hefty 1 to 3 percent of the cost of the wine and is the reason why such labels are reserved for middle- to top-range wines.

Many wine labels include phrasing that may be evocative and at other times will be totally obscure. For a number of years Mission Hill borrowed the Australian practice of assigning bin numbers to wines. Internally, Mission Hill staff knew that Bin ABC Chenin Blanc was made from British Columbia grapes and Bin XYZ Chenin Blanc might be made from Washington state grapes — a distinction that generally eluded the consumer. More typically, wineries seek to distinguish quality levels by designating the best wines as *Reserve* wines. There has been a tendency towards terminological inflation. Mission Hill's top line is called *Grand Reserve*, as typified by the 1992 Chardonnay that won the **Avery's Trophy** in London in 1994. Ironically, when Mission Hill began exporting its Grand Reserve wines to Britain, it was required to drop that designation because the term

is reserved to the Royal Family. There is no industry standardization on label terminology; the consumer has no way to know whether a winery's *Limited Release* or *Private Reserve* is at the middle or top of its range (although price is usually a clue). Quails' Gate estate winery, for example, has a *Limited Release* range positioned between its *Proprietor's Selection* and its *Family Reserve* wines. As a further twist, Andrés puts its premium wines under the Peller Estates brand of which the top cut are bottled as *Limited Showcase* wines.

The expanding universe of wine labels has encouraged the hobby of label-collecting (such a collector is called a *vintitulist*). This is by no means an easy hobby since modern adhesives bond labels to bottles with determined firmness; indeed, white wine and champagne labels are almost impossible to soak off because the producer must assume that some of the wines will be chilled in ice buckets and labels must not float off during dinner. However, wineries usually will provide copies of labels to collectors, some of whom will request that the labels be signed by winemakers.

Artists' labels are especially appealing to some collectors. The best-known series of art labels in the world are those on the labels of Chateau Mouton-Rothschild, one of the great producers in Bordeaux. Almost every year since 1945, a different artist has produced work for the label. While the wines would be collectible on their intrinsic quality, collectors have paid premiums because of the famed artwork on the labels. While wineries in British Columbia have seldom used art labels, Calona Wines since 1991 has been featuring British Columbia artist **Robb Dunfield** on its premium table wines.

LADD, JACK: Successful Kelowna car dealer and city mayor who was president of **Calona Wines Ltd.** from 1941 to 1957, primarily as the genteel front for the immigrant Italians who really ran the place.

LAGNAZ, DANIEL (1954–): The winemaker at **Mission Hill** from 1982 until 1992 when he became the company's Vancouver-based technical manager, Lagnaz was born in the Swiss winemaking district of Aigle. After gaining experience there and in Spain as a vintner, Lagnaz in 1980 joined the Lindemans winery in Australia. He was recruited to Mission Hill two years later, produced a remarkably broad range of wines, ciders and eau-de-vies and quickly had the previously troubled winery winning awards and praise for the quality of its wines.

LAKE BREEZE VINEYARDS: Late in 1994 Swiss-born businessman Paul Moser and his wife, Vereena, purchased a thirteen-acre vineyard south of

Naramata, perched on a bluff overlooking Lake Okanagan and developed a winery named for the breezes from the lake that constantly wash across the vines. The winery opened in 1996. Formerly part of a larger vineyard operated by **Barry and Sue Irvine**, the Lake Breeze property is one of the most attractive natural winery sites in the Okanagan. A perfectionist with an artist's eye, Moser converted the rambling farm buildings into a wine estate transplanted from South Africa's picturesque Cape wine region. Dramatic white stucco walls frame the gate at the driveway into the winery, with the white stucco motif repeated on the buildings that look onto a shaded courtyard with a large picnic area.

"I got into winemaking extensively in South Africa," says Moser, a courtly, bearded man who was born in 1949 in a German-speaking canton in central Switzerland. Growing up in a village of 900, he apprenticed as a toolmaker. As a young man, he wanted to see the world. His first stop in 1969 was South Africa, where toolmakers were in such demand that airline tickets and accommodation were offered to skilled immigrants like Moser. Unlike her husband, Vereena Moser has a wine tradition in her family. Her mother grew up in the winegrowing Italian section of Switzerland and her mother and father had a vineyard at Lensburg, in central Switzerland, where Vereena grew up.

In South Africa the entrepreneurial Mosers — Vereena is both a bookkeeper and a health and beauty therapist — soon launched several manufacturing companies, including one that produced insulating materials. "We supplied most of the wine cellars," Moser says. "That is how I came into contact with the wine

industry. I found it an interesting field and we delved into it more and more." In 1994 the Mosers accepted what Paul describes as an unsolicited "fantastic offer" for their companies. "Now there was a new page in the book," he says. After an extended vacation in France, the Mosers came to British Columbia. He briefly considered starting a plastics company in Vancouver, decided the city was too big and travelled the province until discovering the Okanagan late in 1994. They purchased the Lake Breeze property that November, after a careful six-week research of available real estate, also securing an option to buy the remainder of the vineyard, should the Irvines sell it as well.

The Mosers acquired a property that the Irvines planted in the mid-1980s, choosing grape varieties, notably pinot blanc and pinot noir, that now are the backbone of Okanagan winemaking. Other varieties in the Lake Breeze vineyard include chardonnay, semillon, merlot, cabernet franc and gewurztraminer. Most of the production continues to be sold to **Sumac Ridge Estate Winery**. Moser cautiously started small as a farmgate winery but with the intention of upgrading to an estate winery licence. The winery's initial vintage in 1995, made by young South African winemaker **Garron Elmes**, totalled about 10,000 bottles. Moser's decision to hire a professional, like the craftsmanship lavished expensively on the winery buildings, reflects a determination to be among the best at the very beginning. "I do not believe in trials," says Moser. "From the start of your winemaking career, you should have good wines."

After a life as a toolmaker and

manufacturer, Moser's conversion to winegrower is total. "It is very honest work you do here," he muses. "You walk down the rows and you can see how the grapes turn colour. Day by day, you see how much they grow. You cannot compare it to anything else."

LANG, GUENTHER (1951 –): Born near Stuttgart in Germany, Lang was a junior manager with Daimler-Benz when he and his wife, Kristina, decided to emigrate the year after a 1979 vacation in the Okanagan. He bought a farm near Naramata with a nine-acre vineyard, learned to grow grapes and made his first wine in 1981. A growing list of awards in amateur competitions led him to begin in 1985 applying for a winery licence that was granted five years later, when the new farmgate winery licence had been created.

LANG VINEYARDS: The first of British Columbia's farmgate wineries, Lang Vineyard opened May 25, 1990. Guenther Lang first applied for a winery licence in 1985 but found his nine-acre vineyard was too small for an estate winery, which is required to have twenty acres. When written in 1978, the estate winery rules perversely shut the door on many would-be vintners, since the average Okanagan vineyard was then only fifteen acres; and that average dropped to just eight acres after 1988, when two-thirds of all vines, including several entire large vineyards, were uprooted. Lang lobbied persistently, along with *Adolf Kruger, Vera* and *Bohumir Klokocka* and *Wolfgang Zeller*, until the province created the new farmgate winery category in 1989 for small growers. The Lang Vineyards opening was followed in short order by Kruger's Wild Goose and Klokockas' Hillside Cellars. (Zeller chose to remain a grapegrower and a dealer in specialized winery and vineyard equipment.)

LARCH HILLS WINERY: The Okanagan's most northern winery, Larch Hills was established in 1996 just north of Enderby, taking its name from the district in which it is located. In 1991, owners *Hans* and *Hazel Nevrkla* planted a four-acre vineyard amid the challenging slopes of their seventy-three-acre property. "Most of it is inaccessible for tractors and other equipment because it's too steep," Hazel Nevrkla says. The vineyards are on a southerly slope with a 15 percent grade. The major varieties planted are ortega, siegerrebe, madeleine sylvaner with smaller plantings of madeleine angevine and optima, all early maturing white varieties. Planned for 1996 was a test planting of agria, an early ripening Hungarian red grape also grown on Vancouver Island. Hans Nevrkla, an award-winning amateur winemaker who has taught winemaking courses, produced a modest 400 gallons from the 1995 vintage, the winery's first, with some wines bone dry and others in the off-dry or Germanic style.

LATITUDE FIFTY: Launched in mid-1991, this was the first proprietary white wine from *Gray Monk*. An attractive fruity blend primarily of johannisberg riesling and bacchus, the wine accounted for half of Gray Monk's entire sales within three years. The wine was so named because the 50th parallel of latitude, generally regarded as the practical northern limit for viticulture, actually is a few miles *south* of Gray Monk's vineyard.

LeComte, Albert (1936–): Le-Comte was born in Prince Albert, Sask., into a family with no wine heritage (his father was an electronics technician in the air force). After a business career in automobile repair and electric sign manufacturing in Vancouver, LeComte moved to Oliver in 1975 to represent the sign business he and his brother, Maurice, operated. A home winemaker, he bought a vineyard near Okanagan Falls in 1983 and immediately began developing the *LeComte Estate Winery,* which received its licence in 1986. A restless entrepreneur, LeComte had the winery for sale several times, perhaps because winemaking tasks conflicted with other interests that range from real estate development to fishing in Mexico. The winery was sold in 1995 to a group of investors headed by *Harry McWatters* and *Robert Wareham.*

LeComte Estate Winery: Established in 1986, this winery consistently produces a fine concentrated gewurztraminer from its vineyard on a cool plateau on Hawthorne Mountain above Okanagan Falls. The extensive LeComte offering includes well-made reds from such varieties as chelois, foch and chancellor. The winery also has a full suite of vinifera wines, including merlot, pinot noir, chardonnay, riesling and auxerrois. In 1996 it launched the *Hawthorne Mountain* label for its premium wines.

Lemberger: An Austrian red grape variety known there as *blaufrankish*, this was included among the many varieties imported in 1976 from *Geisenheim* for the *Becker* project. While the variety became important in Washington state, it was not propagated in British Columbia

because the Geisenheim plants were discovered to be contaminated with several viruses.[1] Small plantings have been made in the 1990s from clean vine material.

Lessner, Ivan (1951–): Born in Budapest to a family who had been winegrowers and wine merchants for more than two hundred years, Lessner grew up in Vienna to which his family had fled in 1956 when the Soviet Union crushed the Hungarian uprising. A winemaking graduate of *Geisenheim*, Lessner came to Canada to attend a cousin's wedding in 1980. A social telephone call to a fellow Geisenheimer working at *Jordan & Ste-Michelle* landed Lessner a research job at the winery's St. Catherines, Ont., plant. The following year he became the winemaker at the company's Calgary winery, and in 1984, he was promoted to winemaster at the company's Surrey, B.C., winery. When that winery closed, Lessner established his own company in Whiterock, B.C., IDL Consulting, representing European winemaking machinery and supplies.

At the Surrey winery, the range of wines made by Lessner and winemaker Joseph Vollmer included prize-winning johannisberg rieslings. They also had fun with the wines. In 1986 Lessner, a sportscar buff and a member of the Austin-Healey Club of British Columbia, proudly bottled fifty cases of riesling with an Austin-Healey label for a club rally in Whistler.

Levine, John (1939–): A founder both of the Vancouver American Wine Society and of the Vancouver Playhouse International Wine Festival, Levine grew up in Vancouver amid a typically Canadian isolation from wines, even though his father's businesses included hotels. After getting a hotel and restaurant administration degree at Michigan State University, Levine returned home and in 1961 opened what he describes as Vancouver's first pizzeria. It took him three years to get a liquor licence and when he did, he relied on Wine-Art founder **Stanley Anderson** to draw up the wine list (Anderson's payment was a free pizza). Levine's appreciation of wines began when the liquor board shipped him at a bargain price a better quality Portuguese red than had been ordered for the restaurant. A quick study when it comes to wine, Levine snapped up the remaining twenty cases in British Columbia and put half in his own cellar at home. "It grew from there," Levine said later. "Wine turned into an interest, which turned into a hobby, which became a passion." The cheerfully rotund Levine became a wine writer, educator and critic whose approach to all wines is enthusiastically generous.

The **Vancouver Playhouse International Wine Festival** was created when Levine joined the board of the Vancouver Playhouse, a professional theatre, and found himself on the special events committee which was responsible for fundraising. Levine had recently attended the Monterey Wine Festival in California, was impressed and suggested the Playhouse do something similar. The first festival in 1979, a tasting of Robert Mondavi wines, was spread over four sittings limited to two hundred persons at each. The Playhouse netted $1,000. In its second year, the festival featured the wines of Sonoma's Chateau St. Jean. In 1981, however, forty-five California wineries were enlisted. At the suggestion of the **Liquor Distribution Branch**, British Columbia wineries (as well as others from abroad) were invited to the festival in 1983. By 1996, the festival was so successful that $225,000 was generated for the Vancouver Playhouse. The American Wine Society also was formed in 1979 by Levine, in part to satisfy the festival's insatiable need for volunteer workers.[2]

LIQUOR ADMINISTRATION BRANCH OF BRITISH COLUMBIA: The retailing of alcoholic beverages was conducted under the LAB in the early 1970s. The LAB was effectively the Liquor Control Board under a new name; in 1975, it was split into two bodies, with the Liquor Distribution Branch responsible for retailing from a headquarters in Vancouver and the Liquor Control and Licensing Branch looking after licensing from Victoria.

The New Democratic government of 1972–75 began to open up the distribution of alcoholic beverages in British Columbia by, among other measures, opening new liquor stores. Between April 1974 and February 1975, for example, fourteen new stores were opened and three were relocated. The Social Credit government, which regained office late in 1975, continued to liberalize liquor retailing, moving both branches from the enforcement-minded jurisdiction of the Attorney General to the Ministry of Consumer and Corporate Affairs. The move was not merely symbolic: it represented an attitudinal change by the government. Liquor was returned to the Attorney General's ministry when the New Democrats took office in November 1991.

LIQUOR CONTROL BOARD OF BRIT-ISH COLUMBIA: Under the Moderation Act, the LCB, headquartered in Victoria, was established in April 1921, at the end of prohibition in British Columbia, to control the distribution of alcoholic beverages and to license those establishments where it could be served. The first seventeen stores opened June 15 and within nine months, the board had established fifty-one retail outlets.[3]

Aside from a profit of $1,772,971 in the board's first nine and a half months,[4] the start was hardly exemplary. The Liberal government of the day appointed three members to the LCB, all of them patronage appointments. The first chairman, Archie Mainwaring Johnson, was a New Zealand native who had been an unsuccessful Liberal candidate in the Nelson electoral district in the 1916 election and had then become deputy attorney general. By 1924 the government fired all three after an audit criticized the board's performance. Some of the biggest difficulties had been created by the LCB's freewheeling Vancouver member, J.H. Falconer, who had such good relations with some brewers that he would have barrels of their beers shipped to vendors even if the vendors had not ordered the beer. He was also accused of taking pay-offs from distillers. In addition, Falconer's brother was a shareholder in something called the California Wine Company, whose plant was on False Creek in Vancouver.[5]

The triumvirate were replaced with Hugh Davidson, a tire company executive in Vancouver who served as the sole member and chairman of the LCB. But as Robert Campbell wrote in *Demon Rum or Easy Money:* "Davidson inherited a board with even more patronage potential, for beer parlours [now allowed] had turned the LCB into a licensing agency." And patronage pay-offs became so extensive — distiller Henry Riefel testified in December 1926 that he had contributed nearly $100,000 to Liberal politicians — that the government named a commission under a judge to investigate apparent pay-offs to LCB staff. This was one of several federal or provincial inquiries delving into corruption around the sale of liquor, culminating with one in 1929 (when a new Conservative government had taken power from the Liberals) that recommended "an entire upheaval" of liquor administration. The Conservatives replaced Davidson with a three-person Liquor Control Board, chaired by Henry B. Thomson, who had sat for two terms as a Conservative member of the legislature from Victoria. But in 1932, falling revenues from the LCB during the Depression caused the government to pare the board to one person, William F. Kennedy, who had been the Conservative member for Okanagan North. The LCB finally settled down under Kennedy, who remained chairman until he died in 1951. His successor was the redoubtable *Lt.-Col. Donald McGugan,* who stayed there until 1969 when, at eighty years of age, the government retired him. By that time the LCB was wildly successful as a revenue machine, returning to the province a profit of $56,055,120 in the fiscal year to March 31, 1969. Judge Charles Morrow, in his 1970 liquor inquiry commission report, commented tartly that the population of the province had only increased 400 percent in the forty-eight years since the LCB began while its profits had soared 2200 percent.

LIQUOR DISTRIBUTION BRANCH OF BRITISH COLUMBIA: In 1975, on the advice of management consultants Urwick Currie & Partners, the government separated the retailing function of the Liquor Control Board from the licensing duties. The retail arm became known as the Liquor Distribution Branch, with its headquarters moved to Vancouver from Victoria. Licensing was vested in the newly created Liquor Control and Licensing Branch. For some time there continued to be policy confusion. "I am somewhat alarmed about the confusion that seems to exist in all our minds about who issues official directives on what, relating to liquor," complained Consumer and Corporate Affairs deputy minister *Tex Enemark* in a testy memorandum in September 1977 to the general managers of the two branches.

The government wanted liquor retailing run in a businesslike fashion. Liquor stores had been opened initially in 1921 under legislation called the Moderation Act, with institutional attitudes to match. The stores built during the 1930s and 1940s were as uninspired as small-town bank branches. "Curtains were installed in all front windows so children could not see into the stores," the LDB noted in its 70th annual report. "In the '50s and '60s, the [liquor control] board built many of its own stores and used glass brick extensively, which let in the light, but ensured that the interiors of the stores were not visible to young eyes."

For many years, it went largely unnoticed that a disproportionate number of liquor stores had been opened adjacent to Canada Safeway Ltd. supermarkets in premises owned by the grocery chain. "It is all above board, of course," Enemark explained to his minister in a memorandum in 1977. "In effect, Safeway offers to rent the Liquor Distribution Branch suitable store space adjacent to their stores at what amounts to grossly subsidized rent. The result is a reinforcement of shopper and traffic patterns past Safeway's doors. I have no doubt that this practice has been a major factor in allowing Safeway to become entrenched in the British Columbia market as the price leader."[6]

Under its mandate, the new LDB opened stores and greatly increased the selection of wines and other products available in British Columbia. "Within the last couple of years, for the first time, senior officials of the Liquor Distribution Branch have gone overseas to see what was available and to discuss price and availability with overseas suppliers," Enemark noted in a memo in September 1977. The choice in the liquor stores prior to this time could only be described as abysmal. A 1964 price list included five champagnes and twenty-five other imported table wines, with only one Bordeaux chateau, Chateau Pontet Canet, but several pages of domestic wines, most of them sweet and fortified. By early 1978 the LDB listed 1,470 products, more than double the selection a decade earlier, and it was still adding products. By December 1980, when the LDB opened what it described as the world's largest liquor store at 39th and Cambie in Vancouver, the LDB's 1,962 listings included 1,271 wines, most of which were table wines. The LDB, in fact, has become so attuned to communicating its products that in May 1982 it sponsored what undoubtedly was the first product tasting for wine writers ever organized in the history of the LDB and its predecessors.[7] The LDB put most of its salespeople through product knowledge courses and assigned trained specialists to its major stores, a dramatic improvement from earlier decades. Until the 1960s, sales personnel were discouraged, and sometimes forbidden, to provide product information to customers. The consumer-friendly changes continued in the 1990s. The LDB's 1992 annual report noted proudly that it had inaugurated a toll-free "1-800" number for providing product information; that it had installed three-minute wine chillers in specialty stores (refrigerated walk-in coolers appeared in eight stores in 1994); and that it had begun to allow in-store tastings for customers of LDB products. In the following year, some LDB stores even began selling accessories such as corkscrews, gift bags and wine literature.

The LDB has become one of the largest retailers in British Columbia, with 220 stores in the year ended March 31, 1995, generating sales of $1 billion. In addition to these stores, the LDB also supervised — and got revenues from — 270 agency stores (private beer and wine stores, including a number in small communities and stores operated by wineries,

breweries and distilleries). The total sales from all outlets reported by the LDB was $1.5 billion, a third of which is net profit collected by the government. See also *Tex Enemark, Robert A. Wallace.*

LIQUOR STORES: The British Columbia liquor store with the greatest sales volume by far is the Liquor Distribution Branch's Store 100, also known as the central licensee store in Vancouver. This is the warehouse store where most hotels and restaurants do their shopping. It is not open to the general public. In the LDB's 1994–95 fiscal year, Store 100 achieved sales of nearly $65 million or 6 percent of the LDB's total sales that year.

The LDB opened its flagship store at 39th and Cambie in Vancouver on December 13, 1980, leasing a former Safeway supermarket with enough display space for the 2,000 products offered by the LDB, including the complete selection of specialty wines. Most other large liquor stores in British Columbia subsequently carried almost as many products. All of the LDB's stores will order specialty products requested by customers.

The Top Ten Liquor Stores in 1994–95 by Sales

Orchard Park	Kelowna	$15,672,193
39th St. & Cambie	Vancouver	$14,394,076
Fort Street	Victoria	$12,347,814
Broadway & Maple	Vancouver	$11,468,925
Fourth Avenue	Prince George	$10,787,058
#5	Campbell River	$10,761,100
Terminal Park	Nanaimo	$10,753,089
Langley Willowbrook	Langley	$10,348,243
#12	Duncan	$10,146,527
#113	Vancouver Collingwood	$9,935,528

The smallest store by sales volume in 1994–95 was: Greenwood, $316,743.

LOCHBICHLER, HANS (1940–): Born in Salzburg, Aus., Lochbichler emigrated to Canada in 1982 to get his family away from the tensions of the Cold War and to expose them to North American opportunity. An entrepreneur, he established a chain of family restaurants called Uncle Willy's Buffet, building it to twelve outlets in British Columbia and a number of franchised restaurants across the Prairies before selling the business in 1992.

A friend of Kaleden grapegrower **Toni Jessacher,** Lochbichler eventually began thinking of retiring to the Okanagan and to a small vineyard. "It was always on the back of my mind," he says. In mid-1996 he jumped at the opportunity to buy the **Divino Estate Winery** property south of Oliver. As partners, he enlisted a Vancouver friend, German-born Henry Rathje, another entrepreneur who has owned retirement homes, grown mushrooms and then owned a popular pub in Surrey. The winemaker partner in what then became known as **Hester Creek Estate Winery** was **Frank Supernak,** formerly the winemaker at Vincor.

LOGANBERRY WINE: The first commercial wine in British Columbia was produced from the loganberry, an Oregon-bred hybrid of raspberry and blackberry that thrives especially well on the Saanich Peninsula north of Victoria. Some insight into how the wine was made comes from a prayer card-sized **Growers' Wine Co.** brochure believed written in 1927 and now preserved in the British Columbia Archives: "The original Founders of the Loganberry Wine Industry, was established in 1923, with the co-operation of the Government of British Columbia, for the purpose of making wine on a commercial basis from the juice of the Loganberry, and to create a market for the Loganberry, which at that time was practically unsaleable. The wine made by the Growers' Wine Company, Limited, met with the immediate approval of the public when placed on sale at the Government vendors Stores.

"The wine, which is made mainly from the juice of freshly picked, ripe Loganberries and cane sugar only, is of the Port Class, having a proof percentage of 28. It is delicious in flavour and bouquet and of wonderful colour. The strictest care is used to keep the wine absolutely pure; no chemicals of any kind are used for any purpose and no artificial methods of clarifying or aging are employed. The development of the wine industry by the Growers' Wine Company, Limited, has meant the salvation of the Loganberry growing industry on Vancouver Island."

A Liquor Control Board price list dated October 1, 1934, showed that Growers' was marketing four brands of loganberry wine, each in four different sizes from twenty-six ounces to one gallon. The same durable brands were still available in 1948 (even though more grape wines also were being sold), durable perhaps because they were slightly cheaper. A twenty-six-ounce bottle of Logana Loganberry cost seventy-five cents in 1948 while a similar-sized bottle of Slinger's Grape or Calona Royal Red was eighty cents. Growers' and its successor companies produced and sold loganberry wines across Canada for about fifty years — and even tried, without success, to sell them in Britain.

LONESOME CHARLIE: A so-called "pop" wine with a blueberry flavour produced in the late 1960s and in the 1970s by *Jordan & Ste-Michelle. Joseph Zimmerman,* one of the practical German winemakers who made this and other eccentric products that the winery was selling, refused to call Lonesome Charlie a wine. "It's a refreshment cocktail and beverage," he once said with a dismissive shrug. "You make it efficiently, cheaply and still drinkable." The winery once recruited a less-flexible Californian who resigned after being assigned to make Lonesome Charlie. In 1978 Jordan headlined an advertisement for Lonesome Charlie with these words: "Looking for a friend?" It offended *Tex Enemark*, the deputy minister of Consumer Affairs, who complained to Liquor Control and Licensing Branch general manager *Vic Woodland* that the advertisement "seems to me to fly in the face entirely of our liquor moderation campaign" which was just being launched in November 1978. "Would you please re-examine our clearance of this ad and provide me with some explanation as to why it was cleared?" Enemark asked Woodland.[8] Two decades later Enemark could not recall the outcome of his irritation with an advertisement that, by the standards of the 1990s, would now be unremarkable.

LONGCROFT, PETER M.S. (1936–): The chairman of Sterling Capital Corp. and a wealthy oil industry executive in Alberta, Longcroft developed a two-acre vineyard on the Saanich Peninsula on

Vancouver Island in the mid-1990s. It was intended as the base for a winery tentatively called **Newton Croft Vineyards.**

LOUGHEED, EVANS (1914–1994):

The founder in 1966 of **Casabello,** Lougheed was a businessman whose vision for British Columbia wines was ahead of the times. In 1976 — three years before the first estate winery opened and twelve years before the first farmgate wineries — the prescient Lougheed told one interviewer: "The future lies in the possibility of small individual wineries that can sell their products from their doors."

Born in Outlook, Sask., Lougheed graduated in 1934 from the University of British Columbia with a commerce degree. Six years later, in partnership with his brother Allan and his father, Lougheed developed a chain of junior department stores in British Columbia, ultimately selling the chain in 1951 to F.W. Woolworth & Co. Because he and his wife, Frances, wanted to raise their family in a quieter community, they moved to Penticton where he built the Prince Charles Hotel to provide the city with a medium-priced hotel. An avid sportsman, Lougheed also operated the Penticton Vees amateur hockey team for several years. After suffering his first work-induced heart attack in 1961, he sold the hotel.

Grape enthusiast **Tony Biollo** was Lougheed's wine mentor, schooling his friend with samples of home-made wines until Lougheed had acquired a palate for table wines. With Biollo urging him on, Lougheed assembled about forty investors in 1966 to launch Casabello. While **Mission Hill**, also begun in 1966, was

Evan Lougheed (photo courtesy of John Schreiner)

in near-bankruptcy four years later, Casabello succeeded, in no small meas ure due to Lougheed's careful management. "One of his favourite sayings was look after the pennies and the dollars will look after themselves," recalled long-time Casabello employee **Maurice Gregoire.** "He was good at looking after the pennies." Lougheed enforced a rule that the winery would accept no collect telephone calls. When **Lloyd Schmidt** worked as a Casabello salesman, he was furious when his collect call was refused; Schmidt was driving back from Trail through a blizzard, was late for the Christmas party and had tried to call in from Osoyoos when he arrived in the Okanagan Valley. Fuming, he was determined to give Lougheed a piece of his mind when he arrived at the winery, only to be totally disarmed when Lougheed took him aside and gave him a generous Christmas bonus cheque. When **Harry McWatters** was sales manager at Casabello, he drew Lougheed's ire for running up a $153 photography bill without authorization, even though the photographs supported a successful promotion that sold four hundred cases of wine. Yet when McWatter's wife was in an accident some time later with the new company van, Lougheed brushed aside concern about the van and demanded to know whether Kathy McWatters had been treated at a hospital. Because he was tough but fair, Lougheed got unparalled loyalty from his staff which contributed to the winery's success. By 1972 its rapid growth led Lougheed to accept the Labatt brewing giant as a partner, with a five-year option to buy the winery. When Labatt took over the winery, Lougheed, even though he had had another heart attack in 1977, remained as chairman until he retired in 1982. Retirement did not dim his interest in wines nor his entrepreneurship: he promptly helped establish and manage a furniture factory in Penticton. He also served as president of the British Columbia Automobile Association, having been an active BCAA member since 1946.

[1] Don Allen in interview with author, 1995.

[2] Interview with author, January 18, 1984.

[3] Liquor Distribution Branch, 70th Annual Report, p. 10.

[4] *Report of the British Columbia Liquor Inquiry Commission*, 1970, p.8.

[5] Robert A. Campbell: *Demon Rum or Easy Money*, pp. 59–60. (See SOURCES for complete reference.)

[6] Tex Enemark papers.

[7] Liquor Distribution Branch, 62nd Annual Report, p. 21.

[8] Tex Enemark papers; memorandum to Vic Woodland, November 7, 1978.

MMM

MADELEINE ANGEVINE: A vinifera cross from the Loire which can produce white wines with a hint of muscat fruitiness, this vine is grown primarily in the Fraser Valley and Vancouver Island, since the variety is suited for cool climates.

MADELEINE SYLVANER: A white variety produced by crossing madeleine angevine and sylvaner, to get a variety with more character than the neutral sylvaner. It is grown primarily in the Fraser Valley and Vancouver Island.

MADRONA VALLEY FARMS: See *James Hamilton.*

MADSEN, DIANE: With her husband, Les, Diane Madsen became a vineyard owner when an attractive view property on which they had had their eyes for several years became available. Business entrepreneurs (makers of reinforcing steel and chain-link fencing and ranchers), the Madsens moved to Kelowna in 1971 from Calgary and lived for a decade in a home overlooking an Okanagan Mission area vineyard until the owners, the Dunlop family, sold it to the Madsens in 1981. With Les Madsen involved with the family's other businesses, Diane Madsen, a bookkeeper by training, took charge of the forty acres of grapes, learning viticulture as she went along. Her earliest decision was to replace the varieties then growing (labruscas like bath, patricia and sheridan) with more suitable wine varieties, including Okanagan riesling, white riesling, pinot blanc and pinot noir. The pinot noir, which had half the vineyard, performed poorly — be-

cause it had been planted on poor rootstock, Madsen believes — and was pulled out in 1995. The Okanagan riesling had come out earlier during the 1988 grape pull. However, pinot blanc proved the major success on the site and its acreage is steadily being increased.

MAIR, K. RAFE (1931 –): A Vancouver-born lawyer who practised in Kamloops from 1969 until he became a Social Credit member of the British Columbia legislature in 1975, Mair was Minister of Consumer and Corporate Affairs until late 1978, when he moved to Environment. With his ministry given responsibility for liquor policy which had historically resided with the attorney general, Mair undertook an energetic policy overhaul particularly beneficial to the British Columbia wine industry. In March 1977 the wineries for the first time were permitted to open retail stores in their wineries and to offer tours and tastings. In 1978 the government began licensing "cottage" wineries (subsequently called estate wineries), hoping that new wineries would begin elevating the quality of British Columbia wine. Mair left politics in 1981, becoming a Vancouver broadcaster.

MALLAM, PETER: One of the growers at Okanagan Mission contracted by *Growers' Wines* in the heyday of its expansion. His father, H.C. Mallam, immigrated from England in 1903 and was among the farmers who grew tobacco from time to time in the Okanagan (in Mallam's case, in 1912). Peter

Mallam was a dairy farmer until the early 1960s when, faced with a regulatory requirement to build an expensive new barn to stay in the business, he chose instead to plant fifty acres of grapes.

MALOLACTIC FERMENTATION: This technical jargon of the winemaker describes the process that, in the words of the eminent Bordeaux authority Dr. Emile Peynaud, "produces a considerable improvement in the wine's quality, causing it to become more supple and lose the acid character of new wine."[1] Among the fruit acids found in grapes, malic contributes a green apple tartness which is moderated as grapes mature and which declines further during *fermentation*. After a wine has completed its primary fermentation (in which natural sugar is converted to alcohol), winemakers frequently will allow naturally occurring lactic bacteria to convert a portion of the malic acid to softer lactic acid through the gentle secondary, or malolactic, fermentation. The technique is common in British Columbia because many grape varieties still have relatively high acidity at maturity due to cool-climate growing conditions. Malolactic fermentation is particularly beneficial in softening the acidic bite in red wines, which derive enough edge from natural tannins and do not require as much acidity for structure as do some dry white wines. Malolactic fermentation, which can also be induced, generally occurs immediately after primary fermentation. Winemakers also may inhibit the process in certain wines, either to maintain a more flexible selection of wines for blending or because it is not always desirable to reduce the natural acidity. With muscat grape varieties such as gewurz-

traminer, as an example, the mature fruit is more likely to have too little acidity than too much.

MANAIGRE, ALBERT (1943–): With his wife, Eleanor, Al Manaigre runs Vaseaux View Vineyards near Okanagan Falls, so named because the vines and the Manaigre home dominate a hilltop with a dramatic view of Vaseaux Lake. Born in Thunder Bay and trained in accounting at the University of Calgary, Manaigre's interest in viticulture began in the early 1970s when he volunteered to help a friend pick grapes near Oliver, where Manaigre had a public accounting practice. The Manaigres moved to Vancouver where he joined the administrative ranks of the Liquor Distribution Branch while his wife, who had grown up in Armstrong and had become one of the Royal Bank of Canada's first female managers, pursued a career with Vancouver City Savings Credit Union. They bought raw land for their vineyard in 1983, laid out a three-year development plan and adopted the punishing routine of spending most weekends labouring in the blazing sun to prepare the site. Holes for 10,000 vines were hand-dug in the sandy soil. Weeds were hoed by hand in the steep, terraced vineyard. They strung twenty-one miles of wires when they built trellises for the vines.

Both left their Vancouver jobs in 1987, Al Manaigre to work the vineyard and his wife to become manager of the credit union in Okanagan Falls. Cautiously, they delayed building their soaring open-beam cedar house on the property until their vines had been tested and survived a cold winter. The vines were three years old when that test occurred and only 5 percent were frozen.

The house went ahead.

They had not been cautious in all their moves. Assured there would be ample demand for grapes, they planted without a winery contract, subsequently signing up **Okanagan Vineyards** to buy the first commercial harvest in 1987 — just before Okanagan Vineyards slid into receivership. Manaigre scrambled to sell his grapes to **LeComte** that fall and then negotiated a contract with **Brights**. The vineyard was planted to six acres of vidal and four of white riesling and Brights asked Manaigre to set aside several rows of vidal for **icewine** in 1988. Unfortunately, deer ripped the netting and birds ate most of the fruit; only a few bottles of wine could be made. However, in subsequent years, Brights made a late harvest vidal and two vintages of riesling icewine from the Manaigre grapes. In 1995 **Mission Hill** took over the contract.

Vidal is no longer in demand by the wineries; however, the vidal vines in the Manaigre vineyard became afflicted with what growers called the grape decline disease (because the productive ability of the vines dies over three or four years). Chardonnay and merlot are expected to replace the vidal.

MANNHARDT, RAINER (1926–):
Born in Angola, Mannhardt grew up on a coffee plantation which his parents had established after the First World War in Angola, then a Portuguese colony. When civil war erupted there as it became an independent nation, Mannhardt and his brother Jurgen decided to leave not only Angola but the African continent entirely. "I could see that trouble would occur everywhere in Africa," Rainer Mannhardt said. In his literature research on relocation choices, Canada

appealed to him and he came to the Okanagan in 1975, to be followed a year later by his brother. Both chose to continue careers in agriculture. Unfortunately, Jurgen Mannhardt died a few months after buying the Beau Séjour vineyard at Okanagan Mission when his tractor overturned on a steep slope. Rainer Mannhardt, meanwhile, had purchased an apple orchard and small vineyard on a sandy slope near Westbank, replanting the hybrid varieties in 1977 with ehrenfelser and johannisburg riesling at the request of the **Andrés** winery. Mannhardt then decided to establish a block of virus-free ehrenfelser to support expansion of the variety. He carefully selected seventy plants which, over a two-year period, proved to be the most vigorous; he then had them screened for the most common and devastating viruses, narrowing the selection to ten. These vines then were sent to the **Centre for Plant Health** on Vancouver Island for further testing, with two vines emerging as totally free of viruses. Cuttings from these two established a mother block at the Mannhardt vineyard from which other growers subsequently obtained disease-free plants for their own vineyards. Over the years, Mannhardt has expanded his own ehren-felser plantings to five acres; he also has one acre of riesling. His apple orchard, sixteen acres in size in 1996, was leased to an apple grower.

MARÉCHAL FOCH: A vigorous, early
ripening red hybrid variety, this was the most widely grown red in the Okanagan (some 365 acres) before the 1988 pullout of most hybrid vines. The variety was created by French breeder Eugene Kuhlmann (1858–1932) and was known as Kuhlmann 188-2 prior to

being renamed for one of France's First World War heroes. The deep-coloured, full-flavoured wine was the backbone of many so-called burgundy blends in Canada and continues to be released as a varietal by several farmgate and estate wineries. **Calona** was among the first of the major wineries with a varietal foch (now discontinued). The winery's 1978 Winemasters' Selection Maréchal Foch won a gold medal at the first Okanagan wine festival in 1982 even though the judges found significant variation in quality among the bottles. Many winemakers had difficulty making wines from this variety that remained stable and developed properly in the bottle. **Elias Phiniotis,** when he was making wine at Calona, was one of the few with a reliable touch: Calona's 1981 Winemasters' Selection (2,000 cases were made) was still sound in 1995 when the author chanced to taste a bottle. Perhaps the oldest maréchal foch vines in the Okanagan still producing are a block planted in 1962 at **LeComte Estate Winery.** Another old block was planted in 1969 by **Richard Stewart** on property now owned by **Quails' Gate Vineyards Estate Winery.** While much of the acreage was removed after the 1988 vintage, a handful of vineyards retained foch, either as a blending wine or because the house style — exemplified by the off-dry foch made by **Lang Vineyards** — has developed a following of its own. However, if foch enjoys a revival, much of the credit goes to **Jeff Martin,** an Australian winemaker who joined Quails' Gate in 1994 and who had considerable experience making red wines from old shiraz vines in Australia. With no prejudices against hybrid grape varieties, Martin decided to do "something spe-

cial" when he discovered that the old foch vines were producing small, intensely flavoured berries which, with careful use of oak barrels, yielded rich red wines. He made fewer than one hundred cases of the 1994 Old Vines Foch. It won a bronze medal at the **Okanagan Wine Festival** and sold so well, even at luxury pricing, that almost five hundred cases were produced in 1995. LeComte's winemaker, **Eric von Krosigk**, also continued producing an old vines foch although the winery in 1995 removed three acres of young foch vines to make way for vinifera. The examples from Quails' Gate and LeComte have gone some way to rehabilitating the reputation of the grape.

MARKS, ALAN (1957–): A native of St. Louis, Missouri, and the winemaker at **Summerhill** beginning with the 1994 vintage, Marks started his professional life as a hospital research technician. It was a stop of convenience since Marks had a bachelor's degree in agriculture from the University of Missouri majoring in fruit crops. Soon back at the university's horticultural department for a master's degree, Marks became an assistant in 1982 to the state enologist.

Missouri had been an important wine-growing state a century ago, only to have its industry shrivel during Prohibition. Marks, with a wine culture handed down by his German and Italian immigrant forebears, became absorbed in the rebirth of Missouri wines that was then just beginning. In 1986 he enrolled in the graduate enology program at the University of Arkansas (where the students manage a seven-acre vineyard) and did a doctorate on the chemistry of sparkling wines. In 1988 he became the winemaker at the Hermannhof Winery in Hermann, Missouri, a small winery that had been created in what had been a former brewery by local banker James Dierberg. "The owner gave me free rein to create new wine styles and improve the sparkling wines," Marks says. In short order the winery scored a big win: a white wine Marks made from a New York-developed hybrid called vignoles, somewhat rieslinglike in character, was judged the best new world white wine at an international competition in California. "I had originally planned to go back to the university system after a couple of years of winemaking but then I decided I loved winemaking so much that I could never go back to university and do research and write journal articles."

After five years at Hermannhof, Marks had begun searching for a career-broadening winemaking post in the western United States when he learned from Summerland Research Station scientist Andy Reynolds, a professional acquaintance, that a job was coming open at Summerland. "I came up here for an interview, loved the area and thought it had tremendous potential," Marks said. After the humidity of Missouri, with the attendant vine disease, he recognized that the dry Okanagan climate facilitates healthy grapes. "I had also been very interested in organic and sustainable agriculture," Marks says. "It was a nice bonus that Summerhill was a transitional organic farm." He arrived at Summerhill two days before the early crush in 1994 and was agreeably surprised by the quality of what generally has been recognized now as a stellar Okanagan vintage. "The 1994s surprised me with a richness of maturity and flavour in the grapes and the juice," Marks said. "It made my job a lot easier. Pinot noir has always been my favourite red. I had a 1992 Summerhill pinot noir when I was here for my interview that was the closest to a Burgundian pinot that I had even tasted. The potential of the pinot noir is also a plus." Summerhill continues to specialize in making sparkling wines — one of the reasons Marks was hired — but, under his hand, it has given added attention to barrel-treated chardonnay and pinot noir.

MARTIN, JEFF (1957–): A skilled Australian winemaker, Martin handled the 1994 vintage for *Quails' Gate* and agreed early in 1995 to become the chief winemaker there, resulting in an immediate and positive change in the style and quality of Quails' Gate wines. In Martin's hands, the wines all have become more expressive of the varietal fruit of the grapes, notably with the two signature varieties at Quails' Gate. The chardonnay is crisper and fresher, with a subtle use of oak, while the pinot noir has become deeper in colour and more intense in flavour.

Martin was born at Griffith in the Riverina wine district of New South Wales, the home of a large winery operated by McWilliams, a family-owned company founded in 1877. When Jeff was completing high school, his grandfather, who ran the airport at Griffith, recommended he apply as a winemaker trainee in the winery run by friend Glenn McWilliam, an aviator as well as a vintner. "I didn't know what an enologist was, to be honest," Jeff admitted. He began his career with McWilliams in 1977, helped in the production of the winery's Centenary Vintage Port and concluded that enology was "a great job, basically." McWilliams financed Martin's professional education, a science degree from Australia's Charles Sturt University. By 1989 he had become the chief winemaker at the McWilliams Barwang winery, which specializes in premium red varieties, where Martin produced several award-winning cabernet and shiraz wines.

To broaden his experience, McWilliams sent him to California to work at Carmenet during the 1989 vintage. A two-week camping trip in British Columbia at the end of that vintage left him so enthralled with the natural beauty that, five years later, he decided to return to work here. "I could have gone to any of four places in the world to work," Martin says, noting that Australian enologists and wine technology have been in high demand. With opportunities available in New Zealand, Chile, Bulgaria and the United States, Martin took a sabbatical from McWilliams to handle the 1994 vintage at Quails' Gate. He discovered that this ambitiously run estate winery near Kelowna had the potential to produce fine wines from its vineyard and the money to do it. Martin resigned from McWilliams and, with his wife, Niva, and two daughters, emigrated to British Columbia early in 1995. Martin acknowledges it was a career-risking move to leave a professionally established industry for British Columbia. The attraction is the challenge: "I want to make premium wines, where the challenge is in making the best." He also believes that British Columbia's future requires making premium wines, rather than trying to compete with the low-cost high-volume wine regions elsewhere in the world.

Martin's impact on Quails' Gate was immediate. When the winery started releasing its 1994 vintage, the wines were separated into three tiers. At the top were the super-premium Family Reserve wines, a chardonnay and a pinot noir — the varieties with which Quails' Gate wants to be identified above all others. The next tier were the Limited Release wines which Martin describes as "wines of interest that come from any vintage." The third tier of Quails' Gate wines, Propriertor's Selection, accommodates the generic blends and modestly priced wines that round out the winery's offerings.

It takes a certain amount of hand crafting to achieve this quality segregation. With pinot noir, which is 20 percent of Quails' Gate's production, Martin ferments separately each clone and each significant block of fruit from the vineyard. "By keeping the wines separate, you make sure the cream comes to the top," Martin says. "Those particular batches that come out best in the tank, we keep for our Family Reserve and the rest for the Limited Release pinots. The best pinots go into our best oaks." (Martin prefers French oak for the wine styles he is making.) The more concentrated wines emerging from Quails' Gate from the 1994 vintage reflected numerous changes that Martin introduced to vineyard management and to handling the grapes in the winery. The pinot noir is fermented much more in the Burgundian style, in squat, insulated fermenting vats in which fermentation temperatures are allowed to peak at 30°C, the high temperature helping extract colour from the skins. To achieve this, Martin found a special slow-acting, heat-tolerant yeast that accentuates the flavour of the pinot noir. Indeed, where Quails' Gate (and other wineries) formerly used basically one yeast for red wines and another for white, Martin has begun to use a whole suite of yeast strains to bring out the best from each of the varieties produced at the winery.

MARTINIUK, LANNIS (1949–):

Trained as a nuclear medicine technician, Vancouver-born Lanny Martiniuk enjoys the challenge of leaving the beaten path, whether as a youthful trekker in Nepal or subsequently as a grapegrower. In 1979 Martiniuk and his wife, Julie, a pharmacist whose family were Oliver orchardists, bought a modest orchard south of Oliver with the specific intention of turning it into a vineyard. To learn the art of growing grapes, Martiniuk first began propagating vines in his greenhouses for others. He began planting his own vineyard in 1984, putting in experimental Russian grape varieties like matsvani, rkatsiteli and sereksia chornaya, as well as mainstream varieties such as pinot blanc and müller-thurgau. When most of his plants were killed by a sharp November 1984 cold snap, Martiniuk got more cuttings from *Inkameep Vineyards* and put in the same varieties in 1985; in addition, he planted

oraniensteiner, furmint and schönbeurger. "It appealed to me," he recalls. "Most were not standard. There is something about me — I love experimentation." The disadvantage with this approach is that some experiments fail: after a decade of growing the Russian varieties (made into wine by the *Brights* winery at Oliver), Martiniuk has dropped nearly all. Matsvani produced inconsistent acidity levels from year to year and yielded wines with good aromas but little body. Rkatsiteli was vigorous and easy to grow but usually yielded grapes with too much acidity. Only sereksia chornaya has found a place, yielding fine, dry rosé wines. Oranien-steiner is a vinifera cross produced in Germany; its deficiency is that the vines are prone to fungus disease. Since 1994 Martiniuk's thirty-two acre-property has begun the conversion to less eccentric varieties, including pinot blanc and pinot noir. "Pinot blanc is a grower's grape," Martiniuk has found. "It seems to be able to yield five to seven tons an acre and it can do that consistently without giving you a thin wine." Martiniuk's enthusiasm for grapegrowing extends beyond the vineyard. He has been a director of the *British Columbia Wine Institute* and chairman of the *Grape Growers Marketing Board*.

MAUZ, ALBERT (1935–):

Born on a farm, Mauz was an agricultural consultant in the community of Ostfildern, near Stuttgart, before emigrating to Canada in 1990, six years after a family vacation in the Okanagan attracted the Mauz family to the valley. Mauz purchased and operates a vineyard on the mountainside overlooking Osoyoos on the east side of the valley. The three-acre vineyard is devoted to chardonnay, the variety planted there in the mid-1980s by Tony Dekleva, the previous owner.

MAUZ, REGINA (1965–): With her husband **GERHARD HAMMERL (1955–)**, she operates a nine-acre vineyard south of Oliver, choicely located on what is called the *Golden Mile.* Mauz and Hammerl purchased the vineyard in 1990 from veteran Oliver grower *Peter Serwo* and grow two acres each of merlot, pinot noir, and kerner and one acre each of chardonnay and pinot blanc. The remainder includes cabernet franc and verdelet.

Hammerl and Mauz grew up in Germany's Württemberg wine region, which is just north of the industrial city of Stuttgart, but were pursuing careers outside wine before emigrating to Canada in 1990. Hammerl is an electrician and Regina Mauz is a lithographer. A family vacation to the Okanagan in 1984 attracted them back permanently. "We saw the area here and it was so beautiful," Regina Mauz says. "The idea of grape-growing appealed to us. I guess it happens to a lot of people." Hammerl and Mauz are growers for *Gray Monk* and do not plan their own winery even if they have become capable home vintners. "We do what everybody does," Regina Mauz says. "Once you have grapes, you want to make wine."

MAVETY, IAN (1948–): With his wife, Jane, Mavety is proprietor of *Blue Mountain Vineyard and Cellars.* Born in Vancouver and an agriculture graduate from the University of British Columbia, Mavety became a grapegrower after moving to what is now the Blue Mountain Vineyard at Okanagan Falls in 1971. Regarded by his peers as one of the shrewdest individuals in the wine industry, Mavety was an executive member of the Grape Growers Marketing Board for almost two decades. The Blue Mountain winery was established in 1992. Mavety also continued to grow grapes for other wineries, notably *CedarCreek,* and to operate a nursery from which many other Okanagan growers have purchased vines for their new vineyards.

MCDONALD, ANDREA (1963–) AND HUGH (1960–): The proprietors of *Crowsnest Vineyards,* a farmgate winery that opened in 1995 in the Similkameen Valley near Cawston. Winemaker Andrea McDonald was born in Berne, Switz., the daughter of a food industry executive who took his family to Spain, Chile and Peru before moving to Penticton in 1975. A food-processing graduate from the British Columbia Institute of Technology, Andrea started in the wine industry with *Okanagan Vineyards* in 1985 and subsequently worked in the *Vincor* laboratory at Oliver before leaving to concentrate on Crowsnest and a young family. Husband Hugh McDonald was born in Penticton, grew up on his father's Cawston fruit farm that subsequently became the basis for Crowsnest Vineyards. In addition to nurturing the winery, Hugh McDonald has operated his own trucking firm since 1989.

MCGUGAN, LIEUTENANT-COLONEL DONALD (1889–1974): A legendary regulator, McGugan's career with the *Liquor Control Board* of British Columbia extended from 1923 to 1969 when, at the age of eighty, he finally retired. He joined as Supervisor of Law Enforcement and became chairman and general manager in 1951 when he succeeded William F. Kennedy, who had held the post for nineteen years but who had the misfortune to die of a stroke when he was only sixty-three. The colonel (as he was usually called) summed up his approach when, at the end of his career, he testified before a commission on British Columbia's liquor laws. "I was in the legislature in the formative stages," McGugan said. "It was stated then by the responsible minister that control was the main purpose. Profit was just a circumstance — it was too bad. As far as I'm concerned, the Act was only for control."[2]

McGugan was born in Strathroy, Ont. After graduating from the University of Toronto in 1911 with a degree in mathematics, he moved to Vancouver and then to Victoria, where he practised law. When the First World War began, McGugan joined the Seaforth Highlanders as a private, rising through the ranks to become a much-decorated lieutenant-colonel in France. In 1919, he returned to Victoria and law until joining the Board in 1923.[3]

The colonel became a fixture through his discreet loyalty to his political superiors (he never gave interviews) and his ability to stay above the scandal and controversy that sometimes swirled around the board. H.H. Stevens, who headed a 1952 inquiry into liquor policy, concluded that the Liquor Control Board was inefficiently run. Stevens said later: "I would not want to say anything against my old friend, Col. McGugan, but I am more qualified to be chairman of the atomic commission *of the world* than he is to be chairman of the Liquor Control Board."[4] Author Robert Campbell, in his book, *Demon Rum or Easy Money*, sug-

gested that Premier *W.A.C. Bennett* left McGugan in the chairman's post because "after three decades McGugan knew whose closets held the skeletons, and the astute Bennett left him alone."[5] It is equally probable that Bennett agreed with the colonel's control mentality. The LCB policy of the day "forbade employees to offer any advice or recommendations to customers," author Campbell writes. *Evans Lougheed*, the founder of Casabello, thought McGugan was a "strong autocrat" but also a man with some vision, since the first self-service liquor store operated by any Canadian liquor control board was opened in 1962 at Brentwood Mall in Burnaby by McGugan's board. (By the time the Brentwood store closed twenty years later — nearby liquor stores were enlarged — self-service liquor stores had become the rule, rather than the exception. The convenience also served the criminals: there were 383 shoplifting prosecutions by the Liquor Distribution Branch in 1982 compared with 46 in 1976.)[6]

Unlike Premier Bennett, the colonel by no means was a teetotaler. While he never accepted hospitality from suppliers, he frequently took them to lunch at Victoria's Union Club where, as a lifelong bachelor, he lived for many years. (Charles Keir, who was manager of the LCB stores, also lived at the Union Club — for thirty-eight years, a club record.) Those suppliers who tried to match McGugan's capacity for martinis usually regretted it. Meredith F. Jones, who was a president of *Brights* in the 1950s, staggered back to his hotel room after lunch with the colonel and did not wake up until next morning. Andrés founder *Andrew Peller*, who fashioned a close friendship with the colonel but was never permitted to pay for a drink, recalled one of their lunches: "Cripes, he had six, seven martinis; I had two and my head was spinning."[7] *Vic Woodland,* whom the colonel had named secretary of the LCB, believes the colonel may have had a quiet arrangement with the bartender to water his own drinks. The colonel, far from being befuddled with drink, shrewdly took advantage of his ability to write shorthand to make extensive notes during contentious meetings with suppliers. "It fooled a lot of them," Woodland said.

Woodland usually made the appointments for the colonel and then soothed those who failed to get additional listings. "If someone didn't go to lunch with him, the colonel had a nice chat with him and when he left, he would give him a cigar, a real good cigar because the colonel was a heavy cigar smoker," Woodland recalled. The recipient of a cigar generally assumed he had made some gains with McGugan. "I would never deflate him over a thing like that," said Woodland, who usually would get a perplexed call a few weeks later, with the caller asking when the additional product listings would be coming. Usually, they did not come. The colonel's view, Woodland said later, was that liquor stores "did not have rubber walls. There were 230-some liquor stores. Anytime you changed anything, it changed it through the whole works. And secondly, if you gave some concession to one winery or one distillery, you had every other one coming at you."

The government finally retired McGugan in 1969 (he was succeeded by William Bruce). The colonel's departure and a change of government in 1972

cleared the way for a needed overhaul of the LCB. Within a few years, the LCB was split, with retailing operations placed under a new *Liquor Distribution Branch* in Vancouver while the colonel's beloved control functions remained with a leaner LCB in Victoria.

MCKENZIE, MONSIGNOR W.B. (1887–1967):

Born in Prince Edward Island and ordained in 1919, Father McKenzie was posted as a parish priest in Kelowna in 1931 just as local farmers were planning what later was known as *Calona Wines.* After he suggested it to Archbishop Duke in Vancouver, the diocese had wine from Calona approved for sacramental use in Roman Catholic churches in Canada, supplanting imported Spanish wine. Sales of *St. John sacramental wine,* as the brand was called, contributed materially to Calona's sales in the early years. Father McKenzie, who received a fee for supervising the sacramental wine, retired to Victoria after ill health in 1959 forced him to leave his parish.[8]

MCWATTERS, HARRY (1944–):

Principal owner of *Sumac Ridge Estate Winery,* McWatters is one of the most influential figures in the British Columbia wine scene. His credits include being founding chairman of the *Okanagan Wine Festival* and founder and chairman of the *British Columbia Wine Institute.* Born in Toronto, he grew up in Vancouver after his family was transferred there by his father's employer, the Toledo Scale Company. The McWatters family enjoyed wines ("We always had a gallon in the fridge," McWatters recalls) and Harry began dabbling in home winemaking, making potato "champagne" when he was sixteen. He had a successful career in sales with a moving company when Casabello president **Evans Lougheed**, in what McWatters remembers as a magical day at the winery, convinced him to become Casabello's first salesman in 1968, at half the salary the moving company was paying him. He was at Casabello for thirteen years before leaving to start Sumac Ridge.

MERRIDALE CIDER WORKS LTD.:

Making cider is almost identical to making wine. "The only trick to this is knowing which varieties of apples to blend together," says Merridale proprietor and ciderist **Albert Piggott,** adding with a provocative chuckle: "And I am not going to tell!"

True English cider is a passion with Piggott, who has made fruit wines and apple ciders most of his adult life. He made his first ciders, using acidic cooking apples, when he was twenty. "The cider I made back then wasn't worth drinking," he admits candidly. "I didn't even know what a cider apple was. I had some fruit and I had to do something with it. The cider was pretty bad. If my memory doesn't fail me, I wound up building a small still and distilled it." He marvels that he even developed an interest in cider-making, given the lack of appropriate apples at the time.

Piggott was born in the town of Forfar on the east coast of Scotland. Technically trained in engineering and architecture, he taught shop crafts until he and his wife, Betty, came to Canada in 1954, judging the career opportunities to be better. Here, Piggott continued to teach in Prince George and later on Vancouver Island until retiring at fifty-six to make genuine English cider in a

commercial venture, one of the very few in North America. Merridale Cider, whose rustic buildings are at the end of rural Merridale Road in Cobble Hill on Vancouver Island, is surrounded by a fourteen-acre orchard planted to obscure European apple varieties, good only for making cider, but as perfect for the task as chardonnay is for chablis. Merridale was incorporated in 1987 and began selling cider to the public in 1992, operating under a unique estate cidery licence.

Making apple wine or apple cider was hardly new to British Columbia. **Calona Wines** was established in 1932 initially to make apple wines, discontinuing these products after they showed an unfortunate tendency to referment and blow up the bottles they were packaged in. It is a problem that haunts Piggott as well. Lacking — as Calona did — the fine filters that strip any remaining yeast cells before a wine is bottled, Piggott puts all of his ciders in soft plastic bottles which cannot become dangerous bombs in the rare event that refermentation begins. A successful apple cider was developed in the 1950s by **Dr. John Bowen** at the Summerland Research Station and launched commercially by **Growers' Wines Ltd.** A light, refreshing carbonated beverage now made from apple concentrate, this cider continues to be sold across Canada, along with similar competing ciders.

The style of a Merridale cider is altogether different and it has everything to do with the apples used and how they are blended. The classic European cider, of which Piggott's ciders are an example, requires elements from four types of apples. The necessary acidity is provided by the *sharps:* Piggott, who in 1994 planted three French varieties of high-acid apples, has been relying on tart crabapples grown in the British Columbia Interior. The firm tannic backbone and body in the Merridale ciders are provided by the *bittersweet* varieties. There is a group of cider apples called the *bittersharps* which combine the acidity and the tannin for a balanced product; but the varieties are very difficult to grow, confirming Piggott's view that a single variety cider would not be "economically viable, sensible or feasible." The natural sugar, turned into alcohol during fermentation, comes from a group of apples called the *sweets,* which contribute softness and perfume to the cider. By themselves, these apples would yield flabby ciders because they have insufficient acidity or tannin that the sharps and the bittersweets bring to the cider assembly. Piggott has never had the full panoply of cider varieties available to him, although the selection has improved each year as more varieties have begun to bear in his orchard or in several other Vancouver Island orchards from which he buys fruit.

Processing the apples is not, Piggott says, "a fussy business." After the juice has been pressed from the apples and lightly sulphited to protect it from oxidation, it is inoculated with yeast, typically champagne yeast, and enough yeast nutrient to ensure a reliable fermentation. Because cider apples are harvested in late September and early October, the cider ferments slowly at cool seasonal temperatures and for as long as four months, with a typical Merridale cider achieving 7 percent alcohol. The cider will be bottled and released shortly after fermentation is complete. Piggott believes that cider has its fullest flavour when it is young and

should be consumed within its first year, since the product is not designed by nature to be aged. "But I have cider that is fourteen years old," Piggott adds. "It tastes like a light dry sherry."

Golden in colour, bone dry and crisp in the mouth, Merridale cider has the heft and body of a beverage that demands food with it. In addition to this cider, Piggott also makes a "rough" or tannic cider (alcohol of 9.5 percent) with the traditional name of Scrumpy. In British slang, to *scrump* an apple is to steal it. "We can only assume that farm workers stole from the farm orchard and made their own," Piggott ventures. For the west coast chablis palate, Scrumpy takes some getting used to. Piggott suggests the experience is like moving from a light beer to a full-bodied bitter.

At the other end of the flavour scale is Merridale's Cyser, deliciously sweetened with wildflower honey. Piggott attributes the recipe to a gentleman named Kinelme Digby, who is said to have been the kitchen master to Queen Elizabeth I and the author of a cookbook about 1600 AD, the source of Cyser's formula. Piggott admits he is partial to Cyser, boosting its potency with a few drops of brandy in the winter and using fruit-flavoured sodas to turn it into a refreshing summertime drink.

MERLOT: Very likely the first commercially released merlot in British Columbia was the 1982 vintage from **Uniacke** estate winery. *Tilman Hainle*, who was then the winemaker at Uniacke, was quoted in **B.C. Wines Notes** as predicting that, due to winter damage, this might be the last merlot from that vineyard. "He is not optimistic about the grape's chances in the valley, particularly considering Uniacke has one of the warmer locations."[9] By the mid-1990s about one hundred acres of merlot had been planted in the Okanagan; it had already become the most widely planted red variety in Washington state. True to Hainle's apprehensions, merlot is not as winter-hardy as cabernet sauvignon, even though merlot matures about ten days earlier. However, the wines are richly fruity and accessible and the popularity of merlot, also an excellent blender with cabernet, has propelled growers to plant it. The vines do best in the south Okanagan. The Uniacke vineyard now is owned by **CedarCreek** and, in fact, is not one of the warmer locations, which is why CedarCreek, still a premier merlot producer, expanded its merlot sources in 1995 by planting the warmer **Greata Ranch** on the west side of the Okanagan Lake and by contracting production from the **King Brothers** at Naramata.

MÉTHODE CLASSIQUE: When this phrase or variations such as *Méthode Traditionnelle* appear on the label of a sparkling wine, it means the wine has been made in the same manner as traditional champagne. It is illegal in Europe to call a sparkling wine champagne unless it is made in Champagne. New world sparkling wine producers who believe it is not ethical to call their wines champagne get the message across with these evocative "méthode" terms which are legal.

MICROCLIMATE: This is defined with bureaucratic woolliness in the B.C. Ministry of Agriculture's *Atlas of Suitable Grape Growing Locations* as: "The fine climatic structure of the air space that extends from the very surface of the earth to a height at which the effects of the imme-

diate character of the underlying surface no longer can be distinguished from the general local climate." In plain English, when a grower talks about the microclimate of a section of his vineyard, he's talking about that particular combination of sunlight and protection from frost that makes that section better for grapes than potatoes.

MIKULETIC, ANTON (1933–): Now the operator of a ten-acre vineyard near Westbank, Mikuletic was born in Slovenia in the former Yugoslavia, the son of a farmer, and escaped the Communist regime by stealthily crossing the border at night to Italy. After two years there on a farm, he came to Canada in 1957 and worked at a Winnipeg meat-packing plant until, on a 1971 vacation to Vancouver, he discovered the Okanagan was lush with orchards and vineyards, reminding him of his homeland. He promptly moved to the Okanagan, soon purchasing the Westbank property, then with only a small planting of bath grapes. Since then he has followed the whims of winery demand, first growing reds such as de chaunac and chelois, then switching to whites (primarily verdelet and Okanagan riesling) and in the 1990s to vinifera, including chardonnay, gewurztraminer, white riesling and merlot.

MILNE, ROB (1952–): The owner of **Sunset Vineyard** south of Oliver, Milne is an accountant and a partner in a successful Port Coquitlam plant manufacturing industrial packaging, Interwrap Industries Inc. Milne became enthusiastic about wine after a family vacation in France in 1992 and quickly purchased a former Okanagan vineyard and planted it to preferred vinifera varieties. In 1996

Milne began planning an estate winery to open on Black Sage Road in 1998 as *Kalamalka Estate Winery*.

MIRKO, ROSS (1960–): One of the winemakers at *CedarCreek* since 1990, Vancouver-born Mirko, son of an architect, had his wine interest awakened by an evening wine appreciation course he took while getting a degree in psychology from the University of Auckland in New Zealand. Mirko, who has dual Canadian and New Zealand citizenship, was soon working part-time as a salesman in an Auckland wine shop. On graduating, he spent several more months in Australia, visiting wineries. He had shared his growing fascination about wine with his father, Ivan, who chanced to learn that the *Andrés* winery in Port Moody had a quality control position coming open. In August 1988 psychology graduate Mirko went to work in the laboratory of the winery, undaunted by his lack of formal chemistry. He had, after all, once taken a job (and held it for two years) in a Vancouver scuba diving shop despite having no prior diving experience. "The chemistry required for the position [at Andrés] was basically paint by numbers," he remembered. His mentors at Andrés, winemakers *Ron Taylor* and *Anne Sperling*, "took a lot of time to teach me and feed my enthusiasm for wine. What a learning curve!"

Mirko moved to CedarCreek in May 1990 as what he describes as "a general cellar hand," soaking up more knowledge from veteran winemakers *Elias Phiniotis*, who consulted for Cedar-Creek, and *Helmut Dotti*, then the winemaker there. Sperling followed Mirko to CedarCreek, becoming the senior winemaker in 1991. In early 1994

Ross Mirko (photo courtesy of John Schreiner)

Mirko enrolled at Lincoln University in Christchurch, N.Z., in a postgraduate diploma course in viticulture and enology, the only Canadian in a class of twenty-two. He chose to study there because he believes that New Zealand's cool-climate winemaking is relevant to the north Okanagan. He returned to CedarCreek in November 1994, just after the crush, taking over from Anne Sperling, who moved to Ontario in 1995.

MISSION HILL VINEYARDS INC.: Perched on Boucherie Mountain and commanding a dramatic view of the Okanagan Valley, this winery brought acclaim to British Columbia wines in 1994 when its elegant 1992 reserve chardonnay, made by its talented New Zealand-born winemaker *John Simes,* won the prestigious *Avery's Trophy* at the International Wine and Spirits Competition in London against 220 other chardonnays from around the world. The achievement was all the more remarkable, considering the winery's chequered past.

In 1965, a dynamic Okanagan businessman named *R.P. "Tiny" Walrod*, formerly general manager of B.C. Tree Fruits Ltd., led the development of a California-inspired winery with local investors. Mission Hill Vineyards Ltd., under president W.W. Stewart, would plant grapes while Mission Hill Wines Ltd. would build the winery. Walrod was managing director of both companies. The two soon were consolidated into one public company, with most of the shares held by seven investors: Stewart (who was general manager of Stewart Brothers Nurseries Ltd.); Kelowna doctors D.W. Lim and C. Brian Holmes; Kelowna investment dealers J. Bruce Smith and E.R.F. Dodd; retired investment dealer W.G. Chalmers; and retired banker A.J. Gilroy. To finance a $700,000 winery, they raised $626,500 in a share offering, borrowed $300,000 from the federal government's Industrial Development Bank and secured another $227,500 in federal development grants. Fueling the investment was fast-growing wine consumption in western Canada (Calona Wines sales, for example, roared from $600,000 in 1960 to $3.3 million in 1966).[10] The winery's initial capacity was 325,000 gallons but the investors expected to grow to 1 million gallons within a few years. Unfortunately, Walrod died of a heart attack before the winery opened and the winery faltered. Competitor **Evans Lougheed**, whose Casabello wines reached the market a month before the Mission Hill wines, later maintained that Walrod, with his extensive and influential business contacts, would have secured Mission Hill's success.

The competitors were not happy to see Mission Hill arrive. Doctors Lim and Holmes, besides having money in the winery, also were part owners of Devon Vineyards, the grapes from which were contracted to **Growers' Wines Ltd.** Naturally, they wanted to redirect those grapes to Mission Hill and, in the spring of 1966, Holmes wrote to Growers' general manager **Brian Roberts**, asking that

Nick Clark and Anthony von Mandl at Mission Hill (photo courtesy of Mission Hill Vineyards)

Devon's contract be cancelled even though it had six years to run. Holmes added that Walrod (already deceased) had previously raised the matter with Roberts.[11] Indignantly, Roberts replied that Walrod had never talked to him about it; besides, Growers' expected some loyalty. "Until five years ago, my company was the only company which offered the grower long-term contracts," Roberts wrote. "But for the 40 year policy of my company there would be no grape growing industry in the Okanagan Valley today.... As pioneers of the grape growing industry in the Okanagan Valley, we fail to comprehend why we should be asked to risk our capital and honour over 40 years merely to hand the fruits of our entrepreneurial activity on a platter to a competitor.... That we should be asked to cancel a contract which has collectively involved planning, financing and risk is quite inconceivable to us." Holmes was a dermatologist. One hopes he had a thick skin.

Mission Hill secured grapes from other sources to make wine in the fall of 1966, with Polish-born Henryk Schoenfeld, a winemaker from Ontario, as production manager. The first wines reached the market in September 1967 and within eighteen months, Mission Hill was offering twenty-six wines. These included the durable Caravel and Cabaret brands of red, ruby red, white and sherry. There was vin blanc, vin rosé, vin rouge, Canadian sauterne, claret, burgundy, chablis, medoc; even Canadian Chiantino, described in the company's annual report as "a rich, robust full-bodied, all purpose, Italian type red wine." The range was rounded off with three crackling wines, a port, a sherry and a mulled wine. Despite the shotgun approach to the market, Mission Hill lost $62,636 on sales of $85,505 in the twelve months to June 30, 1968.[12]

By the spring of 1970 the winery, on the edge of bankruptcy, agreed to be taken over by Uncle Ben's Tartan Holdings Ltd., the company through which construction tycoon **Ben Ginter** owned the Prince George brewery. "Your directors very much regret this state of affairs," Mission Hill president Stewart wrote. "There is no single cause. With a number of new B.C. wineries, sales in the early period were not nearly as good as expected. Within a year or so, working capital was used up and advertising and promotion expenses had to be cut down. As a result the company's name did not become well enough known.... We had hoped that the Liquor Control Board prohibitions on general visits to wineries would be relaxed but these still remain. As a result, we were not able to secure advertising value from our location and the memorable view from the winery."[13]

The swashbuckling Ginter took over what was now called Uncle Ben's Gourmet Wines Ltd. just as the other wineries and the newly formed Grape Growers Marketing Board were at an impasse over the board's demand for higher grape prices. Anxious to secure a supply of grapes, Ginter promptly agreed to the board's prices — provided the other wineries paid the same. His move collapsed winery resistance to the board. Ginter also took a shot at his competitors in an interview with the *Vancouver Sun* in August 1970, soon after taking over the winery. "We have got a helluva reputation in Canada for having a rotgut type of wine. Wineries which try to put out a good quality product cannot thrive because people don't accept it more than rot-gut put out by others for a few cents less."[14] Unhappily, winemaking under Ginter's ownership did little to change that reputation. Its products were more notable for outrageous labels (such as Fuddle Duck, Yellow Bird and Hot Goose, all *Baby Duck* copycats) than for quality and the winery slipped into receivership in 1978. When *T.G. Brights & Co.* offered to buy it for $750,000 (some reports say $800,000), Ginter found the resources to top that by $15,000. He operated the winery, now called Golden Valley Wines Ltd., until selling it to *Anthony von Mandl* and partner *Nick Clark* in 1981. They promptly resurrected the original winery name and, within months, dropped Fuddle Duck and the rest of the aviary.

Von Mandl and Clark, who based himself at the winery as president, found the winery's condition deplorable. It needed, in von Mandl's words, "an unimaginable amount of investment."[15] The wine inventory was equally bad. Because the only drinkable wines were port and "old maréchal foch that had been forgotten in some barrels and miraculously turned out good," von Mandl scrambled to purchase bulk wine from California, launching a line of new brands as quickly as the wines could be bottled and labelled. At the time all commercial wineries had the right to sixty-six liquor store listings but Golden Valley had only been using half that number. The re-launched Mission Hill quickly claimed all of its listings since von Mandl and Clark urgently needed cash to upgrade the winery. The workhorse wines that could be made from the imported product or from the limited selection of varietal grapes then available were released under such *pseudo-labels*

as Caves Chauvignon and Klosterberg Cellars. Von Mandl would have preferred not to release these labels of convenience and Mission Hill dropped them later when they were no longer needed to pay the bills. The better hybrid varietals (such as verdelet and chelois) were released under the Pandosy Cellars label, not the Mission Hill label. From the start, the Mission Hill name was reserved for wines primarily made from classic European varieties, starting with a 1981 gewurztraminer and 1981 johannisberg riesling from Okanagan-grown grapes and pinot noir and cabernet sauvignon from Washington state vineyards.

Ironically it was apple cider that enabled Mission Hill to survive. Under Ginter's ownership, the winery was marketing Golden Valley cider but only managed to take 8 percent of market, with the rest of the market firmly in the hands of Growers' cider. Mission Hill in 1982 re-launched a better-quality product under the umbrella of the Okanagan Cider Company, selling 100,000 cases of the product — more than five times what Golden Valley had been selling. Mission Hill also launched a distillery arm, both as a home for poor-quality wines and as a way of garnering cash flow by purchasing distilled products, including scotch whisky, and retailing it under the Great West Distillers label.

After spending more than $100,000 on a new tasting room, the winery offered an aggressive tour program, one year even extending it to helicopter tours of the surrounding vineyards. In the marketplace, Mission Hill hired Canadian actor Bruno Gerussi, formerly a critic of domestic wines, to pitch Mission Hill on television as examples of

British Columbia wines that he proudly served his guests. The marketing worked: Mission Hill shipped 290,000 cases of wine in 1982 compared with 84,000 cases in 1980. By 1983, with Swiss winemaker *Daniel Lagnaz,* Mission Hill began to score victories at wine competitions. The winery now claims that it is British Columbia's most-awarded winery.

None of the awards had more impact on Mission Hill than the *Avery's Trophy,* won in 1994 for the winery's 1992 Grand Reserve Barrel Select Chardonnay, an award that served to draw international attention to British Columbia wines in general and Mission Hill in particular. The genesis of that wine lay in the hiring in 1992 of New Zealand winemaker John Simes. Von Mandl believed that Okanagan grapes had the potential for even better wines if they were put into the hands of a winemaker experienced with cool-climate viticulture. Simes immediately upgraded grape processing at the winery; asked for and got new American oak barrels; and promptly produced the prize-winning chardonnay.

"In terms of our company, the impact has been phenomenal," winemaker John Simes reflected later. "It gave everyone in the organization confidence that we could do it, that the resource existed to make international quality wines, and that if we did, people would pay reasonable dollar values for them that would give us sufficient return to re-invest. Until that wine, the business confidence, from the owner of the company right down to the sales guys, wasn't there." In the year after winning that award, Mission Hill began a $10 million capital expansion program. It included almost

1 million litres of new stainless steel processing equipment and hundreds of new oak barrels. In 1996 the winery purchased vineyard property, its first, at Osoyoos and began planting 150 acres of vines on a sun-baked site on the Canada-United States border. "The chardonnay was the start," Simes said. "The chardonnay is no longer the only wine which has done something worth talking about internationally. We won a huge number of medals in international shows with the 1994s."

MISTRAL VINEYARD: When *Robert and Jenny White* bought a vineyard site south of Oliver in 1992, the constant wind scouring their exposed hillside location led them to name their property after the mistral, the dry wind of the North African desert. See *Robert and Jenny White*.

MITCHELL, DAVID (1940–): With his wife, Susan, Mitchell established *Uniacke Wines* in 1980 (initially, there was a third partner, architectural draftsman David Newman-Bennett, who designed the winery, but who later sold his shares to the Mitchells). A petroleum engineer and a graduate of Dalhousie University, Mitchell was a farmer by avocation. Once while working in Africa, he nearly purchased a farm in Zimbabwe. He and Susan first acquired Okanagan orchard property almost on a whim during a 1974 holiday from Mitchell's oil industry job in Calgary. Mitchell proved to be a capable grower, producing grapes with which Mission Hill produced a number of award-winning wines. However, Uniacke struggled to sell its wines, which were not always distinguished, from a winery then perceived to be well off the beaten track for wine tourists. The winery and vineyard were sold in 1986, becoming *CedarCreek*.

MONASHEE VINEYARDS: See *Ed Wahl* and *John Barnay*.

MONTPELLIER: Established in 1872, the same year as the *Geisenheim Institute*, the L'École Nationale Supérieure Agronomique in this city in the south of France is one of Europe's leading schools for winemakers. Graduates who have worked in British Columbia include *Laurent Dal'Zovo* and *Olivier Combret*.

MOORE, GERARD (1929–): A Vancouver native who spent most of his business life with an industrial machinery dealer in Edmonton, Moore, in what he called semi-retirement, purchased a three-acre vineyard in 1992 on Front Bench Road in Summerland. It had been planted entirely to verdelet in the mid-1980s but Moore has converted most of it to gewurztraminer and muscat, selling both to wineries and amateur winemakers.

MORISSON-COUDERC: This French nursery was the primary source of vinifera vines from Europe that were planted in the Okanagan between 1990 and 1993, when import restrictions were imposed by Canada after some plant viruses were detected. Morisson-Couderc, which was founded in 1880, is a generally well-regarded nursery which exports vines to many markets.

MORROW, CHARLES (1898–1980): Vernon lawyer and judge, he was called to the bar in 1920 and retired in 1972. He chaired the 1970 inquiry into British Columbia's liquor laws whose eminently sensible recommendations were ignored by the government of the day. See also *Inquiries*.

MOSER, PAUL (1949–) AND VEREENA: Owners and operators of Lake Breeze Vineyards, an attractive winery near Naramata. See *Lake Breeze*.

MÜLLER-THURGAU: This variety was created in 1882 at *Geisenheim* by one Dr. Hermann Müller who came from the Swiss canton of Thurgau. In the 1980s it was the most extensively planted white variety in Germany and also came to be planted widely elsewhere in the world, including British Columbia. The variety is productive and ripens early but the wine almost always is unmemorable.

MUNCKHOF, GARY (1951–): He is formally identified on his business card as Gerard Van Den Munckhof but everyone calls him Gary and, informal and easygoing, he does not insist on the *Van Den* part of the title which resonates of distinguished ancestors in Holland, where he was born. His family in Holland had been in the farm machinery business and Munckhof, who emigrated to Canada in 1973, established his own Munckhof Mfg. in Oliver four years later to produce or sell highly specialized machines for orchards and vineyards. To honour a promise to his Dutch-born wife, Tonnie, Munckhof in 1985 bought an apple orchard at one of the highest points of the so-called *Golden Mile* south of Oliver because the property affords a spectacular view from the new house that he built subsequently.

The Munckhofs quickly got rid of the apple trees. "Grapes actually speak more to the imagination," he believes.

Now with a fourteen-acre vineyard and room for another five or six acres, Munckhof planted vinifera from the very beginning, starting with chardonnay, riesling and müller-thurgau. "Everyone was telling me I was nuts," he says. "I wanted to be as modern as possible." Subsequently, he has added pinot blanc, pinot noir and three-quarters of an acre of lemberger, the latter because he favours the variety's deeply-coloured, full-bodied red wines. "Every wine region should have a bit of red wine," he insists. He believes that his vineyard, because of its soils and its elevation high above the valley, yields some of the more flavoursome grapes in the Okanagan. There must be something to that contention since he sells his fruit to *Gray Monk*, an estate winery noted for the juicy style of its wines.

MUSCAT: A large family of grapes exists under the muscat umbrella, often producing wines with distinctive spicy perfume and intense flavour, whether made crisply dry or in the style of dessert wines. The kiss of spice shows up in a number of varieties (such as schönburger) that have been developed from crosses that included muscat varieties. With its Dry Muscat Blanc, *Hillside Cellars* has been a keen exponent of muscat wines.

MUST: This is the winemaking term for crushed grapes at the beginning of fermentation.

1   Emile Peynaud, *Knowing and Making Wine*, John Wiley & Sons, New York, 1984.

2   Robert A. Campbell, *Demon Rum or Easy Money*, p. 134. (See SOURCES for complete reference.)

3   *The Province*, August 1968.

4   Quoted in Campbell, *Demon Rum or Easy Money*, p. 123.

5   Ibid.

6   Liquor Distribution Branch, 62nd Annual Report, p. 35.

7   Interview with author, 1982.

8   Okanagan Historical Society, 31st Report, 1967.

9   *B.C. Wines Notes*, April/May 1984, p. 9.

10   *The Financial Post*, October 7, 1967.

11   Letter dated May 17, 1966, in Lloyd Schmidt files.

12   Annual report in Lloyd Schmidt files.

13   Mission Hill Wines Ltd. letter to shareholders, May 11, 1970; in John Vielvoye's scrapbook.

14   *Vancouver Sun*, August 19, 1970.

15   Interview with author, 1996.

NNN

NEVRKLA, HANS (1946–): With his wife, Hazel, Hans Nevrkla — it is pronounced "never claw" — is the proprietor of **Larch Hills Winery** in Salmon Arm, B.C. Born in Vienna, a city surrounded by wineries, Nevrkla and his British-born wife came to Canada in 1970, young emigrants possessed with a spirit of adventure who settled in Calgary. Nevrkla is an electronics technician who took a winemaking course in Calgary shortly after arriving, embracing the subject so thoroughly that his wines began to win awards and he began to teach both making and appreciating wine in Calgary's school system. During one of their trips to the Okanagan to buy fresh grapes, the Nevrklas were so charmed by the Salmon Arm area that they moved there in 1987 and established a computer consulting business. "We didn't intend at first to grow grapes," Hazel says. "That just happened." Their first vintage for commercial release was 400 gallons of wine made in 1995.

NEWSLETTERS: Several wineries publish regular newsletters available at no charge to customers and friends. While focussed on their own wineries, they also provide information bearing on industry trends. As a bonus, highly original recipes are featured in most. The best newsletters are from **Hainle Vineyards** at Peachland and **Venturi-Schultze Vineyards** at Cobble Hill on Vancouver Island. **Quails' Gate** publishes *The Wine Barrell* while **Tinhorn Creek** launched in 1996 a promising quarterly newsletter called **Tinhorn Tales**.

NEWTON CROFT VINEYARDS: Wine-growing resumes where it began in British Columbia — on the Saanich Peninsula north of Victoria — if a winery proposed by former owners Peter and Wendy Longcroft proceeds. However, unlike the 1920s when the industry was based on loganberries, Newton Croft is expected to make grape wines. The varieties in the compact two-acre Saanichton vineyard include ortega, pinot noir, pinot gris and pinot blanc.

NICHOL, ALEXANDER (1945–): Formerly a professional musician, Nichol now produces harmony from a vineyard planted in 1990 on a one-time pear orchard near Naramata. Born in Calgary, Nichol became a double bass player, starting his professional career in 1961 with the National Youth Orchestra. He subsequently played with the Vancouver Symphony Orchestra and with the Halle Orchestra in Manchester. During a 1979 musical sabbatical in London, Nichol also took a diploma wine appreciation course, returning to Vancouver determined to start his own winery. Nichol's research of his subject including writing a 1983 book, *Wines and Vines of British Columbia*. A self-taught winemaker, Nichol strives to make wines of intense concentration and character, achieved by leaving skins of crushed grapes (even white grapes) soaking in their own juice at cool temperatures for extended periods before, during and after fermentation. His pinot gris, a relatively pale wine in the hands of most other producers, is a bronze-coloured, deeply flavoured wine.

NICHOL, KATHLEEN (1947–): Born in the gold-mining town of Bralorne, Kathleen Nichol has a master's degree in library science and has been a corporate librarian for a bank and a software consultant and marketer. But since she and husband Alexander Nichol bought property near Naramata in 1988 and planted a vineyard, she has become adept at viticulture and at marketing the products of their winery.

NICHOL VINEYARD FARM WINERY: Opened in the summer of 1993, this winery is based on a neatly tended five-and-a-half-acre vineyard whose stony soil abuts a towering cliff of westward-facing rock. The cliff collects the sun's heat, radiating it back over the vineyard at night, allowing owners Alex and Kathleen Nichol to mature syrah, a Rhone variety not usually grown in the Okanagan. Other specialties from this winery include cabernet franc and ehrenfelser.

NICHOLSON, BRUCE (1958–): A native of Niagara Falls, Nicholson is a graduate chemical engineer who, after making wine at home, became so determined to become a vintner that he offered to work without salary at *Inniskillin* just to get his foot in the door of a winery. Before Inniskillin replied, Nicholson was hired in 1986 for the laboratory of the Chateau-Gai winery in Niagara Falls. The next year he was transferred to *Casabello*, Chateau-Gai's sister winery in Penticton, B.C., as an assistant to winemaker Tom Seaver, whom Nicholson succeeded when Seaver was transferred to Ontario in 1989. The Penticton winery closed in 1994 after Casabello (by then operating under the *Cartier* name) was taken over by *Vincor*. Nicholson moved to the Vincor winery at Oliver as an assistant to *Frank Supernak*, then the winemaker there.

NOBLE ROT: This is what winemakers call botrytis bunch rot when, under favourable weather conditions, it attacks mature grapes and dehydrates them, allowing winemakers to produce dessert wines almost as sweet as *icewines* and almost always with more complexity. But if the botrytis infects a vineyard and then it rains, the outcome is grey rot, a disaster that is anything but noble. The rot can be forestalled with sulphur sprays. In the generally dry Okanagan, harvest botrytis is uncommon.

NORDIQUE BLANC: This concept wine was created initially for *Inkameep Vineyards* which invested $100,000 in 1989 to package and market in the United States a crisp, dry white made from ehrenfelser grapes from the 1988 vintage. The name and the package — a clear Bordeaux bottle with clean white label — played on Canada's pristine winter image in the American mind. The object was to create a brand that could compete both internationally and domestically and around which Inkameep could develop a winery, should demand for the vineyard's grapes dry up when winery contracts expired in 1994 at the end of the six-year period of adjustment to free trade. (As it happened, Inkameep had no difficulty renewing grape contracts.) The 1988 Nordique Blanc was made by *Walter Gehringer*; in subsequent years, the production was contracted with various other wineries, including *Andrés*, *Quails' Gate* and *Summerhill*. The first release was a critical success in the United States but at a retail price (generally $5.99 a bottle) too low to make the venture commercially attractive. Ultimately, the brand was licensed by Summerhill, whose owner **Stephen Cipes** was instrumental in marketing the original vintage of Nordique Blanc in the United States.

NOUVEAU: Wines described as nouveau — as in Beaujolais Nouveau — are the new wines of that vintage. It has long been the tradition in Beaujolais (and in Italy where the new wine is called vino novello) that light, fruity red wines are made deliberately in a style that permits them to be released and enjoyed within sixty days of the harvest. These quaffing wines are meant to be consumed by Christmas and certainly no later than the following spring and should not be cellared with the expectation that age will improve them. *Mission Hill*'s 1982 Foch Nouveau, released on November 15, 1982, was the first nouveau wine made in British Columbia. Using maréchal foch grapes grown by *Terry Wells*, then a grower near Oliver, Mission Hill winemaker *Daniel Lagnaz* made 6,000 bottles. *Calona* subsequently also began making a nouveau wine each fall.

OOO

OAK: A hardwood, oak is used to make wine barrels and vats because the wood is strong and watertight. Even more important, many wines (but not all) benefit from what happens to them when they are fermented and/or stored in oak barrels. The traditional and preferred oaks for wine barrels are those from the various forests of France, of which the best known are limousin, nevers, alliers and vosge, names that can be seen burned into the heads of wine barrels. Less preferred, because the wood is more porous, is oak from Slavonia. American oak has both its adherents and its detractors because it imparts sweeter, spicier flavours to wines which some vintners find lacking in subtlety. However, American oak has been gaining ground among wineries in the Okanagan, in part because the barrels are a third the cost of French oak barrels and in part because cooperages in the United States, by applying French barrel-making techniques, are making significantly better barrels. Many winemakers believe that the flavours of oak, if not overdone, add complexity to wines. Wines matured in barrels also develop a softer texture than those aged in stainless steel. Other winemakers have established a style that deliberately avoids oak in order to retain the pure and fresh fruit flavours of the grape. There is validity in either style. See also *Cooperage*.

OAK BAY VINEYARDS: This is the vineyard owned and operated by *Andy Gebert*, a partner with his brother in the *St. Hubertus* winery. The Oak Bay name also serves as the label for premium barrel-aged wines that St. Hubertus began producing with the 1994 vintage when the winery decided to break with its early practice of avoiding the use of oak in its winemaking.

OKANAGAN CELLARS: This label was created in 1977 by *Calona Wines* as the vehicle for some of their dry table wines.

OKANAGAN RIESLING: This heavy-bearing vine once was the most widely planted white grape variety in British Columbia and served as the backbone for many blended table wines and for varietals from several wineries. Production of this variety expanded dramatically during the wine boom of the 1970s, from 385 tonnes in 1970 to 2,800 tonnes in 1978. Some 523 acres of this vine had been planted by 1979 and the growers' affection for it continued, with growers planting so extensively between 1980 and 1983 that the acreage swelled to 900. The last year in which the variety was planted was 1986, when 3.4 acres was added to bring the grand total to 980.6 acres dedicated to Okanagan riesling, about a quarter of British Columbia's total producing acreage.[1] Almost all the vines were destroyed in the vineyard pullout of 1988, with a provincial government survey in 1989 showing that slightly less than five producing acres remained.

The origin of this vine is contentious. In a paper written in 1969 *John Vielvoye* traced the origin back to a vineyard established near Oliver in 1932 by one Joseph Renyi, a Hungarian immigrant and a friend of Dr. Eugene Rittich.

Together, they collaborated in a five-acre vineyard which included riesling, according to Vielvoye. Subsequently, cuttings from this block were transported to other vineyards and the so-called Okanagan riesling took hold because it was so hardy and productive. Vielvoye reasoned that the original vines may have come from the nursery of Hungarian plant breeder Alexander Teleki. It is known that the **Rittich** brothers imported a variety known as *excellent,* which perhaps became the variety later known as Okanagan riesling. "It is a *very old Hungarian variety* and in older times one of the chief grape varieties in Hungary," they wrote in their book, *European Grape Growing.* "It is a wine grape with a *juice* high in sugar and low in acid content when perfectly ripe."[2] Others have speculated that the Okanagan riesling was merely a hybrid with labrusca parentage developed by chance in the Okanagan.[3]

No winemaker misses this variety. **Sumac Ridge**, by dint of diligent effort, won awards for its Okanagan riesling wines, a considerable achievement because, in the hands of most winemakers, the grape produced heavy, coarse wines with unpleasant aromas that recalled old hay barns. The winemakers from Germany who arrived in the Okanagan in the 1970s despised the grape. "It has a foxy flavour," winemaker *Josef Zimmerman* said. "I hate to put the riesling name on it. We ruin the image of riesling."[4]

OKANAGAN VINEYARDS: A small commercial winery south of Oliver, Okanagan Vineyards began life in 1979 as an estate winery called **Vinitera**. The name was changed when the winery was purchased out of receivership in 1984 by Vancouver car dealer **Bill Docksteader.** He sold the winery in 1987 to a group headed by **Alan Tyabji.** Unusual until recently among commercial wineries, Okanagan Vineyards owns a twenty-three-acre vineyard. After the 1988 vine pull, it was entirely replanted to vinifera varieties such as merlot and cabernet sauvignon.

OKANAGAN WINE FESTIVAL: Begun in 1982 as **September,** this annual event is the premier harvest festival and competition for the British Columbia wine industry. Usually beginning in late September and concluding on the Thanksgiving weekend in early October, the festival includes lunches, dinners, tastings and tours at almost every winery. It culminates in a large public tasting in one of the Okanagan's cities at which awards are announced for the wines that have competed.

These wineries have won gold medals at the festival from 1982 through 1995: **Mission Hill** (ten); **Gray Monk** (nine); **Gehringer Brothers** (six); **Sumac Ridge** (six); **Brights/Jackson-Triggs** (six); **CedarCreek** (three plus one platinum award); **Andrés** (three); **Calona** (three); **Blue Mountain** (three); **Casabello** (two); **Quails' Gate** (two); and one each by **Claremont, Hainle, Lang, LeComte, Jordan & Ste-Michelle,** and **Uniacke**. See also **Competitions**.

OLDFIELD, KENN (1955–): Born in Orillia, Ont., Oldfield was a private consultant in process engineering in Red Deer, Alta., until he agreed to become a partner and vineyard manager of **Tinhorn Creek Vineyards Ltd.** in 1992. He had become friends with **Robert Shaunessy,**

Tinhorn Creek's senior partner, when both were students at the University of Waterloo. A shared interest in wines led to the partnership after Shaunessy, an Alberta oil executive, purchased vineyard property in the south Okanagan in 1992.

Sandra Oldfield (photo courtesy John Schreiner)

OLDFIELD, SANDRA (1966–):

The winemaker at *Tinhorn Creek* and the wife (since August 1995) of the winery's manager, Kenn Oldfield, she was born Sandra Cashman in Oakland, Ca., into a family whose only wine tradition was an Italian grandfather who made wine in the bathtub at home. After getting a business administration degree and travelling in Europe, she took a casual job in 1989 in the tasting room at the Rodney Strong winery in Sonoma. In short order, she was moved to the winery's laboratory and to a career decision. "It was immediate," she says. "I knew this was what I wanted to do." She was at the Strong winery through three vintages, learning practical aspects of winemaking. In 1993 she enrolled in the master's program in enology at the University of California's Davis campus. Her thesis,

which involved research in the vineyards of the Robert Mondavi winery, was on the development of flavour compounds as cabernet sauvignon ripens. At Davis, she met Oldfield and agreed to become winemaker at Tinhorn Creek, the estate winery south of Oliver that opened in 1995. She confesses to having been unaware that a wine industry even existed in British Columbia before meeting Oldfield.

OPTIMA: This German white grape was created in 1970 when müller-thurgau was crossed with a sylvaner-riesling cross. The variety ripens early and produces high sugar levels. As a result, it yields richly flavoured dessert wines, particularly in years when the grapes have been touched by *noble rot* (usually identified on the labels as botrytis, for obvious reason).

ORGANIC WINES: These are wines produced from grapes grown organically — that is, without the use of pesticides, herbicides or chemical fertilizers. By 1995 three Okanagan wineries had converted to organic grapegrowing: *Hainle*, *Summerhill* and *Quails' Gate*. The use of chemicals, never extensive in winemaking, is absolutely minimal in organic wines, limited primarily to sulphur dioxide. This is an essential sterilant whose usage is measured in parts per million.

ORTEGA: This white variety, a crossing of müller-thurgau and siegerrebe, is noted for producing full-flavoured grapes with high sugars and is useful in making dessert wines. While the grape was developed in Germany, it is inexplicably named after the Spanish philosopher Jose Ortega y Gasset.

OXIDATION: Careless oxidation is one of the most common of wine faults in table wines, even if it also is one of the most avoidable simply by not exposing wines to air beyond the normal requirements of handling. Wine in barrels or tanks must be protected from the air. The simplest way of doing this is to keep the containers full. The alternative is to displace the air in a partly filled container with either nitrogen or carbon dioxide, both inert gases that form a protective layer above the wines. In traditional winemaking of earlier times, some winemakers protected their wines by floating a thick layer of olive oil on top of them. Oxidized table wines lose freshness and take on dull, metallic flavours.

Deliberate oxidation of wine is another matter. Winemakers such as *Tilman Hainle* espouse what is called oxidative winemaking in which minimal exposure to air is tolerated in order to develop complex, sometimes nutty, flavours in wines. Well-known fortified wines such as sherry also are examples of oxidative winemaking where specific strains of yeast promote the development of complex flavours without spoilage.

---

[1] British Columbia Grape Marketing Board statistics.

[2] Virgil J. and Dr. Eugene A. Rittich, *European Grape Growing*, p. 81. (See SOURCES for complete reference.)

[3] John Vielvoye, "Okanagan Reisling," 1969. (Paper in author's fiels.)

[4] Interview with author in 1978.

PPP

PACIFIC VINEYARDS: In 1965 *Richard Stewart* in partnership with *Calona Wines* developed a two hundred-acre vineyard north of Osoyoos, planting hybrids such as chelois, de chaunac, verdelet and one vinifera, chasselas. Stewart and Calona operations manager *Joe Capozzi* decided on these varieties after seeking advice from growers in Niagara and New York state, who were beginning to enjoy success with the hybrids. Stewart and Capozzi wisely rejected suggestions that they plant concord, a labrusca, which was favoured by the Taylor vineyard in Hammondsport, N.Y. They decided not to chance other vinifera varieties after viewing how the previous winter had ravaged Charles Fournier's pioneering vinifera plantings at the Gold Seal vineyard, also in New York. "Our impression was that he's trying vinifera but you can't grow them here," Stewart said later.[1] The planting of Pacific Vineyards proved to be an adventure in rattlesnake avoidance. One labourer returned from a break to his tractor to find a rattler curled around the gear shift lever. No one suffered a serious snakebite. The Pacific Vineyards partnership also included eight acres of leased vineyard land near Westbank, planted almost equally to labrusca and hybrid varieties. In August 1968 Calona Wines acquired Stewart's interest and became the largest vineyard operator in the Okanagan. After Calona was purchased in 1971 by Standard Brands, Pacific Vineyards was sold to a syndicate of British Columbia investors who ran it until the vines were pulled out after the 1988 harvest.

PACIFIC WESTERN WINES LTD.: This firm was established in July 1959 in New Westminster and acquired that November by Jordan Wines, which changed the name to West Coast Wines Ltd. in 1960 and then to Villa Wines Ltd. in 1967. The first wines listed in government liquor stores were two ports, two sherries, red, white and rosé table wines and a wine called Berry Cup. Later it fleshed out its line with two so-called "mellow" table wines and Loganport, a blend of port wine and loganberry wine. The winery closed in 1970 after its production was merged with that of *Growers'* in Victoria.

PANDOSY, FATHER CHARLES (1824–1891): Oblate missionary Charles John Felix Adolf Marie Pandosy in 1859 arrived in the Okanagan to establish a mission, the first permanent non-native settlement in the British Columbia Interior other than Hudson's Bay posts. "The tillable land is immense," he wrote in his first report to his superiors that October. Credited with planting the first vines in the Okanagan, his name was memorialized as a label for a line of wines produced by Mission Hill in the 1980s. But while the mission farm included the first vines in the Okanagan, viticulture was no more a priority than growing vegetables. The often-repeated claim that Father Pandosy was the founder of the British Columbia wine industry is fanciful. There is no record that he ever sold a bottle of wine.

He was born at Margerdies, a village in Provence near Marseilles, son of a land-owning family; after considering a naval career, he joined the Oblates, an order that had been founded two years after his birth. (The full name of the order is Congregation of Missionary Oblates of Mary Immaculate — *oblate* meaning one who offers himself.) In 1847 he was among a group of Oblates who left France as missionaries to the natives in what is now Washington state. Between 1848 and 1855 there was a series of wars between settlers and Indians, during which American militia, believing the priests in collusion with the Indians, burned one of their Washington missions. The Oblates then closed their other missions in the Washington interior and Pandosy led a group of missionaries to the Okanagan in 1859, opening a new mission just east of modern-day Kelowna the following year.

In one letter Pandosy described the mission site. "It is a great valley situated on the left bank of the great Lake Okanagan and rather near the middle of the Lake.... The cultivable land is immense and I myself believe that if Fr. Blanchet [a fellow Oblate in Oregon] is able to send us next year, some vine cuttings we shall be able to start a plantation, for when Bro. Surel arrives, if he accepts my plans, we shall elevate our little demesne

to the middle of the plain, against a little hill very well exposed...." With the exception of two postings to Vancouver Island (1860–63) and Fort St. James (1882–87), Pandosy spent the remainder of his life in the Okanagan, having become the superior at the mission. "He was a huge, powerfully built man with a booming voice and ready wit," local historian Primrose Upton wrote. "He had large deep-set eyes, well-marked eyebrows, long straight nose, high scholarly forehead, curly black hair and a full beard. He had a very hot temper and was capable of amazing feats of strength, yet was gentle." Upton relates an anecdote of how he frightened off some natives that surrounded his tent during his first night in the Okanagan. He took a butcher knife, cut a target on a tree and from several paces, proceeded to throw the knife to the target three times. Suitably awed, the Indians withdrew quietly.[2]

PARADISE RANCH: This ninety-acre vineyard perches picturesquely above Lake Okanagan north of Naramata. A ranch and orchard homesteaded in 1904, it was acquired in 1975 by the late **Dr. Hu Harries,** an Edmonton consulting economist, who, with his sons Bruce and Jeffrey, began planting vines in 1981. The vineyard was called Koosi Creek, after the creek running along one boundary. The primary variety put in that year was verdelet, Dr. Harries having decided that it would be risky to plant vinifera. In the spring of 1995, the vineyard grafted sixty acres of existing vines (mostly verdelet and two other now-unwanted hybrids, seyval blanc and baco noir) to the more desirable varieties, pinot blanc, pinot gris, chardonnay and merlot. This was the Okanagan's most extensive application of what amounts to a technical shortcut. Rather than ripping out vines and replacing them, the existing vines are cut off at knee level and short canes of the replacement variety are fastened tightly against the cut, forming a bond that enables the new cane to grow and produce grapes. This technique, proven with apple trees and in vineyards elsewhere in the world, allows the replacement canes to benefit from the existing mature root systems. The canes produce about one-tenth the normal crop in the year of the graft and a full crop the following year. Newly planted vines need four years to achieve full production. When done carefully by skilled grafting technicians, the majority of the grafts will bond successfully.

PASSMORE, LARRY (1950–): The senior partner in *Bella Vista Vineyards*, Passmore was born in Vernon and trained as a computer technician. In 1982 he harnessed his experience as an amateur beermaker to open a retail outlet catering to other amateur brewers and vintners. In 1991, when a vineyard on a mountainside above Vernon went onto the market, Passmore enlisted fourteen of his best friends and customers to buy the property. In 1994 the group launched the *Bella Vista* winery, known for the party-time enthusiasm with which the owners welcome visitors to wine tastings.

PELLER, ANDREW (1903–1994): The Hungarian-born founder of *Andrés*

Andrew Peller (photo courtesy of Barry McLean)

171

Wines, Peller was so entrepreneurial that he began his autobiography with a dismissive comment about his unsuccessful bricklayer father. "An intensely religious man ... perhaps he never succeeded because of his conviction that the Almighty did not need nor want his assistance," Peller wrote.[3] After graduating in 1922 from Budapest University in engineering, he left for Canada five years later because discrimination against German-speakers like the Pellers constrained his opportunities in Hungary. He applied his engineering skills as a maintenance technician with a Kitchener brewery and ultimately became a brewmaster and then the owner in 1945 of the Peller Brewing Co. in Hamilton. The ever-inventive Peller got around a government ban on beer advertising by starting an ice company and advertising Peller's ice. The brewery was sold in 1953. The Ontario regulators, humiliated by Peller's "ice-capade," retaliated when he decided to start a winery there in 1960: they would only let him make what they called Rhine wine, clearly too narrow a market for success. Peller headed to British Columbia, which threw up no frivolous limit- ations to his establishing Andrés Wines in 1961. It was built in Port Moody in part because the development-hungry community "practically gave me the property," and in part because he thought it better to be near the market than near the vineyards.[4] The winery's name was Peller's baptismal name in Hungary.[5] By 1974 Andrés had six wineries across Canada, including a large one that became its headquarters in Winona, Ont. Peller's son, Joseph, succeeded his father in 1965 as the company's president and his grandson, John, became president twenty years

after that. Andrew Peller remained the company's chairman until his death.

PELLER, JOSEPH. (1926–):
A 1948 graduate in medicine from the University of Toronto, the eldest surviving son of *Andrew Peller* dutifully took leave in 1965 — he was chief of medicine at Hamilton Civic Hospital — when the management of *Andrés* winery had become too onerous for his father. Andrew Peller, in his autobiography, recalled the conversation with his son: "Here's the situation, Joe. I'm sixty-two years old and I just can't take the strain anymore. It's getting to me. It's all this robbing Peter to pay Paul and not having someone I can trust who won't do me in every time I turn around. You're the only one I can turn to. Would you consider coming with me and taking over the Vancouver plant?" When Andrés purchased its Ontario winery in 1969, Joseph Peller gave up his medical career entirely. "I didn't feel I had much of a choice," he said later. "We were a close-knit European family."[6]

PETRONIO, JOSEPH (1935–):
For seventeen years, until they sold their Oliver vineyard in 1995, Joe Petronio and his wife, Rosaria, were among the most successful growers of chenin blanc in the Okanagan. In 1994 and again in 1995, their grapes were used in excellent *icewines* made by *Vincor*. It began with a dream. During a dozen years as a carpenter in Vancouver, Joe Petronio had had several frighteningly close calls on the job and also had developed arthritis. All of this was preying on his mind one night late in 1977 when — "at 2:20 in the morning to be precise," his wife says — Petronio awakened and asked Rosaria

what she thought about buying a vineyard in Oliver. Joe had been impressed by the quality of grapes he had purchased that fall from the Okanagan for home winemaking. His wife thought it was a good idea. By April 1978, they were living in a new house on an old vineyard south of Oliver.

Both were born in Trieste, in northeastern Italy. Joe Petronio's father had grown grapes but Joe wanted to see the world and he emigrated to Canada in 1957. Rosaria, whom he had met as a student, followed him in 1959. Both were interested in medicine (Rosaria had considered going to medical school before emigrating) and Joe became a medical orderly, switching to carpentry seven years later because it was more lucrative. After the Petronios moved to Oliver, Rosaria became a nurse's aide, successfully juggling that career with helping her husband in the vineyard. They converted an orchard, planting (on the advice of *Casabello*) primarily chenin blanc in the seven-acre vineyard, with modest acreages of chardonnay, white riesling, verdelet and some table grapes. Rosaria made herself expert in viticulture by going back to Italy, for advice and texts. Subsequently she and Joe visited other winegrowing regions as far away as Australia, looking for tips to improve their skills. "You have to have a call from inside of you," she says of the vocation of viticulture. They sold the vineyard suddenly, if reluctantly, in November 1995 (to German immigrants *Ulricke* and *August Flohr*) because Joe's arthritis had returned and Rosaria had injured her back — ironically, not in the vineyard but in the hospital. "I was devastated when the vineyard was sold," Rosaria admitted.

Elias Phiniotis

PHINIOTIS, ELIAS (1943–):

An influential winemaker and consultant (with his wife, Christine) in the Okanagan, Phiniotis was born into a winemaking and grapegrowing family on Cyprus. On a scholarship, he earned a master's degree in chemical engineering (specializing in food chemistry) from the University of Technical Sciences in Budapest, following that with a doctorate in the technology of food chemistry from Budapest's Research Institute of Viticulture and Enology. After three years at a Cypriot winery, he came to Canada in 1976 and spent two years as the technical director of *Wine-Art*, a retail chain of stores dedicated to home winemaking, before becoming the winemaker at *Ben Ginter's* winery near Westbank. Finding the winery excessively dependent on sweet red and fortified wines, Phiniotis expanded the product line to include several successful whites. At the same time, he helped two new estate wineries — *Chateau Jonn de Trepanier* and *Vinitera* — to produce their initial vintages of varietals. He moved to *Casabello* in 1980 and then to *Calona* in 1981. In the mid-1980s when it became evident that more vinifera would have to be planted in the Okanagan, Phiniotis was an early advocate of cabernet franc, now one of the most promising red varieties being grown in the valley. Since 1989, Phiniotis has been a consulting winemaker for several emerging wineries, including *Quails' Gate* and *Domaine de Chaberton.* In 1993 he also established a company called Pannonia Cooperage to import barrels made of Hungarian-grown *acacia* wood, an exotic alternative to oak.

At Calona, Phiniotis was a one-person winemaking revolution. Calona owned a number of large oak vats which had been in use for many years and had become totally encrusted internally with tartaric acids and other deposits. The vats still softened the wine during storage but had long since ceased giving any oak complexity to the wines. Phiniotis had them scraped and shaved; it refreshed the vats and, starting with the 1981 vintage, Calona began producing better reds than it had ever made. He also permitted the red wines to go through *malolactic fermentation*, an established winemaking technique elsewhere but almost unheard of then in the Okanagan. With this technique, Phiniotis softened the Okanagan's naturally tart acids and also added some flavour complexity to his wines. The varietals included chancellor, maréchal foch and rougeon, all of them hybrids. Most acreage of foch and rougeon was pulled out after the 1988 harvest but Calona had such substantial quantities in its vats, particularly of rougeon, that the vintages of the late 1980s stayed on the market, won several awards and became so popular that

Calona subsequently urged some growers to replant the variety.

PHYLLOXERA: This is a tiny insect — the full Latin name is *Phylloxera vastatrix* — that feeds on the roots of grape vines, with disastrous effect if those vines are the classic European *vitis vinifera* variety. In their book on grapegrowing in the Okanagan, the *Rittich* brothers warned that this root louse was the "most harmful grape pest" but that it was then (in the 1930s) unknown in the Okanagan. An occurrence in 1962 was believed to have been eradicated. But a more serious outbreak was spotted in 1971 at *Richard Stewart's* vineyard near Westbank (now the *Quails' Gate* vineyard), panicking the agricultural authorities, who were aware that the louse had nearly wiped out European winegrowing after making its appearance about 1860. Stewart believed that the pest was imported on maréchal foch vines that had been purchased from a nursery in Ontario about 1968. When the vines were in their third year, Stewart noticed that the leaves of many vines had developed galls — scablike growths which, on being opened, were full of larvae. The government horticulturists Stewart called in confirmed this was phylloxera; a check of the vine roots disclosed aphid-like insects feeding on them. The vineyard was quarantined and Stewart was permitted to market the grape crop only after agreeing to fumigate the harvested grapes with methyl bromide before shipping them to a winery. The vineyard workers had to wear protective clothing which was fumigated after each day in the field. The precautions were futile. Now alerted to phylloxera, inspectors and growers soon found evidence of the pest elsewhere in the Okanagan. Undoubtedly, the pest had been imported inadvertently along with the vines from eastern Canada and New York state, perhaps even by *J. W. Hughes* and the *Rittich* brothers. The latter conducted planting trials as early as 1931 at Kelowna with close to fifty European grape varieties.

Phylloxera is a devastating pest. By feeding on the roots, the insect weakens the vine, reducing its productivity and its ability to ripen fruit; the weakened vine is dangerously susceptible to other diseases. The insect is native to the eastern United States. The vines indigenous to that region, notably the *vitis labrusca* and *vitis riparia*, had evolved the ability to tolerate and repair the damage to the roots. The European varieties have no such tolerance. Many plant diseases were unwittingly imported to Europe from the new world both by amateur and by professional horticulturists. Vines infected with phylloxera made it to Europe about 1860,[7] destroying thousands of hectares of French vineyards over the next twenty years until the growers hit on what remains the only effective remedy: grafting the European vines onto North American rootstock. As a result, the roots tolerate the insect while supporting the European vines through a normal life cycle. Unfortunately, infected European vine cuttings were shipped to emerging grapegrowing areas like California and Australia before the nature of phylloxera was fully understood. Consequently, the pest is found in most wine regions with only a few exceptions, notably Chile. Either the Chileans imported their foundation cuttings before the phylloxera outbreak or the insects were unable to survive the very long sea journey in the era before fast steamships.

Even if some phylloxera made it to Chile, the insect would not thrive in Chile's dry and light soils.

Soil type has a bearing on how growers today deal with phylloxera in the Okanagan. Those in the desertlike south end of the valley do not consider the insect a major threat and many have planted European vines on their own roots. (Direct-rooted vines are cheaper than grafted vines and, arguably, are more productive.) Most growers on the heavier soils from Penticton north plant vines grafted onto phylloxera-tolerant roots, since it is well established that phylloxera spreads much more readily in clay-soil vineyards than in sandy-soil vineyards. As the Rittich brothers wrote in the 1930s: "They cannot live on poor sand, and nearly half the Hungarian vineyards are planted on such soil, where the vines are grown on their own roots."[8]

PIGGOTT, ALBERT (1925–): The proprietor of *Merridale Cider Works Ltd.* on Vancouver Island, Piggott was born in the town of Forfar on the east coast of Scotland. Technically trained in engineering and architecture, Piggott taught shop crafts until he and his wife, Betty, came to Canada in 1954, judging the opportunities better. Here, Piggott continued his teaching career on Vancouver Island until retiring at fifty-six to concentrate on a new passion: making genuine English cider. Piggott had been making fruit wines and apple ciders much of his adult life both in Scotland and in Canada. For Merridale — the cidery is at the end of Merridale Road near Cobble Hill — Piggott has an orchard planted with a complex selection of cider apple trees, varieties seldom seen outside France and Britain.

PINOT BLANC: A major vinifera grape widely grown in Europe, pinot blanc emerged from trials during the **Becker Project** as well-suited for producing excellent dry, flinty table wines in British Columbia. The grape has a variety of synonyms. Its Italian name, pinot grigio, is used by **Divino Estate Winery**.

PINOT CHARDONNAY: This was the name once used widely for chardonnay when it was thought, incorrectly, that chardonnay was a member of the extensive pinot family.

PINOT GRIS: A premium vinifera grape for white wine, the variety appears to have been introduced first to the Okanagan by **George Heiss, Sr.** of **Gray Monk Estate Winery**. The same variety flourishes under a variety of names: pinot grigio in Italy; rulander or grauer burgunder in Germany; tokay d'Alsace in Alsace; and szurkebarat in Hungary.

PINOT MEUNIER: This red grape has been planted in the Okanagan primarily as a blender to add fruity flavours to *sparkling wines*, which also is the grape's primary role in Champagne. *Lang Vineyards* at Naramata and *St. Hubertus* near Kelowna are among the handful that have produced varietal table wines from this grape.

PINOT NOIR: By general agreement among winemakers, this is the most challenging of the red vinifera grapes, the Holy Grail of so many vintners aiming for the great pinot noir. When grown and vinified successfully, pinot noir can display a bouquet of rose petals and strawberries and is seductively silken on the palate. Second-rate pinot noir can be a forgettable light wine. The difference between the two begins in the vineyard where the yield needs to be severely limited so that the vines produce concentrated flavours when the grapes are fully mature. In the winery, pinot noir usually is fermented at higher temperatures (up to 30°C) than other red grapes to extract more colour from the skins. Because the flavours are subtle, pinot noir is matured in French oak barrels rather than in the bolder-flavoured American oak. It goes without saying that good pinot noir will be expensive. The specialists in pinot noir table wine in British Columbia have included **Quails' Gate** and **Blue Mountain**. Pinot noir also is important in making **sparkling wine**. Bubblies made entirely with pinot noir were called *blanc de noirs*, literally white from reds (as opposed to chardonnay sparkling wines, called *blanc de blancs*).

PINOT REACH CELLARS: This name was chosen by **Susan Dulik** for a farmgate winery on which development began in 1996 on part of the Kelowna-area vineyard her grandfather **Martin Dulik** acquired from **J.W. Hughes**. The name reflects the winemaker's affection for pinot noir, pinot gris and other members of the pinot family; as well as her determination to reach for excellence.

PIPE: This is the name chosen by **Sumac Ridge** for its port-style wine from chancellor grapes. The name Port is reserved both by tradition and now by international law to fortified wines made in the northern Portugal winegrowing region on the River Douro. The wines are cellared and often bottled in the Portuguese city of Oporto — hence the origin of the wine's name. Pipe is derived from the Portuguese word *Pipa,* referring to a large cask in which the wines are matured. The pipes vary in size from 580 to 630 litres. Sumac Ridge is not the only winery to seek an appropriate term conveying the idea that the wine is made in the style of port, without using that name. The Quady winery in California uses Starboard while **Hainle Vineyards** has adopted **Fathom** for its port-style wine, made in 1993 from baco noir and Andrés calls its version *Dune.*

PLANT QUARANTINE CENTRE: See *Centre for Plant Health.*

POHLE, WALLACE: The wine-maker who was hired by **Andrés Wines** when it opened in 1961, Pohle had twenty-five years' experience with wineries in California. "He was a handsome man with prematurely grey hair," Andrew Peller wrote in his autobiography, describing their first meeting. "He chewed on the end of a cigar without which, I learned, he never appeared.... He really knew the business when it came to building the winery and I depended on him immediately." Peller later wrote that hiring Pohle was a mistake. The winemaker had technical limitations: he recommended against installing temperature controls on the fermentation vats — advice that Peller wisely rejected. For the first vintage Pohle used California grapes — there were no uncommitted wine grapes in the Okanagan — to produce eight different wines, including a medium dry red, a Rhine-type white, a rosé, two sherries and a ruby port. Unfortunately, the wines, when released in 1962, were not stable and began exploding in the liquor board warehouse and had to be recalled. But Pohle and his cigar did not return to California until 1965 when he was of-

fered, and refused, the post of chief winemaker for all three wineries (Port Moody, B.C., Calgary, and Truro, N.S.) that Andrés now operated. "Considering that he had a heart condition and that things were unbearably hectic, I could not blame him," wrote Peller. Pohle also helped **Casabello** with its first vintage in 1966.

POPLAR GROVE FARM WINERY: Located at the end of Poplar Grove Road near Naramata, this winery is based on a vineyard planted in 1993 primarily to merlot and cabernet franc by owner **Ian Sutherland**. A lover of Bordeaux red wines, Sutherland is focussed on red wines.

POTTER DISTILLERIES LTD.: Established in 1958 by Ernest C. Potter and acquired in 1962 by the **Terry** family, the company got into the wine business in August 1983 by opening the modest 100,000-gallon **Beaupré** winery in a Langley industrial park next to the distillery. The winery name was taken from the brand name for a French brandy that Potter was selling. Beaupré made wines from Okanagan grapes and blended some with imported bulk wines to produce undistinguished brands such as Vin Foch & Cabernet Sauvignon. Potter was renamed **International Potter Distilling Corp.** in 1986 after the Terry family sold control. After Potter took over **Calona Wines Ltd**. in 1989, Beaupré was closed. The name was changed again in 1995 to **Cascadia Brands Inc.**, reflecting both the declining sales of distilled products and the company's desire to export its beers and wines under a more generic name.

POTURICA, JOE: A wine buyer who came to Canada in 1953 from Yugosla-

via, Poturica and his sons, Tony and Silvio, began growing grapes in a vineyard south of Oliver in 1967. They opened British Columbia's second estate winery, *Vinitera,* in 1979. The wines were rustic and the winery slipped into receivership in 1982.

POWELL, DEN (1934–): Born in Kelowna, the son of *Henry Dennis Powell,* he learned agriculture by working for *J.W. Hughes,* as his father had done before him. Ultimately, Powell took over the family's vineyard on a farm on Casorso Road, just at the edge of Kelowna.

POWELL, HENRY DENNIS (1905–): Born in Portland, Eng., and raised on his grandfather's dairy farm, Powell came to Canada in May 1928. In Winnipeg, where many immigrants disembarked from the train to register for work, Powell was recruited by *J.W. Hughes,* who gave him a summer job as a teamster on Hughes's Pioneer Ranch near Kelowna. The next spring Powell was rehired by Hughes and, by 1931, was a foreman on the Pioneer Ranch, so named because it had been a large cattle ranch. "He was tight," Powell said of Hughes, "but if you didn't like what he paid, you didn't have to work for him." Apparently satisfied with what he was offered, Powell received 12.5 cents an hour when he started and doubled his salary when he became foreman.[9] In 1944 Powell became the first of Hughes's foremen to agree to terms for purchasing a thirty-acre vineyard portion of Pioneer Ranch over seven years. The vineyard had been planted with a number of labrusca and hybrid varieties, among them Campbell's early, sheridan and patricia, hardy plants to survive the Kelowna cold. "The winters seemed colder then than now," Powell said years later. "You could sit in the house and hear the [frozen] stalks crack — like the crack of a rifle." Even when the shattered trunks died, the vines regenerated from the roots. Powell and his son, *Den Powell,* continued Hughes's practice of selling many grapes into the fresh market as well as to wineries. They also replaced many of the older varieties with the hybrids more in demand for winemaking. "That's what the wineries want," the elder Powell told a Kelowna newspaper in October 1981. "It's getting pretty scientific now and sometimes I feel like we're getting left behind."[10] But after the 1988 vintage, the wine grapes, which made up half the vineyard, were removed, leaving primarily table grapes, with Den Powell devoting himself to operating a trucking business and raising cattle.

PROHIBITION: An Essay

Now the province with the country's highest per capita consumption of wine, British Columbia once voted for prohibition, with the province legally dry for four years.

The temperance movement in Canada began in the Atlantic Provinces in the mid-nineteenth century and thrived there and in Ontario as austere Protestantism sought to curb the harddrinking of frontier Canadians. They drank primarily beer or hard spirits; the immigrants who settled Canada did not come from wine traditions. By the end of the century the temperance movement was so strong that Sir Wilfrid Laurier's Liberals in the 1896 election campaign promised a national referendum. Every province supported prohibition in the 1898 referendum, except Quebec, Laurier's own province, which decisively opposed going dry. Laurier then refused national prohibition but allowed provinces and even individual counties to choose prohibition. Many did so in Ontario and the Maritimes.

British Columbians in the 1898 referendum, with fewer than a third of the eligible voters casting ballots, voted 5,731 for prohibition, 4,756 against. In 1909, another provincial referendum was taken on local option. The majority — 22,771 to 19,184 — favoured the use of local option votes, enabling individual municipalities to go dry. But when nothing much happened, a group calling itself The Prohibition Party for a Prohibitory Act pressured Sir Richard McBride's Conservatives until another prohibition referendum was scheduled in 1916, amid patriotic clamour that giving up alcohol somehow advanced the war effort. Ironically, soldiers overseas also were allowed to vote, with hilarious consequences. A pamphlet written at the time by a Presbyterian temperance advocate in Vancouver, Reverend W.H. Smith, recounted that at least seventy affidavits collected from servicemen admitted fraud. "These showed that men had voted twice, some three or four times, upon the false information that previous ballots had been 'lost,' 'destroyed,' or 'sunk by submarine.'"[11] The government appointed a royal commission which found that 4,697 votes were falsified, including 58 from men who had died in battle *before the voting*. Even so, the prohibitionists still won handily (41,904 for, 36,102 against) and the British Columbia Prohibition Act came into force October 1, 1917, banning the sale of all intoxicating beverages (those with more than 2.5 percent alcohol) with the exception of products sold for medicinal, sacramental or manufacturing purposes. After one doctor gave 4,100 prescriptions in one month and others wrote more than 1,000 each, amendments limited prescriptions to 200 a month by each doctor.

Prohibition in British Columbia was high farce. Because alcoholic beverages still could be sold by prescription, the government opened liquor stores in Vancouver, Victoria, Nanaimo, Prince Rupert, Quesnel, Cranbrook and New Denver. In 1919 these stores had sales totalling $1,579,475. Some 315,177 prescriptions were honoured that year at government and drug stores. The great 1919 flu epidemic alone justified half those prescriptions. "In Vancouver queues a quarter of a mile long could be seen waiting their turn to enter the liquor stores to get prescriptions filled," a secretary to the premier wrote, describing the situation towards Christmas 1919.[12] Even businesses took to getting permits to buy alcohol. "It is very questionable," huffed the government's Prohibition Commissioner in 1920, "if there is any real need for the issuance of any permit to obtain and keep liquor in case of accident or emergency, especially in view of the great number of such establishments who can do without it." Most of the "medicine" that British Columbians bought was rye whisky, but the government stores in 1919 also sold 1,362 gallons of port, 445 gallons of sherry, 35 cases of champagne and 47 cases of St. Augustine wine (a brand used, mostly, for sacramental purposes).[13]

The first Prohibition Commissioner, appointed in 1918, was Walter C. Findlay. Within a few months, he was caught bootlegging, was fined $1,000 and jailed for two years."[14] He was replaced in January 1919 by an individual who signed himself as J. Sclater and who took the job more seriously. He noted in the first report for the office, published in March 1920, that there had been 896 prosecutions under the Act in 1919, leading to 805 convictions, usually for possession of liquor. The government collected $54,659 in fines while fifty individuals got sentences totalling 29¼ years, without the option of fines. These penalties went primarily to people who had been caught selling liquor, where the sentences began with at least six months hard labour for the first offence. Sclater observed that more people might have been nailed if the police and the judiciary had been more sympathetic. "After a close study of the effect of this penalty the commissioner can only state that in his opinion the severity of the penalty is thwarting the very purpose it was intended to serve," he wrote. "There would appear to be grounds for believing that more convictions would be obtained if Magistrates had the option of imposing a fine for the first offense...." [15]

Reverend Smith blamed the problems on the "liquor interests [which] never accepted the Prohibition Act of 1917 as a permanent form of legislation and continued their highly organized propaganda." The Act was ineffective because it did not, and could not, prevent alcoholic spirits being imported from elsewhere in Canada. It would have been necessary for the province to ask the Canadian government to hold a referendum in British Columbia under the Canada Temperance Act which, had the dry side won, would have empowered Ottawa to stop the shipment of alcoholic beverages into British Columbia. Because this was not done, imported spirits were readily available. Indeed, a large number of bonded warehouses were erected, usually close to the American border, from which liquor was smuggled into the United States. As Reverend Smith groused: "The unrestricted importation of large quantities of liquor from the outside and the business of the bootlegger rendered the enforcement of the Prohibition Act difficult, even if such had been seriously attempted throughout the Province." A private member's resolution asking for a plebiscite to make the Canada Temperance Act effective was introduced in the provincial legislature in the spring of 1920 but failed to pass. Instead, the provincial government held a referendum that October, asking the public whether the government should control liquor sales. Social historian James Gray, in a 1972 volume, credited the newly formed British Columbia Moderation League, which he said was bankrolled by brewers, for masterminding the campaign against prohibition. [16]

Whoever inspired this step, the referendum posed a simple question: "Which do you prefer? 1. The present 'Prohibition Act'? or 2. An Act to provide for Government Control and Sale in Sealed Packages of Spiritous and Malt Liquors?" The result was decisive: 92,095 — including a majority of women who were given the franchise for the first time — voted for government control of liquor sales while 55,448 still favoured prohibition. In June 1921, the Liquor Control Board was set up. By the end of the year, the growing network of government stores had sold $4,698,835 worth of alcoholic beverages. Within a year, some sixty liquor stores had been opened around the province.

That British Columbians wanted control, not wide-open drinking, was shown in June 1924 when the government put yet another referendum to the people. "Do you approve of the sale of beer by the glass in licensed premises without a bar under government control and regulation?" it asked. The result: 73,853 said no, just edging out the 72,214 who said yes. In view of the tight result, the government then permitted the sale of beer by the glass in those electoral districts which had voted for it. [17] The first beer parlours opened in March 1925, with the price of a glass of draught fixed at ten cents, a price that, remarkably, stayed fixed for the next quarter-century.

Government control of liquor sales took the momentum away from the prohibitionists. The British Columbia Prohibition Association converted itself into the British Columbia Temperance League (BCTL) and became a diminishing, if still significant, force throughout the 1930s and 1940s. The BCTL failed in an effort to get another provincial referendum on alcohol sales but remained ever vigilant against any liberal moves to make it easier for the public to buy and consume alcohol. In 1952 the BCTL joined with the Vancouver Council of Churches to form the Alcohol Research and Education Council which basically was a lobby to fight against new drinking establishments.

The last hope for any degree of prohibition vanished when the government discovered how much money it could collect from booze sales. When the Second World War broke out, the federal government turned to liquor taxes as one revenue source; federal taxes on domestic still wine went up fivefold during the war. "The British Columbia LCB passed on all of Ottawa's taxes and added hikes of its own," Robert Campbell noted in *Demon Rum or Easy Money.* "By 1943 liquor was earning for the province over $8 million per year, double the pre-depression high. In fact, liquor profits accounted for over 20 percent of provincial revenue in that year." [18] Liquor peaked at 25.6 percent of government revenues in 1947 before other tax sources began to nourish the rising need for government revenues.

In the overhaul of liquor legislation in 1975, the **Liquor Control Board** was stripped of its responsibility for retailing, which was passed to the newly created **Liquor Distribution Branch,** leaving the LCB with all the proper control features — the granting and policing of licences to produce and market alcoholic beverages.

PRPICH, DAN (1931 –): An Okanagan Falls grapegrower interested in developing a winery in his scenic forty-acre vineyard on the east side of Skaha Lake, Prpich was born in Zagreb, the capital of Croatia, part of the former Yugoslavia. A fiercely independent man who chafed under Communism, Prpich deliberately became a ship's engineer and jumped ship in a foreign port in 1952 on his first voyage abroad. He worked in a Hamilton steel mill from 1953 until 1973 when he moved to the Okanagan and became a grapegrower.

PSEUDO-LABELS: This was wine industry jargon for the spate of foreign language labels, beginning in 1977 with Calona's **Schloss Laderheim,** which the industry created to combat the rising popularity of imported table wines. The marketers decided that some consumers were buying wines only by the label and began to generate suitably foreign labels for domestic wines. Other examples: Barbarosso, Klosterberg Cellars, Hochtaler, Alpenweiss, Toscano. The industry rationalized that, since its wines were attempting to become more Euro-

TOSCANO BIANCO
CANADIAN WHITE WINE • VIN BLANC CANADIEN
DRY • SEC
A crisp blended dry white wine,
delicate in body and
fruity in flavour
1L 11% alc/vol
JORDAN & STE-MICHELLE CELLARS LTD.,
SURREY, CANADA

pean in style, the pseudo-labels would best communicate this change. One of the more brazen attempts to pass off a domestic wine as something else was the 1965 release by *Growers' Wine* of a white labelled Canadian Liebfraumilch. This remained on the market for several years until a suit by seven German wineries caused Growers' to drop the label, calling the wine Rhine Castle instead. The winery also tried to release a red called Beaujolais. This time the French cried foul. Growers' finally settled on Beau Séjour as its brand, adopting the same name for its vineyard at Okanagan Mission. See also *Himrod*.

1   Interview with author, 1993.

2   F.M. Buckland, "The Establishment of Okanagan Mission," *Okanagan Historical and Natural History Society*, First Report, Sept. 10, 1926, p. 8; Primrose Upton, *The History of Okanagan Mission*, published in 1958 by the Okanagan Mission Centennial Committee; Primrose Upton, "Father Pandosy OMI," *Okanagan Historical Review*, 26th annual, 1962, p. 141; Denys Nelson, "Father Pandosy OMI," *Okanagan Historical Review*, Second Annual Report, 1927, p. 12.

3   Andrew Peller, *The Winemaker*. (See SOURCES for complete reference.)

4   Interview with author, 1982.

5   Andrew Peller, *The Winemaker*, p. 110.

6   Interview with author, 1982.

7   George Ordish, *The Great Wine Blight*. (See SOURCES for complete reference.)

8   Virgil J. and Dr. Eugene A. Rittich, *European Grape Growing*. (See SOURCES for complete reference.)

9   Interview with author, 1996.

10   *Kelowna Super Shopper*, October 1, 1981; clipping in Gray Monk scrapbook.

11   Rev. Principal W.H. Smith: *The Liquor Traffic in British Columbia* (Board of Home Missions and Social Service, Presbyterian Church in Canada, September 1922); in City of Vancouver Archives.

12   Robert A. Campbell: *Demon Rum or Easy Money*, p. 24. (See SOURCES for complete reference.)

13   *First Report of the Prohibition Commissioner*, for the year ended December 31, 1919; in the B.C. Archives.

14   Robert A. Campbell: *Demon Rum or Easy Money*, p. 24.

15   *First Report of the Prohibition Commissioner*.

16   James H. Gray: *Booze: The Impact of Whisky on the Prairie West*. (See SOURCES for complete reference.)

17   Letter Feb. 27, 1934, by the deputy provincial secretary to A.C. Stewart, the Saskatchewan minister of highways, in the B.C. Archives and Records, file GR 620, British Columbia Provincial Secretary, Policy Manual.

18   Robert A. Campbell: *Demon Rum or Easy Money*, p. 87.

QQQ

QUAILS' GATE VINEYARDS ESTATE WINERY: This winery was established in 1989 on property on the slopes of Boucherie Mountain near Westbank that was homesteaded originally in 1873 by pioneers John and Susan Allison. Their log cabin, substantially modernized, now serves as the winery's attractive tasting room and wine shop. The property was

acquired in 1961 by **Richard Stewart,** a member of another pioneer Okanagan family, who initially planted and marketed table grapes. The first planting in 1963 of quality vinifera grapes, a white variety called chasselas (widely grown in Switzerland), was the result of an error: Stewart had ordered a labrusca variety called diamond from a nursery in Seattle which inadvertently shipped chasselas. Stewart discovered the error several years later and was delighted he had the superior variety. The vines were still producing more than three decades later.

Quails' Gate is operated by Richard's sons, **Ben** and **Tony.** Initially, the Stewarts intended to open in 1984 but were frustrated when bank financing was denied them. Determined to open a winery, Ben Stewart began crushing grapes for wine in mid-September 1989, a week before the government announced the rules for farmgate wineries. Within two years, growing production and sales led Quails' Gate to raise itself to the stature of an estate winery. The signature varieties at Quails' Gate are pinot noir and chardonnay. The first modest planting of pinot noir was made on the property in 1975, with substantial additional acreage added in 1990 and in 1995; in the latter year, the plantings were done under the direction of Pepinieres Guillaume, consultants from Burgundy.

QUALITY STANDARDS: See **Vintners Quality Alliance.**

RRR

RAFFEINER, JOE (1927–): Cellarmaster and winemaker at *Golden Valley* winery, he was retained as cellarmaster in 1981 when the winery was acquired by *Anthony von Mandl* and *Nick Clark* and resumed its original *Mission Hill* name. Gentle and devout, Raffeiner attracted like persons to jobs at the winery. When Clark took over winery management, he concluded that the devotion and work ethic of Raffeiner's band had sustained the operation through the difficulties of receivership and of working under the tyrannical eye of former owner *Ben Ginter*. "One of the most valuable assets is the dedication and the family feeling of the people here," Clark said in 1982. Born near Bolzano in the German-speaking part of northern Italy, the son of a vineyard owner, Raffeiner apprenticed with a winery in Italy and supplemented his training with courses in Switzerland before coming to Canada in 1952. Here he went to work for the Chateau-Gai winery in Niagara Falls, ultimately taking charge of making sparkling wines. In 1967 he was recruited to become assistant winemaker to Henryk Schoenfeld at *Mission Hill*, whom he succeeded when ill health forced Schoenfeld's retirement within a few years.

Raffeiner produced a full range of wines during the Ginter ownership of the winery, including well-regarded fortified wines and a Canadian Medoc, an oak-aged red made from red hybrid grapes. However, he was handicapped by the long-term contracts the original owners had signed for labrusca grapes. "The quality of the grapes was not the best," Raffeiner said in an interview[1] two decades later. "It was discouraging. I like to make good wines." His understatement reflected his unwillingness to speak ill of anyone, not even of Ginter, a man with few fans. Ginter usually telephoned Raffeiner at the end of each working day to discuss business but otherwise left the winemaker alone. "He didn't know anything about winemaking, which was good," Raffeiner said. "He did know something about brewing and I felt sorry for his brewmasters." When von Mandl and Clark acquired the winery, Raffeiner remained as a consultant and still had an office in the Mission Hill winery fifteen years later. He also established a company called Enologica Winery Equipment, importing corks and equipment for wineries in the Okanagan.

RAFTERY, MICHAEL (1942–): British-born wine enthusiast who, while comptroller of the Open Learning Institute in Richmond, authored *The Wine Course* in 1983, one of the first comprehensive wine courses offered by correspondence by any British Columbia educational institution.

RAIKES, EDEN: Veteran grape-grower who also was the first president of the *Grape and Wine Institute of British Columbia* in 1981. He stepped down in the mid-1970s to retire to Hawaii.

RED WINE SURPLUS: Beginning in the late 1970s, consumers began drinking more white wines than red. By 1980, sales of white wines from British Columbia wineries totaled 10.9 million litres compared with red wine sales of 6.4 million litres. The balance shifted even more dramatically by 1984, to 14.5 million litres of white compared with 4.9 million litres of red. But in the vineyards, red varieties still were dominant. Because the commercial wineries in British Columbia had to buy essentially all domestic grapes, they accumulated a large surplus of reds wines which remained unsold despite aggressive discounting. A government funded adjustment program bought the surplus which was distilled while growers were encouraged to switch to white varieties.[2] The imbalance in demand persists. In 1995 the British Columbia wineries sold 9.3 million litres of while table wine compared with 3 million litres of red. However, the sales of red wine increased by almost 11 percent in 1995 compared with the previous year while the volume of white wine sales by the domestic wineries dropped 5 percent. The rebound in the demand for reds — the first significant growth in the decade — was caused by widely published reports suggesting that moderate red wine consumption promotes coronary health.

RESERVE: Wines designated as reserve wines are the winemaker's selection of the better wines from any vintage. The term has no legal standing but rather is a marketing device that suffers such chaotic inflation, as in Limited Reserve, Grand Reserve, Proprietor's Reserve and Vineyard Reserve, to be almost useless to a consumer unfamiliar with a particular winery's nomenclature.

RESIDUAL SUGAR: This technical winemaking term refers to the amount of sugar remaining in a finished wine. The *fermentation* process typically converts almost all of the natural or added sugar to alcohol. The sugar remaining is expressed as grams per litre, with a totally dry wine having perhaps two grams of residual sugar remaining. The label information, when it shows how much residual sugar the wine contains, is not necessarily helpful in alerting the buyer that a wine may taste sweet. High acidity in a wine, such as that found in some riesling table wines, can trick the palate into perceiving a wine as being dry even when it may have as much as 25 grams of residual sugar. On the other hand, intense fruitiness in young white wines grown in cool climates sometimes is perceived as slight (and pleasing) sweetness. Intensely sweet wines such as *icewines* contain several hundred grams per litre. Consumers who are diabetic find it helpful to know what a wine's residual sugar is.

REYNOLDS, DR. ANDREW: Research scientist specializing in viticulture at the *Summerland Research Station* from 1984. He studied plant breeding and genetics at the University of Guelph and got his doctorate at the prestigious Cornell University in New York state. Well regarded by his peers, Reynolds had published forty scientific papers by 1995. However, the Summerland viticultural program was being wound up in 1996, a victim of federal government spending reductions.

RICHMOND WINERY: This company operated briefly as an independent producer of berry wines in Richmond, with Myrtena as the name of its loganberry wine. *Growers'* bought the company in

1925 and maintained the Myrtena brand until the mid-1950s.

RIDDLING: In making bottle-fermented *sparkling wines*, each bottle undergoes riddling after the secondary fermentation is complete. The bottles are put in a rack, called a *pupitre*, with the neck pointed slightly down. Over the next three to four weeks, each bottle is given an eighth of a turn daily, with the heel of the bottle being raised simultaneously. The object is to shake the dead yeast cells into the neck of the bottle. This is hand riddling. It also is done mechanically in several wineries. The plug of yeast sediment is removed after the neck of the bottle is immersed in a freezing bath, leaving behind perfectly clear sparkling wine in a bottle that, when topped up with similar wine, is sealed with a champagne cork and now is ready for market.

RIESLING: When this appears on a British Columbia wine label, it now refers almost invariably to the leading German white vinifera sometimes also called *johannisberg riesling* or Rhine riesling. Formerly, the unrelated *Okanagan riesling* also commanded the riesling name on the label without any of the qualities that make the true riesling one of the world's most distinguished and versatile grapes. Most Okanagan riesling has been eradicated.

RITLOP, JOE (1933–): The owner of the estate winery at the edge of Keremeos which initially was called *Keremeos Vineyards* when it opened in April 1984 and subsequently was reorganized as St. Lazlo. He was born in Slovenia, in the former Yugoslavia, emigrated to Canada in 1954 and settled in British Columbia in 1963. His family operated a twenty-

hectare vineyard in Slovenia, near the Hungarian border. In Canada, he began growing grapes in 1976, choosing a vineyard location in the Similkameen Valley because he believed that its high summer heat units would produce more mature grapes than in the Okanagan. The list of varieties he planted is so extensive that the names sometimes escape him: they have included at various times both classic vinifera like gewurztraminer and chardonnay and hybrids like himrod. A self-taught winemaker, Ritlop has a rustic winemaking style unique among his professional peers. "There's no such thing as a professional," he once snapped. "Professional just means somebody worked on it longer. You don't learn that in school."[3] His favourite boast, as he told the *Vancouver Sun* in 1989, is: "I make totally natural wines. I don't use any chemicals. No preservatives added. I grow my own grapes and I make my own wine and I mind my own business."[4]

RITTICH, DR. EUGENE: Hungarian-born winemaker for *Growers' Wines Ltd.* from 1935 to 1957, Rittich (with his brother) authored the first book on Okanagan viticulture, entitled *European Grape Growing In Cooler Districts Where Winter Protection is Necessary.* It was published in 1934 by Burgess Publishing Co. of Minneapolis. Rittich was instrumental in 1929 in importing a selection of vinifera vines for planting by *J.W. Hughes* in a vineyard near Kelowna.[5] Rittich's main vineyard was north of Kelowna and he, and later his widow, continued to sell grapes to Growers' even if the winery was not always appreciative of the effort. *Brian Roberts*, the winery's general manager, offered this comment in a letter in September

1960 to his Okanagan fieldman, *Lloyd Schmidt*: "Dr. Rittich must be accommodated because he did so much to build up the winery and provide the market which you have today. I never know what he has but my guess is that he may have a few Diamonds this year and some European varieties. We are not interested in keeping his European varieties separate if they are delivered in less than tank load quantities. Just dump them in with varieties of the same colour."[6] On another occasion, Roberts referred to the Rittich vinifera as "miserable European types," which suggests that Rittich may have struggled to grow the grapes to proper maturity. After Rittich died in 1961, most of the European varieties he grew so laboriously were replaced with winter-hardy labrusca and North American hybrid grapes.[7]

RITTICH, V.J.: Brother of Eugene Rittich and a Kelowna grapegrower, he was ahead of his time as an Okanagan viticulturist. In a speech believed to have been made in 1940, Rittich said: "After ten years of experimenting with my brother, I have found that the Okanagan valley is not only perfectly suitable for European grape growing, but its climate is in many respects superior to most vine-growing countries in Middle Europe. It seems to me that the early growers neglected chiefly two things: (1) They did not secure varieties which were suitable to our northern climate and, (2) they did not develop a training method which makes it possible to produce high quality grapes. With my brother I imported about fifty different varieties and planted them on our trial plot." The white wines grapes he recommended were these: müller-thurgau, muscat ottonel, muscat

ferdinand de lesseps, chardonnay, sylvaner and excellent. The latter he described as an old Hungarian variety. The only red he recommended was blau burgunder, an Austrian variety better known today as lemberger; it has been successful in Washington state vineyards. Rittich also recommended as table grapes these varieties: perle of csaba, chasselas, muscat hamburg and sunshine (another Hungarian variety now gone from the Okanagan). In this speech, Rittich disclosed that he and his brother, using a plough, had hilled a winter cover onto the base of their vines each fall as a frost protection. "I would advise not to neglect covering in this country," Rittich said. "Nothing may happen for five or more years, but a cold winter can ruin not only next year's crop, but can throw us back three or four years."[8]

RKATSITELI: This widely planted Russian white grape was among the *Russian grape varieties* given a trial in the Okanagan when it was planted in 1976 at *Inkameep Vineyards*. Experimental lots were vintaged in the 1980s by *Brights* but the variety, notable for its tart acidity, ultimately was dropped, the wine not being as distinctive as the name.

ROBERTS, BRIAN H. (1914–1994): A Johannesburg-born chartered accountant, Roberts was a rising executive with Western Wine, Brandy and Spirit Co. of Worcester in Cape Province, S.A., when he and his family, repelled by apartheid, emigrated to Canada in 1955. After nine months as an accountant in Calgary, he joined *Growers' Wines Ltd.* of Victoria in 1956 and was its gen-

Brian Roberts (photo courtesy of the BC Ministry of Agriculture, Information Branch)

eral manager and ultimately president and chairman until he left in 1976 to become general manager of the **Wine Council of British Columbia** until retiring in 1981. He brought vigorous management to the venerable company, including even an attempt in 1961 to export loganberry wines to Britain. (Several shipments were made but the British did not take to what was being billed as "a new taste sensation.") His boundless boosterism is typified by a comment in the Growers' annual report for 1962: "There is no need for us as Canadians to have an inferiority complex about the quality of our wines. The days of snob appeal of imported wines are fast disappearing and we can all rejoice in our efforts to make our fruit growers prosperous and give more jobs to our wonderful Canadian people."

Roberts was able to expand the winery into new markets from coast to coast: in 1964, after $300,000 was spent on the Victoria winery, Growers' began bottling its popular cider there. Subsequently, the company opened a subsidiary, Castle Wines, in Moose Jaw, Sask., to supply the Prairie markets. But

for Roberts, the Growers' winery might have moved from its old Victoria plant on Quadra Street long before it did in 1978. In the mid-1960s, the company undertook a study of the economics of phasing out the Victoria plant in favour of a winery closer to the vineyards in the Okanagan. Roberts reported to the annual meeting in 1968: "Our own experts and experts brought in by the parent company, Imperial Tobacco, have convinced us that any savings in such a change would be wiped out by having to rebuild on the mainland at present construction and financing costs."

In retirement in Victoria, Roberts indulged in an interest in Shakespeare that had begun after he arrived in Canada, collecting old editions of plays and sonnets. When the first World Shakespeare Congress was held in 1971 at Simon Fraser University in Vancouver, Roberts was a delegate. He attended other congresses. He maintained that *Hamlet* was a "perfect" play and he also had an affection for *Macbeth*. "Well, I love the bloody Scots," he explained to one interviewer.[9]

ROOTSTOCK: While some grape vines flourish on their own roots, many growers choose to graft the fruiting top of a vine, called the scion, onto one of many different grape rootstocks that have been developed to resolve various viticultural problems. Most commonly, vinifera or European grape vines are grafted onto the roots of old North American species that resist *phylloxera*, a seriously debilitating vineyard pest. Rootstocks also have been created to cope with other diseases; to increase or curb a vine's productivity; to tolerate excessive salt or lime in soil; and so on.

Rose, Vern (1927–): Proprietor of *House of Rose*, a farmgate winery north of Kelowna. A retired schoolteacher from Alberta, Rose has been growing grapes at his vineyard since buying it in 1982. Self-taught winemaking skills have been buttressed with short courses taken at the University of California at Davis.

Rotberger: This a German variety developed at *Geisenheim* by crossing the white riesling with the red trollinger: the result was a variety useful for making fresh, dry rosé wines. The first, and so far only, Okanagan winery to produce rotberger is *Gray Monk*, which has an immensely loyal following with standing orders at the winery for each new vintage.

Rougeon: One of the many red hybrid crosses developed by French hybridizer Albert Seibel, rougeon produces a medium- to full-bodied red that sometimes shows spicy notes in the flavour. *Calona Wines* has enjoyed significant success with this variety.

Rülander: This is the German name for *pinot gris*, used occasionally by British Columbia winemakers of German background.

Russian grape varieties: In 1973 cuttings from a number of grapes grown in what was then the Union of Soviet Socialist Republics were brought to British Columbia and planted in the *Inkameep Vineyards* at Oliver. The varieties included: furmint (the variety that predominates in Hungary's sweet Tokay wines), matsvani, rkatsiteli, sereksia rozovaya and sereksia chornaya. For several years in the mid-1980s, *Lynn Bremmer* at Brights made interesting experimental wines from these varieties. When Bremmer left the winery, all were discontinued as varietals. Some of the varieties did not perform as well as hoped in British Columbia but even if they had their tongue-twister names made them unwelcome in the marketing portfolio of a large winery.

---

[1]   Interview with author, 1996.

[2]   Canadian Wine Council statistics.

[3]   Interview with author, October 1985.

[4]   Stephen Hume, *Vancouver Sun,* September 27, 1989.

[5]   Paper by Dr. Bernard W. Hoeter, 1971.

[6]   Letter to Lloyd Schmidt, September 13, 1960; in Lloyd Schmidt files.

[7]   John Vielvoye, "Okanagan Riesling," 1969. Paper in author's files.

[8]   V.J. Rittich, "European Grapes for the Okanagan." Text of address in author's files.

[9]   Various newspaper clippings in author's files.

SSS

SACRAMENTAL WINE: Because Jesus Christ blessed both bread and wine for his disciples at The Last Supper, both are used sacramentally (during church services) by many Christian denominations. Wine is particularly identified with the Roman Catholic Church. However, sacramental wine is also used by the Lutherans, the Anglicans, the Presbyterians, all Orthodox Churches and some Methodist and United Churches. Grape juice is used by some congregations of the latter two Churches; grape juice is used exclusively by Baptists, Mennonites, Pentacostals and congregational free churches. The tradition of sacramental wine predates the Christian era, having played, and continuing to play, a significant role in the Jewish religious tradition as well.

In British Columbia, *Calona* (with a brand called St. John), *Growers'* (with St. Albans) and *Casabello* all produced sacramental wines. Indeed, this is believed to have been Calona's lifeline during the winery's tough early years. In 1936, after Calona began making grape wines, a Kelowna priest, *Father W.B. McKenzie*, suggested to Archbishop W.M. Duke in Vancouver that the Catholic Church in Canada should replace imported wines with Calona wine. A sample of wine and a $45 fee was sent to Dr. Georges Baril, head of the chemistry department at the Université de Montréal, whose analysis confirmed that the wine was canonically acceptable (that is to say, made from natural ingredients). Baril wrote the archbishop that Calona wine could be used "with at

least as much safety (not to say more in my experience of Mass Wine trade) as any imported sweet wine from Spain." The analysis showed that the wine had 14.97 percent alcohol.

Baril further advised that Father McKenzie involve himself closely in supervising the production of the Mass wine. "In North Africa, at the White Fathers' plant, a priest is surveying the wine making. I am informed that they do not allow even a lay-brother (convert) to survey it. In France, many of the Mass Wines are made under the direct supervision of the parish priest." Soon, under the guidance of Father McKenzie, Calona was producing nearly all of the sacramental wine used in Canada.[1] That he was paid for his services is evident from a letter Father McKenzie wrote in 1941 to the then president of Calona, *W.A.C. Bennett*, thanking Bennett for the winery's "generous cheque. I am pleased to co-operate with your winemaker, Mr. Ghezzi."[2]

Less formal ecclesiastical support was given Casabello, whose founder *Evans Lougheed* was a Roman Catholic. When Casabello produced a Saint Anthony's Sacramental Wine in 1971, the bulletin of St. Ann's Parish for August 22, 1971, announced: "The priests of Penticton are proud and pleased that ecclesiastical approval has been given for the use of <u>CASABELLO</u> as Sacramental Wines."[3]

Not even the clergy was spared the inconvenience formerly surrounding the purchase of liquor in British Columbia. As recently as 1968, clerics first bought permits for twenty-five cents from the nearest liquor store or from the Liquor Control Board in Victoria, upon presenting proof of being clergy. Orders could be placed only at the LCB's Davie Street liquor store in Vancouver; or at LCB's Humboldt Street store in Victoria; or at LCB's head office. Once the LCB had been paid, it would advise the selling winery to release the wine to the cleric in question. Out-of-town clerics also had to pay the shipping cost. Typically, the wines, both white and red, were sold only by the gallon. A 1940 receipt in Calona's files showed that the winery charged $2.20 a gallon when it shipped a ten-gallon keg to a Vancouver church. In 1968 Growers' was charging $4 a gallon for its St. Albans.[4]

SALTSPRING ISLAND: See *James Hamilton.*

SAUVIGNON BLANC: A vinifera grape, this produces whites with abundant fruity flavours and, in cool growing conditions, lively citrus and herbal flavours. Prior to the 1990s, it had not been grown successfully in the Okanagan and was considered to be too late maturing and too tender to survive the winters. Vineyard manager **Dick Cleave** disagrees. Sauvignon blanc, he says, is a naturally vigorous vine that, left to its own devices, will overproduce. He advocates limiting both the fertilizer and the water on sauvignon blanc to ensure that the vine matures a reasonable-sized crop early enough in the fall so it has time to become dormant before a hard frost.

SCHERNER, KLAUS: Winemaker at the **Jordan & Ste-Michelle Cellars** Surrey winery in 1980 and 1981. A 1977 graduate of **Geisenheim**, Scherner came from a family who had operated a vineyard on the Rhine since the seventeenth century. He returned to Germany in 1982. His best touch was with the grape varieties he had grown up with, notably riesling. He was so proud of the late harvest 1981 riesling he made that he returned to Germany with five cases of it.

SCHERZINGER, EDGAR (1935–): Born in Germany's Black Forest and, like his father and grandfather, schooled as a woodcarver, Scherzinger emigrated to Canada in 1961, settling in Vancouver until 1974 when he and his wife, Elizabeth, bought a cherry orchard at the outskirts of Summerland. While his wife ran a successful delicatessen in town, Scherzinger tired of losing money on cherries and converted the farm to a vineyard in 1978 by planting gewurztraminer. Until he opened his own winery in 1995, Scherzinger sold his grapes to **Sumac Ridge Estate Winery**.

SCHERZINGER VINEYARDS: German-born wood carver **Edgar Scherzinger** opened this farmgate winery on the western outskirts of Summerland in 1995. It is based on a vineyard tucked away on the edge of Trout Creek Canyon and bordering the historic Kettle Valley Railway. The winery's specialty, aside from the owner's carvings also available in the tasting room, is a spicy gewurztraminer. Also produced: pinot noir and chardonnay.

SCHEUREBE: This is a white vinefera German cross developed by one Dr. George Scheu; hence the name. (*Rebe* is a German word for grapevine.) The variety was introduced to the Okanagan in 1975, one of three white varieties that **Andrés** had planted at **Inkameep Vine-**

yards. **Walter Gehringer,** who vintaged the variety while at Andrés, has since made it one of the regular wines in the **Gehringer Brothers** line. The grape matures well and produces a bouquet of rich flavours, making it excellent for producing dessert wines.

SCHLOSS LADERHEIM: Released by **Calona Wines** in 1977, this wine started as a German-style blend of Okanagan riesling, verdelet and aurora and later included imported blending stock when the wine's popularity outstripped the capacity of the Okanagan's vineyards. In the brand's first year, Calona produced 15,000 gallons; but within four years, production reached 1.5 million gallons. For several years it was the top-selling domestic wine by volume until the Ontario government, alerted by Calona's competitors that Schloss contained almost no Canadian wine in the blend, hit it with the higher import wine markup. The price increase reduced sales but Schloss has continued to be a popular brand. The Schloss concept, quite simply, was to blend and package a domestic wine as if it were imported. The overwhelming success of Schloss inspired other domestic producers to create a riot of *pseudo-label* wines, including Hochtaler, Alpenweiss, Toscana and Tollerkranz.

The Schloss Laderheim label annoyed the German industry which a decade earlier successfully stopped **Growers'** from selling Canadian Liebfraumilch. Once again, the Germans complained to the British Columbia government about a label they believed was misleading. **Tex Enemark,** the deputy minister of Consumer and Corporate Affairs, admitted "some sympathy for

what you have to say with respect to the use of the old gothic print and so forth." But in a January 1978 letter to Germany's Haus des Deutschen Weines, Enemark noted that the label "clearly stated" that the wine was Canadian. "Therefore, I do not agree that anyone will be confused," he wrote. "I am informed that the label in question was granted Canadian trade mark number 221132 June 10, 1977 after being published in the Trade Marks Journal for the requisite period of time during which objections could be filed."[5] Hermann Guntrum of the great Nierstein house of the same name then remonstrated with **Rafe Mair**, the minister of Consumer Affairs, that the Schloss label had "too many German words for a clearly named Canadian product." Enemark suggested that was beside the point: the label misrepresented neither the country of origin nor the manufacturer. "The Calona label to which you refer is not misleading," Enemark wrote to Guntrum in May 1978. "That being the case, we have no legal authority to require that Calona desist from using the label in question."[6]

SCHMIDT, ALAN (1963–): Born in Kelowna, the son of veteran vineyardist Lloyd Schmidt, Alan by age eleven was renting and operating his own small vineyard with a friend. He affirmed his commitment to wine that summer after the **Jordan & Ste-Michelle** winery informed the growers it would not be buying the bath grapes then ripening in various Okanagan vineyards because these labrusca varieties were inadequate for table wines. At that time bath grapes were still widely grown and economically vital to growers. Alan and his grandfather, Frank, made an appointment to see

Jordan & Ste-Michelle general manager **Bob Holt**. Alan Schmidt gravely told Holt that he was planning to go into the wine business but was going to change his mind because of the unfair treatment growers received from wineries. "How can I turn down an eleven-year-old kid?" Holt asked in exasperation. "Send the grapes." The precocious young Schmidt then spent several months working in German vineyards. It was the start of hands on training as a winemaker which ultimately led him, after apprenticing at Napa's prestigious Heitz Vineyards, to become a winemaker at **Sumac Ridge** soon after that winery opened in 1981. He later moved to Ontario where, with his younger brother Brian, he manages the fine Vineland Estates winery at Vineland.[7]

Frank Schmidt (photo courtesy of Paul Ponich Studios)

SCHMIDT, FRANK (1913–1979):

An early Okanagan grapegrower. Born in 1913 in Unity, Sask., he emulated many other farm lads during the Depression by hopping a freight train, arriving in Kelowna in September 1937 for the vin-tage. Schmidt did such a good job picking grapes for pioneer grower **Peter Casorso** that in 1938 Schmidt was given a contract to manage a vineyard, along with a house to live in. Four years later, grower **J.W. Hughes** lured him with an even better package: a house, a car and $100 a month. Subsequently Hughes let Schmidt (and the other vineyard foremen) earn ownership of the vineyards they managed. In 1958 Schmidt became the owner of Lakeside Vineyards, later renamed the Beau Séjour Vineyard, at Okanagan Mission, south of Kelowna on the east side of Okanagan Lake. He retired after the vineyard was sold to **Growers' Wines Ltd.** of Victoria in 1965. He died in Kelowna.

Schmidt had a warm and favoured relationship with Growers' and its general manager, **Brian Roberts**. When the Victoria winery, which had been shipping fresh grapes from the Okanagan since 1932, decided to crush them in the Okanagan and ship the *must* instead, the crushing equipment was installed on the Schmidt vineyard and Schmidt was paid for operating it. "We could have located the crushing depot on neutral soil, but deliberately located it on your farm so that you could get major benefits," Roberts wrote. In January 1960, when Ernest C. Warner bought Growers', Roberts again wrote, offering a benefit: a small number of class B voting shares — never before available — were being offered to friends of Warner and of the winery. "My thought is that the Company's good friends in the Okanagan — the gentlemen who have been growing the grapes for us all these years — might just want to have a few shares in the Company to give them not only a splendid investment, but also a greater interest in the Company which turns their grapes into wines which are sold as far as Ontario and the Yukon.... I will lay my head on the block that the share right now is worth every cent of $10.00, so that it is not really a speculative share." Both Schmidt and his son, Lloyd, became shareholders.[8] See also *Himrod*.

SCHMIDT, LLOYD (1940–): A Kelowna native, son of Frank Schmidt, he quips that he was born under a grape vine. After his 1958 high school graduation, he completed a two-year business college course and applied it to running the accounts for the Beau Séjour Vineyards, as the vineyard was called after his father sold it to *Growers' Wines Ltd*. He was assigned an exhilarating degree of responsibility for a young man — dealing with as many as thirty-five contracted growers, supervising the crush each fall at the vineyard and promoting the wines throughout the British Columbia Interior. Schmidt signed a five-year contract in 1966 and the future looked bright until Imperial Tobacco, which controlled Growers', decided the wine business was insufficiently profitable and in 1969 assigned a cost-cutting executive, *Larry Anderson*, to take over as president of Growers' from the amiable *Brian Roberts*. To this day, Lloyd Schmidt thinks of Anderson as "the hatchet man."

Growers' had paid $480,000 for the picture-postcard vineyard in 1965; Anderson put it on the market for $650,000 because of its real estate development potential even though Schmidt recently had begun a five-year development plan, including $70,000 to put in irrigation. Schmidt erupted angrily in a letter to Anderson in Victoria: "As manager I feel selling any portion of the vineyard is only a short term solution to the companies [sic] overall financial problem. A decision to sell any producing areas of our vineyard will be against the beliefs of myself as manager and would result in my reason for a separation from the company."

But after Anderson held his ground, Schmidt backed down. Anderson then proceeded to clip Schmidt's wings by centralizing in Victoria the enriching administrative tasks that Schmidt had handled at the vineyard. He also ordered Schmidt to lay off one of the vineyard's three employees and not to plant another thirty acres of grapes. Schmidt agreed in September 1969 not to quit while under contract and promised to give enough notice if he did decide to leave for a replacement to be trained. "It is still my belief that selling a portion of the vineyard will in time be a disadvantage to our long term requirements and objectives. However, I also realize that the company is in need of financial releases to insure [sic] the future of its winery operation." By February 1, 1970, Schmidt had had enough: he wrote Anderson that he was not going to renew his contract when it ended April 30, 1971. Anderson replied: "... perhaps, in view of the uncertainty about when and to whom we will sell the vineyard, your decision may be the best one for you personally." When the vineyard was sold to the *Sperling* family, Growers' asked Schmidt to be its consulting field man with other growers still under contract. But Schmidt left the wine industry entirely to run a sporting goods store in Kelowna for two years and then joined the provincial agriculture ministry as a viticulturist.[9] In 1979 he became the field man for the *Casabello* winery, staying there until he and **Harry McWatters** opened **Sumac Ridge Estate Winery** at Summerland in 1981. Schmidt left the partnership in 1985 and moved to Ontario, as the sales manager for Mori-Vin Inc., a major nursery and marketer of grape vines.

SCHULZE, MARILYN (1951–):
The wife of the husband and wife team that owns **Venturi-Schulze Vineyards** on Vancouver Island, Schulze was born in Australia, the daughter of a doctor who emigrated to Canada in 1970. After getting a degree in microbiology, Schulze became a teacher of mathematics and French in Vancouver. She met **Giordano Venturi** when both were in a French immersion course. In 1988 they purchased Maple Glen, a neglected century-old farm in the Cowichan Valley, and set out to create a vineyard and a top quality winery.

SEMILLON:
The white vinifera variety is grown extensively in Bordeaux and in Australia and has taken hold in Washington state. Still planted only in modest quantities in the Okanagan, it can yield table wines with an herbal aroma and with a texture, even in a dry wine, sometimes described as fat.

SEPTOBER:
This was the initial name for the **Okanagan Wine Festival** when it began in 1982, simply because the festival events began in late September and culminated with a wine competition in October. There were forty-seven wines entered in the first competition.

SEREKSIA CHORNAYA:
Of the Russian grape varieties brought to British Columbia for trial in the early 1970s, this is the only one that proved modestly success-ful in a commercial sense. The **Vincor** winery at Oliver produces a fine dry rosé. See also **Frank Supernak.**

SERWO, PETER (1932–):
Because his well-tended vineyard south of Oliver was almost exclusively planted to white grape varieties, Peter Serwo searched German wine literature extensively before deciding on a red variety to plant in 1993. The choice fell on pinot noir, or spätburgunder in the German books, which, Serwo read, described the variety as the king of red wine grapes. He admits that other sources claim the crown for other varieties. "Every gypsy says his horse is the best," he shrugs, falling back on an adage that was current in northern Yugoslavia where he was born and grew up in a German-speaking enclave near the Romanian border.

Being German speakers landed the Serwo (pronounced ser-vo) family in a Communist prison camp in 1945 where Peter Serwo suspects he contracted a mysterious spinal cord infection that was to immobilize him for two years in a body cast in Germany after the Serwo family emigrated there in 1955. While the rest of the family continued to Canada, joining relatives already here, Peter stayed in a Hamburg hospital from 1956 until 1958. Here he met his future wife, Helga, one of his nurses. On recovering his health, he worked in the booming German construction industry until 1966 when he and his wife followed the rest of the Serwo family to the Okanagan. He continued as a builder until 1970 when he bought what Helga described as a hobby farm at Kaleden and planted three acres of Okanagan riesling and de chaunac. Five years later they moved to a peach and apricot orchard south of

Oliver, finely sited on what is today called the *Golden Mile.* Initially he stayed with peaches, discouraged by the difficulty some growers had experienced selling grapes in 1974. Serwo returned to grapes with determination in 1979, not only replacing his peach trees in 1980 with twelve acres of vinifera grapes but buying two nearby vineyards totalling almost thirty acres. These subsequently were sold to leave Serwo with twenty-four acres of vines. In addition to the pinot noir, he grows primarily johannisburg riesling, ehrenfelser and chardonnay, with smaller acreages of bacchus, kerner and optima.

Serwo was one of the early growers in the Okanagan to commit to vinifera grapes. While he was encouraged to do so by *Josef Zimmerman,* then the winemaker at *Jordan & Ste-Michelle,* Serwo credits a fondly remembered visit from a German wine grower in 1980 to "opening our eyes to vinifera." Serwo found that he preferred the vinifera-based German wines tasted with his visitor to hybrid-based British Columbia wines. "If we liked them better, others would, too," he reasoned. Serwo's skill as a grapegrower also caught the eye of *Helmut Becker*, who not only visited the Serwo vineyard but had Serwo visit the *Geisenheim Institute* on the Rhine, where Becker directed plant breeding for many years.

Peter Serwo, the one-time construction worker and peach grower, has been so seduced by the grape that he makes his own wine in a professionally equipped hobby winery, complete with stainless steel fermentation tanks, a laboratory, an air-conditioned storage room and a friendly tasting room. "It's an experimental winery with an un-known time of opening," Helga Serwo smiles, admitting that they have considered establishing a small winery.

SEYVAL BLANC: This white French hybrid, when grown carefully and handled competently in a winery, produces crisp dry whites with more character than the bland verdelet that was planted much more widely in the Okanagan. Seyval blanc acreage are in decline, however, because of little winery interest in the variety.

SHAUNESSY, ROBERT (1953–): A native of Portage La Prairie, Man., and a chemical engineer who co-founded Rio Alto Exploration Ltd., Calgary, in 1988, Shaunessy is the nonresident senior partner in *Tinhorn Creek Vineyards Ltd.*, whose Oliver winery opened in 1995. Shaunessy's interest in wines was fired by touring California vineyards in the 1970s. He acquired choice vineyard property in the south Okanagan in 1993, fifty acres of which is on the so-called *Golden Mile* on the west side of the Okanagan Valley and more than one hundred acres across the valley on Black Sage Road. Both vineyards are committed to vinifera grapes.

SIEGERREBE: A white grape, this was developed in Germany in 1916 by crossing gewurztraminer and madeleine angevine. Because of its spicy flavours and high sugar content at maturity, it serves more typically as a blending grape both in Germany and in British Columbia, where the *Venturi-Schulze* winery's proprietary Millefiori (siegerrebe and ortega) is an example. The vine, being susceptible to fungus diseases, is not popular with growers. The fruit is highly susceptible to wasps. "They seem totally obsessed by the flavour," writes Vancouver Island winegrower Giordano Venturi. "From 1991 to 1994, we lost between 40% and 70% of these grapes to the wasps."

SIMES, JOHN (1950–):

Born in Palmerston North, near Wellington, the capital of New Zealand, Simes at first put his applied science degree to work with an ice cream company. He joined Montana Wines Ltd., New Zealand's largest winery, in 1978 and moved quickly from managing the bottle cellars to become a senior winemaker and vineyard manager. In 1991 *Mission Hill* began wooing Simes, whose wife, Sheilagh, is from Vancouver. The winemaker pondered the offer throughout the first half of 1992, accepting just as the vintage was about to begin in the Okanagan. Simes later regretted giving Montana short notice of his departure, given his seniority there. "I knew that I had to come over here and make the wine for 1992," he says. "How else do you prove you are worthy of being employed as a winemaker?" He proved it dramatically by making a reserve chardonnay that fall that went on to win the prestigious *Avery's Trophy* in a London competition in 1994. He had earlier demonstrated his talent by winning an Avery's Trophy several years previously for Montana with a sauvignon blanc.

Simes arrived at the Mission Hill winery in September 1992, with some of the early grapes already arriving. "Most of the grapes in the Okanagan are harvested at the end of September and into early October. I had a chance to start to get things changed in the way the fruit was processed in the winery," he says. "We totally changed almost everything that happened with the grapes, including when they were picked. I spent a huge amount of time trying to sweet talk the growers into not harvesting, to leave the fruit hanging on the vine." As he inspected the vineyards from which Mission Hill was buying grapes (most of the chardonnay for the award-winning wine came from vineyards in the Oliver area), he formed an appreciation of the fruit quality. "I could tell the fruit was brilliant," he recalls. "I called Anthony [von Mandl, Mission Hill's owner] and I said this fruit tastes as good as I've ever seen chardonnay taste. It cries out for new oak for barrel fermentation." With the immediate green light from *von Mandl*, Simes had about a hundred American oak barrels shipped to the winery in time to barrel-ferment the chardonnay. Some of the chardonnay also was fermented in stainless steel tanks, with a final blend assembled both from this wine and the barrel-fermented wine, an approach that Simes maintains achieves more complexity.

A versatile winemaker, Simes found himself dealing with a range of varieties, including merlot grapes from Washington state and botrytis-affected optima from British Columbia (a wine from the latter also went on to score gold medals). Simes recalls the very fresh and fruity 1992 pinot blanc he made from Okanagan grapes. "The pinot blanc more than the chardonnay told everyone that I was here," he says. "It was a completely different wine to what had been made prior to me. It made a statement." Because he gave the grapes extended skin contact and cold-fermented the juice, the wine was bone dry and yet more packed with flavour than previous Mission Hill pinot blancs that had been finished with some residual sugar.

In barrels, Simes uses both French

and American oak and sees advantages with the latter. "American oak has come of age in the last five to eight years," Simes said in a 1995 interview. "There are several cooperages in the United States that make a premium product. The biggest single change that has occurred with American oak is that some American cooperages that were in the bourbon barrel industry invested in learning how to make a barrel that was suitable for wine. It's a much lower price than French oak, so you can afford to buy many more barrels and have a much greater percentage of your wines sitting in oak. And the quality? I don't have to talk about the quality. The 1992 grand reserve chardonnay was fermented in American oak. That to me is the end of the discussion in terms of the quality."

SIMILKAMEEN SUPERIOR: Table wine brand developed by *Andrés* in the 1970s, it celebrated the Similkameen Valley source of the grapes. It was perhaps the first regionally designated table wine in British Columbia.

SIMILKAMEEN VALLEY: While the valley lies immediately west of the Okanagan, its grapegrowing potential has remained underdeveloped. Former British Columbia Minister of Agriculture Frank Richter, whose constituency included the valley, recounted at Casabello winery's opening in 1967 that his father had grown grapes at Cawston before the turn of the century. "He was successful in growing them but not in marketing them," Richter said. "My mother took a carload to Regina and returned with nothing but the freight bill to be paid."[10]

SLAMKA CELLARS: Farmgate winery established in 1996 by the Slamka family to produce wine from their Boucherie Mountain vineyard. The family has turned what was a three-bay machine shed into an attractive and functional winery, with a fine view from the tasting room. The Slamkas not only purchased good equipment but they also purchased carefully. The winery's original filter was built in 1953, making it older than most of the partners in the winery. The winery's production is to reach 4,000 gallons a year within four years of the 1994 vintage.

SLAMKA, JOE (1923–): Born in the former Czechoslovakia and trained as a machinist, the fiercely independent Slamka left his native land in 1948, just as the Communist government was taking control. He spent several years in Britain, including a stint as an underground miner, before coming to Canada in 1952. Immigration officials directed him to Edmonton to pursue a career in a pipe mill. Ten years later, after a camping trip through the Okanagan when apple trees laden with fruit nostalgically reminded him of his European homeland, Slamka bought an orchard on the slope of Boucherie Mountain. When he discovered that he and his wife, Freya, could not make money with tree fruits, Slamka switched to grapes in 1970, also working ten years at Kelowna's Western Star truck assembly plant to support the farm. The vineyard, now five acres, has been switched from hybrids and Okanagan riesling primarily to vinifera. "Wine is a very interesting phase of agriculture," Slamka has decided.

SLAMKA, PETER (1954–): Born in Edmonton, Peter Slamka is a jack of all trades who moved from Vancouver to live on the family's Boucherie Mountain farm in 1989. He began making wine that year for the family's personal consumption but, noting the success of other farmgate wineries, began researching a similar project. Part of the research included an extended trip in 1993 to winegrowing regions around the world, including a visit with winemaking cousins in Austria. Consultant **Elias Phiniotis** helped Peter Slamka make a scaled-up trial lot of 200 gallons of wine in 1992, a dry run en route to opening a winery. "We have good fruit," he maintains. "It's not hard to make good wine when you have good fruit."

SLAMKA, RICK (1957–): The Edmonton-born silent partner in Slamka Cellars, he is a physics engineer who operates Questek Research & Development in Vancouver and also oversees marketing the wines in Vancouver.

SLAMKA, TIM (1963–): Born in Edmonton and a plumber by trade, Tim Slamka is the vineyard manager at the family winery. He handled the winemaking in 1993, with help from consultant **Gary Strachan**, when his brother was touring wine regions during vintage.

SLINGER, STEPHEN: See **Growers' Wines;** also **Victoria Wineries (British Columbia) Ltd.**

SOMMET ROUGE: When this dry red table wine was released in 1974 by **Calona Wines**, it was a dramatic style shift for a winery known then for its sweet jug wines and potent fruit wines. Blended to the flavour profile of a red Bordeaux, the wine was packaged smartly in a tall-shouldered Bordeaux bottle and sealed with a cork. This suc-

cessful brand was followed the next year with Sommet Blanc.

SOON, HOWARD (1952–): Born in Vancouver, the grandson of a shopkeeper who imigrated from southern China in the 1880s, Soon graduated in biochemistry from the University of British Columbia in 1974. After five years in the brewing industry, he joined **Calona** in 1980 as a quality control supervisor, became assistant winemaker in 1981 and subsequently was promoted to chief winemaker. He and artist **Robb Dunfield** share star billing on the labels of Calona's premium wines.

SOVEREIGN OPAL: This white wine grape was developed at the **Summerland Research Station** and released to growers for trial in 1976. A grape with a dusty pink skin when mature, it is a cross of golden muscat and maréchal foch to create a winter hardy variety capable of maturing with good sugars by early October. *Calona Wines*, the only producer, began releasing a varietal sovereign opal with the 1987 vintage. The wine has a fresh floral muscat character and is best when young. Summerland's grape program in the early 1970s generated a number of new varieties with the common sovereign prefix: Sovereign Gold, Sovereign Tiara, Sovereign Noir, Sovereign Royale and Sovereign Sceptre. Only Opal made it to the consumer as a wine varietal, and it is grown only by August Casorso, who has about ten acres in his vineyard near Kelowna.

SPAGNOL'S ENTERPRISES LTD.: Based on Annacis Island in New Westminster, this is the largest British Columbia dealer in grapes, juices and other supplies for amateur winemakers. The business de-veloped after the Second World War when independent grocer Harry Spagnol began importing fresh California grapes. His son-in-law, Lyle Sproule, gradually took over management in the 1970s. The business began to flourish after the *Wine-Art* chain of stores introduced home vintners to varietal concentrates; it was a short step to seeking out fresh varietals from the grape suppliers, of which Spagnol's emerged as the leader. At first, Sproule found that customers were prone to ordering varietals and then changing their minds, forcing him to sell his surplus grapes to domestic wineries. But by the 1990s, Spagnol's had substantial refrigerated storage for its grapes and a clientele of home winemakers across western Canada.

SPARKLING WINE

Wineries in British Columbia began making "champagne" almost from the start (*Calona's* early lists included one such wine). But until the late 1980s, domestic wines containing bubbles were more likely to be tank-fermented or carbonated than to have come through the difficult technique of fermenting *in the bottle* as is done in Champagne. *Baby Duck* and its many imitators are carbonated. The term *crackling wine* usually, but not always, refers to low-pressure carbonated bubblies. The first premium quality British Columbia sparkling wine made by the classical method was *Sumac Ridge's* Stellar's Jay Cuvée, of which the first vintage was 1987. Subsequently, *Summerhill Estate Winery* has entered the market with its Cipes Brut. *Stephen Cipes,* the owner of Summerhill, objects to the term *sparkling wine* and prefers to call his wines *champagne*, to indicate that his winery is not making cheap carbonated bubblies. He has a point; but even so, none of the classically made premium bubblies made in British Columbia — including those from Summerhill — call themselves champagne. There are two reasons for this: first, the French frequently take legal action against wineries that appropriate what is, after all, a prestigious and legally defined French appellation; second, British Columbia's premium bubblies are good enough to stand on their own feet, as do good sparkling wines elsewhere in the world. In Germany, sparkling wines are called *sekt*; in Spain, *cava*; in Italy, *spumante*. Winemakers in the English-speaking world employ either the phrase *méthode champegnoise* or *classical method*. All that means is that the wine achieved its bubbles by being fermented in the bottle exactly as is done in France. The bubbles were not pumped in later.

The current generation of sparkling wines in British Columbia emerged from trials conducted, starting in 1983, by **Gary Strachan** when he was at the Summerland Research Station. Soon after arriving there from Ontario in 1977, he noticed the wineries all complained that British Columbia grapes were excessively acidic. "Why don't we exploit that and make sparkling wines?" he asked himself. The finest sparkling wines are made from grapes that are slightly more acidic than grapes used in table wines. The acidity, which softens as the wines develop in the bottle, is essential if the wines are to retain their fresh, clean flavours through the prolonged production cycle and during further aging in the consumer's cellar. Ironically, the excessive acidity of grapes of which the wineries complained was caused chiefly by poor growing techniques (typically, over-cropping) which vineyardists since have learned to correct.

Sumac Ridge's **Harry McWatters** was the first producer to cooperate with Strachan's research project, which was funded by a grant from the National Research Council. To a degree, Strachan and McWatters were re-inventing the wheel. After all, Dom Perignon, who died in France in 1715, generally is credited with figuring out how to retain bubbles in wine. However, the French, understandably, have had a long tradition of keeping to themselves the technical nuances of making champagne. "There were lots of books about champagne but they didn't give you the technical background in how to make it," Strachan found. Winemaker **Harold Bates**, who had acquired sparkling wine experience with **T.G. Bright & Co.** in Niagara Falls, helped the inexperienced Strachan in the first year of the Summerland trials. In the second year, technical assistance was provided by **Eric von Krosigk**, a Vernon native who was just completing winemaking studies in Germany that included apprenticeship with a sparkling wine producer. (Subsequently, Bates joined Sumac Ridge and von Krosigk made several vintages of Cipes Brut.) After several trial lots of sparkling wine had been made, Sumac Ridge committed to commercial quantities of sparkling wine, with the first major release coming on July 1991, on the winery's tenth anniversary. The flagship, blended from pinot blanc, pinot noir and chardonnay, is Stellar's Jay Cuvée, named for the raucous blue-feathered creature that is British Columbia's provincial bird.

Cipes Brut has a more complex history. In 1989 Summerhill's Cipes and **Kenn Visser**, who was then managing **Inkameep Vineyards,** invited Jack Davies, owner of California's prestigious Schramsberg Champagne Cellars, to consider investing in a sparkling wine facility in British Columbia. "Jack opened our eyes," Cipes said, recalling the enthusiasm that Davies and his winemaker displayed for the potential of the Okanagan. Strachan secured another research grant and a number of cuvées were produced from grapes grown primarily in the Summerhill vineyard. Davies decided not to get involved but Cipes proceeded on his own, enlisting von Krosigk as the winemaker. The Summerhill vineyard is extensively planted to riesling and this grape, widely used for sparkling wines in Germany, became the basis for Cipes Brut. Subsequently, von Krosigk and his successor at Summerhill, **Alan Marks**, also produced sparkling wines based on pinot noir, chardonnay and pinot meunier, the traditional varieties of Champagne. Okanagan Falls grapegrower **Ian Mavety** had participated in the Schramsberg trial. When Schramsberg withdrew in 1991, Mavety launched **Blue Mountain**

Stephen Cipes (photo courtesy of John Schreiner)

winery, with half of its production committed to sparkling wine.

Stephen Cipes's Summerhill winery, which opened in 1992, devotes between 60 and 80 percent of its production to sparkling wine. "British Columbia actually has superior growing conditions to Champagne," Cipes believes. The advantages, in his view, include clean air, clean water, dry and reasonably disease-free growing conditions, with the added ability of Okanagan growers to tailor vineyard production with the adroit use of irrigation. The Okanagan vineyards are more northerly than those in Champagne; the dry and comparatively cool growing conditions add up to small, concentrated grapes that retain their flavours — evident in fruity Cipes Brut — through the entire processing cycle for sparkling wines.

To make a sparkling wine, the vintner first produces a dry wine, ideally from grapes with good, fresh acidity. Most sparklers are made from white varieties or from light-skinned red varieties, such as pinot noir. When red grapes are used, the grapes are pressed and the juice is drained away immediately from the skins, picking up almost no colour (or very little in the case of a sparkling rosé). Sparkling red wines are seldom made, not being popular because they are perceived as too heavy. Some months after the vintage, when the base wine has been fermented, a dose of sugar and yeast is added and the wine is bottled in the heavy bottles capable of sustaining high pressure and sealed with a crown cap. The secondary fermentation that takes place in each bottle produces the bubbles. Workers in a winery making sparkling wines usually wear protective clothing in the bottle cellar because pressures exceeding 100 pounds per square inch may develop inside the bottles, causing weak ones to explode. The surviving bottles — most of them — will rest two to three years, picking up additional flavour notes (sometimes referred to as toasty flavours) from spent yeast cells.

At the end of this period, the bottles are placed, neck down, into a *pupitre* or *riddling rack*, so called because the practice of giving each bottle a sharp and precise twist by hand daily is called **riddling**. "A good riddler can do 17,000 bottles a day," says Cipes. "That's the number of holes we have on our riddling racks." During twenty-one to thirty days, riddling shakes all the yeast lees into a plug in the neck of the bottle. Then each bottle neck is dipped into an icy-cold solution to freeze the plug, which is then expelled by pressure when the cap is removed; whereupon each bottle is topped up and sealed with the familiar mushroom-shaped cork. During this process, enough pressure has been lost that bottles can be released safely, but because the remaining pressure can expel the cork sharply, each bottle has a wire cage dropped over the cork and tightly fastened under the neck ridges, firmly anchoring the cork.

The labour-intensive process explains why sparkling wines sell at a premium.

There is a cheaper bulk process – the *charmat* process, also developed by the French. *Casabello* employed the charmat method in the early 1970s to make pink, white and red "champagnes" and could state, quite accurately, that "Casabello Champagnes are naturally fermented."[11] The winery had several reinforced tanks in which finished still wines were re-fermented, with the resulting carbon dioxide being contained in the tanks with the wines, which were then bottled directly from the tanks. Making sparkling wine in bulk batches, widely done around the world, is more economical and consistent than making wines in individual bottles. Yet charmat-processed wines, perhaps because they spend less time in intimate contact with the yeast lees, seldom achieve the rich, complex flavours of bottle-fermented sparkling wines, nor are the bubbles as fine and long-lasting in the glass.

Because classic sparkling wines cost more and because they are more dramatic in the glass, they are only served on special occasions. Cipes argues against this positioning of wines that he would prefer to drink most of the time. "Once you get used to champagne, you don't want to drink anything else," he insists. "It goes with every meal."

SPERLING, ANNE (1965–): The only one of the six children of Bert and Velma Sperling to become a winemaker, she joined **Andrés** in Port Moody in 1984 after studying food sciences at the University of British Columbia. She moved to **CedarCreek** where she was the winemaker from 1991 to 1995, when she moved to Ontario. Sperling is an award-winning winemaker whose achievements at CedarCreek included the 1992 merlot reserve, so impressive that the judges at the 1993 **Okanagan Wine Festival** created a platinum medal for it. It was the first time in the competition's history that such a higher-level award was created.

SPERLING, DOUGLAS (1950–): A holder of a bachelor's degree in agriculture from the University of British Columbia, Sperling became a grower when he and his father, Bert, bought the Beau Séjour Vineyard at Okanagan Mission in 1971. Renamed as Balcarra Vineyards, it was a 132-acre property with almost half under vines. "I put Doug

over there and said this is your baby — phone me when you have a problem," Bert Sperling recounted. "He caught on very well." The vineyard portion was sold to other growers twelve years later, while the upper part of the property — too high for grapes — became Balcarra Estates, a housing subdivision. Douglas Sperling established a new vineyard nearby and, after the 1988 grape pull, converted a significant portion of his vineyard to table grapes, including sovereign coronation, a seedless white variety developed at the **Summerland Research Station**.

SPERLING, ENGLEBERT (1928–): Bert Sperling, as he is called, was born in Sedley, Sask., in 1928 but grew up in the Okanagan after his family moved to Kelowna in 1930. After a brief postwar stint in the air force and a decade in road building and construction, he agreed in 1960 to take over Pioneer Ranch, the eighty-five-acre farm just outside Kelowna operated by his father-in-law,

Napoleon Peter **Casorso**, who was retiring and who had not restored vines and fruit trees badly damaged in a winter a decade earlier. Not interested in tree fruits, Sperling replaced the orchard and replanted the existing vineyard, for a total of fifty acres of vines.

The grapes originally were sold to **Calona Wines,** Casorso having been a founding shareholder. Almost all were labrusca varieties, except for perle of csaba, an aromatic early variety whose maturity coincided with the arrival of California grapes at Calona. "By the time Calona would accept them, the wasps would have eaten the grapes right out, leaving just a shell there," Sperling recalled.[12] After several years of quarrelling with the winery about when his perle of csaba would be picked, Sperling angrily switched his contract to **Growers' Wines,** and with this winery's encouragement, converted the vineyard from labrusca to preferred hybrid grapes such as de chaunac. This relationship ultimately led to Sperling and his son, Douglas, buying the Beau Séjour Vineyard from Growers'. The Pioneer Ranch vineyard still grows perle of csaba, along with several other white vinifera varieties, including gewurztraminer. In 1995, finding a surprising demand for the old standby, maréchal foch, Sperling converted all of his verdelet vines by grafting them over to foch.

SPRING HILL VINEYARDS: This was a label introduced in 1984 by **Calona Wines** for premium products made entirely with Okanagan grapes. Unhappily for authenticity, the white was called Chablis and the red Burgundy. The label only lasted a few years.

ST. HUBERTUS VINEYARDS: Estab-lished in 1992 by **Leo Gebert** and his wife, Barbara, this winery is based on one of the Okanagan's historic vineyards at Okanagan Mission and once was oper-ated by **Frank Schmidt** and his son Lloyd as **Beau Séjour** vineyards. All that remains of that history is a far-spread **himrod** vine beside the Gebert family home. The winery's debut white wines, notably pinot blanc, were made in the clean delicate style often associated with the wines of Switzerland, the Geberts's birthplace. The winery name also reflects Swiss heritage, the saint being the Swiss patron for huntsmen. Beginning with the 1994 vintage, St. Hubertus started releasing barrel-aged wines under its **Oak Bay Vineyards** label. The Oak Bay maréchal foch won a silver medal in 1995 at the International World Wine Competition. Other varieties vinified at St. Hubertus include bacchus, chasselas, pinot meunier and gamay.

ST. LAZLO: See **Joe Ritlop.**

STAG'S HOLLOW WINERY & VINE-YARD: This farm winery was opened in 1996 based on a vineyard on Sun Valley Way, south of Okanagan Falls. The name of the winery was inspired when owners Larry Gerelus and Linda Pruegger encountered a shy faun crouching quietly under the vidal vines which yield one of the winery's signature wines. Housed in a building with a striking green roof and a turret suggesting a Loire chateau, the winery is an immediate neighbour to **Wild Goose Vineyards.** See **Larry Gerelus.**

STANDARDS OF WINE GRAPE QUAL-ITY: In 1975 the wineries and the growers agreed for the first time on standards for maturity or brix of grapes at harvest. Brix is one of several measurements of the sugar content in grapes, with twenty-one degrees brix being necessary to achieve an alcohol of about 11 percent in a finished table wine without adding additional sugar during fermentation. The minimum acceptable standard in 1975 was twelve degrees brix and growers were paid only 60 percent of the agreed contract price; the full agreed price was paid only for grapes with between seventeen and twenty degrees brix and a premium was paid for grapes more mature than that. The contracts wineries signed with growers twenty years later for vinifera grapes imposed different and more complex standards, with variation among contracts, in recognition the brix measurement is too narrow. A properly mature wine grape not only has the required brix but the correct acidity to allow winemakers to produce harmonious wines.

STARK, LYNN: See *Lynn, Bremmer.*

STEWART, ANTHONY DAVID (1966–): The business manager at *Quails' Gate,* Tony Stewart chuckles ruefully at the warning that his fellow workers gave him in 1986 when he quit the first full-time job he had had after high school — that of a technician in the ore-processing plant at Cominco Ltd.'s Polaris lead-zinc mine north of the Arctic circle. "They said I would never earn as much money anywhere else," Stewart recalls. Indeed, a decade later the family winery was not paying him nearly as well as the mine; the compensation is in the evident satisfaction Stewart draws from what is already the third career in his young life. When he left the mine, Stewart took a financial management diploma at the British Columbia Institute of Technology and then joined the brokerage firm Burns Fry & Co. in Toronto where he became a commodities trader. In search of the Okanagan lifestyle, Stewart returned to Kelowna in 1992, intending to resume a broker's career there. However, Quails' Gate had just lost its accountant; Tony Stewart stepped in temporarily and stayed on to handle sales and distribution as well as administration. And the winery's prospects have brightened considerably, sales having risen from 8,000 cases in 1992 to 22,000 cases in 1995.

STEWART, BEN (1957–): One of the owners of *Quails' Gate* winery, Stewart was born in Kelowna, a member of a family who immigrated in 1906 from Ireland and has been prominent ever since in Okanagan agriculture and business. After working in the vineyards operated by his father, Richard, Ben Stewart graduated from high school to spend the next five years as a banker in Calgary and Kitimat. He rejoined the family business in 1979 when the Stewarts began planning an estate winery. Lack of banking support frustrated the Stewarts in 1984 but five years later, Ben Stewart was among the early applicants for a farmgate winery licence. A risktaker, Stewart crushed enough grapes that fall for 5,000 gallons of wine before he even had his licence. Quails' Gate subsequently converted to an estate winery.

STEWART, RICHARD (1926–): A member of a family prominent in Okanagan agriculture almost since the beginning of the twentieth century, Richard Stewart first planted grapes in 1963 on property now part of the Quails'

Gate vineyards. As well, he formed a partnership with *Calona Wines* to establish *Pacific Vineyards,* which leased land from the Westbank Indian Band for a vineyard and bought land south of Oliver for a second vineyard. "We believed there was room for growth in the wine industry," Stewart recalled later. Initially he planted what were then considered the established varieties — such North American labrusca grapes as diamond, Campbell's early, sheridan and patricia. A nursery in Seattle, one of his suppliers, misidentified a shipment of what should have been 10,000 diamond vines. Stewart discovered when the vines were growing that he had been shipped chasselas, a vinifera vine that produces far superior fruit than diamond. "We left them in," Stewart chuckled.

In 1964 he and *Joe Capozzi* (in the latter's private aircraft) flew to grape-growing areas in Ontario and New York state to choose varieties for the initial Pacific Vineyards plantings the following year. At Gold Seal Vineyards in New York, one of the early vinifera growers, they found that the previous winter had devastated the vines. That convinced Stewart and Capozzi to play it safe, planting the more hardy hybrid varieties, including de chaunac, chelois, verdelet and maréchal foch. After managing Pacific Vineyards for several years, Stewart sold his interest to Calona Wines and concentrated on developing the vineyard near Westbank that now supports Quails' Gate.

Stewart was a founding member in 1961 of the Association of British Columbia Grape Growers (with *Frank Schmidt* and *Martin Dulik*), set up to lobby government for favourable policies. He was not an original member of the Grape Growers Marketing Board but soon joined this price-negotiating body and subsequently became its chairman. Interested more in grapegrowing than winemaking, Stewart encouraged his son Ben to establish Quails' Gate.

STRACHAN, DR. GARY (1938–):

An influential figure in British Columbia wine, Strachan has contributed widely, as a scientist, as an organizer of wine-judging panels, and even as a wine tour guide through Okanagan Wine Tours, launched in 1993 with partner Nancy Johnson. And as owner of Oliver Technologies Ltd., Strachan has been a consulting winemaker for many British Columbia wineries and aspires to launch his own winery.

Born in Toronto, he has a bachelor's degree in dairy science from Guelph and a master's in nutrition and food science from the Massachusetts Institute of Technology. He was about to begin a doctorate at MIT when his father, who owned a substantial dairy products trucking business just outside Toronto, alerted Gary to another dairy trucking firm for sale in the Guelph area. Strachan bought it and ran it for ten years before selling it. "I used to pick up milk from 2,000 farms," he recalls. "I was the best educated milk trucker in Ontario." Strachan had sold his dairy trucking business when he enrolled at the University of Guelph to do post-graduate work on yeast genetics.

Again, he did not complete his doctorate: one of his professors urged him to apply for a research scientist job with the Canada Department of Agriculture at the *Summerland Research Station* in 1977. Summerland had just begun the *Becker* project to evaluate better wine grape varieties and Strachan was soon making small batches of wine from the Becker grapes and from other trial plots, in what amounted to a crash course in winemaking. It did not take him long to become totally involved in wine. In 1981, he was one of the founders of what became the ***Okanagan Wine Festival*** and for many years he supervised the judging panel. In the 1980s he wrote the early drafts of what subsequently became the industry's quality standards. After leaving the research station in 1990, he established his consulting firm. He also planted a small vineyard at his farm on the outskirts of Summerland, a first step towards his own winery. "I'm looking at semillon-pinot blanc blends; I feel they are a very good pairing for the valley," Strachan believes. "I think it should make a dynamite wine. I've never seen one, but conceptually, it should be very good."

STYLE: The evolution of wine in British Columbia

The taste of the wines of a region or of an individual producer is the *style* of the region or of the producer. For example, the commonly understood style of Chablis is that of a crisply fresh white wine with the varietal character of chardonnay, the only variety permitted for producing true Chablis.

Is there a British Columbia style so easily identified? The answer is no: the wine-producing area is too extensive, covering differing soil types and — in the example of Vancouver Island compared with the Okanagan — dramatically differing climates. The only defining characteristic of grapes grown in British Columbia, notably the white varieties from the cooler sites, is piquant acidity, giving zest to the flavours of the wines. There are many house styles of winemaking among the producers, but with the general stylistic element of wines that are fresh, full of fruit, with the lively kiss of natural acidity that comes with cool-climate viticulture.

Winemaking in British Columbia tramped a long and inglorious journey to reach the point where one can seriously discuss the style. In 1976 a Vancouver wine enthusiast named Roland Morgan authored what likely was the first guide, tasting and rating most of the wines (and other products) then available in British Columbia liquor stores. His *Sterling B.C. Wine & Spirits Guide* was well ahead of its time for there were hardly enough products in the liquor stores worth rating to even justify a guide. However, Morgan's insights into the style of British Columbia wines at that time provides a benchmark for progress since.

A wine can never be better than the grapes from which it is made, as Morgan understood. "The vast bulk of these [British Columbia] wines are still made from North American hybrid grapes which have a distinctive taste as hard to remove as cheap perfume. The taste has a name: 'foxy'... " The familiar concord grape exemplifies the taste and aroma associated with the so-called foxiness of North American grapes; it has nothing to do with the pungent aroma of a fox but rather because early settlers, it is said, called native varieties fox grapes. "The best remedy for the foxy flavor is sugar," Morgan wrote. "Thus, the sweeter the wine, the more passable the taste." Many wines made in British Columbia well into the 1970s relied on varying degrees of sweetness to make the wines acceptable to consumers. It must be said that many of those consumers were not discerning.

Morgan tasted the formidable group of reds that were sold by the gallon or half-gallon. "These are basic, unpretentious B.C. reds, blended towards the sweetness rating," he wrote, alluding to the scale of one to ten by which the liquor board ranked wines, the sweetest being ten. Most British Columbia table wines were rated three to five. In discussing British Columbia whites, Morgan advised: "Go by the sweetness rating, bearing in mind that this range *does not include a satisfactory dry wine.*" (Emphasis added.)

When Morgan wrote his guide, the selection of imported table wines in British Columbia was abysmal. "Here they are," Morgan wrote at the head of that section. "Sixty imported listings [including only] three Californians, when we lie only an hour's air freight from the world's second best wine district." Shortly after he wrote that arguable proposition, the **Liquor Distribution Branch** was carved out from the liquor control apparatus by the government and given the green light to offer consumers a serious choice of imported wines. In no time at all, consumers learned to discern decent wines and the wineries of British Columbia began to lose market share. In turn, that triggered the first change in style away from cloying sweet table wines in the history of British Columbia winemaking.

The drying out of tables wines became possible because growers in the 1970s switched to the so-called French hybrid varieties such as de chaunac, foch, chelois, and verdelet. None are great winemaking grapes but all were substantially better than the "foxy" varieties. The wineries sought to retain consumers by making wines as dry (one or even zero rating) as those being imported from France, Italy and elsewhere. Most wineries underlined this style shift by giving foreign-sounding names (the so-called **pseudo-labels)** to the wines. Thus, **Calona**'s list of wines with a zero (dry) rating included San Pietro Italian Red and Haut Village white. **Andrés** responded with Moulin Rouge; **Casabello** with Gala Italian Red; **Jordan & Ste-Michelle** with Toscano Rosso; and so on. But the majority of the wines were only partly dried out, to be positioned with rankings of two or three, since most consumer palates were nowhere near appreciating zero. The most successful white table wine launched in the late 1970s, Calona's **Schloss Laderheim,** had enough sweetness to rate as a two.

The continuing sweet style of British Columbia wines at the beginning of the 1980s, while reflecting where consumers were on the learning curve, also flowed from the deficiencies of the grape varieties then available. The Okanagan riesling, the backbone of the original Schloss and of many other whites, was a mischievous variety that retained overly high acidity until fully mature and then developed foxy notes to the flavour and aroma. Winemakers chose to balance the acidity with a dose of sugar, avoiding the foxiness of full maturity. Only when the winemakers were able to obtain properly mature vinifera, were they able to make totally dry table wines that still were appealing. In 1981, for example, Jordan & Ste-Michelle was marketing a chenin blanc and a zinfandel, both made from imported vinifera grapes and both rated zero. Throughout the 1980s, an increasing number of dry table wines (zero or one) were released as acreages of better wine grapes increased.

House styles began to emerge with the estate wineries. From its very beginning, **Gray Monk** consistently has produced wines with expressively fresh and juicy fruitiness in the aroma and in the taste. Similarly, the majority of wines from **Gehringer Brothers** have maintained a consistent style, showing clean, delicate fruit flavors, often with a hint of sweet fruit obtained by blending a tiny quantity of sweet reserve (unfermented juice) into the finished wines. The hallmark of wines from **Hainle Vineyards** has been their austere, dry structure and the complexity of the flavours. **Sumac Ridge**, because of its larger and changing repertoire of wines, developed less of a house style in its initial years except with its flagship gewurztraminer wines, generally richly fruity with good spicy flavours appropriate to the grape. These styles are sufficiently individual that experienced tasters at times will pick out the wines in blind tastings. These styles developed for two reasons. First, these wineries control their vineyards (either owning them or having contracts with growers) and can begin to shape the wines in the field. Second, the winemaking philosophy has been unchanged from the start, with experienced or adequately trained winemakers at the controls at all times.

In the 1990s winemaking styles in British Columbia have undergone a paradigm shift. An international "pattern" of wine styles has been laid over British Columbia wine, drawing on winemaking experience of France, California, Australia and New Zealand which has added to the strong German influence that dominated the better wines of the previous decade. Both the established wineries and the newer wineries are no longer trying to compete globally with dated products masquerading under foreign-sounding labels. The 1990s is the first decade in which the vineyards have become widely replanted with quality vinifera vines to provide winemakers with the fruit necessary for good wines. This also is the first decade in which wineries have committed seriously to new French or American oak barrels and to the sophisticated grape-processing equipment found in fine wineries elsewhere. In short, from the vineyard through to the bottling lines, the winemakers of the 1990s now have the tools to make great wine.

Mission Hill winemaker **John Simes** is acknowledged as the winemaker upon whom the paradigm shifted. Already well regarded in New Zealand when he was hired by **Mission Hill**, Simes arrived in the Okanagan just as the 1992 vintage was beginning. The grand reserve chardonnay he produced from that vintage won the **Avery's Trophy** at a London competition in 1994, perhaps the most prestigious international award won up to that time by a wine from British Columbia. "As a wine, it seems to have given an impetus to the industry which is extraordinary for one wine," Simes says. "In a few years we'll know what the real impact of that wine was on the industry." The New Zealand winemaking style from which Simes emerges makes wines, whether red or white, with clean, mouth-filling fruit; the oak will be evident but not overwhelming in those wines fermented in or matured in barrels. Increasingly, this has emerged as the overall style of British Columbia wines since winemakers like **Ross Mirko** at **Cedar-Creek** and **Mark Wendenburg** at Sumac Ridge have New Zealand experience while **Jeff Martin** at **Quails' Gate** is an experienced winemaker from Australia. Also coming to play are elements of French winemaking, notably at **Domaine Combret** and at **Blue Mountain**. The Domaine Combret winery is operated by the Combret family whose winemaking tradition in France is three hundred years old. Blue Mountain's complex Burgundian-style wines are made by *Ian Mavety*, a native-born British Columbian who had the good sense to employ as his consultant a French-trained vintner working in California.

The winemakers of the 1990s espouse a holistic approach much more rooted in the vineyard than ever before in British Columbia. Olivier Combret and his father, Robert, speak almost obsessively about the *terroir* in their vineyard and how it has governed the choice of grapes they planted. Mavety, a skilled vineyardist, achieves the concentrated flavours of the Blue Mountain wines by limiting production much more severely than he ever did when he was growing the prolific hybrids for commercial wineries in the 1970s. "Winemaking is a chain," Simes maintains. "For a wine that wins a top international award, there's a chain from the bottle back to the vineyard. Everything in the chain has to be there. Good winemaking won't make up for rotten garbage grapes. And brilliant grapes will not make a brilliant wine without good winemaking and good systems in the winery and good barrels and all the rest. They all have to fit."

SULPHUR: Used in minute concentrations, sulphur is one of the most universal winery sterilants and preservatives. Sulphur-based sprays also are used in the vineyard to protect the vines against mildew. Winemakers have learned to reduce the use of sulphur to a minimum but seldom do without it. Sulphur-free wines are prone to oxidizing.

SUMAC RIDGE ESTATE WINERY: Established in 1980, this estate winery emerged from a nine-hole golf course and clubhouse on the northern edge of Summerland. The golf course fairways were interplanted with vines, not always an easy co-existence. However, the brilliance of the site was not the vineyard but the winery's ready accessibility for visitors. In its first season after opening to the public, the winery was sold out and was serving coffee to visitors after Christmas. The winery's popularity with wine tourists has never flagged.

The founding partners were *Harry McWatters* and *Lloyd Schmidt*, who had worked together at *Casabello* wines, in whose winery Sumac Ridge produced its initial vintage while building its own winery. When Schmidt left the partnership, his place was taken for five years by an Okanagan businessman named Bud Richmond, who in turn sold his interest to *Bob Wareham,* another of the friends that McWatters made at Casabello. In each case, the dynamics of the partnership have been designed to permit McWatters to pursue his strong suit as a much-travelled salesman while the stay-at-home partner deals with the mundane affairs of the vineyard and the banking relationships. Clearly, the formula has worked.

Sumac Ridge initially established its reputation as one of the best producers of gewurztraminer in British Columbia. Throughout its first decade and a half, Sumac Ridge laboured hard to turn chancellor into the most distinguished of the varietals made from a red hybrid grape, and was perhaps on the cusp of success with that grape when the winery began releasing its merlots and cabernet sauvignons. The superior quality of these reds reminded everyone that the hybrid varieties simply lack the character to rise beyond a utility status. In the 1990s Sumac Ridge, in addition to its Bordeaux reds, has become a leading exponent of pinot blanc, both as a dry table wine and, in the example of its Stellar's Jay Cuvée, in a sparkling wine. While the winery still retains the golf course vineyard, now somewhat shrunken in size, it relies increasingly on grapes grown near Oliver on the *Black Sage Vineyard*, which is controlled by Sumac Ridge's partners. Some of these partners, including McWatters and Wareham, also bought *LeComte Estate Winery* in 1995.

SUMMERHILL ESTATE WINERY:

Opened in 1992 by former New York real estate developer *Stephen Cipes*, Summerhill has set out to be the single largest producer of classical method (Champagne-style) *sparkling wines* in British Columbia. The winery's flagship Cipes Brut, made entirely from riesling grapes in the style of a serious German sekt, quickly became a best seller, due both to the wine's consistent quality and to its clever promotion. During a 1993 summit meeting of the American and Russian presidents in Vancouver, Cipes managed to get his sparkling wine served on the yacht on which the two presidents toured the Vancouver harbour. The winery is located at Okanagan Mission, a short drive east of Kelowna, and is based on a thirty-eight-acre organic vineyard. In its early years Summerhill made and sold its wines from makeshift quarters protected from the weather by a massive blue tarpaulin; others in the industry sardonically began calling it the Blue Tarp winery. But early in 1996 Summerhill opened a grandly sited and fully modern winery building with a tasting room commanding a fine view

of the Okanagan Valley. Perhaps the most important building on the property, however, is a pyramid in which Summerhill ages virtually all of its wine. Cipes subscribes to the belief that pyramid-aging definitely improves the quality of the wines.

SUMMERLAND RESEARCH STATION:

Properly called the Canada Department of Agriculture Research Station, this was established in 1914 as the Dominion Experimental Station south of Summerland, on a bench on the west side of Okanagan Lake. Test plantings of grapes began in 1928, consisting of *labrusca* warhorses like niagara, concord, and campbell's early. This round of trials ended in 1948 by which time 112 varieties had been tested. The station had eliminated many for their tenderness or susceptibility to powdery mildew, including cabernet sauvignon.[13] In 1957, when it became apparent that interest in wine grapes was rising, the station once again resumed trials of varieties, this time including both *vinifera* and *hybrid* vines. The trials were directed by Donald V. Fisher, who later became Summerland's director from 1971 to 1974 when he retired. With a doctorate from Iowa State University, Fisher had begun working at the station in 1933, primarily in pomology but ultimately also acquired expertise in viticulture. He brought in at least seventy different grape varieties, mostly hybrids, that were planted in test plots around the Okanagan. The few tested vinifera included some of today's stars — gamay, pinot blanc and pinot noir. They flunked them either because growers still could not control powdery mildew or because the vines were thought insufficiently hardy. In a 1974 paper, Fisher wrote: "The most outstanding two grapes to emerge from this testing program were Seibel 9549 [de chaunac] and foch, now both widely grown in this area."[14] In spite of his expertise, Fisher's views echoed the cautious, risk-averse advice from the professionals that deterred growers for years from planting vinifera. "The wineries are pressing the growers to grow exotic varieties that will make good wine but are alarmingly risky from a commercial point of view," Fisher said in a 1982 interview. "The best grape we grow here is the Hungarian riesling."[15] He was referring to the Okanagan riesling, believed by some to have been imported from Hungary by the **Rittich** brothers and planted in 1932. Most of the variety was ripped out in 1988 because the quality of the wine is poor.

Summerland's finest hours were those when it coordinated the so-called **Becker** project, a trial of grape varieties from the **Geisenheim Institute** of Germany between 1977 and 1985. The varieties were grown in test plots near Kelowna and Oliver, with the grapes turned into wine at Summerland by staff enologist **Dr. Gary Strachan** and viticulturist **Dr. Andy Reynolds**. The wines were assessed regularly by professional industry tasting panels and the results, coordinated with the field performance of the varietals, enabled Okanagan growers for the first time in their history to make properly informed planting decisions. The Becker project ended because government funding ran out.

Summerland's on-again, off-again relationship with viticulture went off again with the federal government's 1995 budget, which cut $51 million in base funding from Agriculture Canada's re-search budget over a two-year period. Those cuts included eliminating the viticulture program because, as provincial grape specialist **John Vielvoye** put it in his industry newsletter in April 1995, "Returns to investment (value of dollars spent on staff vs. returns to industry) are said to be lower in these programs than in other programs." The decision means there will be no federal research in viticulture anywhere in Canada by 1997. "There will be," Vielvoye wrote, "a general dependency on other areas [of the world] for viticulture research and local use of trial and error to evaluate such practices."

SUNSET VINEYARD: This ninety-five-acre vineyard adjacent to the **Black Sage Vineyard** and formerly part of the Shannon and **Pacific** vineyards north of Osoyoos, was purchased in 1993 by **Rob Milne**, a Coquitlam, B.C., entrepreneur, after a vacation in France fired an interest in good wine. Under the management of **Dick Cleave**, seventeen acres of vinifera (including cabernet sauvignon, merlot and chardonnay) were planted in 1994. Difficulty in importing vines from France prevented the planned 1995 plantings of the rest of the vineyard and delayed Milne's plan to build a winery here. Expected to open in 1998, the winery will be known as **Kalamalka Estates Winery**.

SUPERNAK, FRANK (1961 –): Born in Nanaimo, Supernak joined the **T.G. Brights & Co.** Oliver winery in 1984, shortly after graduating in microbiology from the University of British Columbia. During his first four years at the Oliver winery, a federal government grant funded intensive research and

Frank Supernak (photo courtesy of James O'Mara)

evaluation of trial varieties, with Supernak gradually taking over making the wine from those grapes. He found that the Russian whites produced good wines, but not consistently so; the matsvani, for example, made fruity wines one year, neutral wines the next. Eventually, the winery dropped all the eccentric varieties except the sereksia chornaya, an excellent rosé, which was re-launched in 1992 as Blanc de Noirs. The renaming of that wine was necessary because the Brights marketing department found it too difficult to sell the Russian tongue twisters. Supernak, who took over the winemaking at Oliver in 1992, describes the purple-skinned sereksia chornaya as "the most interesting grape I have ever worked with." However, he had the winery now focussed on mainstream varietals, including chardonnay, riesling and ehrenfelser, usually vinified into crisply dry wines. The baco noir was dropped, with the winery now concentrating on vinifera varietals only. The major red varietal made in 1992 by Supernak was a merlot with grapes from the Columbia Valley in Washington state; ultimately, adequate supplies of merlot have become available in the Okanagan. Supernak left **Vincor** (as Brights had become known) in May 1996, to become the winemaking partner of **Hester Creek**, the winery formerly operating as **Divino** at Oliver.

SUTHERLAND, IAN (1952–):

A man of many interests, Montrealer Ian Sutherland trekked much of the world from Norway to Nepal before settling in the Okanagan in 1976 where he learned to make beer and then wine. By trade he is a welder and boilermaker; by passion, he has become a winegrower. In 1992 he and his wife, Gitta, a nurse, purchased an eight-acre apple orchard on Poplar Grove Road near Naramata and almost immediately began converting some of the acreage to vines for a winery to be called, suitably enough, **Poplar Grove**.

Sweeney Cooperage Ltd.

Founded in Victoria in 1889 and later relocated to Vancouver, this company claimed to be the biggest barrel-maker in the British Empire. The company's motto was: "Barrels — we roll 'em all over the world." Leo Sweeney, the energetic and ambitious son of the founder, ran the company in its salad days and became one of Vancouver's more prominent and well-travelled businessmen from the 1930s through the 1950s. "I have traveled over a million miles in the last thirty years and on one trip covered 12,000 miles by water, another 14,000 miles by air, and on still another trip 16,000 miles by various transportation methods," Sweeney boasted in a 1944 speech to the annual meeting of the Associated Cooperage Industries of America.[16] At one time the owner of cooperages in Montreal, Seattle and Portland as well as Vancouver, he became in 1939 the second president of the one-year-old Canadian Cooperage Association (his uncle from London, Ont., Frank Forristal, was the founding president).

The business peaked from the 1940s through to the mid-1960s, when the company had the capacity to make more than 2,000 barrels a day. But business declined rapidly when barrels were displaced by cardboard and plastic containers. Sweeney's, which had once employed four hundred, laid off ninety employees in Vancouver in 1968; four years later, rising labour and material costs led to the closure of the sawmill where staves and barrel heads had been fashioned. Until the cooperage closed entirely in 1980, barrels for the dwindling remaining demand were assembled with components imported from Europe. "Our operation was unique in the world, processing from log to stave under one roof," Jack Sweeney, one of the former managers, told a Vancouver journalist in 1972. "It's the last of its breed."[17] The plant, with its century-old tools, was termed "the biggest anachronism on False Creek" by Dr. Robert Collier, a University of British Columbia planning professor who campaigned briefly to have the cooperage turned into a museum. The ten-acre site on which the plant stood is now the home of B.C. Place Stadium.

The founding Sweeney was Michael, who was born and grew up in Carbonear, Nfld., where he learned the craft of coopering in a seven-year apprenticeship with a local barrel-maker. He took his skill first to Boston and then to London, Ont., where his brother-in-law, Frank Forristal, had a cooperage. "Mike didn't like the eastern winters," journalist Archie H. Wills wrote in a 1971 profile of Sweeney's. "When British Columbia was featured on the completion of the Canadian Pacific Railway, he decided to see what the place was like."[18] He discovered a demand for barrels from fish processors and sealers and began to craft barrels in a shed in Victoria. His use of locally grown fir enabled him to produce barrels that were cheaper than traditional oak barrels, since the oak had to be imported; fir was suitable for most of the applications to which barrels were put in an age when wood was the leading packaging material. In a few years, Sweeney bought a property at 162 Johnson Street with a stable that was converted into a four-barrel-a-day assembly plant. With the Klondike gold rush in 1897, there was an additional demand for whisky and food barrels. The cooperage moved to new industrial quarters on Victoria's Inner Harbour just before the First World War, when business boomed. By 1924, with the company aggressively run now by his son, Leo, capacity was six hundred barrels a day.

Leo Sweeney in the Carribbean (photo courtesy of Ed Sweeney)

When fire destroyed the plant that year, it was rebuilt immediately. James K. Nesbitt, a veteran Victoria journalist and amateur historian, described Michael Sweeney, who stepped aside as president in 1920, as a "plain, simple, kindly man, not greatly interested in dollars, happy in his eight hours labor, glad the good Lord gave him strength to work that way in old age. At night, he liked to sit, pipe going full blast, around his dining table, before a roaring stove fire, reading the newspapers and talking of the old days in Newfoundland with cronies from his homeland."[19]

By contrast, his son Leo (1886–1977) was a barrel-chested dynamo who started in the cooperage when he was eleven, also finding time to star, and often captain, Victoria lacrosse, rugby, rowing and cycling teams. He was twenty-seven when he was made managing director in 1913. Seven years later, in partnership with Western Cooperage Inc. of Portland, Leo Sweeney moved to Vancouver to run a new barrel-assembly plant called Canadian Western Cooperage Co., going after the burgeoning market for barrels in Vancouver and the Fraser Valley. Located at False Creek in a building and on land leased from Canadian Pacific Ltd., it made barrels with staves and barrel heads supplied from the Sweeney plant in Victoria. In 1940, after Sweeney purchased the Portland company's shares, the Vancouver plant changed its name to Sweeney Cooperage Ltd. Ultimately, Leo Sweeney also took over Western's cooperages in Seattle and Portland. In 1946, a sawmill to make barrel staves and heads was opened at the False Creek site, primarily to save the freight costs of shipping barrel components from Victoria. The Victoria operation was closed the following year.

Many of the barrels produced by Sweeney Cooperage were sold to industrial or food-processing customers in more than forty countries around the world. Anaconda was a steady buyer of small barrels in which it stored arsenic at its Montana mining operations. The cherry growers in Oregon bought barrels for shipping cherries in syrup. The citrus fruit processors in the Caribbean used Sweeney barrels for orange concentrate. Meat packers in eastern Canada — Sweeney bought the John Paxton Co. cooperage in Montreal in 1941 — shipped meats this way. Access to tight-grain, knot-free Douglas fir gave Sweeney's a competitive advantage which was preserved by close attention to quality in the plant. The company once calculated that each barrel stave was handled by as many as fifteen different persons: many were scrutinizing the wood to prevent defects from slipping through.

Wineries and distilleries required oak barrels. Where new barrels were needed, Sweeney's bought American oak from the southern United States where, because the trees grow evenly through all the seasons, the wood has a consistently tight grain. What little Canadian oak that might have been available in eastern Canada (most was sold to furniture makers) proved too porous for barrel-making because the dramatic seasonal variations cause the trees to grow unevenly, laying down alternately tight and loose rings of growth. The cooperage seldom used European wood for barrels until the 1970s, when rising prices for Douglas fir led to the import of beechwood barrel components from Holland.

For the barrels sold to wineries in Canada and in California, Sweeney procured used bourbon barrels from American distillers. To be called bourbon, the whisky must be aged in new American oak. Each year Leo Sweeney would buy boxcar loads of used barrels (he had multi-year contracts with some distillers). His coopers in Vancouver would check each barrel for soundness, replacing leaking or broken staves, and the barrels then would be sold, typically to Canadian distillers, to wineries and, in surprising quantity, to home winemakers. During Prohibition in the United States, which ended in 1933, there also was a market there for re-coopered whisky barrels, for it was never illegal for individuals to make wine for their own consumption. British Columbia's postwar influx of European immigrants, notably from Italy and Portugal, included a vast number of home vintners who turned to Sweeney's for barrels. (Sweeney's also relied on immigrants for trained coopers, hiring a number who came from Britain, Germany, Portugal and Italy, including the entire Donatiello family.) One year in the 1960s, as the demand for barrels moved past its peak, the distillers found themselves with such a surplus that Sweeney was able to buy used barrels for twenty-five cents each. He bought more than 100,000 of them. When they arrived in Vancouver, they were stacked on the False Creek property in a pile whose top was level with the deck of the adjacent Cambie Street bridge. Sweeney's needed several years and some fanciful marketing to work through this inventory. Leo Sweeney's suggested applications even included dog houses fashioned from bourbon barrels.

More prized by winemakers than used whisky barrels were used port and sherry barrels, with the British Columbia Liquor Control Board being one source of the latter. For many years, the board imported both fortified wines and spirits in bulk, bottling them in Vancouver, and selling the empty barrels. Edward

Sweeney, one of the three sons of Leo Sweeney who joined their father in the business, recalled his first business trip to Victoria with his father to negotiate the annual barrel purchase contract with the redoubtable **Lt.-Col. Donald McGugan**, who ran the board. Edward Sweeney remembered the colonel as a gruff man who warmed up once business was concluded. On this particular trip, the colonel invited the Sweeneys to lunch with him at the Union Club. When he asked what they would like to drink, the youthful Edward declined. "That's not very good for the liquor business," McGugan snorted unhappily.

Sweeney's winery customers included **Calona Wines**, which was so short of money when it started in 1932 that **Cap Capozzi** talked Leo Sweeney into accepting shares in the winery in payment for barrels. Sweeney sold the shares after the war when he needed cash to expand the cooperage. "I'm not sure my father made an awful lot of money on those shares," Edward Sweeney said.[20] The domestic wineries that opened in the 1960s were not always major buyers of barrels, with the exception, perhaps, of barrels purchased for decorative purposes around the winery, but for **Casabello** which bought a large number of Sweeney's barrels. Most wineries relied on stainless steel tanks or concrete vats for wine storage.

A program for the cooperage company's seventy-seventh annual meeting showed that Leo Sweeney had held some executive title in the company since 1913, succeeding his father as president in 1920 and remaining in that job until 1964 when he promoted himself to chairman and sales director. The same program indicates that he also drew most of his eight children into the business, with his three daughters as directors. Jack Sweeney, born in 1929, was made a vice-president in 1957 and president in 1964. Edward Sweeney, born in 1930, started to work in the cooperage, like his father, at age eleven, became assistant general manager in 1957 and vice-president in 1965. Frank Sweeney, born in 1934, was sent in 1957 to run the Seattle cooperage that Sweeney's had acquired. He returned to Vancouver after the Seattle plant was closed in 1972, and he took over running the company in its declining years, his brothers having left to pursue other businesses once the cooperage no longer supported them all. (The other Sweeney sons, who were not interested in barrel-making, entered the priesthood.)

With a large family looking after the cooperage, Leo Sweeney could spend a good deal of time travelling, so much so that the odds caught up with him. He was involved in two train wrecks, the first, a serious wreck between Quebec City and Montreal in 1941, in which there was one fatality (a trainman) and forty-one injured passengers (but not Sweeney). In the second, his train in the United States was involved in a minor collision with Thomas Dewey's campaign train. Both of these events made the Vancouver newspapers, for Sweeney was a Vancouver celebrity through five or six decades — and he was aware of his celebrity, for he (or more likely his secretary) saved his press clippings in voluminous scrapbooks. Sweeney headed various service clubs, including Kiwanis, Gyro and Knights of Columbus. During the war years, he was president of the British Columbia Automobile Association. But he was best known for his Vancouver boosterism, both when he headed the Vancouver Tourist Association and as a private citizen. Refusing to acknowledge that Vancouver ever had inclement weather, Sweeney often wore a straw boater in winter, arranged to have the press photograph him smelling roses in Stanley Park at Christmas and claimed never to have owned an umbrella. "Never apologize for the rain," he said in 1948. "It washes away germs, it makes the flowers beautiful, and the grass green."

Leo Sweeney once ran for a seat on the Vancouver Park Board and, in 1953, stood as a Liberal candidate in the provincial election. He was unsuccessful on both occasions, a testimony perhaps to his talent for saying things that were not politic. For example, soon after returning from one of his trips to Europe, Sweeney reported on his impressions to the Gyro Club in Vancouver in a speech on January 3, 1938, that was covered by all the city's newspapers. "I would advise Prime Minister Mackenzie King and Premier T.D. Pattullo to put a little bit of Nazi into their governments with some authority behind it in order to deal with unemployment," Sweeney said. "Having reduced unemployment from 7,000,000 to 500,000, Hitler has solved the problem to a large extent.... Hitler is also keeping his people physically fit. Perhaps he is keeping them fit for war — and if it comes to that, why shouldn't we keep our people fit, too, if we have to fight sometime?" The remarks drew ridicule (he was greeted with cries of *Heil Sweeney* by members of the Kiwanis Club, of which he was then president) and criticism. Almost a decade later, when the cooperage was involved in a labour dispute with the International Woodworkers of America, the union reminded the public of those remarks.

The labour problems for Sweeney began after the IWA certified the Sweeney sawmill in Victoria in the spring of 1946 and then struck for a forty-hour week and a raise of twenty-five cents an hour. The rising labour costs appeared to have triggered the subsequent decision to close that sawmill in September 1948, for Leo Sweeney complained to the press about "the trend in labor nowadays to take things easy and just not work very hard." A dispute with the IWA led to a seven-week closure of the Vancouver plant in 1952 (Sweeney threatened to close it for good before getting a settlement) and a strike in 1969. The resulting rising labour costs led to the 1972 closure of the Vancouver sawmill, where procedures were too labour intensive and the technology too obsolete for a barrel-stave mill to pay wages similar to those paid at the increasingly automated neighbouring lumber mills. With barrels on the way out as a general-purpose container, the cooperage had no hope of paying competitive wages nor even of staying in business long enough to see the wine industry-led revival in demand for barrels in the 1990s.

SYRAH: This vinifera makes densely dark wines in the south of France and in Australia, where the variety also is called shiraz. In the Okanagan the variety has been planted only in the warmest sites because the grape needs plenty of heat. The first winery to release a varietal syrah was *Nichol* vineyards. In cooler vintages, the winery produced a gutsy rosé. In years of abundant sun, the grapes yield a wine that is satisfyingly big and dense.

1. *Calona Wines: Golden Anniversary,* published in 1982 by Calona Wines Ltd.

2. Letter in Calona Wines files.

3. Clipping in Evans Lougheed scrapbooks.

4. Memorandum by Brent Langley, a marketing manager at Growers', in March 1968; in Lloyd Schmidt files.

5. Tex Enemark papers; letter January 16, 1978, to Dr. Franz Werner Michel at the Haus des Deutchen Weines.

6. Tex Enemark papers; letter May 23, 1978, to Hermann Guntrum.

7. Information on the Schmidt family from interviews in 1994 with Lloyd Schmidt.

8. Lloyd Schmidt files.

9. Correspondence in Lloyd Schmidt's files.

10. *The Province,* August 19, 1967.

11. Quoted in a 1972 sales brochure preserved in the Lougheed scrapbooks.

12. Interview with author, May 1995.

13. Association of B.C. Grape Growers, *Atlas of Suitable Grape Growing Locations,* p. 3. (See SOURCES for complete reference.)

14. D.V. Fisher, "History of Grape Growing in the Southern Interior," *British Columbia Orchardist,* March 1974, pp. 12–14.

15. Interview with author, 1982.

16. *The National Coopers' Journal,* June 1944, p. 93; clipping in Edward M. Sweeney's scrapbooks.

17. R.M. Shaw, *Vancouver Province,* September 30, 1972.

18. Archie H. Wills, *Victoria Colonist,* April 25, 1971.

19. J.K. Nesbitt in the *Vancouver News-Courier,* 1948; clipping in Edward M. Sweeney's scrapbook files.

20. Interview with author, March 4, 1995.

TTT

TANNINS: These naturally occurring chemicals occur in grapes in their skins, seeds and stems. The palate sensation of overly tannic wine recalls the dry, puckering impact of a mouthful of strong, black tea. However, tannins in the proper degree are important to the structure and longevity of red wines; because white wines are rarely fermented on the skins, the tannin content is insignificant. The amount of tannin in the wine depends on how long the wine has remained in contact with the skins, with wines crafted for long life usually being given longer skin contact. The amount of tannin varies with the grape variety. In general, the red hybrid varieties are lower in tannin than the red vinifera; and certain vinifera grapes, such as gamay, are lower in tannin than cabernet sauvignon, for example. Winemakers try to avoid the harsh tannins found in seeds by crushing grapes gently. Wines containing the soft tannins found in the skins have a mouth feel that is rounder and more luscious.

TARTRATES: When wines are chilled, the naturally occurring tartaric acids drop out as crystals, which are also called wine diamonds because they resemble diamonds. Most wines have been chilled before being bottled to remove the tartrates, which are not harmful but are unwanted only because consumers tend to reject bottles of wine containing what look like bits of broken glass. However, wines stored in a cool cellar or in a refrigerator may also precipitate wine diamonds which may fall to the bottom of the bottle or adhere to the cork.

TAXATION: According to the "Strategic Plan for the British Columbia Wine and Grape Industry," done in 1994 by the Chancellor Partners, a Vancouver consulting firm, "the taxes which Canada applies on wine are the highest in the world, more than twice the level applied by the next highest wine producing country (New Zealand), and over three times the level in the main wine producing nations." The report concluded that consumers in British Columbia would have a high preference for British Columbia wines if taxes and markups were reduced. "However," the authors lamented, "the requirements of government for revenue are not relaxed...."[1]

Ron Taylor (photo courtesy of John Schreiner)

TAYLOR, RON (1942–): The mentor of many Okanagan winemakers, Vancouver native Taylor, with a microbiology degree from the University of British Columbia, was hired by **Andrés** in 1970 to fill in for an ailing assistant winemaker. Taylor soon became the senior winemaker at the Port Moody winery and stayed there until 1992. Besides grooming young winemakers like **Walter Gehringer, Anne Sperling** and **Lynn Bremmer**, Taylor was able to stretch his talents from the production of proprietary blends like Hochtaler to well-crafted Okanagan varietals, with a 1987 botrytis-affected late harvest ehrenfelser among his achievements.

TEMPERANCE: See **Prohibition.**

TERRY, FRANK LENNARD: Chairman of **Potter Distilleries Ltd**. until December 1986 when he and brother Bill, the vice-chairman, stepped down after selling control of the company. Frank and Bill were sons of Captain Harold J.C. Terry.

TERRY, CAPTAIN HAROLD J.C.:
Terry was born in Australia in 1897, went to sea when he was fourteen and ultimately ended up sailing and then owning coastal freighters in British Columbia. Northland Navigation Co., of which he was chairman, was the leading coastal shipping company when he sold it in 1963. He had acquired **Potter Distilleries** in 1962 from Ernest C. Potter. Potter's, which had begun operating in 1959 from a small plant on Annacis Island, opened a larger distillery in Langley in 1967 to take advantage of a strong demand in the United States for Canadian rye whisky. The **Beaupré** winery, named for a brand that Potter's conveniently owned, opened next to the distillery in 1983. The Terry family sold control of Potter's in 1986. Both the winery and the distillery moved to Kelowna in 1989 after **Calona Wines** merged with Potter's.

THORPE, RICK (1946–): Hard-driving accountant Thorpe, a native of Byron, Ont., ran the **Cartier** winery (formerly **Casabello**) in Penticton from 1989 until it closed in 1994; then he became general manager of the **Okanagan Wine Festival.** Having a full plate of work is his style. "I have this tendency," he says. "Hard work always wins." He joined the Labatt brewing company in 1967 as an accounts payable clerk. He combined work with the courses that saw him become a certified management accountant in 1972, at which point he had had his fill of number-crunching and asked his boss for an interesting assignment. He spent the next three years turning around and running a Labatt-owned food-processing company in Trinidad, followed by three years running a brewery in Israel which also had problems to be resolved. Back in Canada, Labatt gave him several other tough management assignments. He succeeded at each one but there was a price: in April 1988, at age forty-two, Thorpe had a heart attack in his office. When he recovered and went back to work nine months later, he vowed to retire by the time he was fifty. Thorpe was Labatt's director of national sales in 1989 but agreed to join the winery management group that purchased the winery group from Labatt that June. While he stepped aside after Vincor bought and bought and closed Cartier, he did not retire at fifty. Instead, he won a seat in the British Columbia legislature in 1996 as a Liberal.

TINHORN CREEK VINEYARDS LTD.:
Located south of Oliver and up No.

Seven Road off the highway, this winery is near the end of a daunting, narrow road climbing uphill towards the mountain. The reward is a tasting room with one of the best views in the south Okanagan. The winery, which debuted in September 1995, with merlot and chardonnay and a kerner icewine, draws its name from an occasionally dry creek running through the property. In the late nineteenth century, the Tin Horn Quartz Mining Co. produced gold and silver from a mine, long since exhausted, in the hills above the vineyard.

TOKIOS, JOHN (1924–): Hungarian-born Tokios, who came to Canada in 1951, worked seventeen years in a silver mine at Beaverdell in British Columbia before planting grapes in 1968 on his property south of Oliver on the so-called *Golden Mile*. He had purchased the site in 1963 as raw Crown land at a government auction and considered planting fruit until persuaded by the new wineries in the valley to put in vines. Tokios planted Okanagan riesling — the grape, he was told, had come from Hungary like himself — along with de chaunac, chancellor and seyval blanc. Subsequently, the Okanagan riesling and the chancellor came out, to be replaced by vinifera, including gewurztraminer, merlot and pinot noir. Tokios has about nine acres under vine. In his spare time, he is also an accomplished wood carver.

TOSCANO: This Italian place name for Tuscany was registered in 1976 in Canada by *Jordan & Ste-Michelle Cellars* as the trademark for generic white and red table wines that subsequently sold well, especially in British Columbia. In 1983 a Tuscan wine producer released a Toscano Bianco and a Toscano Rosso — and Jordan went to court to protect its Canadian trademark. A judge in Ontario threw the case out, saying that the place name should not have been registered as a trademark in the first place. Jordan reconciled itself to co-existing with the Italian wines.

TOSTENSON, IAN (1955–): Born in North Vancouver and raised in Kelowna, Tostenson went to work for the Bank of Montreal as a management trainee after receiving a commerce degree in 1978 from the University of British Columbia. He turned down his first chance to enter the wine business when, six months into his banking career, *Calona Wines* sought to hire him as a salesman. However, by the fall of 1981, when Calona offered him the job a second time, Tostenson decided that a career in wine might be more exciting. "My sales territory when I started was New Westminister all the way to Prince Rupert," he recalled. "I thought this was the most incredible environment in which to develop a career against what I saw in the Bank of Montreal, which was very disciplined. My personality type was such that I needed to be in an environment that was much more innovative and open-ended than the bank."

Tostenson's personality is that of the cheer-leading coach who is up even when the team is down. At Calona Wines over the next dozen turbulent years, that positive attitude was essential. About three months after he joined the company, the first of many management shakeups swept through headquarters. "That was very disheartening," Tostenson found. The company, owned since 1971 by Standard Brands of Montreal, now was buffeted by successive ownership changes of its parent company. Calona found itself with a new president roughly every second year and sometimes with no president at all; and with the decisions being made in Toronto or New York or wherever the parent company happened to be headquartered at any one time. "Frankly, we became an orphan," said Tostenson, who kept on selling wine and rallying his colleagues. "I remember standing at a Christmas party with the staff in Calona, many of whom had been with the company for years, and as the sales manager, having to address them because there was no other manager around. I can remember saying 'You know, gang, we've got great products, we've got a great company and most of all we have each other to keep this thing moving.' That was the underlying culture. If our parents were going to continue to leave this house, we were going to keep the lawns cut and keep the house painted. That gave us the strength to get through all sorts of nonsense and to continue."

In 1989 ownership of the winery came back to British Columbia when it was acquired by *International Potter Distilling Corp.* If anything, this exacerbated Calona's orphan status. Tostenson, by then Calona's vice-president, recalls having to shout for attention at corporate meetings even though the winery accounted for half of the group's sales. Potter also had its historic spirits business and two breweries, both of which had difficulty generating profits. In addition, Potter's chairman was the flamboyant Harry Moll, a controversial Vancouver stock promoter. He attracted a mysterious group of Swiss investors to several of his companies, including Potter. The winery was not high on any manager's priority but Tostenson's. In 1991, just days before the company's annual meeting, Potter's president Robert Hunt took exception to some accounting manoeuvres dictated from Switzerland and resigned abruptly. Tostenson's reaction was typical: he told his fellow managers, "We've got one choice here — we've got to keep this thing moving." That evening after dinner, a Potter's director telephoned Tostenson and offered him the presidency. "It wasn't easy," he recalls of his early incumbency as president. "The senior management, I don't think, had bought into me because I was this loud kid from the winery." The corporate turbulence continued for another two years until promoter Moll and the original Swiss investors were forced out. Control of Potter settled with a major and stable Swiss conglomerate and the name of the company changed in April 1995 to *Cascadia Brands Inc.*, a name that helps move the company away from its recent difficult past. The stable ownership provided the opportunity for Calona in 1995 to begin taking a longer-term view of its future.

Boardroom instability was not Tostenson's only problem. After the Canada-United States Free Trade Agreement became effective in 1989, "nobody believed that the wine industry was anything but doomed," he recalled. The strategy at Calona was adjusted accordingly. "We headed down the road of bottling imports to keep the volume through the winery and we were not really taking a longer-term view," he said. "One model showed that the amount of British Columbia wine produced in British Columbia would go from about 60 percent of the market to 25 percent of the market, as this great influx of cheap imports were going to take over." That was not what happened. In the face of that challenge, the wineries formed the **British Columbia Wine Institute,** launched the *Vintners Quality Alliance* program and began a dramatic overhaul of wine quality.

At Calona, Tostenson shifted gears when he recognized the VQA's premium wine program was creating a profitable market for good quality wines made from grapes grown in the Okanagan. In 1995 Tostenson (who also became chairman of the Wine Institute that year) signed an eight-year contract for premium grapes from the vast **Burrowing Owl** vineyard near Oliver. "We can make great generic wines in great packages but we are putting that behind us," he said in 1995. "The effort is into the VQA, 100 percent British Columbia-produced product." To underline that shift in direction, the Calona name has been replaced by *Okanagan Cellars* on the labels of such warhorses as Royal Red, with the winery's name increasingly associated with VQA wines and with the imported varietals bottled at the winery under its "Calona Vineyards International" line.

That also represents a shift in thinking about the Calona name. Some of the managers who preceded Tostenson consciously played down the historic name; in the early 1980s, a line of wines appeared under the Spring Hill Vineyards label. "Should we abandon our heritage?" Tostenson asked himself. "Where we are solidly now is saying 'No!' We'll take our shots but we'll take the leadership. I sometimes think it would be easier to create a concept. But [we want to be seen] as a winery that is rich in heritage and experience and determination."

TRAUT, LOTTIE (1918–): The owner of Mission View Vineyards Ltd., just south of Kelowna at Okanagan Mission, Traut sells a patented system of permanently fixed bird netting to protect vineyards, including her own five-and-a-half-acre vineyard. Born at Ludwigsburg north of Stuttgart in Germany, she came to Canada in 1957 with her husband, Wilhelm. After a brief stint in construction in Vancouver, they settled on a small orchard north of Kelowna, soon branching into other businesses. While she imported ceramic tile from Germany, her husband began developing houses, one of which they traded for a vineyard near Rutland. When frost wiped out the grapes a few years later, the Trauts simply subdivided the land and sold the lots. In 1964 they purchased what has become the Mission View Vineyards property and Wilhelm, who died in 1974, cleared the land and planted vines. His widow has carried on, primarily growing prodigious tonnages of seyval blanc and verdelet. She developed her netting system, which can be raised and lowered like a curtain, after trying to protect the vines with used fish nets. They worked, but handling them damaged the vines.

TRIGGS, DONALD L. (1944–): The president of *Vincor International Inc.*, Canada's largest winery, Triggs was born and raised on a large grain and cattle farm at Trehern, Man., a community midway between Winnipeg and Brandon. His undergraduate degree from the University of Manitoba was in agriculture but a subsequent master of business administration degree at the University of Western Ontario led him off the farm to a career in business, starting as a salesman for Colgate Palmolive. In 1972 he was hired as national marketing director for an Ontario winery called Parkdale and later known as Chateau Cartier. Parkdale had been acquired in 1965 by John Labatt Ltd., the first of five Canadian wineries and one American winery that Labatt scooped up during a decade of expansion into the industry. In 1978, Triggs was made president of the Labatt Canadian wine group. With a rising reputation as a troubleshooter, he was dispatched in 1979 to California to run the Lamont winery, a near-bankrupt former cooperative bulk wine producer in Bakersfield, Ca., that Labatt bought the year before. This gave Triggs invaluable experience in running a large facility since Lamont crushed between 120 and 180 tons of grapes each year. Much of the wine was distilled and sold as brandy.

In 1982 Triggs left the winery to move to Vancouver as president of the subsidiary of a British chemicals' giant called Fisons Plc. Triggs, who had circulated a petition in favour of the new Canadian flag when he was a university student, made that career move simply because he wanted to bring his family back to Canada. Ironically, Fisons transferred him on January 1, 1989, to its British headquarters in Ipswich, as the chairman of its worldwide horticultural division. He returned to Canada seven months later when his former colleagues in the Labatt wine group invited him to join them in buying the group from the brewery and becoming its chief executive. The wine group was renamed Cartier Wines; in 1992 it ac-quired Inniskillin, Canada's oldest estate winery; and in 1993, it merged with the much larger *T.G. Brights & Co.*, adopting the *Vincor* name the following year.

Buying the Labatt wine group was classic, risk-taking entrepreneurship by Triggs and the group's managers. Labatt received two offers for the group, the other being from *Andrés Wines Ltd.* which bid $25 million and was so confident of having won that it announced this internally to a sales meeting. But the Triggs group matched the Andrés bid. "We had no money, let's be clear about that," Triggs says. "I sold my chalet at Whistler and we all borrowed the maximum on our homes." Triggs and the managers raised $2.2 million and borrowed the rest from the Canadian arm of Germany's Dresdner Bank (Canadian banks declined to lend the money). "It was true entrepreneurship," Triggs says. "If we had not been successful, we would all have been working ourselves out of bankruptcy." The outcome has been otherwise: Vincor now is among the ten largest wineries in North America with projected sales of $150 million in 1996.

TURKOVICS, FRANK (1926–):

At one time Hungarian-born Turkovics operated one of the Okanagan's busiest nurseries at his farm near the upper end of Glencoe Road above Westbank. His nursery propagated thousands of vines from cuttings, either from his own vineyard or from other vineyards, selling the plants to vineyards from one end of the Okanagan to the other. The nursery ultimately proved more successful than the Turkovics vineyard. When he converted the property to vinifera varieties, the wind-swept elevation of the farm — about 350 feet above Okanagan Lake —

proved unsuitable for them.

A shopkeeper in Hungary, Turkovics grew up near Lake Balaton, a premier winegrowing region in Hungary; both his father and his father-in-law grew grapes. He and his wife, Mary, left Hungary during the 1956 uprising against the Soviet Union and arrived in Kelowna in the spring of 1957 to join grapegrower George Nemeth, his wife's uncle. Nemeth, who had emigrated to Canada in 1923, not only was a foreman for **J. W. Hughes**, one of the Okanagan's pioneer growers; Nemeth also had married the widow of **Eugene Rittich,** the other pioneer grower. Through Nemeth, Turkovics went to work for Hughes, spending nine years on the Hughes payroll even though his employer was notoriously tight. "He never paid up-to-date wages," Turkovics recalled. When he pressed for a raise in 1964, Hughes instead rented him Lakeside Ranch near Okanagan Mission. Now a park, it was then the last Hughes's property not sold to Hughes's foremen. It was the break Turkovics needed: he arrived home from signing the rental contract to find **Ed Wahl,** his first customer, waiting at the Lakeside Ranch nursery with an order for bath vines.

Turkovics ran Lakeside Ranch until 1969. Meanwhile, he purchased his eighteen acres on Glencoe Road, a property so rugged that 180 truckloads of rocks had to be removed to prepare it for planting in 1965, entirely to bath. This was a labrusca variety that was soon to be supplanted by the preferred (by wineries) French hybrids. "From 1965 to 1986, I changed the varieties four times," Turkovics says. The vineyard went from bath to de chaunac to foch; to Okanagan riesling; and then after the 1988 pullout program to vinifera, including gewurztraminer, pinot blanc and pinot noir. He even tried a Hungarian variety, perle of zala, before conceding that his vineyard lacked the heat units to mature the vinifera fully. (Even bath, a late-ripening variety, was decimated by frost one year.) "I wanted to keep grapes but it was a big mistake," he found. "This is a windy and cold place," he says of his farm. By 1991 Turkovics had pulled out most of his grapes, keeping only some patricia and a hedge of bath, reminders of his early days. Turkovics also operated a second vineyard, twenty-three acres in size, near Peachland, from 1967 when he bought it until 1988 when the vines, most of them French hybrids, were pulled out and, in part, replaced with apple trees.

TYABJI, ALAN (1944–): A one-time professional jockey who now breeds horses, Tyabji is a Kashmiri-born accountant who came to Canada in 1966. When the financial performance of **Calona Wines** was suffering in 1973, Tyabji was a member of the turnaround team dispatched to Kelowna by McGuinness Distillers, the company through which Calona Wines was controlled by Standard Brands. He remained for seven years as vice-president of operations until another shakeup ordained by head office swept out Tyabji (and four other of the winery's executives). After an unsuccessful attempt to get Cinzano of Italy to finance an Okanagan winery, Tyabji managed a fruit cooperative in Creston, B.C., until 1984 when Vancouver car dealer **Bill Docksteader** acquired bankrupt **Vinitera Estate Winery** of Oliver and asked Tyabji to be the general manager of what was now called **Okanagan Vineyards Ltd**. After two years Docksteader and Tyabji parted company, with Tyabji joining a fruit cooperative in Oliver. But in October 1987, Docksteader sold the winery to investors headed by Tyabji (but financed primarily by Amir Mangat, a London hotelier and a friend of the Tyabji family). Subsequently, the winery re-planted its vineyard to quality vinifera grapes and substantially upgraded its wines.

TYABJI, JOSEPHINE (1966–): The daughter of *Alan Tyabji,* she was born in Calcutta and trained as an account-ant. She is the general manager of *Okanagan Vineyards* where she has worked since 1987. "My love of wine has come with the business," she says, "but I tend to stay more to the business side."

TYME TECHNOLOGIES INC: Consult-ing company operated by *Lynn* and *John Bremmer.*

---

1 "Strategic Plan for the British Columbia Wine and Grape Industry," The Chancellor Partners, May 1994, p. 25.

UUU

ULRICH, WAYNE (1937–) AND HELENA: The proprietors of Cherry Point Vineyards on Vancouver Island, the Ulrichs came to winegrowing as a mid-life career change. Wayne Ulrich, who grew up on his family's farm at Dundurn, Sask. and graduated in engineering from the University of Saskatchewan, became a development officer based in Victoria with Agriculture Canada in 1981. A passionate wine interest developed in 1989 when he was processing a grant application from *Blue Mountain Vineyard and Cellars* at Okanagan Falls. Ironically, that application was turned down by the government but Ulrich, ignoring the message he himself had delivered to a struggling start-up winery, quit his secure government job to buy a small mink farm in the Cowichan Valley and turn it into a vineyard. Netherlands-born Helena, who is trained as a laboratory technician, shared her husband's enthusiasm and sold a successful lamp shop in Victoria to pitch into the development of Cherry Point. The mink were replaced with sheep and a vineyard was planted in 1990. The planned opening of the winery was delayed one year, to 1994, because the Ulrichs were unprepared to protect their first significant harvest in 1992 from a sudden bird onslaught at harvest. The vineyard now is entirely protected with nets.

Helena and Wayne Ulrich (photo courtesy of John Schreiner)

UNCLE BEN'S GOURMET WINES:
This was the slightly ludicrous name that **Ben Ginter** gave to **Mission Hill** in the early 1970s; he was already using the Uncle Ben's tag for other parts of his beer and soft drink empire. After Ginter retrieved the winery from receivership in 1978, it was given the more sedate name of **Golden Valley**.

UNIACKE WINES: This was the original name for an estate winery established at Okanagan Mission by David and Susan Mitchell in 1980; it became **CedarCreek Estate Winery** after the property was acquired in 1986 by **Ross Fitzpatrick**. The Uniacke name commemorated one of Mitchell's forebears, Robert John Uniacke, the first attorney general of Nova Scotia. A geologist who had graduated from Dalhousie University in Halifax, Mitchell was a farmer by avocation, giving up a career in petroleum exploration in 1974 to buy a small acreage in the Okanagan. In 1978 he acquired a 180-acre vineyard and orchard on Lakeshore Road, south of Kelowna and on the east side of Lake Okanagan. The upper portion was sold for residential development while the vineyard, with the significant addition of vinifera grapes, formed the basis for the estate winery. The varieties planted in 1978 included gewurztraminer, johannisberg riesling, chardonnay, merlot and pinot noir, all grapes that now produce distinguished wines for Cedar-Creek. Mitchell also planted sauvignon blanc, a tender variety that failed to survive a hard winter in 1981. "Almost everything is planted on its own roots," Mitchell said in a 1983 interview. "It may be highly dangerous, but we may get knocked off by a cold winter before we get knocked off by *phylloxera*."

A skilled farmer, Mitchell produced grapes with which *Mission Hill*, to which he was a contract grower, created award-winning wines. Uniacke, however, struggled for recognition. The winery failed to develop a consistent style, perhaps because, as Mitchell said in that 1983 interview, "we've never gotten a [full-time] winemaker." **John Bremmer** and **Lynn Stark**, then at Brights, provided initial consulting help. **Don Allen**, an experienced home vintner, helped with the 1980 and 1981 vintages. In 1982 **Tilman Hainle** became the consulting winemaker and was available for several vintages, helping Mitchell learn the art. Wine sales suffered from poor distribution in the market and from the winery's perceived isolation. Allen said that in one of Uniacke's early years, only six visitors came out to the winery during July. The 1983 withdrawal of partner David Newman-Bennett (the Mitchells acquired his interest) added to the financial burden of the winery. Finally, the Mitchells sold the winery in 1986.

VALI VINTA: One of the three brands in 1967 in what was called the Castle (*Growers'*) family of wines. The other brand families were Beau Séjour and Ste. Michelle. The Vali Vinta wines included Slinger's Grape, Logana, Bon White, Bon Red, and several fruit wines. The Beau Séjour wines were pitched slightly higher in the price point. The Ste. Michelle was reserved primarily for varietals and upscale brands, including chardonnay, rougelais and an infamous Canadian Liebfraumilch. See also *Himrod.*

VALLEY OF THE VINES: An eighteen-minute film produced by *Castle Wines Ltd.* (as *Growers'* called itself briefly) as a 1967 Centennial project. It was described as a "permanent record of the development of the grape growing industry in the Okanagan Valley." Scripted by Doug Smith & Co., a Vancouver public relations firm, most of the footage was shot at the *Beau Séjour* vineyard, which spent $278.56 to host the premiere in a Kelowna hotel on May 15, 1967. The cost was chiefly the buffet dinner.[1]

VALLEY WINE MERCHANTS LTD.: With *Harry McWatters* of Sumac Ridge as the principal shareholder, this company was formed in 1989 to market bulk wines (mostly Okanagan wines but also some imported wines) from an outlet in Vancouver called Winery on Broadway. The wines were packaged initially in stainless steel, fifty-eight-litre beer kegs, for sale to restaurants and pubs. Individuals also were able to bring their own large containers to be filled, an economical way of selling wine. While this concept is common in France and Italy, it failed to catch on in Vancouver and the store closed in 1991.

VANCOUVER ISLAND: The grape-growing potential on Vancouver Island has been explored at least since the 1960s. The federal experimental farm at Saanichton began trials with vinifera grapes in 1964 and found in the first harvest in 1966 that the varieties matured with sugar levels between sixteen and twenty-two brix, despite a cool summer. "The outlook for growing grapes on a commercial scale in this area is promising," said the farm's director, Harry Andison.[2] The federal Department of Indian Affairs and *Growers' Wines Ltd.* jointly embarked on planting what should have been a five-acre vineyard on Indian Reserve land in the Cowichan Valley. The project appears to have been abandoned soon after its 1968 launch. It was the more determined vineyard trials near Duncan in the 1980s by *Dennis Zanatta* and *John Harper* that established the basis for the modest grape industry that has developed, primarily in the warm and relatively dry Cowichan Valley on the east coast of the island. Grapes also have been planted successfully on the Gulf Islands and on Bowen Island near Vancouver.

VANCOUVER PLAYHOUSE INTERNATIONAL WINE FESTIVAL: Begun in 1979, this annual fund-raiser for Vancouver's senior professional theatre has grown into one of North America's biggest consumer and trade wine-tasting events. The Robert Mondavi winery from Napa in California was the single featured winery in 1979. Now, more than 125 wineries from around the world participate in a four-day orgy of tastings, brunches, lunches and dinners which attract between 4,000 and 5,000 people. In 1996 it raised $225,000 for the Playhouse. British Columbia wineries were first invited to join the festival in 1983. See also *John Levine.*

VARIETAL: This term generally is used to mean a wine made from a specific grape variety, e.g., chardonnay or merlot. Wines blended from several varieties may appear under generic labels, such as proprietor's reserve, or under trademarked proprietary labels like Latitude 50 or 49 North.

VARIETIES IN VINEYARDS: The vineyards of the Okanagan have been replanted again and again since the 1950s, as tastes and the needs of wineries changed. In 1952, a provincial government grape survey of the Okanagan found that European varieties accounted for slightly under 10 percent of the 424 acres then in grapes. The leading varieties, both reds, were the ubiquitous labrusca variety, the concord (89 acres) followed by Campbell's early (80 acres), an American hybrid that, curiously, also was widely planted in Japan. The leading white variety, with 40 acres, was diamond, a labrusca/vinifera cross.

By 1960, Campbell's early (94 acres) had moved ahead of concord (77 acres). But diamond now was growing on 166 acres, by far the most important variety. Popular with growers, it was the single most widely planted vine during the 1960s, peaking at 376 acres in 1966.

A red variety called bath put on a

charge during the 1960s, accounting for 302 acres in the 1970 survey. The variety was almost as strong in labrusca character as the concord. While diamond still was most widely planted in 1970, the French hybrid red grapes now figured significantly. The de chaunac accounted for 328 of the 2,414 acres under vine in British Columbia in 1970. Farmers also had 166 acres of chelois and 100 acres of verdelet. During the latter half of the 1960s, the wineries — especially the new ones — set out to produce table wines rather than fortified wines and the growers gradually switched away from the varieties with strong labrusca flavours. There was one exception: the Okanagan riesling, perhaps because it was thought a superior European wine grape, was planted so quickly that it covered 179 acres in 1970 compared with 2 acres a decade earlier.

The 1979 survey of a total of 3,236 acres of vineyard showed that Okanagan riesling had emerged on top with 608 acres, followed by maréchal foch at 604 acres and de chaunac at 553 acres. The durable diamond had slipped to fourth place with 186 acres.

Plantings in the 1980s were dominated by the hybrid varieties. By 1983 Okanagan riesling, at 919 acres, accounted for almost a third of all the plantings in the valley. In second place was foch at 593 acres and de chaunac at 359 acres.

Vineyard plantings changed dramatically after two-thirds of the vines were pulled out after the 1988 harvest, leaving about 1,000 acres. The leading variety in 1989 was white riesling (143.5 acres) followed by verdelet (121 acres). Now the classic European varieties began to emerge, including pinot blanc (78 acres), gewurztraminer (66 acres) and chardonnay (53 acres). When the next vineyard census is done, it will show that in 1996, with more than 1,500 acres now planted, European varieties dominate while verdelet has fallen into disfavour. The leading red vinifera in 1996 appeared to be merlot, with nearly 100 acres planted, followed by pinot noir, cabernet franc and cabernet sauvignon. A sudden demand for red wines in the mid-1990s saved red hybrids such as foch, chancellor and rougeon from being abandoned altogether.[3]

VASEAUX CELLARS: Named after a nearby lake, this is a label created in 1983 by the *Brights* winery in Oliver, used initially on wines made from experimental grape varieties that were sold only at the winery. Later the label was used more widely for blended wines and varietals from British Columbia grapes.

VASEAUX VIEW VINEYARDS: See *Albert Manaigre.*

VENTURI, GIORDANO (1941 –): The Italian-born co-proprietor of *Venturi-Schulze Vineyards*, Venturi brings to whatever he does such an uncompromising search for excellence that strangers sometimes take it for arrogance. Wine was made in the family home in Italy to the amateur standards that Venturi later came to deride. He emigrated to Canada in 1967, became an industrial electrician, got a university degree and ultimately became an electronics teacher in Vancouver. He and his wife, *Marilyn Schulze,* moved to a heritage farm on Vancouver Island in 1988, looking for a country lifestyle and independence based on winegrowing. Venturi is a daring and creative winemaker. For example, he has turned normally bland müller-thurgau into a complex and interesting wine by,

Giordano Venturi and Marilyn Schulze (photo courtesy of John Schreiner)

unconventionally, letting it rest on and pick up flavours from its lees. Venturi also makes balsamic vinegar, carrying on a fine tradition of the Modena region in northern Italy where he grew up, and is a highly original chef for the winery's occasional winemaker dinners.

VENTURI-SCHULZE VINEYARDS: Established in 1993, this farmgate winery, named for owners Giordano Venturi and Marilyn Schulze, is at a heritage farm on the Island Highway just south of Duncan. The vineyard is small and, as a result, the wines sell out almost as quickly as they are released, making it necessary to call ahead before visiting in case the empty-shelved tasting room is closed. The wines include madeleine sylvaner, müller-thurgau, siegerrebe and kerner, along with pinot noir, sparkling wines and imaginative blends such as Millefiori ("one thousand flowers") made from siegerrebe and ortega. The winery also hosts gourmet dinners to show off its wines and the owners' cuisine, and produces remarkable balsamic vinegar.

VERAISON: This word, with French roots, is the term growers use to describe when grapes begin to turn from hard, green berries into fleshy and coloured mature fruit.

VERDELET: This productive and hardy white hybrid was planted extensively in the Okanagan during the 1980s to fill a burgeoning demand for white wines. The wines are bland at best and slightly herbaceous at worst, and few wineries want it for anything other than a blending wine.

VICTORIA WINERIES (BRITISH COLUMBIA) LTD.: Exclusively a producer of loganberry wines, this company was formed in 1927 as Brentwood Products Ltd. to process Saanich Peninsula loganberries into jams, juices and syrup. The company soon found itself confronted with far more fruit than the confectionery market would absorb. "To deal with a large output of fruit," President William O. Wallace wrote his shareholders in March 1928, "the logical method is a winery, and your directors have been working on this for at least six months. We are fortunate in having with us a well known wine maker, Mr. S.B. Slinger, who has thrown his lot in with us. He will be our Manager for the next three years, and on his efforts will depend the success of our efforts." Stephen Slinger was then operating a small winery, also processing loganberries, in Chemainus.

For its winery, the company paid $8,000 to buy the former Queens Hotel, not far from the downtown of modern Victoria, and spent another $2,000 on equipping it. Wallace and his directors figured that the investment was sound simply on its real estate value, for the hotel had been built some years before for $50,000 and had traded as high as $85,000 before Victoria property values crashed. "Some day," Wallace wrote, "it may be worth a great deal more than we have paid, and then we might think of a new winery on a larger scale than we think at present."

The company contracted with growers for 100 tons of berries and planned to produce between 10,000 and 20,000 gallons of wine in 1928, the first year of production. When more berries than expected were offered, closer to 30,000 gallons of wine were made. The value of this wine inventory was $23,940. This drained the company's resources;

more money was raised from the shareholders to enable the purchase of berries and sugar in 1929 since no wine sales were expected until the initial vintage had almost two years of maturity. With more wine than jam in inventory, the company changed its name from Brentwood — it had originally been based in Brentwood Bay — to Victoria Wineries in April 1929. By the end of the company's next financial year, November 30, 1929, the inventory of wine was valued at $77,640, not a drop of which had yet been put onto the market. Yet the company continued to expand. A letter to shareholders at the end of 1929 said: "Your directors have purchased a site for a new Winery in Saanich and will probably build early in 1930 to take care of the 1930 production." The Victoria and Chemainus wineries also remained opened. A progress report to shareholders in March 1930 said that the company planned to make 100,000 gallons of wine that summer.

The first of Victoria Wineries' products to reach the market, sometime in the first quarter of 1930, was Slinger's Loganberry Wine, with a banana-yellow oval label with black and red type. It was available in bottles ranging from twenty-six ounces (at fifty cents a bottle) and forty ounces (at seventy-five cents) through to one gallon in size. Sales averaged 2,100 gallons a month in 1930, for a total of $26,333.75 in the financial year ending November 39, 1930. But there now was another $120,362.50 worth of wine in inventory. "For your information," shareholders were told in a letter in February 1931, "we have in our wineries more than 160,000 gallons of wine in excellent condition." Once again, however, the ninety-nine shareholders were

asked to subscribe for more shares to repair the stretched balance sheet. "The Loan account is higher than it should be and the auditor and Banker both point out that the capital is too low for the extensive operations carried on," Secretary J.E. Sladen wrote.

The sales in 1931 averaged about 3,000 gallons a month "in spite of bad times," Sladen told shareholders in a letter November 16, 1931. He continued: "We have manufactured this year nearly four times the quantity sold. Our sales must therefore increase very considerably in the next six months, or it will be necessary to curtail our manufacture next year." Sladen also urged the shareholders to get out and hustle the wine. "Your company is doing very well and is in a strong position, as you will see by your next Balance Sheet, but the Directors want your help to do better, especially in advertising our products.... A suggestion for Xmas. Buy a carton of six, Chateau Patricia, at $3.50, and distribute among your friends."[4] The shareholders found a better solution: shortly thereafter, they sold their winery and its brands to Herbert Anscomb's better-financed *Growers' Wines Ltd.*

VIDAL: This white hybrid grape was planted by some growers in the 1980s but fell out of favour with wineries in the 1990s even though it can yield attractively fruity wines. It is a useful grape for making *icewine* because its thick skin resists disease and because of the wine's room-filling aroma of tropical fruit.

VIELVOYE, JOHN (1942–): The amiable grape specialist for the British Columbia government, Vielvoye was born in Hillsberg, a Dutch town just outside Rotterdam. His father was a versatile jack-of-all-trades (milkman, gardener, landscaper, pastry chef and Dutch resistance fighter) who brought his family to Vancouver in 1952 and established a successful landscaping and greenhouse business. With that upbringing, John Vielvoye naturally took a University of British Columbia bachelor of science degree in ornamental horticulture. On graduation in 1965 he joined the federal ministry of agriculture as a plant products' inspector in Toronto until October 1966, when he returned to British Columbia and a posting in Kelowna as an assistant provincial horticulturist. "They immediately gave me the grape industry and the fruit industry," he says, recalling having to learn on the job with counsel from veteran growers like *Frank Schmidt* and Eden Raikes. By 1970, however, Vielvoye was actively gathering viticultural information from Washington state and from Ontario, where experimentation had begun earlier, and passing it on to the new growers in the Okanagan. Essentially, his career spans the entire modern history of grapegrowing in British Columbia. That includes such milestones as the development of *Inkameep Vineyards* beginning in 1968; the *Becker* project; grape trials on Vancouver Island; the 1988 pullout program and the dramatic shift to vinifera varieties in the 1990s.

VIGNETI ZANATTA: The first farmgate winery on Vancouver Island, Vigneti Zanatta opened in the fall of 1992 in the pleasant country setting of the Glenora district, just south of Duncan. The first wine to be released, a 1991 ortega, was in such limited supply that the winery was closed by Christmas. Since then a substantial vineyard has been developed by proprietors *Dennis Zanatta* and his winemaker daughter, *Loretta Zanatta*. By the middle 1990s the winery was evolving into Vancouver Island's first estate winery.

VINCOR INTERNATIONAL LTD.: The name chosen in 1994 for the successor to *T.G. Brights & Co.*, after the 1993 merger of Brights and *Cartier & Inniskillin Vintners Inc.* With sales projected to exceed $150 million in 1996, Vincor is Canada's largest winery. In British Columbia, it operates a winery at Oliver in which *Inniskillin Okanagan* also produced several of its initial vintages.

VINEYARD AT BOWEN ISLAND BED AND BREAKFAST: This farm winery, planned to open in 1997, is based on a vineyard and a bed and breakfast inn operated on Bowen Island, near West Vancouver, by *Lary Waldman* and his wife, Elena.

Vineyard Production in British Columbia:[5]
In short or 2,000 LB tons

Year	Production	Year	Production
1930	135	1963	2,050
1931	259	1964	2,870
1932	259	1965	185
1933	415	1966	3,001
1934	462	1967	3,733
1935	552	1968	6,162
1936	433	1969	1,714
1937	813	1970	9,038
1938	976	1971	9,107
1939	738	1972	10,028
1940	1,117	1973	6,404
1941	868	1974	12,142
1942	1,267	1975	12,589
1943	705	1976	12,678
1944	1,632	1977	11,713
1945	1,326	1978	18,404
1946	971	1979	10,437
1947	1,000	1980	13,755
1948	1,326	1981	11,674
1949	955	1982	15,629
1950	555	1983	15,130
1951	857	1984	13,810
1952	1,213	1985	15,119
1953	1,095	1986	13,212
1954	823	1987	16,260
1955	968	1988	18,397
1956	217	1989	3,830
1957	1,096	1990	5,094
1958	1,159	1991	4,045
1959	1,273	1992	5,267
1960	634	1993	9,085
1961	1,600	1994	6,438
1962	1,634		

VINIFERA: This is the vine species to which all the finest wine grapes belong. The vinifera varieties, such as chardonnay and cabernet, often are called European grapes because they achieved their winemaking importance in Europe and spread to the New World through cuttings from European vines. In fact, vinifera is thought to have originated south of what is today the Black Sea and the vine cuttings spread to the Mediterranean and Europe as humanity spread. Until the 1980s most growers and government agriculturists in British Columbia doubted that vinifera grapes could grow successfully in the Okanagan because of occasionally severe winters. Growers since have discovered which vinifera varieties can be grown in British Columbia and have evolved techniques for dealing with the occasional challenges of climate.

VINITERA ESTATE WINERY: British Columbia's second estate winery, it was opened in 1979 south of Oliver by the **Poturica** family. The winery went into receivership in 1982, with an inventory of unsold wine approaching 50,000 gallons, much of it white made with Okanagan riesling. The winery was revived in 1984 as Okanagan Vineyards under new owners, the car-dealing **Docksteader** brothers of Vancouver. They managed to squeeze that wine inventory onto the market but the wine's rustic quality ruined what reputation remained and the car dealers soon exited the wine business. But with another change of ownership and a totally replanted vineyard, the winery, now known as **Okanagan Vineyards,** rebuilt its reputation in the excellent 1994 vintage.

VINTAGE HOLDINGS INC.: This Calgary-based firm of investors acquired **Hillside Cellars** in 1996.

VINTNERS QUALITY ALLIANCE: Usually referred to as VQA, this is the system for governing quality standards for British Columbia wines in a manner consistent with the appellation designations in other winegrowing regions. Administered by the **British Columbia Wine Institute,** the VQA standards became effective in May 1991 upon an order by the British Columbia cabinet. The standards parallel the VQA program begun earlier in Ontario. Wines that meet the standards are entitled to be sold with a VQA symbol on each bottle. A VQA wine must be made entirely from grapes grown and vinted in British Columbia; 85 percent of the wine by volume must be from the grape variety named on the label and 95 percent by volume must be from the year shown on the label. All VQA wines must first be approved by a wine-tasting panel whose membership includes British Columbia winemakers.

VIOGNIER: A vinifera grape, the viognier produces richly complex, golden-hued white wines in the Rhone even though, paradoxically, it is not widely grown. Some modest plantings were planned in the Okanagan in the mid-1990s.

VIOLET, CLAUDE (1935–): The Parisian-born proprietor (with his German-born wife, Ingeborg) of **Domaine de Chaberton** estate winery in Langley, Violet comes from a family who owned vineyards in France as early as 1644. The family money was made producing a fortified aperitif called Byrrh; the family company was merged in the 1950s with the producers of Dubonnet and Cinzano. After training to become a banker, Claude Violet became a wine merchant in Switzerland in 1968. He and his wife emigrated to British Columbia in 1981, settling in Langley where they converted a farm into the largest vineyard in the Fraser Valley. The winery, named after a Violet family farm in the south of France, opened in 1991.

VIRUSES: See **Centre for Plant Health.**

VISSER, KENN (1950–): Born in Kirwood, Mo., the son of an advertising executive, Visser studied food service management at the University of Missouri and worked in hospital dietary departments before coming to the Okanagan in 1979 and, in a dramatic career change, becoming an orchard manager. From 1986 to 1990 he was the general manager of **Inkameep Vineyards Ltd.** With the assistance of **Stephen Cipes**, Visser launched the **Nordique Blanc** label in June 1989, beginning with a New York tasting of British Columbia wines to gauge whether any of the wines would be taken seriously. Encouraged by the reception, Visser was able to book an initial order for 1,000 cases of Nordique Blanc that fall. Another 4,000 were shipped to various American markets the following year.

Eric von Krosigk (photo courtesy of John Schreiner)

VLCEK, TONY (1966–):

Andrés winemaker Vlcek (pronounced vol-check) was only two when his family left Czechoslovakia in 1968 and came to Vancouver. The son of a steelworker, Vlcek began studying chemistry at the University of British Columbia but, finding that discipline dull, switched to food sciences. Graduating in 1989 he went backpacking in Europe. "Travelling on a shoestring budget, I found that wine in Europe was the cheapest beverage," he says. On his return to Vancouver in 1990 he took a job as a quality control technician at the **Andrés** winery in Port Moody and subsequently became one of the winemaking team there.

VON KROSIGK, ERIC (1962–):

Self-confident about his talent, Vernon-born von Krosigk once refused a job as an assistant winemaker at **Sumac Ridge** by saying he did not intend to be anyone's assistant. Instead, he became the first winemaker at **Summerhill** in 1991 where he produced several vintages from a primitive former garage without the benefit of adequate hot water. The wines were prizewinners, all the same. In 1995 von Krosigk took over as winemaker at

LeComte after that Okanagan Falls winery had been acquired by a group headed by Sumac Ridge's owners. LeComte had adequate running water but a ramshackle winery and von Krosigk had one more difficult vintage under primitive conditions before he got modern equipment. Indeed, 1996 was his first Okanagan vintage without significant equipment handicaps.

Von Krosigk comes from an old and distinguished German family; a great-grandfather was an admiral and an uncle was the German finance minister in the Weimar Republic. Eric's father, Buko von Krosigk, who escaped from East Germany after the Second World War, managed a Vernon ranch until he founded the Okanagan Springs brewery in Vernon in 1985. Eric's interest in winemaking flourished in high school and in 1983 he went to Germany, first to apprentice with wineries there and later to enrol at **Geisenheim.** Here, he became the first Canadian to head the student association. Unfortunately, the time consumed by student politics prevented him from completing his chemistry studies and he left there in June 1991 a credit short of a degree. During his studies, von Krosigk apprenticed with several German producers of sparkling wine. He also spent two summers, 1988 and 1989, back in the Okanagan, working on Sumac Ridge's *sparkling wine* venture. All this experience with bubblies led to him joining Summerhill, a winery that has specialized in sparkling wines. Not surprisingly, when von Krosigk moved to LeComte, one of his first initiatives was to launch the production of sparkling wine there.

VON MANDL, ANTHONY (1950–):

The Vancouver-born owner of *Mission Hill Vineyards Inc.* acquired the reputation of being an *enfant terrible* from the very start of his career in 1972 as a wine merchant when he was barely old enough to drink and looked even younger. Von Mandl grew up in an elegantly cultured family. His Vienna-born father, who owned textile plants in Czechoslovakia, had come to Vancouver to escape the Nazis but returned to Europe after the war, living in Switzerland and sending young Anthony to private schools there, in Austria and in Germany. When the family returned to Canada, von Mandl completed a commerce degree from the University of British Columbia. He next learned the wine trade by apprenticing with Josef Milz, a respected Mosel winery owned by one of Germany's oldest wine families. Milz was not selling in North America at the time and backed von Mandl to form Josef Milz International Ltd. The Milz family not only allowed von Mandl to own 51 percent of the marketing company but for a time supported him with $1,000 a month. With that, von Mandl rented a 100-square-foot office in downtown Vancouver for $19.95 a month and set out to sell wine. His first break was a sale of Milz wines to Canadian Pacific Airlines.

But British Columbia Liquor Control Board chairman William Bruce, a protégé of *Lt.-Col. Donald McGugan,* simply brushed off von Mandl's applications for liquor store listings. In frustration, von Mandl complained to the *Vancouver Sun's* influential columnist, Jack Wasserman, whose column backing the wine merchant got von Mandl blacklisted by the British Columbia board. He had Milz wines listed in Saskatchewan and Ontario before they were ever available in his home province, and then only after a new government in Victoria in 1973 overhauled the retailing of alcoholic beverages and encouraged new listings of imported wines. When the retailing functions were given to the newly formed Liquor Distribution Branch in 1974, the McGugan think-alikes warned the LDB that the young von Mandl was an "SOB." Keith Warnes, the first general manager of the LDB, found von Mandl "impatient" but came to admire him. "He is not only the pushiest [agent], he is also the sharpest," Warnes said later.[6] *Nick Clark*, the LDB's aggressive new purchasing manager, not only was receptive but became a close friend of von Mandl. By 1978 von Mandl purchased the other 49 percent of Milz International from the Milz family and renamed the company Mark Anthony Wine Merchants Ltd.

The dream of an Okanagan winery began in the early 1970s when von Mandl and the Milz family discussed such a project. That venture never advanced but von Mandl remained alert for an opportunity and in 1981, when he learned from Clark that the Mission Hill winery was for sale, he and Clark formed a partnership to buy it. "Mark Anthony Wine Merchants was doing so well at the time," he says, recalling why he had the confidence for the move. "I really believed that someone was going to, and would, make world calibre wines in the Okanagan." Neither he nor Clark had the resources to build a major winery from scratch and he was not interested in a smaller estate winery. "I determined early on that estate wineries are, in the business sense, mom and pop operations," von Mandl says. "If you and your spouse ran the operation, you could make a living. But I didn't believe that, as a going business concern integrated with Mark Anthony Wine Merchants, that was an economic model that I thought was feasible." In any event, he was a bachelor at the time.

The winery von Mandl and Clark bought was more "concern" than "going." Built in 1966 and modelled on the finely sited wineries in California, Mission Hill had been in receivership once and close to it twice. In 1981 it was known as Golden Valley Wines and the owner was **Ben Ginter**, an autocrat who had mounted both a cutout of his image above the bottling line and his portrait inside the back door. "The whole strategy behind negotiating with Ben was that Ben was clearly a rogue and his behaviour could never be accounted for," von Mandl says. "To keep him happy and at the table, you needed a bottle of Glenlivet because he wouldn't drink anything else." In the final purchase negotiations, which lasted late into the night in a law office boardroom in Vancouver, von Mandl and Ginter found themselves $200,000 apart. Remembering that Ginter liked to gamble, von Mandl suggested they flip a coin, each flip being

worth $25,000 to the winner. Von Mandl won the majority of the eight tosses. The final price of the winery was $2.9 million.[7] At the final closing of the deal, Ginter was dissuaded from backing out only by a confrontation with von Mandl's lawyer so ugly that Clark and von Mandl lost all desire to open the celebratory bottle of champagne they had put on ice. "That's the last time I ever saw Bin Ginter."

The brash von Mandl's inspection of the winery before buying it amounted to a superficial walk-through; he was only dimly aware of how rundown it was. On June 1, 1981, the day he and Clark took possession, von Mandl found himself on a winery catwalk above the stainless steel tanks, hosing off the filth and the fruit flies, quite convinced that he had made a terrible mistake. "I was going to lose everything I had," he remembers telling himself. "The place was absolutely disgusting," he recalls, and the wine inventory was "a catastrophe." Publicly, von Mandl maintained a brave face. "When I look out over this valley," he said in a slightly purple speech at the winery's first public function in October 1981, "I see world class vinifera vineyards winding their way down the valley, numerous estate wineries each distinctively different, charming inns and bed and breakfast cottages seducing tourists from around the world while intimate cafes and restaurants captivate the visitor in a magical setting. In short, the dream is the Napa Valley of Canada, but much more!"[8]

What must have seemed improbable to most of von Mandl's guests that day became a reality in the 1990s, with Mission Hill turned into one of the Okanagan's best wineries, able to boast that it is "British Columbia's most awarded winery." In 1994, a Mission Hill 1992 Grand Reserve chardonnay, competing against 220 other chardonnays from around the world, won the *Avery's Trophy* as the best chardonnay that year in the International Wine and Spirits Competition in London. "I can't describe how significant an event that was for Mission Hill and, in my mind, for the entire Okanagan Valley," von Mandl says, comparing it to the 1976 Paris tasting when a 1973 Stag's Leap Wine Cellars cabernet sauvignon outscored four top Bordeaux wines and put the California wine industry on the map. "It was the watershed in consumer confidence here in British Columbia and in other parts of Canada that wines that we were now producing at Mission Hill were truly of top international character. It gave me personally, and all of us, a huge inspiration. It took twelve years to get there. This was really the key that we'd been searching for to open the door to what I believe, going back to my talk in 1981, is the real future for the Okanagan valley."

VON WOLFF, HARRY (1934–):

The proprietor of *Chateau Wolff* winery in Nanaimo, von Wolff was born in Riga, the capital of Latvia, a member of a family who were prosperous landowners until war and the Soviet occupation of Latvia left the father in a Siberian prison camp and the rest of the family postwar refugees. Von Wolff, with his mother and grandmother, emigrated to Canada in 1953. Von Wolff worked on an uncle's ranch in British Columbia's Peace River

country for a year and then began a peripatetic career through fifty-eight other jobs over eleven years, including a hotel management course in Switzerland and a career in the hotel business that fostered his interest in wines. With his wife, Helga, von Wolff settled in Nanaimo in 1977; they developed a prosperous retail store specializing in western clothing and footwear. Von Wolff now became a competent amateur winemaker and, after planting a few vines at his home, purchased a small farm at the outskirts of the city where he established a vineyard to support a planned winery. An admirer of the wines of Burgundy, von Wolff grows pinot noir and chardonnay in the best site on his vineyard.

VQA: See *Vintners Quality Alliance.*

[1] Lloyd Schmidt files.

[2] *Victoria Daily Colonist*, November 7, 1966.

[3] Statistics taken from the files of John Vielvoye, the B.C. government grape specialist in Kelowna.

[4] Victoria Wineries file; in British Columbia Archives.

[5] Association of B.C. Grape Growers, *Atlas of Suitable Grape Growing Locations.* (See SOURCES for complete reference.) B.C. Ministry of Agriculture figures reproduced in a 1980 report on the B.C. wine industry by Robin Burns, a marketing consultant for Simons Resource Consultants. Burns noted that the BCMA collected figures in 1952, again in 1962, then in alternate years to 1974; then in 1979. Intervening years represent estimates.

[6] Interview with author, 1981.

[7] Author interview with Anthony von Mandl, March 15, 1996.

[8] Address by Anthony von Mandl, October 2, 1981; in author's files.

W W W

WAGNER, DAVID (1952–): The owner of *Carriage House Wines* on Black Sage Road south of Oliver, Wagner was born in New Westminster but grew up in the Okanagan where his father, an agricultural feed salesman, operated a feedlot at Okanagan Falls. Wagner entered the University of British Columbia to become a veterinarian but dropped out after his first year to work as a letter carrier. A brewery strike in 1972 started him making beer; when he moved to a small farm in the Fraser Valley a few years later, he began making rhubarb and blackberry wines, joined an amateur winemaking club in Abbotsford and even planted a few vines on his own property. In 1986 Wagner enrolled at Simon Fraser University, taking as many science courses as he could over the next three years with the aim of transferring to the enology program at the University of California's Davis campus. He was deterred by the absence of winemaking jobs in British Columbia after the 1988 vine pullout and instead became a field service representative (meter reader and bill collector) for BC Hydro.

But Wagner had been truly bitten by the desire to produce wine. He and his wife, Karen, searched for a suitable vineyard, first in the Fraser Valley and then in the Okanagan until, in April 1992, they purchased an eight-acre orchard (apples, apricots) on Black Sage Road. "The original idea was to run the orchard for several years," Wagner recalls. "But the apples were costing us money." In 1994, the fruit trees were taken out, to be replaced with vines: kerner, chardonnay and pinot blanc that

year and merlot, pinot noir and cabernet sauvignon in 1995. The vines came from grower **Lanny Martiniuk**, who also leased his kerner vineyard to Wagner for the 1994 vintage, enabling Wagner to produce the wines to launch Carriage House, a farmgate winery, in 1995.

"Kerner, to my mind, is one of the undiscovered grapes," maintains Wagner, who has a large block of it at his vineyard. "Because of the fruit notes in the kerner, it is an appealing wine." Carriage House is one of the very few producers of this wine and, Wagner believes, the only producer to make the wine fragrantly dry.

WAHL, ED (1915–): The principal operator of Monashee Vineyards Ltd., once the largest vineyard in British Columbia, Wahl was born in the Ukraine, the son of a teacher/bookkeeper. The Wahl family came to Canada in 1924, first to Saskatchewan and in 1930 to Kelowna. Wahl earned a master's degree in geography, wrote a geography text and taught school. Early into a four-year teaching assignment in Nigeria between 1961 and 1965, Wahl, on a vacation home, struck a partnership with his two brothers and Kelowna businessman Douglas Shaw to invest in property in the Okanagan. With Kelowna land prices out of reach, they purchased 265 acres of sagebrush-covered virgin land south of Osoyoos. Balthaser Bachmann, a family friend who had grown grapes in the Ukraine, supervised planting the first forty acres. Ed Wahl managed the vineyard for two years when he came back from Nigeria and then, when offered a teaching post at

Okanagan College, hired **John Barnay** to run the vineyard. Barnay was given a 10 percent interest in Monashee and was the manager until all the vines were pulled out in 1988.

Monashee (named for a nearby range of mountains) began with such varieties as bath, Okanagan riesling and various labrusca vines, reflecting the historic demand from wineries. By the time the bath grapes were producing, however, the wineries no longer wanted the variety. The vineyard gradually converted to red French hybrids; but one of those varieties, the de chaunac, proved to be a poor performer in Monashee's sandy soil. However, Wahl never switched to vinifera (although he would maintain that Okanagan riesling was a vinifera). The sheer expanse of Monashee forced Wahl in 1973 to purchase the first mechanical harvester in Okanagan, bought from a California supplier. "Our labour pool was too small," Wahl said. "We needed eighty-five to a hundred pickers and we couldn't get them." The machine only needed a crew of four. Within five years, four other vineyards also had acquired mechanical harvesters.[1]

When growers were compensated in 1988 to remove nonpremium varieties, Wahl and his business partners decided it was time to retire. "We didn't want to start all over again," he said later.[2] Subsequently the property was sold to Goldie Smitlener, the owner of *Chateau Ste. Claire,* who briefly considered ginseng and then resold the land. Monashee has been parcelled out among several grapegrowers and now is producing vinifera.

WALDMAN, LARY (1952–): With his wife, Elena, Waldman operates the Vine-yard at Bowen Island Bed and Breakfast, where the hospitality is supported by a six-and-a-half-acre vineyard. Born in Winnipeg, Waldman moved to Vancouver in the 1970s and onto Bowen Island in 1978. While Waldman runs a transport company that hauls equipment for bands and stage productions, his interest in wine was fired by an earlier foray into the restaurant business. When he concluded that his Bowen Island property, with its good southern slope, was a microclimate suitable for viticulture, Waldman in 1994 began planting a vineyard with cool-climate varieties including pinot noir, pinot gris and pinot blanc. He believes the vineyard will support a production ultimately between 60,000 and 80,000 bottles a year, with patrons of the guest house at the vineyard among the consumers.

WALLACE, ROBERT A. (1924–): When he was interviewed in 1978 to become general manager of the Liquor Distribution Branch, Wallace demurred: "If you're looking for a wine expert, that's not me!"[3] In fact, Wallace was hired from among eighty-nine applicants for his well-oiled administrative abilities, needed to restore stability to the LDB after Keith Warnes, the previous general manager, had been asked to resign. *Tex Enemark*, the Victoria deputy minister who interviewed the leading applicants, summarized Wallace's qualifications in a memo to his minister: "Firstly, he has the reputation of being a sound, tough, excellent manager of substantial programs. Secondly, he has an excellent knowledge of how government works, Federal and Provincial."

The son of a Manitoba farmer, Wallace earned a master's degree in agriculture at the University of Manitoba in 1953, became a soils specialist with the provincial department of agriculture and was the deputy minister a decade later. With a rare ability to be even-handed and nonpartisan, Wallace served as secretary to the Manitoba cabinet's planning and priorities committee under both Conservative and New Democratic governments. From 1973 to 1978 he was Canada's assistant chief statistician in Ottawa, sorting out problems with the timely processing of census information. His wine education only began when he took over the LDB, with Wallace, a hands-on administrator, participating in product tastings and trips to wineries. By the time he retired in 1988, Wallace had graduated from the German Wine Academy (a thorough one-week course), visited most major wine regions and settled on France's Chateau D'Angludet as one of his favourite wines.

At the LDB Wallace walked into a substantial challenge. "The Branch is in desperate need of superb management and the bringing to it of modern management tools," Enemark wrote to his minister. Enemark had discovered how desperate when he stepped in as acting general manager after the departure of Warnes in February 1978. "While there is apparently no evidence of widespread theft or disappearance, the control systems are simply so bad that it would be relatively simple for us to be robbed blind and we would not even *know it* for probably 10 weeks," Enemark said in a long memo in March 1978. "There have simply been *no* training programs and in fact the former General Manager gave *no priority* whatever to training matters.... [There had been] a large number of failures in the area of internal communications ... this week, for the first time in the history of the LDB, there was a meeting of store managers, area managers and some of the senior executives of the Branch."[4]

Wallace, who took over July 1, 1978, energetically carried out his mandate to correct the problems and turn the LDB into an efficient commercial operation. In 1978 the LDB operated 205 stores and had assigned another 21 to private operators as agency stores. (Agency stores include those in small or remote communities where full LDB stores would not be economic, stores in wineries and the so-called cold beer and wine stores.) By 1988, the LDB operated 217 stores, *all of which* had been remodelled or replaced or were new entirely, all with bright decor to replace the gloomy appearance of earlier decades. In addition, the number of agency stores had expanded tenfold to 219.

Within the stores, there had been a revolution. Wallace did away with what had been a virtual ban against women employees in liquor stores; by the time he retired from the LDB, six of its managers and twenty-one of its assistant managers were women. There were 600 products listed in 1978; while this was a vast improvement since the start of the decade, wines were not displayed by country of origin but rather by order of price. By the end of the Wallace decade, 1,500 products were listed, all displayed by country of origin. In-store merchandising displays were permitted and even in-store tastings; Wallace received some sharp media criticism for the tastings but he did not back down. The LDB developed a product knowledge course for its front-line employees. "Prior to 1978," Wallace recalled, "the store staff were prohibited from talking to customers about products, beyond price." Indeed, in 1978, the price list was the only consumer information available from the LDB — and it was seldom on display. Soon after Wallace became general manager, the LDB started publishing a product guide, freely giving copies to customers.

Tiny Walrod (photo courtesy of B.C. Tree Fruits)

WALROD, R.P. (TINY): A nephew of grapegrower *J.W. Hughes*, Walrod was the plant foreman and food technologist with Modern Foods Ltd., a Kelowna apple processor that was taken over in 1946 by B.C. Fruit Processors Ltd. and later became known as Sun-Rype Products Ltd. Walrod, who had worked on developing juices and other apple products, managed Sun-Rype and in the 1950s also became general manager of the renamed B.C. Tree Fruits Ltd. A very large man — hence the nickname — the energetic Walrod had many interests: he had a fine singing voice, played the

organ, painted, learned to fly and prodded Sun-Rype to create ever more products using local fruit. Success with apple products led Walrod to explore the opportunity for grapegrowing and wineries in the Okanagan. In 1964 he left B.C. Tree Fruits to develop the *Mission Hill* winery, with financing from Kelowna businessmen. Walrod's research took him to California and he came back promoting a dramatically designed winery on a site with fine views of the Okanagan Valley. "I can recall Tiny talking about the opportunities of a mission type winery where visitors would come to view the plant as well as enjoy the beautiful scenery and use picnic table facilities," writes Ian Greenwood, who succeeded Walrod as chief executive at B.C. Tree Fruits. "It is obvious that he was ahead of his time." Walrod did not live to see his ideas transformed into the winery on Boucherie Mountain. "He passed away with a massive coronary [while] actually sketching potential vineyard property just north of Kelowna," Greenwood writes.[5] Walrod was only fifty-seven years old.

WAREHAM, ROBERT (1946–): A partner at *Sumac Ridge Estate Winery*, Wareham was born in Newfoundland, the son of a prosperous Placentia Bay fish merchant. After getting a commerce degree from Memorial University, Wareham became an accountant and was recruited by John Labatt Ltd. in 1970. Four years later he was transferred to Saskatchewan and in 1976 he moved to Chateau-Gai, the Ontario winery that Labatt had purchased. When Labatt took over *Casabello* in 1977, Wareham moved to Penticton as vice-president and general manager, a promotion he welcomed.

"I don't enjoy accounting," he admits. "I enjoy making things happen."

Wareham relished the tutelage of Casabello founder *Evans Lougheed*. But in 1981, after Lougheed had retired, Wareham left Casabello on a matter of principle: he refused to "stretch" wines beyond 250 gallons to a ton of grapes. Stretching was an infamous practice in the British Columbia wine industry at a time when wineries salvaged immature but over-priced grapes with a judicious, but profitable, addition of water and grain alcohol. "Back in those days the commercial wineries were not shy about putting the hose in the tank," Wareham recalls. Properly matured grapes should yield 125 to 150 gallons of wine to the ton. Wareham thought he was diluting quality enough. "I'm not here to ruin this company," he snapped at his boss.[6] His successor, he recalls wryly, once managed to get 600 gallons from a ton. After a brief and unsuccessful stint as a land developer, Wareham became the director of retail operations in 1983 for the Saskatchewan Liquor Board. Evidently, Labatt appreciated men of principle, for he became the brewer's Alberta sales manager from 1986 to 1989. Wareham then spent a year with a Calgary fish merchant before returning to Penticton in June 1991 to succeed Bud Richmond as *Harry McWatters's* partner at *Sumac Ridge*. They had known each other since Casabello. "We were business associates before we became good friends," Wareham notes. "I usually do a lot of the planning stuff and the implementation of things. Harry does public relations and sales."

WARNES, N. KEITH: The first general manager of the Liquor Distribution Branch when it was set up in 1975, Warnes resigned in February 1978 at the request of *Tex Enemark*, the deputy minister to whom he reported in Victoria.

WARREN, MICHAEL: A South African-born accountant who emigrated to Canada in 1975, Warren joined the British Columbia government in 1978 to manage a federal-provincial program funding development projects in agriculture. One of the first clients for whom Warren processed a loan was *Marion Jonn*, who opened the first estate winery in the Okanagan. Warren subsequently became manager of the beverage division in the Ministry of Agriculture, a modest title that does not do justice to his powerful influence over winery policy in British Columbia. Warren was involved in writing regulations for estate wineries, where he argued successfully against an initial proposal to limit these wineries to an annual production of 7,500 gallons a year. "I said that was ridiculously low," he recalls. An initial maximum of 30,000 gallons was set and has been raised several times since to improve the economic viability of the wineries. In 1985 Warren helped craft the adjustment program to deal with the Okanagan's *red wine surplus* and in 1988 he helped designed the even larger adjustment program that enabled many growers to exit the industry after the free trade agreement with the U.S. When the *British Columbia Wine Institute* was established in 1991, Warren was appointed the government member. What sets Warren apart from the usual "control" attitude towards wine among bureaucrats is his refreshing view that wine should be regarded as a food.

WARWICK PAUL (1941−): With a vanity vehicle licence plate reading *GEWURZ*, wine educator Paul Warwick puts his enthusiasm for wine in general and love of gewurztraminer in particular on display for all to see. Born in Winnipeg and raised in Edmonton where he was an automobile parts salesman, Warwick joined the Opimian wine-tasting society in Vancouver in the late 1970s and became such an ardent student of wines that, on entering a wine-tasting competition in 1979, he breezed through to the national level and finished sixth. He has been teaching wine appreciation and cooking courses in the Vancouver area ever since, at venues ranging from Capilano College to Vancouver Community College. He was a member of the committee that directed the Pacific National Exhibition's wine competitions and served as the competition chairman in 1990. In 1994 he applied for a licence for a winery called Wolf Creek Cellars, intending to establish a facility on East Second Avenue in Vancouver that would sell both inexpensive bulk wines blended from imported wines and upscale wines made from British Columbia grapes. The initial application failed because the proposed site was just down the street from a detoxification centre and funding for the project subsequently evaporated.

WASPS: These insects are considered vineyard pests, and not just because of the searing pain of the wasp sting. In the late summer, wasp swarms will gorge themselves on early-ripening grapes, especially the aromatic muscat varieties such as siegerrebe, sucking out the juice and leaving damaged clusters to become diseased. Insecticides have made it easier to deal with wasps than was the case in the 1930s when the *Rittich* brothers were dispensing advice on wasp control in their book, *European Grape Growing*. They suggested putting a mixture of sugar water and beer into partly filled small bottles tied on low trellises or stakes in vineyards. This bait attracted wasps who then perished inside the bottles. Some orchardists, they added, preferred cages covered with fine wire netting, with small openings. The bait in this case was rotting fish. Wasps who got into the cages rarely found their way out.

WATTS, TIM (1958−): A Victoria-born exploration geologist, Watts is one of the partners at *Kettle Valley Winery.* From 1987 he was the senior geologist at the Nickel Plate gold mine near Hedley, an hour-long commute from his Naramata vineyard, where Watts lives and where the winery is based.

WEINSBERG: A leading German school for winemakers, notable for its practical bent, is based in this community in the wine region of Württemberg. Graduates currently active in British Columbia include *Tilman Hainle, George Heiss, Jr.* and *Gordon Gehringer.*

WELLS, TERRY (1940−): Born in Penticton, Wells grew up in Osoyoos and settled into a career in teaching after getting a master's degree in educational administration in 1972 at the University of British Columbia. Within two years he was vice-principal at Sir Winston Churchill Secondary school in Vancouver and was on the fast track for top administration posts in the systems. By the end of the decade, however, he had tired of administration. In a 1980 career change, he and his wife, Halina, purchased what they called the Tin Horn Creek vineyard south of Oliver, intending a small estate winery there one day. He knew a bit about grapegrowing, his father having had a hobby vineyard, while an interest in good wines developed at university, where Wells joined the Opimian Society (a national wine club run from Montreal). They purchased their vineyard after an extensive search of sites in the Okanagan, with Wells prudently examining crop insurance records of available properties and staying away from those with a history of claims. The twenty-acre Tin Horn Creek vineyard (named for the creek that flows through it) had only had one claim, during the exceptionally cold winter of 1978–79. The grapes then being grown included foch, de chaunac, verdelet and newly planted chenin blanc, a variety that Wells came to regard as his favourite grape.

Chenin blanc, a white variety propagated from vines that came from Washington state, acquired the reputation of being a "tender" variety after the provincial agriculture ministry's test planting was killed in the 1978–79 winter. In March 1983 Wells, who had four and a half acres of chenin blanc, learned to his dismay that the variety, which had become insurable in 1981, was now being deleted from the eligible list. Wells protested that Peter Humphry-Baker, the director of the provincial crop insurance branch, had "toured our chenin blanc block last summer and commented upon how healthy and vigorous the plants were." He demanded the reason for the deletion. "Chenin blanc is no longer insured because its average pick date is after October 15," explained William Somer, the chairman of the **Association of B.C. Grape Growers** crop insurance

advisory committee. "The latter pick date is derived by Mr. **John Vielvoye** using both horticultural and local frost data. Local crop insurance officials rely on Mr. Vielvoye for horticultural information." Wells was outraged. In 1982 he had harvested 13.8 tons of chenin blanc grapes on October 9, while a neighbour had harvested another 7.3 tons five days later. Furthermore, it was the third-largest vinifera variety then grown in Washington state. Wells insisted that the variety could grow successfully "in the SOUTH Okanagan." Under pressure from the Grape Growers association, Humphry-Baker agreed to keep the chenin blanc insured but for 1983 only. Wells won on a technicality: the crop insurance board had failed to tell him of insurance changes before November 1, 1982, as required under the rules. "In future," Humphry-Baker wrote on July 6, 1983, "six months notice will be given of any varietal changes that are made to our lists of eligible varieties."[7] His battle propelled Wells into grapegrower politics; he become a director of the Association that fall. In 1986 he became a member of the Grape Growers Marketing Board, which he chaired during the three critical years from 1988 to 1990 when the board negotiated the compensation for growers uprooting their vineyards. Wells also was a founding director of the **British Columbia Wine Institute** in 1990. As for his beloved chenin blanc, much of it was uprooted (along with foch and verdelet) during the 1988 grape pull when no winery would contract the variety. Wells went into his house, tearfully, while the chenin blanc vines were pulled out because he could not watch the destruction. The foch and verdelet were replaced with chardonnay and merlot while Wells in 1991 returned to teaching at the high school in Oliver. The vineyard was sold the following year and now, under a modified spelling, anchors **Tinhorn Creek** winery.

Wells also recalls the 1988 pullout because of an improbable incident. One day in late summer a Toronto advertising agency telephoned with the request to buy half an acre of foch vines, with the grapes still on them. Suspecting a practical joke, Wells demanded cash in advance. It was not a prank. The agency paid him and sawed off at ground level two large refrigerated truckloads of vines which were delivered along with dwarf apple trees from a Creston orchard to a wheat field in Alberta. There the agency filmed a commercial for a new Nabisco cereal containing raisins, apples and wheat.

WENDENBURG, CHRIS (1924–):
A grower with one and a third lush acres of pinot blanc in a steeply pitched vineyard on the southeast edge of Penticton, Wendenburg grew up in the Harz Mountains of Germany where his family were substantial agriculturists until dispossessed of their property by the war and the subsequent Communist government of East Germany. Wendenburg settled on his Penticton property, then an orchard, in 1960. He planted grapes in 1982, making the unfortunate choice of Okanagan riesling and several hybrids. Three years later, on the recommendation of a winery, he converted to pinot blanc.

WENDENBURG, MARK (1961–):
Born in Penticton in 1961, the son of German-born vineyardist Chris Wendenburg, Mark returned to Germany to qualify as a winemaker and apprentice with wineries there. Since 1987, he has worked at wineries in New Zealand, Australia and Switzerland (where he met his wife) until in 1992 he joined the winemaking staff at **Sumac Ridge**, specializing in the production of sparkling wines. He also has a half-acre of chardonnay vines planted near his father's vineyard.

WHITE, ROBERT (1930–) AND JENNY:
The owners since 1992 of the **Mistral Vineyard** on Black Sage Road, south of Oliver, the Whites are retired adventurers embarked on the new adventure of grapegrowing. Toronto-born Robert White, a professional forester, accepted an early retirement package in 1987 from Domtar Inc. That allowed him and his Winnipeg-born wife, Jenny, to pursue a passion for ocean sailing. They leased out their Vancouver home and sailed south in a thirty-three-foot sailboat , spending the next four years either in the Caribbean or in the Pacific off Central America. Tiring of being nomads, they sailed back to British Columbia in 1991, exchanged the sailboat for a recreational vehicle and spent the winter panning for gold in Arizona. When even success at that pursuit did not ward off boredom, they bought a twenty-five-acre parcel of what had been a former Okanagan vineyard and built a house. Of course, the house took up only half an acre; on the advice of neighbour **Dick Cleave,** the remaining land was planted to vines, beginning in 1993. Tending the 22,500 vines in what Jenny White calls "the big garden" has left no time for boredom. The vineyard is planted, in almost equal acreages, to chardonnay, pinot noir, merlot, pinot gris and, surprisingly, to rougeon. While the

latter is one of the red hybrid varieties generally pulled out in the Okanagan after the 1988 vintage, the Whites were talked into replanting it by *Calona Wines*. The winery, having scored a surprising success with its 1987 rougeon, had developed a following for the wine, forcing it to contract new supplies of the variety in order to retain the market niche. White was able to replant because some old rougeon vines on his property had been overlooked during the pullout and these provided the cuttings from which new vines were propagated. Ever curious, White also has planted about a dozen zinfandel wines, one of California's oldest red varieties. "I thought if these plants survive, I can make a little wine for myself," says White who, even though he had no more than average interest in wine, became a capable self-taught vintner once the Mistral Vineyard was in production. The Whites are not planning a winery but the possibility of a winery one day at Mistral Vineyard cannot be ruled out. The Whites have six children and fifteen grandchildren; perhaps one will be attracted by the winegrower's lifestyle.

WHITE RIESLING: This is the increasingly common way to refer to *Johannisberg riesling*, the widely planted classic white vinifera grape.

WHITEHEAD, FRANK: A viticulturist widely respected by growers, he was the field man for *Jordan & Ste-Michelle* when that winery convinced its contract growers in the late 1970s to plant johannisberg riesling and other vinifera varieties.

WHITNEY, JARVIS (1938–): Born in Shellbrook, Sask., Whitney has authored the longest-running wine column in Vancouver with his column in *The Province* which began in 1970. His journalism career began as a news reporter and broadcaster with CKOM in Saskatoon. From there he moved to Prince George, B.C., where he edited *The Citizen* for five years. Whitney joined *The Province* in 1963 as a copy editor. His interest in wine began when he was assigned to a wine tour sponsored by the Italian government. Nearly all of the other two dozen journalists from around the world on the tour were established wine writers and Whitney, a quick study, got a cram course on wine during three weeks on a bus, visiting wineries the length and breadth of Italy. "I was hooked on the subject," he recalled. His reportage on that tour blossomed into his weekly column. On occasion, various of Whitney's editors suspended the column, only to reinstate it after a deluge of letters and telephone calls from readers.

WILCOX, W.J.: Farmer at Salmon Arm, B.C., who in 1907 planted a small vineyard (variously reported as from three-quarters of an acre to two acres in size) with varieties including Campbell's early, concord, niagara, white mountain, delaware, clinton, thompson seedless, hamburg and agawam. The grapes were sold as fresh fruit.[8]

WILD GOOSE VINEYARDS: One of the original farmgate wineries in 1990, it is operated near Okanagan Falls by *Adolf Kruger* and his family, who began planting the vineyard in 1984. The winery got its name from a flock of geese Kruger discovered on the property when he first walked around it in 1983. The wines include riesling, gewurztraminer, pinot blanc and, among the reds, pinot noir and one of the few maréchal foch wines still made. The winery's off-dry Autumn Gold, a blend of riesling and vidal, has been a bestseller even though it was developed by chance when a partially full tank of riesling was topped up with vidal, the only wine at hand.

WILSON, GEORGE (1946–): Few have more earth from Okanagan Falls vineyards under their nails than George Wilson. Born in Penticton, he grew up on an Oliver orchard but joined the navy in 1965 to get away from picking fruit. Unhappily, Wilson was severely sick every time he went to sea and, in 1968, he left the navy, studied electronics for a year and than returned to the south Okanagan to work with his stepfather, Gordon Tubbs, on the so-called SYL Vineyard near Okanagan Falls. Grapes have been in his blood ever since; and Wilson has worked with and for most of the Okanagan Falls growers since.

The SYL Vineyard was developed by **Major Hugh Fraser,** so named because his British bride after the First World War lived there only briefly before she decided it was far too remote; she left after penning a brief note that she would "see you later." The first grapes were planted about 1965 by Bill Fraser, the major's son, who sold the property in 1974. After several changes of ownership it was acquired by **LeComte Estate Winery.** Tubbs retired in 1974 but Wilson continued working the SYL vineyard until 1980 when he bought an eleven-and-a-half-acre property on Rolling Hills Road — now an Okanagan Falls address for half a dozen small vineyards. On the five plantable acres, Wilson put in Okanagan riesling and verdelet in 1981. The former was replaced with auxerrois after the 1988 vintage and the verdelet was replaced by pinot gris in 1996.[9]

The lean, laconic Wilson, who favours pickup trucks and ten-gallon hats, says he chose to grow grapes initially because he figured that was where the money was. Subsequently, doing his books on a good computer accounting program convinced him otherwise. "But this is a beautiful place to live," he says of his property. "And there are other advantages. I just like the lifestyle."

Guy Wilson (photo courtesy of John Schreiner)

WILSON, GUY TUNSTALL (1945–): Most hope to end in Paradise. Guy Wilson can claim to have begun there, having been born at home on Paradise Ranch, a dramatically beautiful 635 acres wedged between Okanagan Lake and the mountains, four miles north of Naramata. Matthew Wilson, his grandmother Florence's second husband, homesteaded here in 1904 and his father Victor added extensive tree fruit plantings. There also were some grapevines but the property was operated as a ranch with Black Angus beef cattle. When Victor Wilson sold the property in 1963, his son went to sea with the Canadian navy for three years and then went travelling by car across the continent until, in a lonely bar in the Bahamas in 1967, Guy Wilson decided he wanted to be back in the Okanagan, growing grapes. After all, grapes were in his blood. His grandmother and her first husband, W.J. Waterman, had planted grapes at a farm they purchased at Okanagan Falls in 1904 and where she lived until 1916.[10]

Wilson's mentor was **Tony Biollo**, the Penticton vineyardist, who in 1962 had advised that Paradise Ranch was suited for grapes. While Wilson scavenged vine cuttings from **Den Dulik**'s Kelowna vineyard that winter, he never got around to propagating them. Now, on returning from the Bahamas, Wilson consulted Biollo about vineyard work and was hired by **Casabello**, first as a cellarman and later as production manager. On the side, Wilson began growing grapes (Okanagan riesling and verdelet) on the fourteen-acre vineyard just south of Paradise Ranch that had remained in the Wilson family when the ranch was sold. In 1971 he won the coveted trophy for the best Okanagan grapes, sponsored by **Andrés** at the annual Penticton Grape and Harvest Fiesta. Subsequently, he won the trophy in 1979 again at his own vineyard; in 1985, 1986 and 1987, the trophy was won by Paradise Ranch Vineyards, which Wilson then was managing; and in 1990 it was won by the **Summerhill Estate** vineyard, again with Wilson as manager. "I had a natural feel for the land," he said later.

Wilson left Casabello in 1974 to spend eight months travelling the wine regions in Australia before coming home to tend the Wilson vineyard. In the spring of 1976, while walking the beach at nearby Paradise Ranch, he encountered the new owner, Edmonton economist and rancher **Hu Harries**. They hit it off instantly, with Wilson, a lean and wiry horseman with a taste for western garb and rodeos, being hired to manage the ranch where he was born. When Harries decided to grow grapes in 1980, Wilson supervised planting a large vineyard during the next four years. He managed Paradise Ranch until 1988, leaving to manage the Summerhill vineyards for a year.

His own small vineyard in 1981 was operated in partnership with **Sumac Ridge Estate Winery,** and the partnership only dissolved in 1992 after Wilson sold the vineyard. He sold reluctantly, unable to secure long-term winery contracts during the gloomy period after 1988. He had pulled out his Okanagan riesling and his verdelet; in the absence of a winery commitment, he looked seriously at planting ginseng before selling the property. (The new owner planted neither, preferring to pasture horses.) Subsequently, Wilson has set up his own viticultural consulting company, based in Naramata.

WILSON, WAYNE (1952–): The curator of the **Wine Museum** in Kelowna, Wilson was born in Lillooet, the son of a teacher and the grandson of an Oliver orchardist. After earning a master's degree in geography from the University of British Columbia, Wilson joined the Kelowna Museum in 1978, just in time to play a role in the preservation of the Laurel Packinghouse, the heritage building near downtown Kelowna that now houses both the Orchard Museum and the Wine Museum. One of the few remaining examples of several fruit industry buildings that had been erected in 1917 and 1918, the brick-clad Laurel was destined for demolition in 1979 when the City of Kelowna, under public pressure, agreed to preserve the building and put it under the administration of the museum. Wilson was assigned to do the first historical survey on the building. "It was a hulk," he recalled later. "The attic was full of sawdust and dead pigeons." More than $500,000 was raised to refurbish Laurel Packinghouse, turning it into a well-utilized community arts building. The Orchard Museum opened in 1989 and the Wine Museum in 1996.

WINE-ART SALES LTD.: See *Stanley Anderson*.

WINE COUNCIL OF BRITISH CO-LUMBIA: An organization formed in the late 1970s, it promoted the interests of the commercial wineries. It was of limited effectiveness because it never had all of the commercial wineries in its membership at any one time and it subsequently was dissolved.

WINE MUSEUM: Established in 1996 as a satellite to the Kelowna Museum, the 1,000-square-foot museum is located in Laurel Packinghouse, a heritage building. The museum is dedicated primarily to British Columbia wine, including the sponsorship of events that promote the industry. Its first function even before opening was the sponsorship in September 1995 of the first British Columbia wine label awards. Curator *Wayne Wilson's* imaginative agenda for the wine museum includes operating a wine club, selling premium wines at the gift shop and permitting wineries to launch new wines in the museum. "We want to offer the museum

as a start or as a conclusion to wine tours," Wilson says.

WINTER DAMAGE: "Low temperature damage to vineyards is the single most limiting factor for grape production in British Columbia," according to the provincial government's *Management Guide for Grapes*.[11] Research has identified -23°C as the threshold temperature that causes damage to both the buds and the trunk of a grapevine during winter. But less severe cold also causes serious damage if it occurs too soon after harvest or if there is no or inadequate insulation from snow cover. In the 1955–56 winter, repeated cold waves began November 11 and continued, with the lowest temperature recorded at Kelowna being -22°C in February. Damage to vines was so extensive that the 1956 vintage was 78 percent lower than 1955. *The Atlas of Suitable Grape Growing Locations* commented: "A temperature of -12°C on or before November 15 has been identified as the temperature which will begin to cause damage to grape vines early in winter. More severe damage to vines occurs as winter temperatures drop to -20°C."

Other winters in which vines were damaged or killed by extreme weather included 1949–50, when production was reduced to 42 percent of the previous vintage. In January 1950, the temperature got down as low as -32°C for nearly a week, too severe for vines even with the good snow cover that existed that year. In December 1964, when -26°C was recorded at Summerland, production collapsed by a devastating 94 percent. In 1968–69, killing frosts reduced grape production in the 1969 vintage to just over a quarter of the previous year's production. In 1972–73, mid-September freezes stripped the leaves from vines in the Oliver/Osoyoos area. Vines need to retain leaves for several weeks after harvest to enable them to store carbohydrates and "harden" for winter. The September freeze thus left the vines vulnerable to colder weather later. The most serious damage that winter was to vines in the adjoining Similkameen Valley, where 75 percent of the vines were damaged when temperatures plunged to -20°C on December 7, 1972, and even lower in January.

The winter of 1978–79 also is notorious. "On October 23 it froze and we didn't come out of the freeze until late in February," vineyard manager **Dick Cleave** recalls. More than half of the vines in the southern Okanagan and the Similkameen were killed by the cold, combined with high winds that dried out the vines.[12] The devastation was so severe because the 1978 vintage had been very large, with many growers over-cropping the vines which were burdened generously with fruit. The high tonnages had to be left on the vines well into late autumn so that the grapes could reach acceptable maturity for winemaking. "We were still harvesting grapes into the first week of November," recalled **John Bremmer,**[13] who was harvesting the Similkameen vineyard that he and partner **Robert Holt** had purchased that summer. At the time, few growers understood that it is essential to give vineyards a post-harvest watering to protect the roots from desiccation in the very dry south Okanagan winter. Vines already stressed by overproduction and sitting on desiccated roots could not survive the winter. "We didn't get rain until the following April," Bremmer said. "The plants didn't die of cold — they

died of desiccation. We didn't know enough that it was very important to soak the vineyard down. The damage would not have been nearly as bad." Equally devastating, most vines had not gone properly into dormancy before the first serious frosts; one large vineyard in the south Okanagan, using a mechanical harvester, only harvested *after* a freeze swept across the vineyard, having waited too long for its grapes to reach adequate sugar.

Irrigating after harvest if the soil is dry has since become one routine in protecting vines from winter damage, along with windbreaks to shield vines from the dry, dehydrating winds of winter. There are other methods for warding off frost damage in the spring or in the autumn. Bare earth between vine rows, because it absorbs the sun's heat, can be made to serve as a heat sink in certain vineyards. Those vineyards with overhead sprinklers turn them on when there is a frost warning since a thin crust of ice on the vines offers some protection. The reason: when water freezes, it releases enough heat to raise the vine temperature by one to one and a half degrees Celsius. Because the coldest air pools in low spots of a vineyard (called frost pockets), some growers warm up these spots with smudge pots or install wind machines whose huge propellers mix warmer air with the cold. A hovering helicopter does the job well but at an exorbitant cost.[14]

WOLF CREEK: An apparently unlucky name, it was the name of a vineyard planned in the 1970s but never developed near Osoyoos; and in the 1990s it was the name for a planned Vancouver-area winery that failed to get either financing or licensing.

WOOD, GLEN (1943–): The laconic, silver-haired general manager at **Cedar-Creek Estate Winery,** Wood is a farmer by avocation even though he comes from a Nova Scotia fishing family. The Vancouver-born Wood, after a taste of university, formed a 1968 partnership with a brother-in-law to grow apples, grapes and cherries near Rutland. He left that partnership twenty years later to manage CedarCreek's vineyard, becoming the winery's general manager in 1994.

WOODLAND, VIC (1917–): The primary author of the rules that launched the cottage wineries in 1979, Woodland was the ex-military bureaucrat whose career in the **Liquor Control Board of British Columbia** spanned not only the control era of **Lt.-Col. Donald McGugan,** but after the Board was separated into two branches, encompassed the expansionist modern era of the **Liquor Control and Liscensing Branch.** Born in the Edmonton suburb of Strathcona, Woodland taught physical education until he joined the Royal Canadian Air Force in 1940. He spent the war years on the RCAF disciplinarian staff and was a sergeant major when the war ended. He earned a commerce degree at the University of British Columbia and, after several private sector jobs, became an inspector with the **Liquor Control Board** in 1953. "It was a terrific basic grounding in liquor administration and the problems with liquor," recalled Woodland, who was based in the Fraser Valley. At that time the government kept a black list of individuals not allowed, for various reasons, to buy alcoholic beverages, names that were entered in the LCB minutes. Getting off the interdiction list required getting the endorsement of the police or a magistrate. Woodland recalled one woman, anxious to get off the list, writing a poignant plea. "She would swear over a Bible — and also on the government liquor act — that she would never have a drinking problem again," Woodland remembered, marvelling: "The government liquor act had more authority than the Bible." The list was abandoned in the 1960s.

Evidently, Woodland caught the attention of his superiors. In 1958 he was summoned to Victoria to meet with Lt.-Col. McGugan whom Woodland remembers as a man economical with words. The colonel got right to the point: he offered Woodland a promotion to secretary of the Liquor Control Board and gave Woodland overnight to think about. Woodland accepted promptly. His initial assignment was to do the first complete overhaul of liquor regulations since the LCB had been formed four decades earlier.

When the government licensed three new wineries in the 1960s, Woodland insisted that the domestic wineries use predominantly British Columbia grapes. Without that requirement, the burgeoning wineries might easily have relied on California grapes and the subsequent vineyard expansion in the Okanagan would not have occurred. In *Demon Rum or Easy Money,* Robert Campbell writes: "Woodland regularly met with the growers to encourage them to expand their acreage using better grapes."[15] Campbell also notes that Woodland in 1977 recommended that the government enhance the protection for British Columbia wineries by giving them lower markups than those applied to imported wines, along with guaranteed listings in liquor stores. He also recommended that wineries be allowed to operate their own stores, a privilege extended to estate wineries as soon as they opened but not extended to commercial wineries until 1985. Woodland retired in 1981.

WYSE, JAMES (1938–): Cycling through the Loire in 1984 and in subsequent years through Italian wine country fired an interest that culminated in the **Burrowing Owl Vineyards,** Wyse's 220-acre vineyard in the Okanagan Valley north of Osoyoos. One of the largest vineyards in the Okanagan, it is on property formerly known as *Pacific Vineyards* before the 1988 vine pullout. Unlike Pacific, Burrowing Owl is planted entirely in vinifera grape varieties, including three Italian ones (sangiovese, barbera and nebbiollo) never before tried in the Okanagan.

Born in Toronto, Wyse became a civil engineer like his father and spent the first four years of his professional career building roads and bridges for the Ontario highways department. He then acquired an MBA, spent two years selling isotopes for Atomic Energy of Canada and came to Vancouver in 1968 as a management consultant. Wyse established his own real estate development company in 1973, with projects as far afield as Denver and Whistler. While working on a project in Vernon in 1991, Wyse learned that the **Chateau Ste. Claire** winery might be for sale. After checking it out, he decided to invest in a vineyard rather than jumping straight into a winery. In late 1993 he put together two syndicates, one representing his family and one representing a group of sixteen investors, to acquire the two neighbouring properties that have now become Burrowing Owl.

The vineyard is named for the owls, endangered birds, that live in deserted badger holes in the ecological reserve adjoining the vineyard. There is a strong green streak to the vineyard's management by **Dick Cleave** and Robert Goltz, the resident managers. For example, a number of boxes designed as bat habitat have been erected around the vineyard; this should improve the survival of the flying rodents who will return the favour by eating leaf hoppers, a common vineyard pest. The Burrowing Owl vineyard also is surrounded by twenty-eight bird boxes for mountain bluebirds. "Just for fun," Wyse explains. Burrowing Owl also became the first vineyard in 1995 to experiment with protecting its grapes from starlings with sunlight-degradable netting. In a controlled test of a ten-acre section of vines, half was draped with netting and the other half was left exposed so that the vineyard could measure just how much the birds actually eat. "If the starlings are eating more than 10 percent of the grapes, then this netting is a useful expenditure," Wyse says.

When Wyse took over Burrowing Owl, the vineyard had two modest blocks of pinot blanc vines, believed to have been planted in 1985. As well, **Albert LeComte**, who had owned the vineyard for a year before Wyse bought it, had begun planting vinifera where hybrids once had grown. Wyse has continued those plantings, with a heavy bias to red varieties such as merlot and pinot noir, since he believes the southern Okanagan soils and climate are suited to red varieties. "There is no point doing whites if we can do reds," he believes. Seventy-five percent of the production is contracted to **Calona Wines**, a seren-dipitous outcome given that Calona was an original partner in developing Pacific Vineyards.

The other 25 percent of grapes? It seems there is a high point at the back of the vineyard, with views of the valley, that cries out for a premium estate winery. Wyse has received most of the approvals for a winery building expected to be ready by the fall of 1997.

1 Interview with author, 1978.

2 Interview with author, 1995.

3 John Schriener, "The Vancouver Wine Festival's Bob Wallace," *BCL Guide,* February 1990, p. 106.

4 Tex Enemark papers; memorandum March 17, 1978, to Consumer Affairs minister Rafe Mair.

5 Letter by Ian Greenwood to author, September 1982.

6 Interview with author, 1995.

7 Correspondence in Terry Wells's personal files.

8 John Vielvoye, "History and Future of the Grape Industry in the Okanagan," *Canadian Horticulture and Agriculture,* January 1971, p. 21.

9 Interview with author, 1995.

10 Okanagan Historical Society, *Okanagan History: 49th Report of the Okanagan Historical Society,* p. 104.

11 B.C. Ministry of Agriculture, Fishers and Food, *Management Guide for Grapes for Commercial Growers, 1994-5 Edition* (Victoria: author).

12 Association of B.C. Grape Growers, *Atlas of Suitable Grape Growing Locations*, p. 79. (See SOURCES for complete reference.)

13 Interview with author, 1995.

14 B.C. Ministry of Agriculture, *Management Guide for Grapes*, p. 5.

15 Robert Campbell, *Demon Rum or Easy Money*, p. 159. (See SOURCES for complete reference.)

Y Y Y

YOUNG, ROBERT (1928–): With his wife, Maryke, Young cultivates the modest four-acre Okanagan Mountain Vineyard on a rugged twenty-five-acre property clinging onto the side of Okanagan Mountain, southeast of Kelowna. Born in Britain but raised on a Kelowna orchard and dairy farm to which his parents emigrated in 1939, Young pursued several careers before becoming a grapegrower. He served for eighteen years in the Canadian navy, retiring with the rank of lieutenant-commander. For five years he then ran a dairy farm on the outskirts of Kelowna until urban sprawl led him to sell the property in 1969. After a few years in real estate, he joined the Federal Business Development Bank, retiring from that job in 1994. The Youngs had purchased their Okanagan Mountain property in the early 1980s. "The land was actually waste land until I planted something," he said. He chose grapes on the advice of a *Calona Wines* fieldman who compared the rocks and gravel of the property to vineyards in Sicily. Young planted Okanagan riesling in 1983 and harvested a bounteous 21 tons of grapes in 1987. That variety, no longer wanted by wineries, subsequently was removed and replaced, on the advice of the nearby *CedarCreek* winery, with two acres of auxerrois. The remaining plantable area was devoted to table grapes. Because the property is adjacent to a park, the terraced vineyard is encircled with a ten-foot-high deer fence and an electrified, three-stranded bear fence. He laments that these defences do not always work. "One year, I had six bears in here at one time."

ZZZ

ZANATTA, DIONISIO (DENNIS) (1929–): When he immigrated from Treviso in northern Italy in 1959, a relative in Vancouver suggested his new Canadian neighbours would find his given name tough to spell. An agreeable man, Zanatta adopted Dennis as a more accessible first name. He settled on a farm just south of Duncan in the Cowichan Valley on Vancouver Island, establishing a dairy herd but, because fruit trees were already growing, also starting an experimental plot of grapevines in 1970 with varieties such as leon millot, a red French hybrid, obtained from the federal government's plant health centre at Saanichton. In 1983 Zanatta extended his trial plot, cooperating with the B.C. government in the so-called Duncan Project, a six-year trial in which more than a hundred varieties were tested for their suitability on Vancouver Island. Midway through the trial, Zanatta began a five-acre planting of ortega, a white variety suited to the long, cool growing season of the Cowichan Valley. It formed the basis for the *Vigneti Zanatta* farmgate winery that opened in 1992 when his daughter, Loretta, completed her training as a winemaker in Italy.

Subsequently, Dennis Zanatta extended the vineyard to a full thirty acres, by far the largest vineyard on Vancouver Island, big enough to support the estate winery from a new facility planned to be built in 1996. Pinot gris (thirteen acres) and auxerrois (eight acres, some of which was planted as early as 1980) make up most of the plantings. The other significant varieties are three acres of muscat and two acres each of pinot noir, madeleine sylvaner and cabernet franc. The vineyard is on well-drained sandy soil, with a gravel knoll reserved for red varieties and for the family home, with views that take Zanatta back to the vineyard country in which he grew up.

ZANATTA, LORETTA (1963–): The enologist at family-owned *Vigneti Zanatta*, she holds a bachelor's degree in plant science from the University of British Columbia and a graduate degree in winemaking in 1990 from an agricultural college at Piacenza, south of Milan in Italy. She also gained practical experience at a sparkling wine producer in Italy owned by her mother's cousin. Not surprisingly, given that background, a sparkling wine fetchingly called Glenora Fantasia, made from a New York hybrid grape called cayuga, was one of the early releases at Vigneti Zanatta. (Glenora refers to the district south of Duncan where the winery and vineyard are located.) The vineyard's three-acre planting of muscat grapes also affords her the opportunity to make a wine in the style of Italy's well-known Asti Spumante sparkling wines.

ZELLER, DANIEL (1973–): Born in Germany, Daniel Zeller apprenticed as a toolmaker, specializing in production machinery, with Daimler Benz before joining the family firm, Zeller & Sons Enterprises Ltd., in Naramata.

ZELLER, KARL-HEINZ (1963–): Born in Germany, his college education was interrupted when father *Wolfgang Zeller* emigrated to Canada with the Zeller family. He is now a partner in the family firm, Zeller & Sons Enterprises Ltd., and also is the chief winemaker, producing wines for the family's consumption from their vineyard.

ZELLER, WOLFGANG (1938–):

Born in the old German university town of Tubingen into a family who had grown grapes for generations, Wolfgang Zeller, since his emigration to the Okanagan in 1983, has become a major source of vineyard and winery equipment in British Columbia. Soft-spoken and courtly, Zeller apprenticed in Germany as a machinist and mechanical engineer with an employer whose foreign sales afforded considerable travel opportunities. Appetite whetted, Zeller decided to emigrate to the United States, with Canada as a temporary staging point. As it happened, Zeller and his family put down roots near Naramata when his machinery import business, launched in 1984, quickly succeeded.

After visiting the Okanagan in 1981, Zeller settled his family — wife Martha and six children, with a seventh born later in Canada — on what was a ranch property with an appealing view over Okanagan Lake to the west. After levelling the site in 1983 for a vineyard, Zeller found himself caught up in the absurd bureaucracy formerly practised by the British Columbia Grape Growers Marketing Board. The Board refused to give him a licence until he had a contract from a winery while the major wineries refused him a contract until he got a licence. Finally, on the assurance that *T.G. Brights & Co.* would give him a contract later, Zeller took the risk of planting some vines. He planted what he wanted,

not what the wineries advised. He was told to plant de chaunac, vidal and Okanagan riesling; instead, he started with johannisberg riesling and pinot noir, telling the wineries that he might be a newcomer but he knew something they did not. After the Second World War, his parents in Germany replaced vinifera grapes in their vineyard with hybrids at the urging of the American occupation authorities. Within three years, Zeller recalls, they ripped out the hybrids. He had no intention of making the same error in Canada. In 1988, as a result, nothing had to be pulled from the Zeller vineyard at Naramata and, with the immediate shortage of good wine grapes after the pullout, he had no difficulty selling his fruit to wineries. By then his eight-acre vineyard had been expanded to include müller-thurgau, ehrenfelser and the mother block of 2,000 oraniensteiner vines, a German white variety obtained for Zeller by Brights, which later lost interest in making a varietal wine from it.

Along with Guenther Lang, Adolf Kruger and Vera Klokocka, Zeller campaigned for the right to open a farm winery. By the time the farmgate licence was created in 1989, Zeller & Sons Enterprises Ltd., his machinery import company, had become too successful for him to consider a winery. "We can't have two full-time businesses running," he decided. He and son Karl produce excellent wine from their grapes for the Zeller household but they are content to sell most of their production to other wineries. The import business was started because it was evident to Zeller there was a need in the Okanagan for modern vineyard equipment and not much supply available. Zeller tapped his contacts in Germany in 1983 to source equipment. Within three years the company had begun re-exporting viticulture and other horticultural machinery to the United States and extended the selection until customers ranged from Florida citrus growers to Hawaiian palm groves. "We are very hard-working," Zeller says simply. "We can't have a winery."

ZIMMERMAN, JOSEF (1949–): His family traces its winemaking heritage back at least four hundred years but it is unlikely that any Zimmerman made wine in circumstances as hostile to good wine as those endured by Josef Zimmerman during the final two vintages at the historic *Growers'* winery on Quadra Street in Victoria. "I encountered so many things which were unrealistic," he remembers. "I have *never* heard that a winery can have a wooden floor."

Born into a grapegrowing family in Guldenthal, Ger., Zimmerman graduated from *Geisenheim* in 1975 and went on to do wine research in Baden until he and his wife, then a student in advanced mathematics, decided they were "financially burned out." In search of a career, Zimmerman replied to an advertisement from *Jordan & Ste-Michelle* to make wine in Canada — even though it had never occurred to him before that Canada even could grow grapes. (Later he found that the so-called viticultural experts in Canada also doubted that Canada could grow decent grapes; Zimmerman had a hand in teaching them otherwise.) Late in 1976 Zimmerman arrived in Victoria as an assistant to *Dieter Guttler*, another Geisenheim graduate who had been recruited several years before to make wine at the Victoria winery. Guttler recalls the old

winery — now a Keg restaurant not far from downtown Victoria — as a "shithouse." Zimmerman is less blunt but would never dispute his mentor's assessment. The winery had been designed initially to make fortified wines on a modest scale and was expanded in such a piecemeal fashion that it was completely inefficient. The sanitation problems alone occupied a crew of four people much of the time, scrubbing down floors and tanks with iodine and other disinfectants, with the winemaker scrambling to ensure that the disinfectant was not cascading from upper floors into tanks of wine below. The winery was so inefficient that it employed a cellar crew of three dozen people to handle what eight people later did when Jordan & Ste-Michelle in 1979 opened its large, modern Surrey winery.

In addition to its antiquated state, the Victoria winery's location on Vancouver Island also gave Zimmerman endless headaches during the two vintages he suffered there. Fresh grapes from California arrived by truck; if the winery was lucky, the driver telephoned he was on the way when he crossed the Washington state/British Columbia border. It was even better luck if the driver then caught the next available ferry since, at that time of the year, there may be two hours between sailings. The best luck required that the driver call from the border, make the ferry as planned — and then not get lost in downtown Victoria with a truckload of grapes while Zimmerman and his unionized production crew were standing by, expensively idle. "It was literally a nightmare," Zimmerman remembers, the bizarre scheduling problems at the winery caused by its location so inconveniently far from the raw materials. "But it is my style and my personality that I didn't throw in the towel." Everyone shared the frustration of working in these utterly inadequate circumstances, an experience that created its own team spirit. "The level of frustration kept people working together," Zimmerman believed.

Zimmerman believed that the Okanagan actually had advantages over German wine regions, including more sunshine and far less risk of killing spring frosts. Zimmerman believed that some Okanagan growers had poor sites and once sarcastically advised one to solve a viticultural problem by replacing the vines with broccoli. He also disliked the undisciplined way in which some grew hybrid varieties which were easily overcropped to yield mediocre wine. "With hybrids, you have to select the grower before you select the variety," he believed. He became chief winemaker at the new Jordan & Ste-Michelle winery in Surrey in 1978 when Dieter Guttler moved to the Jordan winery in St. Catharines, Ontario. In 1980, Zimmerman transferred to the Jordan winery in Ontario, succeeding Guttler, who had left to develop an estate winery.

ZIP: The brand name for a gin-flavoured wine beverage released by West Coast Wines, a small winery that operated briefly in New Westminster in the early 1960s. These beverages enjoyed explosive popularity after Jordan Wines in Ontario introduced Zing in August 1962, a beverage with 20 percent alcohol sold at perhaps half the price of real gin. Zing was the largest selling wine in Ontario within four months. Competitors quickly jumped aboard the trend, with Zip and Calona's Silver and Gold being west coast brands. Sales of the category peaked in 1965 and then died slowly, with Zing being discontinued in 1978.

ZIRALDO, DONALD (1948–): Born in St. Catharines, Ont., of Italian parents, he received a bachelor of science in horticulture from the University of Guelph. Ziraldo was the co-founder in 1974 and remains president of Inniskillin Wines Inc., the first new winery established by Ontario since 1929 and Canada's first so-called "cottage" winery. Its early success inspired the emergence of estate wineries both in Ontario and in British Columbia. Ziraldo established **Inniskillin Okanagan** in 1994; this winery produced its initial vintages at the **Vincor** winery at Oliver since Inniskillin has been part of the Vincor corporate group since 1992. Ziraldo was one of the architects of Canadian wine quality standards and has been a long-time chairman of the Vintners Quality Alliance in Ontario.

SOURCES

BOOKS

Association of British Columbia Grape Growers. *Atlas of Suitable Grape Growing Locations in the Okanagan and Similkameen Valleys of British Columbia.* Kelowna: Agriculture Canada, 1984.

Campbell, Robert A. *Demon Rum or Easy Money: Government Control of Liquor in British Columbia from Prohibition to Privatization.* Ottawa: Carleton University Press, 1991.

Casorso, Victor. *The Casorso Story: A Century of Social History in the Okanagan Valley.* Okanagan Falls: Rima Publications Ltd., 1983.

Givton, Albert. *Wine Wise.* Vancouver: Brighouse Press, 1988.

Gray, James H. *Booze, The Impact of Whisky on the Prairie West.* Toronto: Macmillan of Canada, 1972.

Nichol, Alexander. *Wines and Vines of British Columbia.* Vancouver: Bottesini Press, 1983.

Ordish, George. *The Great Wine Blight.* New York: Charles Scribner's Sons, 1972.

Peller, Andrew. *The Winemaker, The Autobiography of Andrew Peller, founder of Andrés Wines Ltd.*, as told to S. Patricia Filer. Published for Andrés Wines Ltd., 1982.

Raftery, Michael. *The Wine Course.* Richmond: Open Learning Institute, 1983.

Rittich, Virgil J., and Dr. Eugene A. Rittich. *European Grape Growing in Cooler Districts Where Winter Protection is Necessary.* Minneapolis: Burgess Puglishing Co., 1934.

Robinson, Jancis. *Vines, Grapes and Wines.* London: Mitchell Beazley International Ltd., 1986.

Schreiner, John. *The Wineries of British Columbia.* Victoria: Orca Book Publishers, 1994.

Schreiner, John. *The World of Canadian Wine.* Vancouver: Douglas & McIntyre, 1984.

Wenzel, Jan-Udo. *Ginter.* Prince George: The Caitlin Press, 1993.

NEWSLETTERS AND PERIODICALS

B.C. Wine Country, published annually by Blue Moose Publications, Kelowna.

B.C. Wine Notes, published and edited by Nicholas Grimshawe. Ceased publication in 1985.

British Columbia Wine Trails, published quarterly by B.C. Wine Trails, Summerland.

British Columbia Ministry of Agriculture, Fisheries and Food. *The Leading Edge: Grape and Wine Industry Newsletter*, 1690 Powick Road, Kelowna, BC, V1X 7G5.

Hainle Vineyards Newsletter, published by Hainle Vineyards Estate Winery, Peachland, BC.

Okanagan Historical Society, *Okanagan History*. Published annually.

Venturi-Schulze Vineyards Newsletter, published by Venturi-Schulze Vineyards, Cobble Hill, BC.

The Wine Barrel, published by Quails' Gate Estate Winery, Westbank, BC.

The Wine Consumer — A Wine Buyer's Guide for Canadians, published by Turnagain Enterprises Ltd., Burnaby, BC; edited by Albert Givton. Ceased publication in 1990.

OTHERS

Scrapbooks were made available by Gray Monk Estate Winery, dealing primarily with Gray Monk's history; by Frances Lougheed, dealing with Casabello's history; by Stanley F. Anderson, dealing with Wine-Art; and by Linda Ben-Hamida, dealing with Calona Wines and the Ghezzi family. Edward Sweeney made available his extensive scrapbooks on the Sweeney Cooperage.

Personal files on the history of Growers' Wines were made available by Lloyd Schmidt of Mori Nurseries, Niagara-on-the-Lake, Ont. Ted Brouwer provided his files on the history of Inkameep Vineyards. Tex Enemark provided his files of his two years as deputy minister of Consumer and Corporate Affairs. R. A. Wallace provided files and notes on his decade as general manager of the Liquor Distribution Branch.

John Schreiner was born in 1936 at Indian Head, Saskatchewan, and grew up on a wheat farm. After graduating in arts from the University of Saskatchewan, he joined the *Regina Leader-Post* as a reporter and subsequently became the newspaper's chief political reporter in the Saskatchewan Legislature. In 1961, Schreiner joined the staff of *The Financial Post* in Toronto. In 1973, he became that newspaper's bureau chief in Vancouver. He has written about a wide range of business matters. His 1989 history of BC Sugar, *The Refiners: a Century of BC Sugar*, was the runner-up and a $5,000 prize winner in the National Business Books awards in 1990.

Schreiner's passion for wine began in 1959 with his first bottle of French Sauternes and flourished into a catholic interest that includes membership in four wine-tasting societies and more than two decades of experience as an award-winning home vintner. He is a veteran wine writer whose work has been published in *Wine Tidings*, *The Financial Post*, *Vancouver Magazine* and the *British Columbia Liquor Distribution Product Guide*. He is a graduate of the German Wine Academy, has judged wines and has visited virtually all of the world's major wine growing regions.

Schreiner's major interest is Canadian wine. His previous works include, *The World of Canadian Wines* (Douglas & McIntyre, 1984), and *The Wineries of British Columbia* (Orca Book Publishers, 1994).